NORTH AMERICAN TREES FOURTH EDITION

NORTH AMERICAN TREES FOURTH EDITION

Exclusive of Mexico and Tropical Florida

Richard J. Preston, Jr.

IOWA STATE UNIVERSITY PRESS / AMES

TO MY WIFE
Bernice Boynton Preston

Richard J. Preston, Jr., is professor emeritus of forestry, North Carolina State University, Raleigh.

© 1948, 1961, 1976, 1989   Iowa State University Press

Manufactured in the United States of America

First edition, 1948
Second edition, 1961
Third edition, 1976
Fourth edition, 1989

Library of Congress Cataloging-in-Publication Data

Preston, Richard Joseph, 1905–
    North American trees : exclusive of Mexico and tropical Florida / Richard J. Preston, Jr.—4th ed.
    p. cm.
    Includes index.
    ISBN 0-8138-1171-6.—ISBN 0-8138-1172-4 (pbk.)
    1. Trees—United States—Identification.   2. Trees—Canada—Identification.   I. Title.
QK110.P74   1989
582.16097—dc19   89-1944

CONTENTS

INCREASING NUMBERS of people are becoming interested in the trees and forests of North America. Regional manuals of our native trees are available for the different sections of the United States and Canada. *North American Trees* is a simple, yet complete, up-to-date manual for the entire area.

This book covers the trees of North America with the exception of Mexico and tropical Florida. Care has been taken to include all species native to this area (except for 35 species of hawthorn and 16 usually shrubby willows that, for the most part, can be distinguished only by specialists) as well as naturalized or commonly planted exotic species.

This handbook has been designed to meet the needs of an interested general public as well as those of students and scientists. Concise descriptions of botanical and silvical characters have been included for species of trees that are important or of general interest, while additional, less important species are briefly described or included in the complete keys. The terminology has been kept as simple as possible without sacrificing scientific accuracy. Basic information on characters and techniques used in identifying trees appears in the introduction, and a comprehensive glossary defines necessary technical terms that might not be generally understood. Anyone interested in knowing how to identify the native trees will find this manual understandable and easily used.

Plant families are arranged according to apparent geneological relationships based on reproductive processes and the structure of reproductive organs, proceeding from the simpler to the more complex. In general this grouping is based on the pioneer system of Eichler, later modified by Engler and Prantl and successive International Botanical Congresses. Occasionally an unimportant species does not follow this arrangement but is inserted in a box elsewhere in the book to save space.

This fourth edition follows the scientific and common names appearing in USDA Agriculture Handbook 541, *Check List of Native and Naturalized Trees of the United States*, 1979. This has resulted in numerous changes in nomen-

PREFACE

clature and accepted species. Distribution maps have been improved through use of the excellent maps prepared by Elbert L. Little, Jr., in USDA Misc. Publ. 1146, *Atlas of United States Trees,* vol. 1, 1971; vol. 3, 1976; and vol. 4, 1977. Keys have been revised and descriptions improved.

Included in this manual are 161 full pages of distribution maps and plates detailing descriptive characters for important species. Sixty-nine of these drawings are original, the work of Bruce Eastman or Robert Lorenz. Twelve were redrawn for the second edition by Tom Olive and three by Anne Kiser. The remainder of the drawings are from the following sources:

1. United States Forest Service. All the drawings of conifers except those on pages 10, 18, 22, 34, 56, 68, 82, and 110; also the drawings on pages 162, 174, 176, 188, 190, 214, 240, 276, 308, 322, 326, 338, 342, 350, 360, 362, 366, and 380. The map showing Forest Regions also was secured from the United States Forest Service.

2. Otis, *Michigan Trees.* The drawings on pages 18, 22, 56, 68, 110, 124, 134, 140, 144, 146, 148, 152, 154, 156, 166, 168, 170, 172, 184, 194, 196, 200, 202, 220, 222, 226, 230, 232, 238, 242, 246, 250, 252, 254, 264, 266, 268, 278, 280, 282, 288, 294, 304, 306, 310, 314, 328, 336, 340, 356, 358, 360, 362, 368, and 378.

3. Illick, *Pennsylvania Trees.* The drawings on pages 244, 292, 298, 318, 332, 344, 346, 350, and 366.

4. Hanzlik, *Trees and Forests of Western United States.* The drawings on pages 10 and 82.

5. North Carolina Agricultural Extension Service. AG42. The drawings on pages xvi, 183, and 290, by Valerie Wright.

6. Sargent, *Manual of the Trees of North America.* The drawings on pages 270 and 296.

Both the author and publisher wish to thank the individuals and organizations involved for permission to make use of these drawings.

Ginkgo • Maidenhair Tree

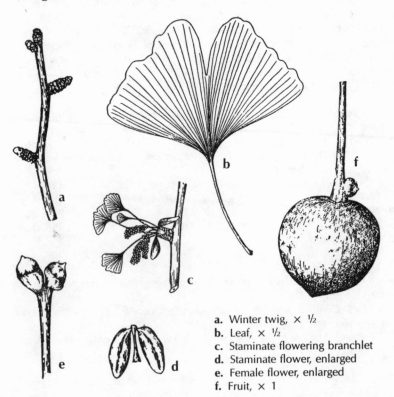

a. Winter twig, × ½
b. Leaf, × ½
c. Staminate flowering branchlet
d. Staminate flower, enlarged
e. Female flower, enlarged
f. Fruit, × 1

INTRODUCTION

Natural Relationship of Trees

Trees, with the exception of tropical tree ferns, belong to one of two major plant groups: the forms with naked seeds commonly subtended by a scale, called Gymnosperms, and the forms containing an ovary that encloses the ovules, called Angiosperms.

Two of the four orders of Gymnosperms contain trees that grow in temperate climates, and by far the most important of these are the cone-bearing trees, such as the pines, spruces, and cedars known as conifers (*Coniferales*). The members of this group have distinctive needlelike, linear, or scalelike leaves and are often known either as evergreens (in spite of the fact that some shed their needles annually) or as softwoods (although several have hard, dense wood). Fifteen genera of conifers containing 94 species are native to North America. These and 13 exotic species are treated in the first section of this book.

The other order of Gymnosperms present in tree form is represented by a single surviving species, the ginkgo or maidenhair tree (*Ginkgo biloba* L.) of China. This interesting tree is extensively planted through all but the coldest parts of the United States and is remarkably free from disease or insects and very tolerant of city smoke. Ginkgo forms a slender, spirelike tree with fan-shaped, fernlike, deciduous leaves borne either spirally on the twigs or at the ends of spurlike shoots. The flowers are dioecious and of interest botanically because of the free-swimming antherozoids. The fruit is orange-yellow to green, about 1 inch in diameter, and resembles a plum. Its fleshy, ill-smelling, outer pulp encloses a large, edible, silvery pit.

The Angiosperms likewise divide into two groups—the Monocotyledons and the Dicotyledons. The first of these, while containing many tree forms in the tropics, is represented in this text by one palm, three palmettos, one nolina, and nine yuccas. These monocotyledonous plants are characterized by parallel major veins in the leaf, flower parts in threes or sixes, and fibrovascular bundles scattered through the stem. While trees in this group are important in the tropics, they are of little use in the temperate zones.

The Dicotyledons contain our most common and widespread trees, such as the oaks, maples, and elms, and they are frequently referred to as broadleaf trees or hardwoods. They differ from the Monocotyledons in having prominent, branched (pinnate or palmate) major veins in the leaves; floral parts usually in fours or fives; and fibrovascular bundles disposed in a ring around a pith. While most of the dicotyledonous trees are deciduous (drop their leaves each fall), many are evergreen and have leaves that persist for two or more years. In this text 142 genera of Dicotyledons are covered, and 500 species are either described or included in the complete keys.

Forest Regions of North America

As a result of differing conditions of moisture, temperature, and soil, the forests may vary from one section of the country to another, both in the species of trees present and in the type or character of the forest. In North America six broad, natural forest regions can be easily recognized. Two are restricted to the eastern part, two to the western part, and two are transcontinental. These regions are described in the sections immediately following. Foresters generally subdivide these six major regions into a larger number.

Within each region are several smaller natural associations or "forest types." These are usually defined and named by one or more dominating tree species, such as the oak-hickory type in the Central Hardwoods region or the lodgepole pine type in the Rocky Mountain region. More than 150 such forest types are recognized in the United States alone. The regions will be briefly described as well as the important species found in each. The principal forest types for the United States are shown on the Forest Service map on page 1.

TROPICAL FOREST REGION. In southern Florida and extreme southern Texas, Arizona, and California are forests made up largely of tropical species. While unimportant, this small area of tropical forests contains many interesting botanical forms. The tropical forest in Florida and east Texas is humid in character and is the northernmost range for many species typical of the deep tropics. Some 100 tropical tree species native to these areas are not included in this manual. Southern Arizona and California, on the other hand, have a desert climate with largely endemic species and these are included.

SOUTHERN FOREST REGION. This region covers the coastal area from Maryland to Texas, extending north along the river bottoms into Missouri, Arkansas, and Oklahoma. The area is characterized by abundant rainfall and mild temperatures and is one of the most important timber-producing areas on the continent. The seven species of pine are found largely on the uplands or flatlands, while baldcypress, Atlantic white-cedar, and numerous hardwoods are typical of the extensive swamps and bottomlands. Among the important hardwoods are the sweetgum, tupelo gums, numerous oaks and hickories, beech, river birch, and several ashes and elms.

CENTRAL HARDWOOD FOREST REGION. There has been a greater decrease in the amount of forested land in this region than in any other due to the large percentage of fertile agricultural land. However, large quantities of high-grade hardwood lumber still remain. This region embraces the central portion of the eastern United States (except for the Appalachian Mountains) and extends into southern Canada. It is characterized by a very large number of species and many types. The climate is humid and generally moderate. Oaks are the dominant species, with hickories, ashes, elms, maples, gum, beech, yellow-poplar, walnut, cottonwood, sycamore, and dogwood also important.

NORTHERN FOREST REGION. This is by far the largest of the forest regions, extending from Georgia north along the Appalachian Mountains to New York, New England, and the northern portions of the Great Lake states in the United States and north in Canada to the limits of tree growth. In Canada this region is transcontinental, extending in a continuous belt across the northern limits of the Great Plains and through the interior of Alaska. The southeastern part of this region is characterized by highly valuable timber species, such as white, red, and jack pine; hemlock; red and white spruce; birches; beech; basswood; maples; and red oak. The northern transcontinental portion of this region is enormous but is largely composed of small-sized trees of white and black spruce, balsam fir, larch, paper birch, aspen, balsam poplar, and willows.

ROCKY MOUNTAIN FOREST REGION. This vast region is spread over the mountains and high plateaus of the western interior from Mexico into northern Canada, where it merges with the Northern Forest region. It is bordered on the east by the Great Plains and on the west by the Pacific Coast Forest. The forests are not continuous in this region, but are limited to the more humid, higher areas interspersed between large treeless stretches occupying the arid lowlands.

The forests characteristically are grouped in conspicuous life zones or belts determined by the moisture, temperature, and topography. These zones tend to increase in altitude as they become more remote from polar regions, so that trees typical of the Northern Forest in northern Canada at elevations of a few hundred feet above sea level might be found at elevations of 8,000 feet in Montana, 10,500 feet in Colorado, and 12,500 feet in Arizona. In the higher, colder, and more humid belt, often called the Canadian zone, are dense forests of Engelmann spruce, alpine fir, western white and lodgepole pine, aspen and balsam poplar, and many other species closely resembling those found in the Northern Forest. Below this belt, in the transition zone, the characteristic tree is ponderosa pine, along with less important species such as western larch, Douglas-fir, various oaks, narrowleaf cottonwood, and water birch. This zone is warmer and drier, being intermediate between the humid Canadian zone and the arid Sonoran zone. The Sonoran zone is semitropical and ranges from high plains and foothills in the south to low plains and valleys further north; it is typified by pinyon-juniper forests, broad-leaved cottonwoods, mesquite, and numerous other shrubby tree species.

PACIFIC COAST FOREST REGION. Many highly important, very large trees growing in dense stands characterize this region, which contains the major portion of our remaining saw timber. This region, bounded on the east by the Rocky Mountain Forest, includes the Pacific Coast states plus the coastal portions of British Columbia and Alaska. Numerous forest types are recognized, including one or more of such species as the coast redwood, Douglas-fir, ponderosa pine, sugar pine, Jeffrey pine, western hemlock, true firs, cedars, spruces, cypresses, red alder, maples, myrtle, and oaks. While some of the southern portions are dry, the greater part of the coastal forests lies in a zone of heavy rainfall. The largest trees in the world (giant sequoia), the tallest trees in the world (redwood, with a maximum height of 372 feet), and the most important timber species in the world (Douglas-fir) are found in this region.

Tree Characters

A brief discussion of the structural and silvical characters, an understanding of which is necessary in identifying trees, is presented here to aid readers without previous botanical training.

DEFINITION OF A TREE. There is no clear-cut line of demarcation between a tree and a shrub, and it is often impossible to place a plant definitely in one group or the other. Frequently a species, treelike under favorable environmental conditions, will be shrublike over most of its range. In general, the height, form, and diameter must be taken into account in determining the classification of a doubtful form. In this handbook a tree is defined as a woody plant having one well-defined stem, a more or less definitely formed crown, a minimum height of 15 to 20 feet, and a diameter of not less than 3 inches.

TERMINOLOGY. While appearing cumbersome to the beginner, the use of technical terms is describing characters is often necessary for a concise, accurate description. A glossary explaining such terms has been included, and their use has been avoided wherever their omission does not impair meaning. Students should learn the more commonly used terms early in their study of the trees.

NAME. The unit used in classifying trees is the *species*. A species is a collection of individuals that so closely resemble one another that they suggest a common parentage. Individuals within a species that exhibit prominent yet minor variations are regarded as *varieties* of the species. A group of related species constitute a *genus,* and a number of related genera, a *family*. Most species of trees have been given one or many common names, which usually describe some character of the tree and are easily learned. Unfortunately, these common names have many limitations. Some are merely local, others apply to two or more entirely different species, and some apply to trees belonging to different genera. Because of this, while common names may be useful and convenient, it is essential that each species have a definite, individual name that can be accepted throughout the world and cannot be applied to any other species.

Botanists and scientists as a whole have agreed that these scientific names should be in Latin, as this is a dead language and not subject to change. Botanists have further agreed that the name of a tree should consist of three parts: (1) a generic name, which is italicized and begins with a capital letter, that refers the species to the group to which it belongs; (2) a specific epithet, which is italicized and begins with a small letter, that refers to the single species; and (3) the full or abbreviated name of the authority or person first describing the plant. Thus, the scientific name of ponderosa pine is *Pinus ponderosa* Laws. When a variety of a species is recognized, the varietal name follows the specific name; in the case of Arizona pine (a southern variety of ponderosa pine), the scientific name is *Pinus ponderosa* var. *arizonica* (Engelm.) Shaw. When the names of two authorities are given, with one appearing in parentheses, the species was first described by the authority in the parentheses, but in a different group of the same rank or in a different rank, and the second author was the one who effected the change. This is the case with the western hemlock, *Tsuga heterophylla* (Raf.) Sarg.

HABIT. Habit refers to the general appearance of a tree, usually as seen from a distance. The size; appearance and form of trunk; shape, density, and size of crown; and number, size, and direction of growth of branches are all factors helpful in distinguishing trees. In the conifers the trunk typically extends to the top of the tree without dividing (*excurrent*), while in most of the hardwoods the trunk breaks up into several large branches (*deliquescent*). The crown and branches may vary greatly in the same species, depending upon whether the tree is growing in the open or in a dense stand where it is shaded on the sides by its neighbors.

LEAVES. Since leaves display characteristic patterns, they are probably the most useful organs in identifying trees (Fig. 1). Leaves consist of an expanded portion (*blade*), a supporting stalk (*petiole*), and small leaflike or scaly structures (*stipules*) attached in pairs at the base of the petiole. Leaves having no stipules are termed *estipulate*, and those without petioles are called *sessile*. Evergreen species can be identified by their leaves throughout the year, while species that shed their leaves annually (*deciduous*) must be identified by other characters during the winter months. Leaves may be arranged with one leaf attached to the twig at a certain point (*alternately*), as two leaves emerging at opposite sides from the same place on a twig (*oppositely*), as more than two leaves emerging from one node on the twig (*whorled*), or as a number of

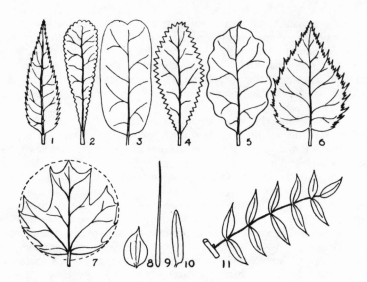

Fig. 1. Leaf patterns. Leaf shapes: lanceolate (*1*), oblanceolate (*2*), oblong (*3*), elliptic (*4*), oval (*5*), ovate (*6*), orbicular (*7*), scalelike (*8*), acicular (*9*), and linear (*10*). Leaf margins: serrate (*1*), crenate (*2*), entire (*3*), dentate (*4*), sinuate (*5*), doubly serrate (*6*), and lobed (*7*). Leaf apices: acuminate (*1*), rounded (*2*), emarginate (*3*), acute (*4*), rounded (*5*), cordate (*6*), and truncate (*7*). Leaf types: simple (*1–10*) and pinnately compound (*11*).

leaves emerging in a cluster or bundle (*fascicled*). They may be made up of a single blade or expanded portion (*simple*) or of several individual leaflets (*compound*). If the leaflets in a compound leaf are arranged along each side of a common axis (*rachis*), the leaf is said to be *pinnately compound,* while if the leaflets all arise from the apex of the petiole, the leaf is termed *palmately compound.* Other characters used in identification are the shapes and the types of margin, apex, and base. Texture, color, and surface, whether smooth or hairy, are also useful characters.

FLOWERS. All trees have flowers, although frequently they are small and inconspicuous. These are the reproductive organs by means of which the species is perpetuated. Floral characters are the most accurate means of identifying many trees, although they are little used in the field because the period of bloom is so short. Flowers vary greatly in form, structure, and size. A *complete* flower (Fig. 2) is usually made up of leaflike *sepals* (*calyx*); often brightly colored *petals* (*corolla*); *stamens,* the male organs that bear the *pollen* in saclike *anthers*; and a *pistil,* the female organ consisting of a terminal *stigma* that catches the pollen, a *style,* and an *ovary.* The ovary may consist of one or

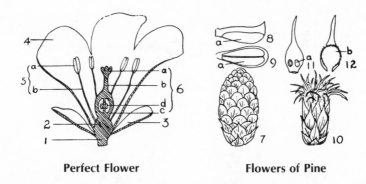

Perfect Flower   **Flowers of Pine**

Fig. 2.   Flower structure: peduncle (*1*), receptacle (*2*), sepal or calyx (*3*), petal or corolla (*4*), stamen (*5*), anther (*5a*), filament (*5b*), pistil (*6*), stigma (*6a*), style (*6b*), ovary (*6c*), ovule (*6d*), staminate conelet (*7*), stamen or pollen-bearing scale showing side and lower surfaces (*8* and *9*), seed-bearing conelet (*10*), seed-bearing scale showing inner and outer surfaces (*11* and *12*), ovule (*11a*), and bract (*12b*).

more compartments (*cells*) and contain one to many *ovules* that later mature into seeds.

If the ovary is inserted on top of the other flower parts, it is *superior,* while if it appears below the origin of sepals, petals, and stamens, it is *inferior.* Flowers may be *perfect* (containing both stamens and pistil) or *imperfect* (containing one sex but not the other). Plants having imperfect flowers can either have both sexes present in different flowers on the same plant (*monoecious*) or each sex borne on a different plant (*dioecious*). When the only functioning sex organs in an imperfect flower are stamens, the flower is termed *staminate,* while one in which the pistil is the active organ is *pistillate.* Plants that bear some perfect and some imperfect flowers are termed *polygamous.* Flowers may appear singly or in clusters (*inflorescences*) (Fig. 3). In Gymnosperms the pistil is replaced by a seed-bearing scale that does not enclose the seed.

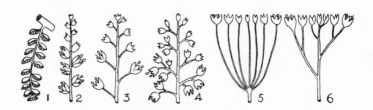

Fig. 3.   Types of inflorescences: ament (*1*), spike (*2*), raceme (*3*), panicle (*4*), umbel (*5*), and corymb (*6*).

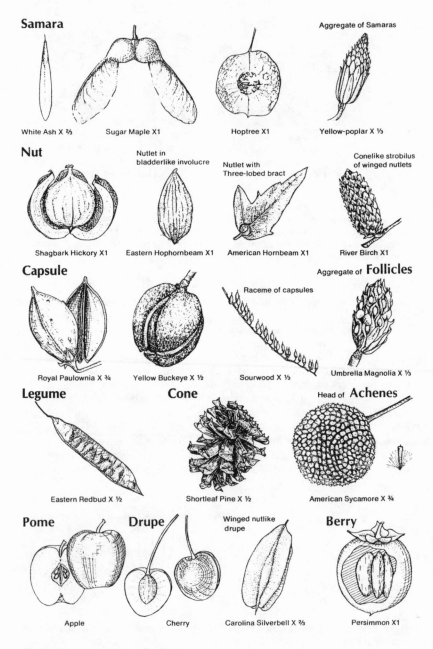

Samara

White Ash X ⅔ Sugar Maple X1 Hoptree X1

Aggregate of Samaras

Yellow-poplar X ⅓

Nut

Shagbark Hickory X1

Nutlet in bladderlike involucre

Eastern Hophornbeam X1

Nutlet with Three-lobed bract

American Hornbeam X1

Conelike strobilus of winged nutlets

River Birch X1

Capsule

Royal Paulownia X ¾ Yellow Buckeye X ½

Raceme of capsules

Sourwood X ⅓

Aggregate of **Follicles**

Umbrella Magnolia X ⅓

Legume

Eastern Redbud X ½

Cone

Shortleaf Pine X ½

Head of **Achenes**

American Sycamore X ¾

Pome

Apple

Drupe

Cherry

Winged nutlike drupe

Carolina Silverbell X ⅔

Berry

Persimmon X1

Fig. 4. Descriptive terms for fruits.

FRUIT. Fruits vary greatly in type and appearance and are thus very useful in identification. The different types of fruits are pictured in Fig. 4, discussed in the text, and defined in the glossary. The seeds included in the fruit contain the embryonic plant. To the layman these are generally of secondary utility in identification.

TWIGS. The color, stoutness, central pith, or surface coverings and markings may be very useful in identifying trees, especially during the winter months (Fig. 5). As buds, stipules, and leaves fall off, they frequently leave characteristic scars on the twig. Buds are conspicuous on most twigs and helpful in identification. The shape, size, color, number of scales, arrangement, and the presence or absence of a terminal bud are important diagnostic characters.

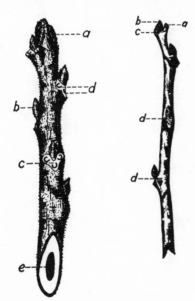

Fig. 5. *Left,* winter twig of black walnut: terminal bud (*a*), lateral bud (*b*), leaf scar (*c*), bundle scars (*d*), and pith (*e*). *Right,* winter twig of red mulberry: tip scar (*a*), lateral bud (*b*), leaf scar (*c*), and stipule scars (*d*).

BARK. The appearance of bark, while varying greatly with age and environment, is often a useful character in identification. Color and thickness of the bark; whether it is furrowed, scaly, or smooth; and even its taste are helpful features.

WOOD. The character of the wood forms a separate means of identification that is more technical and difficult to use than are the external characters. In this handbook only the outstanding wood characters are given, such as the weight, color, and arrangement of large pores (*ring-porous* wood has pores in a definite ringlike zone and *diffuse-porous* wood has pores scattered throughout the wood). A statement as to importance and use of the wood is also included.

SILVICAL CHARACTERS. The tolerance, sites, associates, reproduction, enemies, roots, life zones, and altitudinal distributions of species are often helpful in identification and have been included wherever possible.

In identifying trees it must be remembered that characters are variable and often overlap with those of closely related trees. Wherever possible, identification should not be based on a single character but on as many as are available.

KEY TO THE GENERA

The Use of Keys

Keys provide a useful method of identifying unknown trees. Any feature of a tree that distinguishes it from other trees may be used in a key; however, those characteristics that are readily observable and commonly present are the most useful. The keys in this book stress leaf characters where these are distinctive enough to separate the tree into its genus and species, but fruit, flowers, twigs, buds, and bark are also used when helpful. A key to the genera follows. Keys to the species appear in the handbook where several species are listed in a genus.

The key is based on the principle of alternate choice. At each step in the key there are two contrasting characters between which the user must choose. Through these successive choices, the genus is reached. Once the genus is reached, the page number is given to the generic description and the user is provided with the means of checking the determination. If the tree does not fit the generic description, an error was made in a choice in the key and the material should be rerun through the key.

Key to the Genera

Based Largely on Leaf Characters
1. Seeds not in ovary; flowers unisexual; leaves fan-shaped, linear, needlelike, or scale-like .... **GYMNOSPERMS** (see p. xix)
1. Seeds borne in a closed ovary that becomes the fruit at maturity **ANGIOSPERMS**
    2. Leaves narrow with parallel veins; flower parts in 3's or 6's; stems without central pith or annual wood layers; embryo with 1 cotyledon ....
    .... **MONOCOTYLEDONS** (see p. xx)
    2. Leaves generally broad or rarely wanting, with netted veins; flower parts usually in 4's or 5's; stems with pith and annual wood layers; embryo with 2 cotyledons .... **DICOTYLEDONS** (see p. xxi)

GYMNOSPERMS

1. Leaves fan-shaped with numerous fine veins radiating from petiole, deciduous; twigs with spur shoots; fruit a drupelike seed .... **Ginkgo,** p. viii

1. Leaves linear, needle-shaped, or scalelike, with 1 vein, usually persistent . . . .
   . . . . **Conifers,** p. 3
   2. Leaves needle-shaped, in fascicles of 1–5 each enclosed at base by a sheath
      . . . . **Pinus,** p. 3
   2. Leaves single, linear or scalelike 3
3. Leaves mostly linear; leaves and fruit scales spirally arranged 4
3. Leaves mostly scalelike; leaves and fruit scales opposite 14
   4. Fruit a woody or papery cone of seed-bearing scales 5
   4. Fruit a single seed partially or wholly surrounded by a fleshy aril 13
5. Cone scales thin, terminally attached; seed terminally winged, 2 to each scale . 6
5. Cone scales peltate; seed laterally winged, 2 to many per scale 11
   6. Twigs with spur shoots; cones upright 7
   6. Twigs without spur shoots; cones upright or pendent, maturing in 1 year . . 8
7. Needles deciduous; cones maturing in 1 year . . . . **Larix,** p. 44
7. Needles persistent; cones maturing in 2 or 3 years . . . . **Cedrus,** p. 45
   8. Base of leaves persistent on twigs as peglike projections (sterigmata) 9
   8. Leaves not leaving peglike bases on twig upon falling 10
9. Leaves sessile, 4-angled or flattened . . . . **Picea,** p. 50
9. Leaves stalked, flat or rounded in cross section . . . . **Tsuga,** p. 66
   10. Leaves sessile; cones erect, scales deciduous from axis at maturity; buds
       rounded, resinous (except A. bracteata) . . . . **Abies,** p. 74
   10. Leaves narrowed at base into stalk; cones pendent with exserted bracts; buds
       pointed, nonresinous . . . . **Pseudotsuga,** p. 65
11. Leaves deciduous (persistent in tropical T. mucronatum); 2 seeds under each scale;
    southeastern . . . . **Taxodium,** p. 95
11. Leaves persistent; 2–9 seeds per scale; Pacific 12
    12. Leaves on lateral shoots linear, 2-ranked . . . . **Sequoia,** p. 91
    12. Leaves ovate, appressed . . . . **Sequoiadendron,** p. 93
13. Leaves ½–1 in. long; fruit or seed partially enclosed in scarlet aril, maturing in 1
    year . . . . **Taxus,** p. 121
13. Leaves 1–3½ in. long; fruit a drupelike seed enclosed in green or purple fleshy
    covering; maturing in 2 years . . . . **Torreya,** p. 119
    14. Cone berrylike; leaves scalelike or awl-shaped, both types usually present; seed
        wingless . . . . **Juniperus,** p. 108
    14. Cone woody or leathery; leaves scalelike; seed winged 15
15. Cones globose with peltate scales; 2–20 seeds per scale 16
15. Cones oblong, thin-scaled; 2–3 seeds per scale 17
    16. Cone woody, over ½ in. across, of 6–12 scales; 6–20 seeds per scale; branch-
        lets angled or rounded . . . . **Cupressus,** p. 96
    16. Cone leathery, ¼–½ in. across, of 4–8 scales; 1–5 seeds per scale; branchlets
        flattened . . . . **Chamaecyparis,** p. 96
17. Cones ¾–1½ in. long, 6-scaled . . . . **Libocedrus,** p. 105
17. Cones ⅓–½ in. long, 6- to 12-scaled . . . . **Thuja,** p. 107

MONOCOTYLEDONS
Leaves with Parallel Veins, Alternate, Simple, and Persistent

1. Leaves lanceolate and long; fruit a large capsule . . . . **Yucca,** p. 379
1. Leaves fan-shaped, large; fruit a drupelike berry 2

2. Leaf stalks armed with spines; southwestern .... *Washingtonia,* p. 381
2. Leaf stalks unarmed; southeastern .... *Sabal,* p. 381

DICOTYLEDONS
Leaves with Netted Veins or Rarely Absent

1. Leaves and buds opposite
    2. Leaves compound .... I, p. xxi
    2. Leaves simple .... II, p. xxi
1. Leaves and buds alternate
    3. Leaves compound .... III, p. xxii
    3. Leaves simple
        4. Leaves persistent .... IV, p. xxiii
        4. Leaves deciduous .... V, p. xxiv

LEAVES OPPOSITE, COMPOUND, AND DECIDUOUS

1. Leaves palmately compound; fruit a capsule .... *Aesculus,* p. 316
1. Leaves pinnately compound or 3-foliate 2
    2. Leaflets entire or finely toothed; fruit a samara .... *Fraxinus,* p. 352
    2. Leaflets deeply and sharply toothed 3
3. Flowers yellow, showy; fruit a linear capsule 4–8 in. long; southwestern ....
    .... *Tecoma,* p. 371
3. Flowers small; fruit a double samara, drupe, or capsule 4
    4. Fruit a double samara in racemes; terminal bud present *Acer negundo,* p. 315
    4. Fruit drupaceous or capsule 5
5. Fruit in dense clusters of small, drupelike berries; twigs red-brown ....
    .... *Sambucus,* p. 375
5. Fruit a bladdery, inflated capsule; twigs greenish striped ...... *Staphylea,* p. 323

LEAVES OPPOSITE AND SIMPLE

1. Leaves persistent, entire, thick; fruit a drupe; southeastern coastal plain ....
    .... *Osmanthus,* p. 367
1. Leaves deciduous, not leathery 2
    2. Leaves palmately lobed; fruit a double samara .... *Acer,* p. 302
    2. Leaves not lobed, fruit not a double samara 3
3. Leaves entire 4
3. Leaves toothed 11
    4. Leaves heart-shaped, 5–12 in. long 5
    4. Leaves linear to ovate, less than 5 in. long 6
5. Leaves 5–10 in. long, densely hairy below; flowers purple; capsule leathery, ovoid,
    1–2 in. long .... *Paulownia,* p. 369
5. Leaves 8–12 in. long, slightly hairy below; flowers white; capsule linear, 8–20 in.
    long .... *Catalpa,* p. 369
        6. Leaves linear to lanceolate; fruit a linear capsule 7–12 in. long; southwestern
        .... *Chilopsis,* p. 371
        6. Leaves suborbicular to elliptic 7
7. Exfoliating bark; showy fall flowers; fluted trunk .... *Lagerstroemia,* p. 377
7. Bark not exfoliating; spring flowers; trunk not fluted 8

LEAVES ALTERNATE AND COMPOUND

LEAVES ALTERNATE, SIMPLE, AND DECIDUOUS

Leaves Scalelike, Inconspicuous, or Wanting (p. xxiv)
Leaves Lobed (p. xxv)
Leaves Entire (p. xxv)
Leaves Toothed (p. xxvi)

LEAVES SCALELIKE, INCONSPICUOUS, OR WANTING

4. Twigs without cushionlike processes 5
5. Twigs with lateral spines; fruit a legume .... *Dalea,* p. 272
5. Twigs ending in spine; fruit a berry .... *Koeberlinia,* p. 331

LEAVES LOBED

1. Leaves 4-lobed; bud large with valvate scales; fruit an aggregate of samaras .....
.... *Liriodendron,* p. 239
1. Leaves not 4-lobed; bud scales not valvate 2
   2. Leaves entire or 1- to 3-lobed , all types usually present; aromatic; fruit a blue
   drupe on red stalk .... *Sassafras,* p. 243
   2. Leaves more than 2-lobed, not strongly aromatic 3
3. Leaves palmately 3- to 7-lobed; fruit in multiple heads 4
3. Leaves not palmately 3- to 7-lobed; fruit not in heads 5
   4. Leaves finely toothed; terminal bud scaly; twigs with corky wings; fruit of
   capsules .... *Liquidambar,* p. 245
   4. Leaves coarsely toothed; terminal bud absent, lateral enclosed in enlarged leaf
   petiole; fruit of achenes; bark characteristically mottled .... *Platanus,* p. 247
5. Terminal bud absent; sap milky; fruit a berrylike multiple of drupes 6
5. Terminal bud present; sap watery; fruit simple 7
   6. Leaves velvety-hairy below; fruit globose, orange ..... *Broussonetia,* p. 231
   6. Leaves smooth to hairy below; fruit ovoid, purple, dark red, or white ......
   .... *Morus,* p. 231
7. Twigs with sharp thorns; fruit a small, red pome .... *Crataegus,* p. 257
7. Twigs unarmed (sometimes spinescent in *Malus*) 8
   8. Leaf scars with many bundle traces; fruit an acorn .... *Quercus,* p. 178
   8. Leaf scars with 3 bundle traces 9
9. Leaves toothed; fruit a pome; buds small .... *Malus,* p. 248
9. Leaf lobes entire; fruit a capsule; buds large .... *Populus,* p. 122

LEAVES ENTIRE

1. Leaves, twigs, and drupes silvery-scurfy 2
1. Plants not silvery-scurfy 3
   2. Leaves elliptic to oblong .... *Shepherdia,* p. 339
   2. Leaves lanceolate .... *Elaeagnus,* p. 339
3. Leaves heart-shaped; fruit a legume .... *Cercis,* p. 279
3. Leaves not heart-shaped; fruit not a legume 4
   4. Sap milky; twigs with sharp axillary thorns; fruit a globose multiple of drupes
   4–5 in. across .... *Maclura,* p. 233
   4. Sap watery; twigs and fruit not as above 5
5. Leaves obovate-lanceolate, 10–12 in. long; stipules absent; buds minute; fruit a
berry 3–5 in. long .... *Asimina,* p. 297
5. Leaves and fruit not as above 6
   6. Terminal bud present, conspicuous 7
   6. Terminal bud absent; lateral buds often minute 14
7. Terminal bud large, with single caplike scale; leaves 4–30 in. long; fruit conelike
aggregate .... *Magnolia,* p. 234
7. Terminal bud scaly; leaves 1–7 in. long; fruit simple 8
   8. Stipules present; fruit an acorn .... *Quercus,* p. 178
   8. Stipules absent; fruit not an acorn 9

LEAVES TOOTHED

FOREST REGIONS AND PRINCIPAL TYPES
OF FORESTS IN THE UNITED STATES

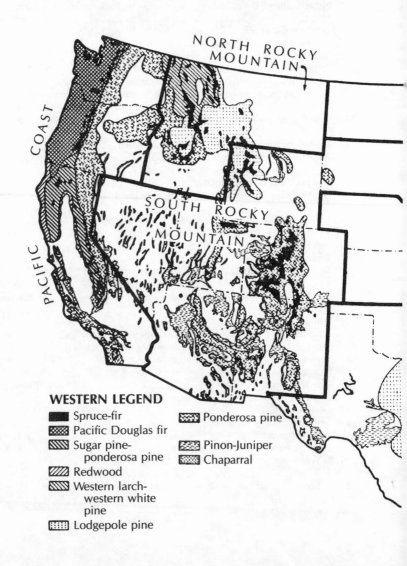

NORTH ROCKY
MOUNTAIN

COAST

PACIFIC

SOUTH ROCKY

MOUNTAIN

WESTERN LEGEND
- Spruce-fir
- Pacific Douglas fir
- Sugar pine-
  ponderosa pine
- Redwood
- Western larch-
  western white
  pine
- Lodgepole pine
- Ponderosa pine
- Pinon-Juniper
- Chaparral

NORTH AMERICAN TREES FOURTH EDITION

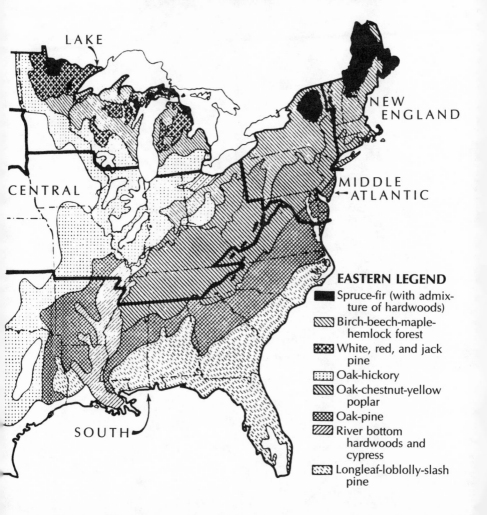

LAKE

NEW ENGLAND

CENTRAL

MIDDLE ATLANTIC

SOUTH

EASTERN LEGEND

- Spruce-fir (with admixture of hardwoods)
- Birch-beech-maple-hemlock forest
- White, red, and jack pine
- Oak-hickory
- Oak-chestnut-yellow poplar
- Oak-pine
- River bottom hardwoods and cypress
- Longleaf-loblolly-slash pine

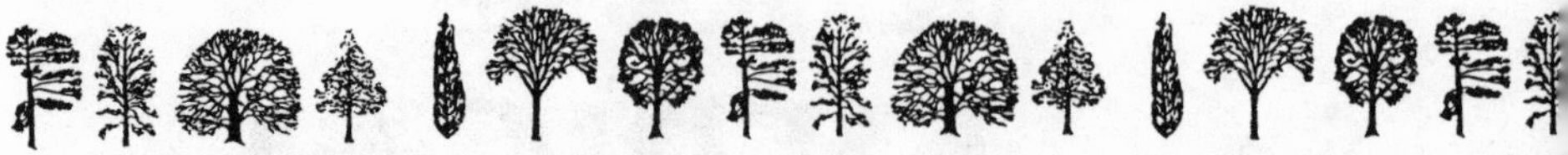

PINACEAE

The Pines

Characteristics of the Genus *Pinus* L.

HABIT. Evergreen trees with straight, unbranched, cylindrical trunks and whorled, spreading branches.

LEAVES. Needlelike; fascicles or bundles of 2–5 (1 in single-leaf pinyon); enclosed in bud by 6–12 scales forming a persistent or soon-deciduous basal sheath; usually with several lines of stomata on each surface; juvenile leaves on young shoots differ, being spirally arranged, single, and scalelike.

FLOWERS. Monoecious; male, or pollen-producing, consisting of spirally arranged, sessile anthers, yellow, orange, or scarlet; female, or cone- and seed-producing, small, conelike bodies consisting of numerous spirally arranged, 2-ovuled scales, each subtended by a small bract.

FRUIT. A cone, usually pendent, composed of the hardened, woody scales of the flower; scales more or less thickened on the exposed terminal surface (the apophysis) with the ends of the growth of the previous year appearing as a terminal or dorsal, brown protuberance or scar (the umbo), which is often armed with a prickle; maturing in 2 (rarely 3) seasons. Seed: 2 borne at the base on inner face of each fertile scale; thin, terminal, papery wing or wingless.

BUDS. Variable in size, shape, and color; covered by fringed or papery-margined overlapping scales; these component scales each protecting a tiny bud that, after the main bud unfolds, develops into a fascicle of leaves or occasionally into a female flower.

WOOD. Among our most important trees; properties extremely variable; numerous, large, easily visible resin ducts; resinous scent. Some species produce naval stores and edible nuts in addition to lumber.

GENERAL. The largest and most important genus of conifers, including about 95 species widely scattered over the Northern Hemisphere; 36 species are native to the United States and Canada; the North American species can be conveniently grouped into the soft or white pines and the hard, pitch, or yellow pines.

KEY TO THE SPECIES OF PINES

1. Needles in clusters of 5 (except pinyons), cluster sheath deciduous, absent on mature needles; 1 fibrovascular bundle in needle cross section; cone scales without prickles (except foxtails) . . . . **soft pines**
    2. Needles in clusters of 1–4; cones globose, few-scaled; seed large and edible, without wing; western . . . . **pinyon pines**
        3. Needles single; Idaho, Nevada, Utah, Arizona, California . . . .
           . . . . *P. monophylla,* **singleleaf pinyon,** p. 17
        3. Needles predominantly in 2's; Colorado, Utah . . . . . *P. edulis,* **pinyon,** p. 17
        3. Needles in 3's; southern Arizona, New Mexico, Texas . . . .
           . . . . *P. cembroides,* **Mexican pinyon,** p. 17
        3. Needles predominantly in 4's; southern California . . . .
           . . . . *P. quadrifolia,* **Parry pinyon,** p. 17
    2. Needles in clusters of 5; cones many-scaled.
        4. Cone scales thin, without prickles; seeds long-winged; needles slender, 2–4 in. long, persistent 2–4 years . . . . **white pines**
            5. Cones 4–8 in. long, scales flexible; eastern Canada to Iowa, Illinois, Georgia . . . . *P. strobus,* **eastern white pine,** p. 11
            5. Cones 5–11 in. (most about 8 in.) long; scales flexible; western Canada to Montana and California . . . . *P. monticola,* **western white pine,** p.11
            5. Cones 12–18 in. long; scales rigid; Oregon, California, Nevada . . . .
               . . . . *P. lambertiana,* **sugar pine,** p. 9
        4. Cone scales thick; needles stout, 1–3 in. long, persistent 5–17 years; western.
            6. Cone scales without prickles; seed wing absent or short; needles 1½–3 in., persistent 5–8 years . . . . **stone pines**
                7. Cones 1½–3 in. long, subglobose, remaining closed; alpine, southern Canada to California and Wyoming . . . .
                   . . . . *P. albicaulis,* **whitebark pine,** p. 13
                7. Cones 3–10 in. long, subcylindrical, opening at maturity.
                    8. Cone scales not or only slightly reflexed; widely scattered through West . . . . *P. flexilis,* **limber pine,** p. 13
                    8. Cone scales strongly reflexed; Mexican border . . . .
                       . . . . *P. strobiformis,* **southwestern white pine,** p. 13
            6. Cone scales with prickles; seed with long wing; needles 1–1½ in. long, resin-dotted, persistent 10–17 years . . . . **foxtail pines**
                9. Cones with long, slender prickles; alpine, Colorado to California, south
                   . . . . *P. aristata,* **bristlecone pine,** p. 15
                9. Cones with minute, incurved prickles; California alpine . . . .
                   . . . . *P. balfouriana,* **foxtail pine,** p. 15
1. Needles in clusters of 2 or 3 (5 in Torrey and Arizona pine), cluster sheath persistent (deciduous in Chihuahua pine); 2 fibrovascular bundles in cross section of needle; cone scales usually armed with prickles . . . . **hard pines**
    2. Eastern hard pines (northeastern and central states, some extending south)
        3. Needles in 3's, or 2's and 3's, 3–5 in. long, twisted; cones 1½–3½ in. long, persistent on branch.
            4. Needles in 3's, rigid; cones ovoid with stout prickles; New Brunswick and Ontario to Georgia . . . . *P. rigida,* **pitch pine,** p. 23
            4. Needles in 2's and 3's, soft and flexible; cones oblong with weak prickles;

New York to Missouri and south . . . . . *P. echinata,* **shortleaf pine,** p. 25
3. Needles in 2's.
    5. Needles 4–6 in. long; cones symmetrical.
        6. Cones 2–3½ in., persistent several years, falling entire; scales yellow-brown, short spine; widely planted exotic . . . . *P. nigra,* **Austrian pine,** p. 19
        6. Cones 1½–2½ in. long, falling in 1 year, leaving basal scales on limb; scales red-brown, unarmed; southern Canada to Minnesota and West Virginia . . . . *P. resinosa,* **red pine,** p. 19
    5. Needles 1–3 in. long.
        7. Bark distinctly orange-colored; cones 1½–2½ in. long, unsymmetrical, opening at maturity, falling when ripe; scales often pyramidally thickened; widely planted and naturalized in Northeast . . . . *P. sylvestris,* **Scotch pine,** p. 19
        7. Bark not distinctly orange-colored; cones long persistent; scales not pyramidally thickened.
            8. Cones 2–3½ in. long, heavy; scales much thickened at ends, armed with conspicuous sharp spurs; Appalachian Mountains, New Jersey to Georgia . . . . *P. pungens,* **Table Mountain pine,** p. 31
            8. Cones 1½–2 in. long, thin-scaled, slender or minute prickles.
                9. Cones strongly incurved, commonly remaining closed; scales irregularly developed; Canada to New York, Indiana, Wisconsin, Minnesota . . . . *P. banksiana,* **jack pine,** p. 21
                9. Cones symmetrical, opening at maturity; New York to Indiana, south to Georgia, Mississippi . . . . *P. virginiana,* **Virginia pine,** p. 21
2. Southern yellow pines (Gulf and South Atlantic states).
    3. Needles 6–18 in. long, in 3's (2's and 3's in slash pine).
        4. Cones 2–2½ in. long and broad, often remaining closed, long persistent; needles 6–8 in. long; New Jersey to Florida . . . . *P. serotina,* **pond pine,** p. 23
        4. Cones 2–10 in. long, much longer than broad, opening at maturity and not persistent.
            5. Needles 8–18 in. long; cones 6–10 in. long; conspicuous thick twigs, large silvery-white buds; Virginia to Florida to Texas . . . . *P. palustris,* **longleaf pine,** p. 29
            5. Needles 6–12 in. long; cones 2–6 in. long; twigs not conspicuously stout; buds red-brown.
                6. Needles in 3's, 6–9 in. long; cones light brown, stout spine; New Jersey to Oklahoma, Texas . . . . *P. taeda,* **loblolly pine,** p. 27
                6. Needles in 2's and 3's, 8–12 in. long; cones chocolate-brown, small spine or prickle; South Carolina to Louisiana . . . . *P. elliottii,* **slash pine,** p. 31
    3. Needles 1½–5 in. long, in 2's (2's and 3's, shortleaf pine).
        7. Needles 3–5 in. long, in 2's and 3's, widely distributed on dry soils; New York to Missouri and south . . . . *P. echinata,* **shortleaf pine,** p. 25
        7. Needles 1½–3½ in. long, in 2's.
            8. Cones 2–3½ in. long, often remaining closed and persistent for years; dry sandy soils in Florida. . . . . *P. clausa,* **sand pine,** p. 27
            8. Cones ½–2 in. long, opening at maturity and falling in few years;

coastal bottomlands, South Carolina to Louisiana . . . .
. . . . *P. glabra,* **spruce pine,** p. 25
2. Western yellow pines (region west of Great Plains).
    3. Needles in 5's.
        4. Needles 5–7 in. long; cones thin-scaled, 2–3½ in. long; Arizona and New
        Mexico . . . . *P. ponderosa arizonica,* **Arizona pine,** p. 33
        4. Needles 8–13 in. long; cones thick-scaled, 4–6 in. long; southern Cali-
        fornia . . . . *P. torreyana,* **Torrey pine,** p. 43
    3. Needles in 2's and 3's, or 3's.
        5. Cones massive, 6–14 in. long, clawlike spines; needles in 3's.
            6. Cones yellow-brown, 10–14 in. long; seeds shorter than wings; south-
            ern and lower California . . . . *P. coulteri,* **Coulter pine,** p. 39
            6. Cones red-brown, 6–10 in. long; seeds longer than wings; dry California
            foothills . . . . *P. sabiniana,* **digger pine,** p. 39
        5. Cones not massive; without clawlike spines.
            7. Cones unsymmetrical with thickened scales, often remaining closed and
            persistent for years.
                8. Needles in 2's, 1–3 in.; cones under 2 in.
                    9. Cones with knoblike scales and long prickles.
                        10. Needles 1–1½ in. long; small contorted tree of coastal area
                        . . . . *P. contorta,* **shore pine,** p. 37
                        10. Needles 1–3 in. long; straight, slender, mountain tree
                        throughout West . . . .
                        . . . . *P. contorta latifolia,* **lodgepole pine,** p. 37
                    9. Cones with thin scales and minute prickle; Canada and northeast-
                    ern United States . . . . *P. banksiana,* **jack pine,** p. 21
                8. Needles 3–7 in. long; cones 2–6 in. long; Oregon, California
                    11. Needles in 2's; cones 2–3½ in. long, with stout, spurlike prick-
                    les . . . . *P. muricata,* **bishop pine,** p. 43
                    11. Needles in 3's; cones 3–7 in. long, without spurlike prickles.
                        12. Thickened cone scales flattened, pyramidal; dry foothills,
                        California, Oregon . . . *P. attenuata,* **knobcone pine,** p. 41
                        12. Thickened cone scales rounded, domelike; California coast
                        . . . . *P. radiata,* **Monterey pine,** p. 41
            7. Cones symmetrical, thin-scaled.
                13. Needles in 3's, 2–4 in. long, cluster sheath deciduous; cones 1½–2
                in. long, maturing in 3 years, long-stalked, often remaining closed,
                long persistent; southern Arizona, southern New Mexico . . . .
                . . . . *P. leiophylla,* **Chihuahua pine,** p. 37
                13. Needles over 4 in., sheath persistent; cones 2–15 in., maturing in 2
                years, short-stalked, opening, deciduous, basal scales remaining on
                twig.
                    14. Cones 2–3½ in long; needles 4–6 in.; rare and local in Washoe
                    County, Nevada . . . .
                    . . . . *P. washoensis* M. & S., **Washoe pine,** p. 35
                    14. Cones 3–15 in. long; needles 4–15 in. long.
                        15. Cones 5–15 in. long; needles 4–9 in. long, persistent 6–9
                        years; twigs purplish, lemonlike odor; buds not covered
                        with resin droplets; California, Oregon . . . .
                        . . . . *P. jeffreyi,* **Jeffrey pine,** p. 35

15. Cones 3–6 in. long; needles persistent 2–3 years; twigs orange to red, turpentine odor; buds often covered with droplets.
    16. Needles 4–11 in. (mostly 5–7 in.) long, in 2's and 3's, yellow-green; throughout West . . . .
    . . . . *P. ponderosa,* **ponderosa pine,** p. 33
    16. Needles 8–15 in., in 3's (rarely 2–5), dark green; Arizona, New Mexico . . . .
    . . . . *P. engelmannii,* **Apache pine,** p. 35

Sugar Pine

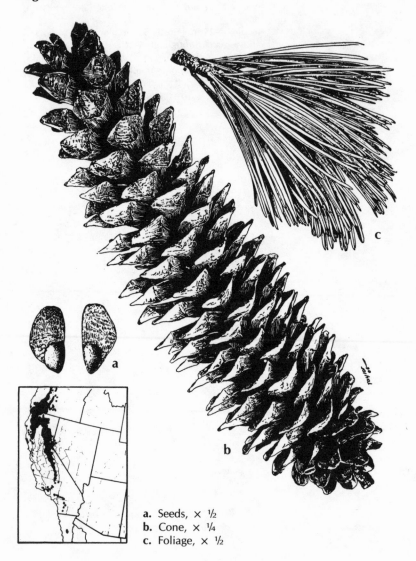

a. Seeds, × ½
b. Cone, × ¼
c. Foliage, × ½

Sugar Pine

Pinus lambertiana Dougl.

HABIT. The largest American pine, commonly 175–200 ft high and 3–5 ft in diameter (max. 246 by 10 ft); on good sites with a long, clear bole and a short crown of large, often contorted, horizontal branches.

LEAVES. In fascicles of 5; 2–4 in. long; stouter than in white pine; twisted; blue- to gray-green; persistent 2–3 years; sheath deciduous; margin with minute teeth; often silvery with conspicuous white lines of stomata.

FLOWERS. Male yellow; female bright pink with purple scale margins.

FRUIT. Cones long-stalked; 10–26 in. long and 4–5 in. in diameter; scales slightly thicker and more rigid than in white pine, unarmed and with terminal umbo. Seeds: ½ in. long; dark brown to black; wings 1–1½ in. long.

TWIGS. Slender to stout; at first rusty-pubescent, later smooth and orange-brown. Winter buds: ⅓ in. long; sharp-pointed; chestnut-brown.

BARK. On young stems thin, smooth, and gray-green; on mature boles 1½–4 in. thick, in thick platelike ridges covered with purplish to reddish scales.

WOOD. Very important; similar to white pine but coarser in texture; sash, door, pattern work, etc.; a sweet, sugarlike substance called pinite exudes from wounds and gives the tree its name.

SILVICAL CHARACTERS. Intolerant; reaches maturity in 200–350 years (extreme age 623 years); reproduction generally sparse; tree windfirm with well-developed tap and lateral root system; blister rust and bark beetles cause damage.

HABITAT. Transition zone; altitudinal range 3,000–10,000 ft; best development on west slopes of Sierra Nevada at 4,500–5,500 ft; in mixed stands with ponderosa and Jeffrey pines, Douglas-fir, and other conifers; on cooler and moister sites than associated pines.

White Pine

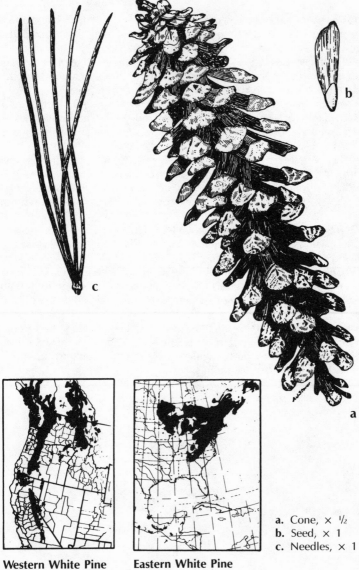

Western White Pine

Eastern White Pine

a. Cone, × ½
b. Seed, × 1
c. Needles, × 1

Western White Pine

Pinus monticola Dougl.

HABIT. A tree 90–180 ft high and 2½ ft in diameter (max. 200 by 8 ft); on good sites a tall bole with narrow, symmetrical crown and slender, drooping branches.

LEAVES. In fascicles of 5; 2–4 in. long; slender; twisted; blue-green; persistent 3–4 years; sheath deciduous; margin with minute teeth; all sides marked by stomata.

FLOWERS. Male yellow; female red-purple in clusters.

FRUIT. Cones long-stalked; 5–15 (mostly 8–11) in. long; narrow; scales thin, unarmed, with terminal umbo. Seeds: ¼ in. long; wings about 1 in. long; red-brown.

TWIGS. Slender; at first rusty-pubescent, later smooth and red-brown to purple-brown. Winter buds: ½ in. long; oblong-ovoid.

BARK. On young stems thin, smooth, and light gray; on mature trees rarely over 1½ in. thick in square or rectangular, dark gray plates.

WOOD. Very important; soft, light in weight, and not strong; light brown heartwood; similar to eastern white pine; planing mill products, building, construction, patterns, etc.

SILVICAL CHARACTERS. Tolerant when young, becoming intolerant with age; reaches maturity in 200–350 years (extreme age 400–500 years); reproduction generally sparse; tree windfirm with well-developed tap and lateral root system; fire, blister rust, and bark beetles cause damage.

HABITAT. Canadian zone; altitudinal range 2,000–7,000 ft; best on rich, porous, moist soils; often forming extensive pure forests, in mixtures elsewhere with other conifers.

Eastern White Pine

Pinus strobus L.

Until about 1890 this species was the most important forest tree in North America. It is still an important species and very similar in appearance to western white pine, from which it can be distinguished by its distribution, the cone length varying from 4 to 8 (mostly about 5) in. long, and needle persistence of 2 (rarely 3) years.

Limber Pine

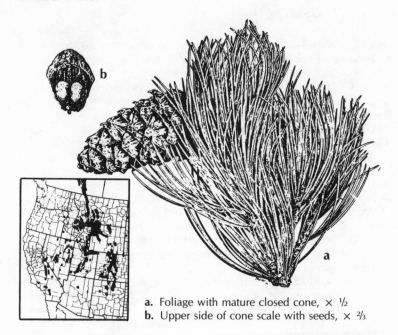

a. Foliage with mature closed cone, × ½
b. Upper side of cone scale with seeds, × ⅔

Whitebark Pine

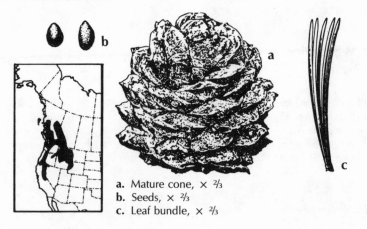

a. Mature cone, × ⅔
b. Seeds, × ⅔
c. Leaf bundle, × ⅔

Limber Pine

Pinus flexilis James

HABIT. A tree 25–50 ft high (max. 85 by 6⅓ ft); crown broad, open, with large, plumelike, often drooping branches.

LEAVES. In fascicles of 5; 1½–3 in. long; stout; rigid; dark green; persistent 5–6 years; sheath deciduous; margins with minute teeth; marked on all sides by rows of stomata.

FLOWERS. Male red; female clustered red-purple.

FRUIT. Cones short-stalked; 3–10 in. long; subcylindric; open at maturity; scales greatly thickened and often slightly reflexed, with terminal unarmed umbo. Seeds: ⅓–½ in. long; wingless; thick, light brown shell.

TWIGS. Stout and tough; smooth and silver-white or gray. Winter buds: ⅓–½ in. long; broad-ovoid and pointed.

BARK. Characteristically thin, smooth, white-gray.

WOOD. Unimportant; moderately light and soft; close-grained; used locally for mine props, railroad ties, etc.

SILVICAL CHARACTERS. Very intolerant; slow-growing; reaches maturity in 200–300 years; tree very windfirm with taproot; fire, blister rust, and bark beetles cause damage.

HABITAT. Upper Sonoran to Hudsonian zones; altitudinal range 4,000–11,500 ft; adapted to wide variety of sites, but typical of summits and rocky foothills.

Southwestern White Pine

Pinus strobiformis Engelm.

This species of the Mexican border has been considered a variety of *P. flexilis*. It differs in having strongly reflexed cone scales.

Whitebark Pine

Pinus albicaulis Engelm.

A subalpine tree almost indistinguishable from limber pine except for its very characteristic cones.

FRUIT. Cones short-stalked; 1½–3 in. long; subglobose; closed at maturity and opening by disintegrating at the axis; purple-brown; scales thick with stout, pointed umbos.

Bristlecone Pine

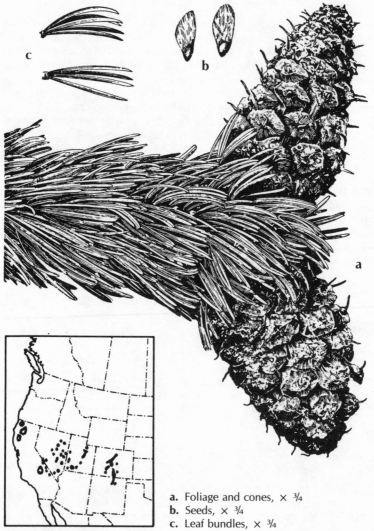

a. Foliage and cones, × ¾
b. Seeds, × ¾
c. Leaf bundles, × ¾

**Bristlecone (solid) and
Foxtail Pine (open)**

Bristlecone Pine

Pinus aristata Engelm.

HABIT. A subalpine tree 30–40 ft high and 1–2 ft in diameter (max. 60 by 3 ft); bole short, stocky, and commonly malformed; crown dense, irregular, bushy in appearance, and frequently clothing the stem nearly to the ground.

LEAVES. In fascicles of 5; 1–1½ in. long; stout and curved; deep green; persistent 10–17 years; in dense, often appressed, clusters; sheath deciduous; lustrous on back, marked on lower or ventral surfaces by numerous rows of stomata; usually showing conspicuous whitish exudations of resin.

FLOWERS. Male dark orange-red; female purple.

FRUIT. Cones short-stalked; 3–3½ in. long; ovoid-oblong; open at maturity; scales thick, with dark chocolate-brown apophysis; umbo dorsal, with long, bristlelike, fragile, incurved prickle. Seeds: ¼ in. long; long terminal wing.

TWIGS. Stout; orange-colored, becoming nearly black; long tufts of foliage at ends. Winter buds: ⅓ in. long; brown.

BARK. Thin, smooth, and gray-white on young stems; ½–¾ in. thick on mature trunks; red-brown and furrowed.

WOOD. Unimportant; moderately soft; heartwood pale red-brown; used locally for fuel and mine props.

SILVICAL CHARACTERS. Very intolerant; slow-growing; reaches maturity in 200–250 years; attains great age, some trees over 4,000 years old and possibly the oldest living organisms; reproduction sparse and scattered; tree windfirm.

HABITAT. From typical Hudsonian to Transition zones; altitudinal range 7,500–10,800 ft; typical of exposed sites; usually in mixture with limber pine, fir, and spruce.

Foxtail Pine

Pinus balfouriana Grev. & Balf.

This California subalpine species closely resembles *P. aristata* except for its cones, which are dark purple, 3–5 in. long, and armed with a minute, incurved, deciduous prickle.

Mexican Pinyon

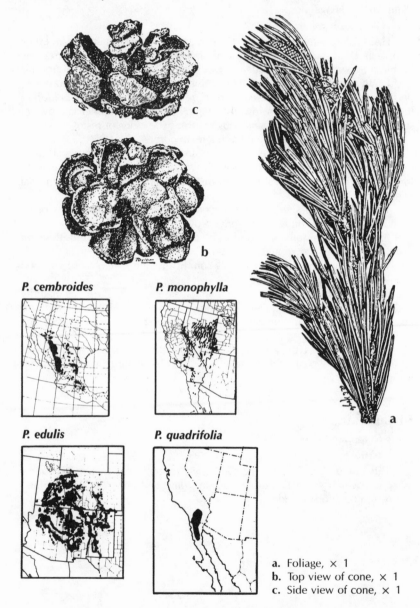

P. cembroides

P. monophylla

P. edulis

P. quadrifolia

a. Foliage, × 1
b. Top view of cone, × 1
c. Side view of cone, × 1

Mexican Pinyon • Nut Pine

Pinus cembroides Zucc.

HABIT. A tree 10–40 ft high and 1–2 ft in diameter (max. 50 by 3 ft); bole often divided with a spreading, rounded crown, giving the tree a bushy appearance.

LEAVES. In fascicles of 3, or 2 and 3 (rarely 1–5); 1–2 in. long; moderately slender (less than 1 mm); blue-green; incurved; sharp-pointed; persistent 3–4 years; margins with minute teeth; fascicle sheath only partially deciduous.

FLOWERS. Male yellow in crowded clusters; female red.

FRUIT. Cones 1–2½ in. long; ovoid to globose; scales few and unarmed. Seeds: ½–¾ in. long; wingless; edible; hard-shelled.

TWIGS. Moderately stout; orange-colored to brown.

BARK. Rarely over ½ in. thick on mature trees; divided into ridges separated by shallow fissures; light red-brown.

WOOD. Unimportant; rather hard; fine-textured; light yellow heartwood; used locally for fuel, ties, and posts.

SILVICAL CHARACTERS. Very intolerant; growth slow; reaches maturity in 250–350 years; reproduction generally sparse and scattered; tree very windfirm.

HABITAT. Upper Sonoran zone; arid, gravelly slopes; usually in mixture with junipers and scrub oaks.

SIMILAR SPECIES. The following species are very similar to *Pinus cembroides but differ from it in distribution and certain characters.*

Pinyon • Colorado Pinyon

Pinus edulis Engelm. (*Pinus cembroides* var. *edulis* Voss)

LEAVES. In fascicles of 2 (rarely 1 or 3); over 1 mm thick; yellow-green; persistent 3–9 years; margins entire.

FRUIT. Seeds thin-shelled, easily cracked with teeth.

Singleleaf Pinyon

Pinus monophylla T. & F. (*Pinus cembroides* var. *monophylla* Voss)

LEAVES. Single (rarely in 2's); over 1 mm thick; pale green; persistent 4–12 years; margins entire.

Parry Pinyon

Pinus quadrifolia Parl. (*Pinus cembroides* var. *parryana* Voss)

LEAVES. In fascicles of 4 (rarely 3–5); over 1mm thick; blue-green; persistent 3 years; margins entire or toothed.

Red Pine

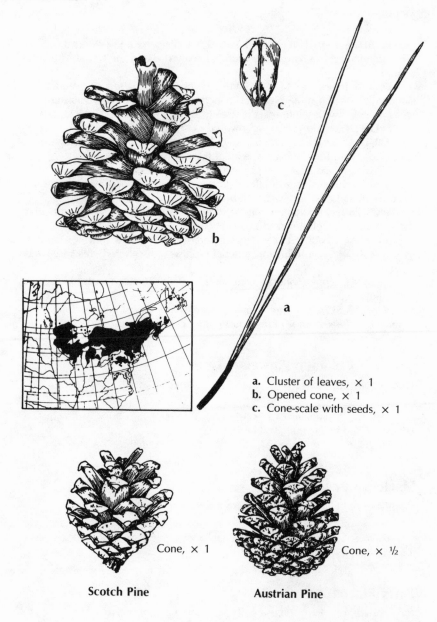

a. Cluster of leaves, × 1
b. Opened cone, × 1
c. Cone-scale with seeds, × 1

Scotch Pine — Cone, × 1

Austrian Pine — Cone, × ½

Red Pine

Pinus resinosa Ait.

HABIT. A tree 60–80 ft high and 2–3 ft in diameter (max. 120 by 5 ft); bole symmetrical, clear; crown broad, rounded, open.

LEAVES. In fascicles of 2; 4–6 in. long; slender; straight; brittle; dark yellow-green; persistent 4–5 years; margins with minute teeth; basal sheath persistent.

FLOWERS. Male purple; female scarlet.

FRUIT. Subsessile; 1½–2¼ in. long; ovoid-conic; chestnut-brown; umbo dorsal and unarmed; in falling leaves basal scales on twig. Seeds: ³⁄₁₆ in. long; wings ⅔ in. long.

TWIGS. Stout; rough; orange to red-brown. Winter buds: ½–¾ in. long; scales red-brown with white fringed margins.

BARK. 1–1½ in. thick; light red-brown; broken into scaly plates.

WOOD. Important; rather light and soft; heartwood light red-brown; used for construction, ties, etc.

SILVICAL CHARACTERS. Intermediate in tolerance; moderate rate of growth; reaches extreme age in about 350 years; roots widespreading with taproot; reproduction vigorous; hardy and resistent to enemies.

HABITAT. Light, sandy soils; in pure stands, or mixed with white pine on better sites and jack pine on poorer.

Scotch Pine

Pinus sylvestris L.

The Scotch pine has become naturalized in the Northeast. This species is easily identified by its twisted needles, 1½–3 in. long, in clusters of 2; by yellow-brown cones 1–2½ in. long with flat or pyramidally thickened scales; and by bark that is distinctly orange in color.

Austrian Pine

Pinus nigra Arnold

Another related Eurasian pine, Austrian pine, has escaped from cultivation. It resembles red pine in its needles, but can be distinguished by its dark brown bark; silvery-white buds; and yellow-brown cones 2–3 in. long, armed with a short spine, and falling intact from the twigs.

Jack Pine

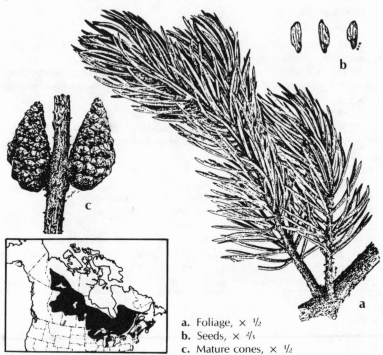

a. Foliage, × ½
b. Seeds, × ⅔
c. Mature cones, × ½

Virginia Pine

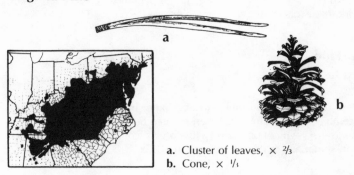

a. Cluster of leaves, × ⅔
b. Cone, × ⅓

Jack Pine

Pinus banksiana Lamb.

HABIT. A tree rarely 60–80 ft high (max. 90 by 2 ft); bole often crooked; crown open, irregular, scraggly.

LEAVES. In fascicles of 2; ¾–1½ in. long; divergent; stout; twisted; yellow-green; persistent 2–3 years; margins with minute teeth; basal sheath persistent.

FLOWERS. Male yellow; female dark purple; clustered.

FRUIT. Sessile; 1½–2 in. long; oblong-conic; unsymmetrical; often remains closed and on tree for years; scales irregularly developed, unarmed or with minute deciduous prickle. Seeds: ¹⁄₁₂ in. long; black; wings about ⅓ in. long.

TWIGS. Thin, tough; flexible; becoming rough and red-brown; Winter buds: ¼ in. long; ovoid; pale cinnamon-brown; very resinous.

BARK. Thin; dark red-brown; shallowly ridged.

WOOD. Moderately important; light and soft; heartwood light brown; used for pulp, fuel, posts, etc.

SILVICAL CHARACTERS. Very intolerant; short-lived; widespreading roots with a taproot; reproduction vigorous.

HABITAT. Essentially Canadian, extending farther north than other pines; dry sterile soils; mostly in pure stands.

Virginia Pine

Pinus virginiana Mill.

This species is similar to jack pine in habit, twigs, bark, wood, silvical characters, and site; it differs from jack pine in distribution and the following characters:

LEAVES. In fascicles of 2; 1½–3 in. long; divergent; stout; twisted; gray-green; persistent 3–4 years; margins with minute teeth; short-needled trees hardly distinguishable from jack pine.

FLOWERS. Male orange-brown; female pale green tinged with rose.

FRUIT. Subsessile; 1½–3 in. long; ovoid-conic; symmetrical; opens at maturity but persists on twigs 3–4 years; scales think, flat, with persistent prickle and deep purple inner lip. Seeds: ¼ in. long, pale brown, with wing about 1 in. long.

Pitch Pine

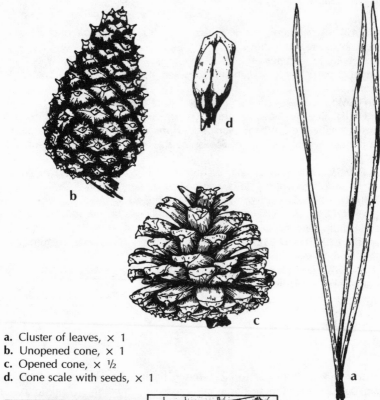

a. Cluster of leaves, × 1
b. Unopened cone, × 1
c. Opened cone, × ½
d. Cone scale with seeds, × 1

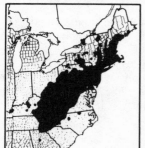

Pitch Pine

Pond Pine

Pitch Pine

Pinus rigida Mill.

HABIT. A tree 40–60 ft high and 1–2 ft in diameter (max. 100 by 3 ft); on good sites; straight bole; open, irregular crown of large, nearly horizontal branches.

LEAVES. In fascicles of 3; 3–5 in. long; stout; stiff; usually twisted; standing out at nearly right angles to twig; yellow-green; often produced on trunk; persistent 2–3 years; margins with minute teeth; basal sheath persistent.

FLOWERS. Male yellow; female red-green.

FRUIT. Short-stalked; 1½–3½ in. long; ovoid-conic; opening at maturity but persistent for many years; scales armed with short, rigid prickle. Seeds: ¼ in. long; dull black; winged.

TWIGS. Stout; rough; gray-brown. Winter buds: ½–¾ in. long; scales chestnut-brown and fringed; resinous.

BARK. Thick; dark red-brown; flat plates separated by furrows.

WOOD. Of little importance; light and soft; heartwood light brown; used for lumber, ties, props, fuel.

SILVICAL CHARACTERS. Very intolerant; short-lived; taproot in youth; reproduction vigorous; young trees produce sprouts.

HABITAT. Typically dry, sterile sites; pure or mixed stands, with scrub oak, red maple, gray birch, etc.

Pond Pine

Pinus serotina Michx. (*Pinus rigida* var. *serotina* [Michx.] Loud.)

This closely related southern species found in swamps and low, wet flats differs from pitch pine in having flexible needles 6–8 in. long and nearly globose cones that remain closed for several years and armed with weak, deciduous prickles. Pond pine closely resembles *P. taeda* when persistent cones are lacking but may be distinguished by its very resinous buds, less upright needle orientation, and frequent presence of trunk sprouts. It has remarkable ability to sprout following fire.

Shortleaf Pine

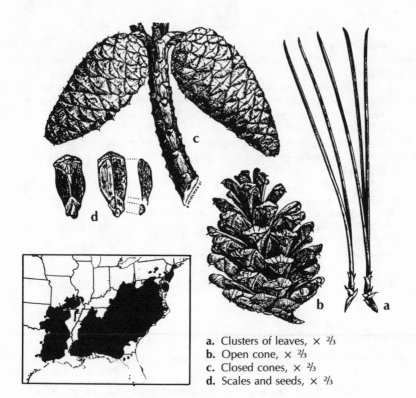

a. Clusters of leaves, × ⅔
b. Open cone, × ⅔
c. Closed cones, × ⅔
d. Scales and seeds, × ⅔

Spruce Pine

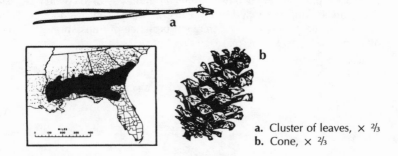

a. Cluster of leaves, × ⅔
b. Cone, × ⅔

Shortleaf Pine

Pinus echinata Mill.

HABIT. A tree 80–100 ft high and 2–3 ft in diameter (max. 130 by 4 ft); long, clear bole; narrow, pyramidal crown.

LEAVES. In fascicles of 2 and 3; 3–5 in. long; slender; flexible; yellow-green; persistent 2–4 years; often produced on trunk; basal sheath persistent.

FLOWERS. Male pale purple; female pale rose color.

FRUIT. Nearly sessile; 1½–2½ in. long; oblong to conic; opening at maturity and persistent several years; red-brown; scales thin, armed with small sharp prickle. Seeds: 3/16 in. long; brown with black markings; wings ½ in. long.

TWIGS. Slender; flexible; roughened; red-brown. Winter buds: ¼ in. long; red- to gray-brown; not highly resinous.

BARK. Thin; nearly black and scaly on young trees; later becoming red-brown and scaly-plated; characteristic resin holes or pockets.

WOOD. Very important; intermediate between longleaf and western pines in strength and hardness; many uses.

SILVICAL CHARACTERS. Intolerant; fast-growing on good sites; deep tap-root system; reproduction aggressive; young trees capable of producing sprouts if stems killed.

HABITAT. Typical of dry, light soils in pure or mixed stands.

Spruce Pine

Pinus glabra Walt.

Nowhere common, this unimportant medium-sized tree is found scattered among hardwoods on moist sandy loams. It is very tolerant and resembles shortleaf pine.

LEAVES. In fascicles of 2; 1½–3 in. long; slender; dark green.

FRUIT. Similar to shortleaf, but more globose and smaller, with weak, small, often deciduous prickle.

BARK. Thin; gray; smooth on twigs and young stems.

Loblolly Pine

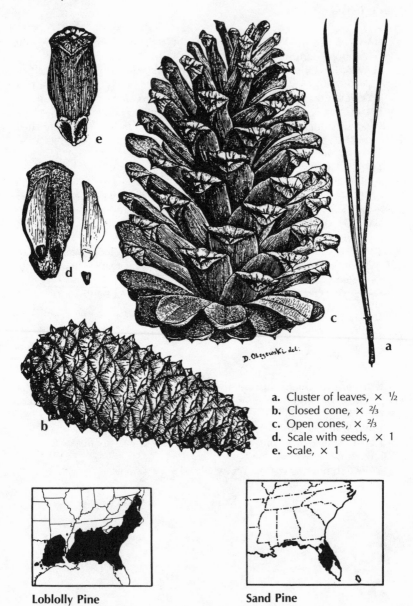

D. Olzgewski del.

a. Cluster of leaves, × ½
b. Closed cone, × ⅔
c. Open cones, × ⅔
d. Scale with seeds, × 1
e. Scale, × 1

Loblolly Pine

Sand Pine

Loblolly Pine

Pinus taeda L.

HABIT. A tree 90–110 ft high and 2–3 ft in diameter (max. 150 by 5½ ft); long, clear bole; crown rounded, dense.

LEAVES. In fascicles of 3 (rarely 2); 6–9 in. long; slender; yellow-green; persistent 3 years; basal sheath persistent.

FLOWERS. Male yellow; female short-stalked, yellow.

FRUIT. Sessile; 2½–6 in. long; typically oblong-conic; opening at maturity and falling next year; dull, pale, red-brown; scales thin, armed with a stout, sharp spine. Seeds: ¼ in. long; brown with black markings; wings ¾ in. long.

TWIGS. Moderately slender; roughened; yellow- to red-brown. Winter buds: ½ in. long; red-brown scales with free tips.

BARK. Thin; becoming ¾–2 in. thick; scaly and nearly black on young trees, becoming bright red-brown and scaly-plated.

WOOD. Important; intermediate between longleaf and western pines in strength and hardness; marketed as shortleaf pine.

SILVICAL CHARACTERS. Most tolerant of important southern pines; very fast-growing; windfirm; reproduction very aggressive; not resistant to fire; in pure or mixed stands.

HABITAT. Typical of wet bottomlands; aggressive on drier cutover or abandoned areas when protected from fire; in pure stands or mixed with pines and hardwoods.

Sand Pine

Pinus clausa (Chapm.) Vasey

This unimportant small tree is common in Florida on very dry, sterile, sandy soils; it comes in aggressively after fires. It is easily identified by its needles and characteristic cones.

LEAVES. In fascicles of 2; 2–3½ in. long; slender; dark green.

FRUIT. Short-stalked; 2–3½ in. long; some cones remaining closed and persistent for years; yellow-brown; scales armed with short prickle.

Longleaf Pine

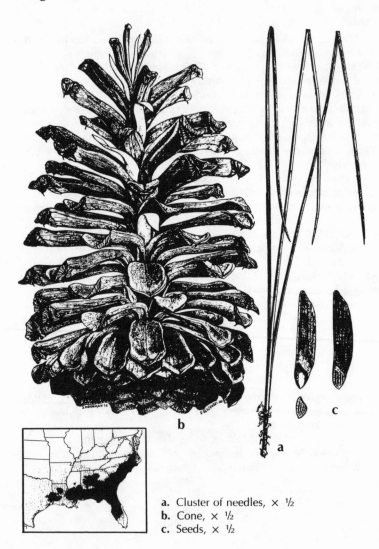

a. Cluster of needles, × ½
b. Cone, × ½
c. Seeds, × ½

Longleaf Pine

Pinus palustris Mill. (*Pinus australis* Michx.)

HABIT. A medium-sized tree 80–120 ft high and 2–3 ft in diameter (max. 150 by 4 ft); long, clear bole; small, open crown with needles in dense tufts at ends of branches.

LEAVES. In fascicles of 3; 8–18 in. long; slender; flexible; bright green; persistent 2 years; basal sheath persistent, ⅓–½ in. long.

FLOWERS. Male dark rose-purple; female dark purple.

FRUIT. Nearly sessile; 6–10 in. long; narrowly ovoid-cylindric; opening at maturity; in falling, leaves basal scales attached to twig; red-brown; scales thin, with an incurved prickle. Seeds: ½ in. long; pale with dark blotches; wings 1½ in. long.

TWIGS. Very stout, the terminal leader up to 1 in. in diameter; roughened by leaf bases; orange-brown. Winter buds: ½–1 in. long; conspicuously white, covered by silvery, lustrous, fringed scales that make the bud remarkably resistant to fire.

BARK. Thin; becoming ¾ to 1½ in. thick on old stems; orange-brown; in rough, scaly plated.

WOOD. Very important; heavy, hard, and strong; used for construction timbers, lumber, flooring, boxes, ties, posts, poles, etc.; the chief source of naval stores.

SILVICAL CHARACTERS. Very intolerant; generally slow-growing; reaches maturity in about 150 years with extreme age of 300 years; practically no above-ground growth for 3–6 years while taproot becoming established; windfirm with deep taproot system; reproduction vigourous and plentiful; very resistant to fire and disease.

HABITAT. On variety of sites but typical of dry, sterile, sandy sites; usually in pure stands or with scrub oak. The only tree that will produce timber over much of its range.

GENERAL. A hybrid between longleaf and loblolly pines has been named *P.* X *sondereggeri* H. H. Chap. This has been reported as not uncommon in Louisiana, North Carolina, and Texas.

Slash Pine

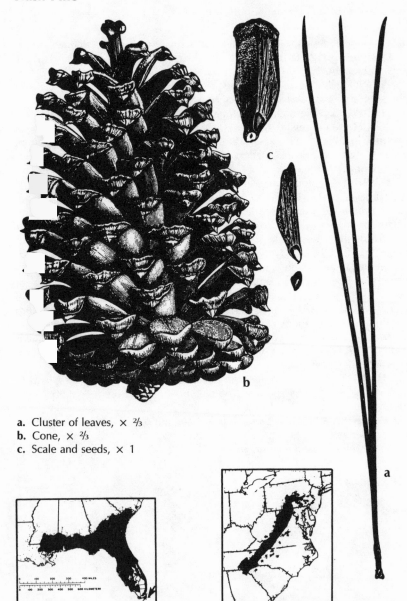

a. Cluster of leaves, × ⅔
b. Cone, × ⅔
c. Scale and seeds, × 1

Slash Pine

Table Mountain Pine

Slash Pine

Pinus elliottii Engelm. (*Pinus caribaea* Morelet)

HABIT. A tree 80–100 ft high and 2–3 ft in diameter; long, clear bole; crown rounded, dense.

LEAVES. In fascicles of 2 and 3; 8–12 in. long; stout; glossy, dark green; persistent 2 years; basal sheath persistent.

FLOWERS. Male dark purple; female pink.

FRUIT. Stalked; 2½–6 in. long; ovoid-conic; opening at maturity and falling following year; chocolate-brown, shining as if varnished; scales thin, armed with small sharp spine. Seeds: ¼ in. long; black; wings about 1 in. long.

TWIGS. Stout; roughened by leaf bases; orange-brown. Winter buds: ½–¾ in. long; scales silvery-brown.

BARK. Thin; becoming ¾–1½ in. thick; orange to purple-brown plated; peeling off in thin, papery, characteristic layers.

WOOD. Important; heavy, hard, and strong; marketed as longleaf pine and used for same purposes; important source of naval stores.

SILVICAL CHARACTERS. Intolerant, but less so than longleaf pine; very fast-growing; windfirm on deep soils; reproduction aggressive; not resistant to fire.

HABITAT. Old stands in low, wet sites because of fire damage; aggressive on cutover areas if protected; pure or mixed stands. The southern Florida variety with very dense wood and grass stage seedlings is designated *P. elliottii* var. *densa* L. & D. This species was incorrectly listed as *P. caribaea* Morelet, a species of the Bahama Islands.

Table Mountain Pine

Pinus pungens Lamb.

This unimportant species, characteristic of the tablelands of the Appalachians, is a small, intolerant tree. It is easily identified by its needles and characteristic cones.

LEAVES. In fascicles of 2; 1½–3½ in. long; yellow-green; rigid; twisted.

FRUIT. Sessile; 2½–3½ in. long; light brown; ovoid; serotinous and persistent for years; heavy; thick scales armed with conspicuous, sharp, hooked spines or claws.

Ponderosa Pine

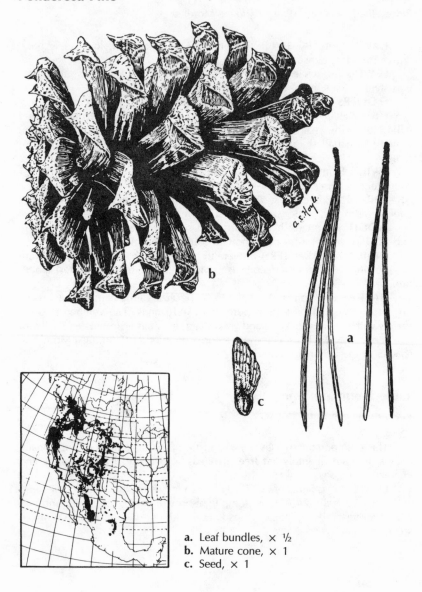

a. Leaf bundles, × ½
b. Mature cone, × 1
c. Seed, × 1

Ponderosa Pine • Western Yellow Pine

Pinus ponderosa Laws.

HABIT. A tree 150–180 ft high and 3–4 ft in diameter (max. 232 by 8 ft on Pacific Coast); bole symmetrical, clear; crown short, conical or flat-topped.

LEAVES. In fascicles of 3, or 2 and 3 (rarely 1–5); 3–11 in. long (mostly 4–7 in.); stout; dark to yellow-green; persistent 2–7 years (usually 4–6 years); cross section shows 2–5 resin ducts; basal sheath ¼–¾ in. long, persistent.

FLOWERS. Male yellow; female red, clustered or paired.

FRUIT. Subsessile; 2½–6 in. long; ovoid; open at maturity; basal scales remaining attached to twig when cones shed; scales thin, armed with short prickles. Seeds: ¼ in. long; brown-purple, often mottled; wings 1 in. long.

TWIGS. Stout; orange-colored; turpentine odor when bruised. Winter buds: about ½ in. long; often resinous.

BARK. Black and furrowed on young trees; on old trunks 2–4 in. thick; yellow-brown to cinnamon-red; in large, flat plates.

WOOD. Very important; rather light and soft; sapwood very thick with properties of white pine; heartwood light brown; uses include construction, planing mill products, and ties.

SILVICAL CHARACTERS. Intolerant; slow-growing; reaches maturity in 350–500 years (extreme age 660 years); reproduction vigorous; long taproot; fire and bark beetles cause damage.

HABITAT. Transition zone; large altitudinal range, 2,000–8,000 ft; exceedingly drought resistant; in open pure stands or more commonly the most abundant tree in mixed coniferous stands.

GENERAL. The Rocky Mountain variety is designated *P. ponderosa* var. *scopulorum* Engelm. Arizona pine, *P. ponderosa* var. *arizonica* (Engelm.) Shaw of southern New Mexico, Arizona, and northern Mexico differs in having needles in fascicles of 5 and cones less than 3½ in. long.

Jeffrey Pine

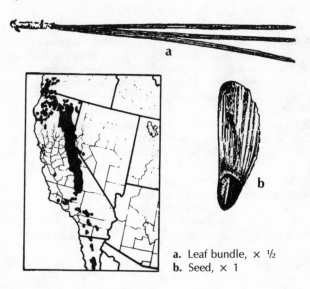

a. Leaf bundle, × ½
b. Seed, × 1

Apache Pine

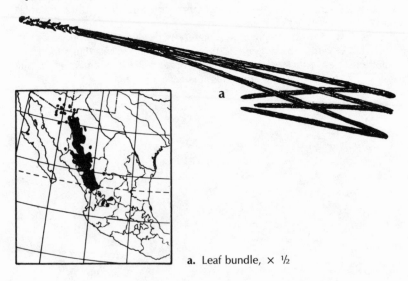

a. Leaf bundle, × ½

Jeffrey Pine

Pinus jeffreyi Grev. & Balf. (*Pinus ponderosa* var. *jeffreyi* Vasey)

This tree is similar in most of its characteristics to *P. ponderosa* but differs from it in the following ways:

HABIT. A tree 100–180 ft high and 4–6 ft in diameter, not quite reaching the proportions of ponderosa pine; lumber is sold as ponderosa.

LEAVES. In fascicles of 3, or 2 and 3; 4–9 in. long; blue-green; persistent 6–9 years.

FRUIT. 5–15 in. long; scales thin, armed with a stout, long, incurved prickle.

TWIGS. Stout; purple; pineapplelike odor when bruised. Winter buds: not resinous.

HABITAT. Endures greater extremes of climate than ponderosa; mixed with ponderosa pine and other conifers.

Apache Pine

Pinus engelmannii Carr. (*Pinus apacheca* Lemm.)

This tree is similar in most of its characteristics to *P. ponderosa* but differs from it in the following ways:

HABIT. A tree 50–60 ft high and 1–2 ft in diameter (max. 75 by 3 ft).

LEAVES. In fascicles of 3 (occasionally 2–5); 8–15 in. long (mostly about 10 in.); dark green; conspicuously fringed margins; persistent 2 years; cross section shows 11–14 resin ducts; basal sheath ¾–1 in. long.

HABITAT. Transition zone; altitudinal range 5,500–8,200 ft; otherwise similar to ponderosa pine.

GENERAL. Some authors consider this tree a synonym of *P. ponderosa*. It is characterized during its first few years by development of a very deep taproot and little height growth.

Washoe Pine

Pinus washoensis Mason & Stock.

This rare and local species was described from Washoe County, Nevada, in 1945. It is related to *P. jeffreyi*.

Lodgepole Pine

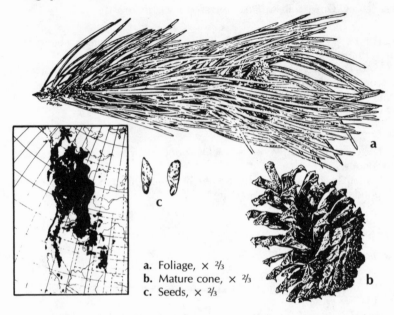

a. Foliage, × 2/3
b. Mature cone, × 2/3
c. Seeds, × 2/3

Chihuahua Pine

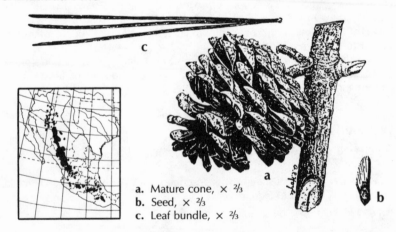

a. Mature cone, × 2/3
b. Seed, × 2/3
c. Leaf bundle, × 2/3

Lodgepole Pine

Pinus contorta Dougl.

HABIT. A tree 70–80 ft high and 1¾–2½ ft in diameter (max. 150 by 3 ft); long; slender bole; short crown.

LEAVES. In fascicles of 2; 1–3 in. long; stout; often twisted; bright yellow-green; persistent 4–6 years; margins with minute teeth; basal sheath persistent.

FLOWERS. Orange-red; male in spikes; female clustered.

FRUIT. Subsessile; ¾–2 in. long; ovoid; frequently remaining closed and on the tree for many years; scales at base knoblike, armed with long prickle. Seeds: ⅙ in. long; thin, dark red-brown shell; wings ½ in. long.

TWIGS. Stout; light orange-brown, becoming black. Winter buds: ¼ in. long; ovoid; dark chestnut-brown; resinous.

BARK. Very thin, rarely over ⅖ in. thick; orange-brown to gray; covered by thin, loosely appressed scales.

WOOD. Moderately important; soft; fine-textured; sapwood thick; heartwood pale brown; tangential surface with many indentations; used for lumber, ties, poles, and mime timbers.

SILVICAL CHARACTERS. Intolerant; slow-growing; reaches maturity in about 200 years; shallow root system; reproduction vigorous, typically form-ing dense stands following fires; fire, bark beetles, and mistletoe cause dam-age.

HABITAT. Canadian zone; altitudinal range 6,000–11,000 ft; adapted to variety of soil types; in pure, dense, even-aged stands, or in mixture with various conifers.

GENERAL. Three geographical varieties are distinguished: shore pine, *P. contorta* var. *contorta*, a stunted, short-leaved, twisted cone tree of the Pacific Coast; lodgepole pine, *P. contorta* var. *latifolia* Engelm., the taller Rocky Mountain tree described above; and *P. contorta* var. *murrayana* (G. & B.) Engelm., of the Pacific Coast mountains.

Chihuahua Pine

Pinus leiophylla var. *chihuahuana* (Engelm.) Shaw

This small, essentially Mexican tree is unique in that it matures its cones in 3 years and is a hard pine with a deciduous basal sheath. The needles are in clusters of 3, 2–4 in. long, and persistent 4 years. The cones are 1½–2 in. long, long-stalked, ovoid, and often remaining closed. It is characteristic of poor, dry sites.

Coulter Pine

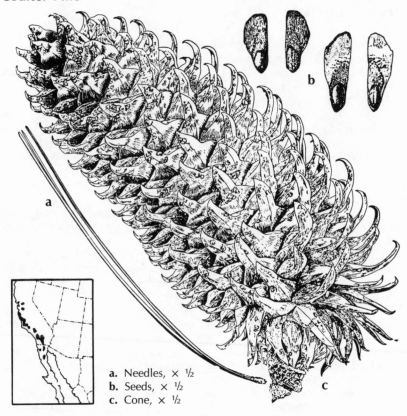

a. Needles, × ½
b. Seeds, × ½
c. Cone, × ½

Digger Pine

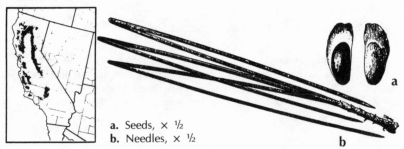

a. Seeds, × ½
b. Needles, × ½

Coulter Pine

Pinus coulteri D. Don

HABIT. A small tree 40–50 ft high and 1–2½ ft in diameter (max. 80 by 3½ ft); large, open unsymmetrical crown.

LEAVES. In fascicles of 3; 6–12 in. long; dark blue-green; rigid; persistent 3–4 years; basal sheath persistent.

FLOWERS. Male yellow; female dark red-brown.

FRUIT. Short-stalked; 10–14 in. long; oblong-ovoid; opening at maturity and persistent several years; light yellow-brown; thick scales terminating in large claw; the largest American pinecone, weighing up to 5 lb. Seeds: ½ in. long; thick-shelled; wings longer than seeds (about 1 in.).

TWIGS. Very stout; rough; orange-brown. Winter buds: ½ in. long; brown.

BARK. Nearly black; 1½–2 in. thick; broad, scaly ridges.

WOOD. Unimportant; soft and weak; used for fuel.

SILVICAL CHARACTERS. Intolerant; reaches maturity in about 150 years; slow-growing; wide, deep roots; reproduction scanty.

HABITAT. Dry, rocky slopes 3,000–7,000 ft; pure or mixed stands.

Digger Pine

Pinus sabiniana Dougl.

HABIT. A small tree 40–50 ft high and 1–2 ft in diameter; bole often forked; open, sparsely foliaged crown.

LEAVES. In fascicles of 3; 7–12 in. long; pale blue-green; flexible; pendent; persistent 3–4 years; basal sheath persistent.

FLOWERS. Male yellow; female dark purple.

FRUIT. Similar to Coulter pine but smaller (6–10 in. long) and chocolate-brown. Seeds: ¾ in. long; thick-shelled; edible; wings about half as long as seeds.

TWIGS, BARK, WOOD, and SILVICAL CHARACTERS. Similar to Coulter pine.

HABITAT. Dry foothills 100–5,000 ft; able to survive on exceedingly dry sites; in pure stands or mixed with oaks.

Knobcone Pine

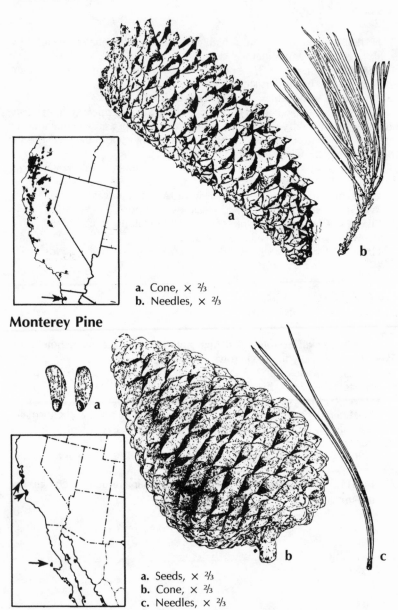

a. Cone, × ²/₃
b. Needles, × ²/₃

Monterey Pine

a. Seeds, × ²/₃
b. Cone, × ²/₃
c. Needles, × ²/₃

Knobcone Pine

Pinus attenuata Lemm.

HABIT. A small tree 20–60 ft high and 1–2 ft in diameter (max. 100 by 3 ft); open, sparse crown.

LEAVES. In fascicles of 3; 3–7 in. long; yellow-green; slender; persistent 4–5 years; basal sheath persistent.

FLOWERS. Male orange-brown; female fascicled, purple.

FRUIT. Short-stalked; 3–6 in. long; ovoid-conic; light yellow-brown; unsymmetrical with outer basal scales pyramidally knoblike; remaining closed and persistent many years, with clusters characteristically encircling stems of even small trees. Seeds: ¼ in. long; wings 1¼ in. long.

TWIGS. Slender; smooth; orange-brown. Winter buds: ½ in. long; brown.

BARK. Thin; gray-brown; low, scaly ridges.

WOOD. Unimportant; soft and weak; used locally for fuel.

SILVICAL CHARACTERS. Intolerant; short-lived; fast-growing; wide, deep roots; reproduction aggressive, especially following fire.

HABITAT. Very dry mountain slopes to 5,000 ft; pure or mixed stands.

Monterey Pine

Pinus radiata D. Don (*Pinus insignis* Dougl.)

HABIT. A handsome tree 40–100 ft high and 2–5 ft in diameter; rounded, open crown; common ornamental.

LEAVES. In fascicles of 3; 4–6 in. long; bright green; slender; flexible; persistent 3 years; basal sheath persistent.

FLOWERS. Male yellow in spikes; female dark purple.

FRUIT. Short-stalked; 3–7 in. long; ovoid; yellow-brown; unsymmetrical, with outer basal scales round, thickened, and domelike; remaining closed and persistent. Seeds: ¼ in.; wings ¾ in.

TWIGS. Slender; dark orange. Winter buds: ½ in.; brown.

BARK. Thick; red-brown to nearly black; furrowed.

WOOD. Unimportant in the United States; soft and weak.

SILVICAL CHARACTERS. Moderately tolerant; short-lived; fast-growing; prolific seed production. An important forest tree in Australia, New Zealand, and South Africa.

HABITAT. Dry soil (less than 17 in. rain annually) but humid air; in pure stands or mixed with bishop pine and cypress. This species is rare, native only at three localities on the coast of California and on Guadalupe Island, Mexico. These localities are indicated on the map by arrows.

Bishop Pine

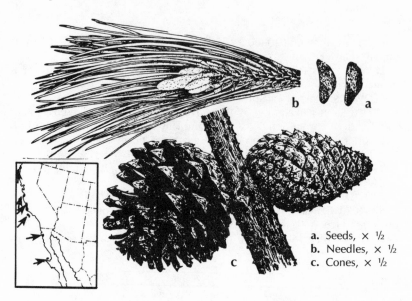

a. Seeds, × ½
b. Needles, × ½
c. Cones, × ½

Torrey Pine

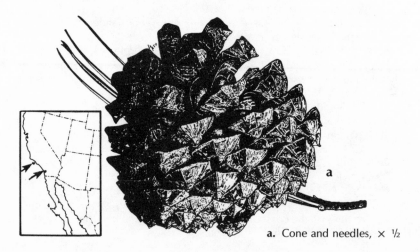

a. Cone and needles, × ½

Bishop Pine

Pinus muricata D. Don

HABIT. A tree 30–80 ft high and 1–3 ft in diameter; handsome, rounded crown of dense, tufted foliage.

LEAVES. In fascicles of 2; 4–6 in. long; dark yellow-green; thick; rigid; persistent 2–3 years; basal sheath persistent.

FLOWERS. Male in orange-colored spikes; female in whorls.

FRUIT. Sessile; in clusters of 3–7; 2–4 in. long; ovoid; yellow-brown; unsymmetrical, with outer basal scales knoblike and extended into spurlike spines; often remaining closed and persistent for years. Seeds: ¼ in. long; black.

TWIGS. Stout; rough; orange-brown. Winter buds: ½ in. long; brown.

BARK. Thick; purple-brown; rough; furrowed.

WOOD. Unimportant; moderately light and strong; lumber and fuel.

SILVICAL CHARACTERS. Moderately tolerant; short-lived; fast-growing; reproduction aggressive, especially following fire.

HABITAT. Variety of sites from wet clays and peat bogs to dry, sandy ridges; pure stands or mixed with lodgepole, madrone, and oaks; commonly planted ornamental. This species is local on the California coast and on the Santa Crux and Santa Rosa islands. It is also local in Baja California. These localities are indicated on the map by arrows.

Torrey Pine

Pinus torreyana Parry

HABIT. A rare, local tree 25–60 ft high and 8–14 in. in diameter; few, stout, spreading branches; rounded crown.

LEAVES. In fascicles of 5; 7–13 in. long; dark yellow-green; rigid; persistent 3–4 years; basal sheath persistent.

FLOWERS. Male yellow in heads; female on long stalks.

FRUIT. Long-stalked; 4–6 in. long; broad-ovoid; chocolate-brown; thick-scaled; persistent 3–4 years. Seeds: ¾ in.; wings ½ in.; edible.

TWIGS. Very stout; smooth; green first year, becoming black.

BARK. About 1 in. thick; red-brown; rough; furrowed.

WOOD. Unimportant; too rare to be of any use.

SILVICAL CHARACTERS. Intolerant; short-lived; reproduction abundant.

HABITAT. Dry soil (less than 15 in. rain annually) but very humid air; in pure, open groves; smallest range of any American pine, on Santa Rosa Island and north of San Diego as indicated on the map by arrows.

The Larches

Characteristics of the Genus *Larix* Mill.

HABIT. Tall, pyramidal trees; open crowns, with slender, irregularly disposed, horizontal or pendulous branches; dwarfed, short, spurlike lateral branchlets.

LEAVES. Deciduous; needle-shaped or linear; produced in dense false whorls or clusters or spurlike lateral branches; solitary and spirally arranged on new shoots; numerous lines of stomata on all surfaces; 2 resin canals in cross section.

FLOWERS. Monoecious; terminal; single; appearing with leaves; male naked, globose to oblong, consisting of several yellow, spirally arranged scales, each bearing two pollen sacs; female erect, consisting of few or many rounded, red-purple scales in the axes of much longer scarlet bracts, each scale bearing 2 small inverted ovules.

FRUIT. Woody, erect, short-stalked cones; maturing in one season; cone scales thin, persistent, concave, longer or shorter than their long-pointed bracts. Seeds: 2 under each scale; triangular and light brown; large terminal wing.

TWIGS. Smooth and glaucous, or hairy. Winter buds: subglobose; small; nonresinous; accrescent inner scales that mark lateral spur branches with prominent ringlike scars.

WOOD. Rather strong and durable; small scattered resin ducts; thin, white sapwood and sharply defined, red to russet-brown heartwood.

SILVICAL CHARACTERS. Intolerant; slow-growing; found on a variety of habitats; extensive forests occasionally destroyed by larch sawfly (*Nematus erichsonii*).

GENERAL. This genus contains about 10 species scattered through the Northern Hemisphere. In North America 3 species are native. The European larch (*L. decidua* Mill.), an important tree, has been planted in the United States for ornamental purposes. It can be identified by its puberulous cones, 3/4–1 1/2 in. long, with inserted bracts and 40–50 suborbicular scales. It has become naturalized in the northeastern states.

KEY TO THE SPECIES OF LARCHES

1. Cones with bracts shorter than scales and usually concealed; twigs slender, yellow-ish, glabrous.
    2. Cones ½–¾ in. long, composed of 12–15 glabrous scales; twigs glabrous, covered at first with glaucous bloom; eastern, far northern . . . .
    . . . . *L. laricina,* **tamarack,** p. 47
    2. Cones ¾–1½ in. long, composed of 40–50 hairy scales; twigs without bloom; ornamental exotic . . . . *L. decidua,* **European larch,** p. 44
1. Cones with bracts conspicuous and exserted beyond the 40 or more scales; twigs stout, brownish, hairy; western.
    3. Twigs with pale hairs, brittle; bark thick, red-brown, plated and deeply furrowed; cones 1–1½ in. long; needles flatly 3-angled; western . . . .
    . . . . *L. occidentalis,* **western larch,** p. 49
    3. Twigs densely woolly, tough; bark thin, gray, scaly; cones 1½–2 in. long; needles 4-angled; western alpine . . . . *L. lyallii,* **subalpine larch,** p. 49

The Cedars

Characteristics of the Genus *Cedrus* Trew.

The name cedar, though improperly applied to trees in several native genera, is correctly used for four closely related species in the genus *Cedrus,* none of which are native to the Americas. All have linear needles arranged spirally and scattered on new shoots and in dense false whorls on lateral spur branches, as found in the larches; however, the needles are persistent. The upright cones resemble those of *Abies* but require 2–3 years to mature.

The deodar or Himalayan cedar, *C. deodara* (Roxb.) Loud., with pendulous, densely pubescent leading shoots and branchlets, is widely planted in warmer sections of the United States. The biblical cedar of Lebanon, *C. libani* Loud., with stiff, nearly glabrous shoots, is less commonly planted as an ornamental, as are Atlas cedar, *C. atlantica* Man., and Cyprus cedar, *C. brevifolia* Henry, both of which differ from the two species above in having needles less than 1 in. long and cones less than 3 in. long.

Tamarack

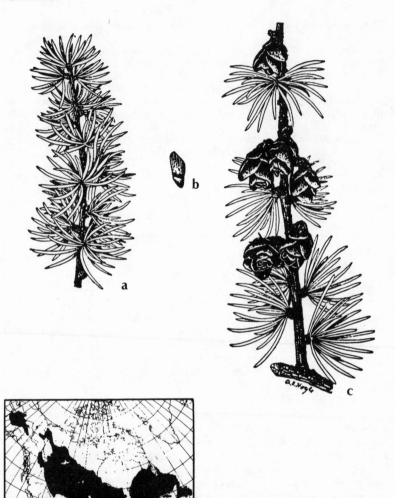

a. Foliage, × 1
b. Seed, × 1
c. Branchlet with cones, × 1

Tamarack • Eastern Larch

Larix laricina (Du Roi) K. Koch (*Larix alaskensis* Wight)

HABIT. A small to medium-sized tree seldom over 60 ft high and 1–2 ft in diameter (max. 100 by 2½ ft); long, clear, cylindrical bole; open, pyramidal, irregular crown with slender horizontal branches.

LEAVES. Linear; triangular in cross section; ¾–1¼ in. long; bright blue-green; falling in September or October; in clusters of 12–20.

FLOWERS. Male subglobose and sessile; female oblong and short-stalked.

FRUIT. ½–¾ in. long; short-stalked; oblong–subglobose; chestnut-brown; falling during second year; cone scales fewer than 20, slightly longer than broad, erose at margin, glabrous and lustrous and twice as long as their bracts except at base of cone. Seeds: ⅛ in. long; wings about ¼ in. long; light chestnut-brown.

TWIGS. Slender; smooth; glaucous at first, becoming orange-brown during first year. Winter buds: conspicuous; globose; small; lustrous; dark red.

BARK. Thin and smooth on young stems; ½–¾ in. thick, red-brown, scaly on mature trunks.

WOOD. Heartwood yellow-brown; medium texture; strong, hard; heavy; durable; not widely used, chief uses being poles, railroad ties, and rough lumber.

SILVICAL CHARACTERS. Intolerant; moderate in growth, reaching maturity in 100–200 years; reproduction vigorous on favorable sites; shallow root system; larch sawfly and fire cause serious damage.

HABITAT. Hudsonian and Canadian zones; restricted to sphagnum bogs or swamps in southern part of range and making best growth on moist beaches and well-drained uplands farther north; chiefly with black spruce, also balsam fir, aspen, birch, and jack pine; extending northward to limits of tree growth.

Western Larch

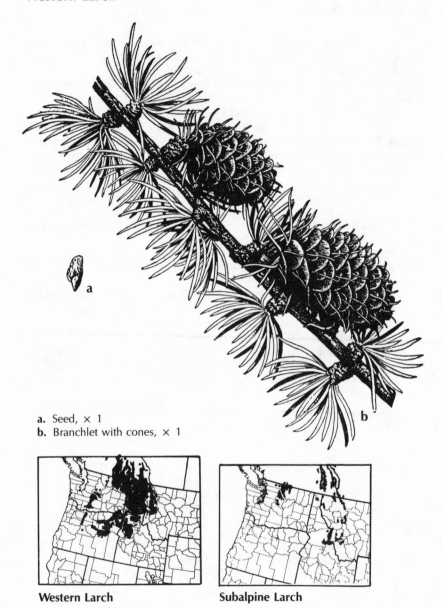

a. Seed, × 1
b. Branchlet with cones, × 1

Western Larch

Subalpine Larch

Western Larch

Larix occidentalis Nutt.

HABIT. A tree 140–180 ft in height and 3–4 ft in diameter; long, clear, cylindrical bole, often with a swollen butt; short, open crown of small, horizontal branches.

LEAVES. Linear; flatly triangular in cross section; 1–1¾ in. long; light pale green, becoming yellow; falling in early autumn; in clusters of 14–30.

FLOWERS. Male short, oblong; female oblong, subsessile.

FRUIT. 1–1½ in. long; short-stalked; oblong; purple-red to red-brown; falling first year; cone scales 40 or more, broader than long, sometimes toothed at reflexed apex, usually white-woolly on the outside, and shorter than exserted long-tipped bracts. Seeds: ¼ in. long; wings ½ in. long.

TWIGS. Stout; brittle; at first with a pale pubescence, soon becoming glabrous and orange-brown. Winter buds: ⅛ in. in diameter; subglobose; chestnut-brown.

BARK. Scaly on young stems; 4–6 in. thick, plated, deeply furrowed on old trunks; red-brown to cinnamon-red.

WOOD. Heartwood red-brown; heavy; strong; durable; similar to and sold as Douglas-fir for lumber, poles, ties, etc.

SILVICAL CHARACTERS. Intolerant; rather slow-growing, reaching maturity in 300–400 years (trees over 700 years reported); reproduction vigorous, competing with lodgepole pine on burned areas; windfirm with deep, wide-spreading root system; fungi and mistletoe often cause damage.

HABITAT. Transition zone; altitudinal range 2,000–7,000 ft; best development on deep, moist soils but does well on dry, gravelly slopes; in nearly pure stands or with Douglas-fir; western white, ponderosa, and lodgepole pines; western hemlock; Engelmann spruce; and alpine and grand fir.

Subalpine Larch

Larix lyallii Parl.

This is a small timberline tree in regions of heavy snows that fall early and remain late. Its range lies within that shown for western larch. It is characterized by densely woolly twigs and cone scales; cones 1½–2 in. long with exserted bracts; 4-angled needles; and thin, furrowed, scaly bark.

The Spruces

Characteristics of the Genus *Picea* Dietr.

HABIT. Evergreen trees with sharp-pointed, pyramidal crowns, and straight, tapering trunks; branches in regular whorls.

LEAVES. Spirally arranged; linear; sessile; stiff; single; extending from all sides of twigs; persistent 7–10 years but deciduous when dried; 4-angled or flattened; in falling, leave basal peglike projections (sterigmata) on the twig.

FLOWERS. Monoecious; catkinlike; solitary; male, or pollen-bearing, axillary, yellow to red or purple, ¾–1 in. long, consisting of numerous spirally arranged scales, each bearing 2 pollen sacs; female, or cone- and seed-producing, terminal, erect, yellow-green or red, ¾–1¼ in. long, consisting of numerous 2-ovuled, bracted scales.

FRUIT. Woody, pendent cone; matures in 1 season; borne mostly near top of crown; scales numerous, thin, unarmed, persistent, much longer than bracts. Seeds: 2 under each fertile scale; small; compressed; highly buoyant with thin wings.

TWIGS. Roughened by sterigmata. Winter buds: ovoid or conical; of overlapping scales; usually not resinous.

BARK. Thin and scaly (furrowed on old trunks in blue spruce).

WOOD. Light; soft; resilient; fine-textured; long-fibered; straight-grained; small, scattered resin ducts; not resinous; high satiny luster; strong for weight; highly important for paper pulp, lumber, boxes, etc.

SILVICAL CHARACTERS. Tolerant; no taproot; generally shallow-rooted. Natural enemies: fire; leaf aphid (*Adelges abietis*), which causes conelike gall; spruce budworm (*Harmologa fumiferana*), which often destroys young stands; white pine weevil (*Pissodes strobi*).

HABITAT. Cool, moist sites; typically in swampy areas or along the margins of streams and lakes.

GENERAL. This genus contains about 30 species, largely restricted to cooler regions in the Northern Hemisphere. In North America there are 7 indigenous species. The Norway spruce, *P. abies* (L.) Karst., characterized by cones 4–7 in. long, is commonly planted throughout the United States and has become naturalized in the East.

KEY TO THE SPECIES OF SPRUCES

1. Cone scales rounded at tip, smooth or wavy (erose) on margin.
   2. Cones under 2 in. long; needles 4-sided.
      3. Cones ½–1½ in. long, ovoid, purple, persistent many years; scales stiff, rigid, brittle, with wavy margins; twigs hairy; needles blunt-pointed; transcontinental and northern .... *P. mariana,* **black spruce,** p. 55
      3. Cones 1¼–2 in. long, oblong, brown, falling in 1 year; scales smooth on margin or nearly so; needles pointed.
         4. Cone scales stiff and rigid at maturity; twigs more or less hairy; eastern United States and Canada .... *P. rubens,* **red spruce,** p. 57
         4. Cone scales soft and flexible at maturity; twigs not hairy; transcontinental and northern .... *P. glauca,* **white spruce,** p. 53
   2. Cones 2–4 in. long; scales with entire margins; needles flattened; alpine in California and Oregon .... *P. brewerana,* **Brewer spruce,** p. 61
1. Cone scales wedge-shaped at tip, margin wavy (erose).
   5. Cones 4–7 in. long; drooping foliage; needles 4-sided, not prickly; common European ornamental .... *P. abies,* **Norway spruce,** p. 50
   5. Cones rarely 4 in. long; native and western.
      6. Needles flattened, not prickly, yellow-green; cones 2½–4 in. long; Pacific Coast area .... *P. sitchensis,* **Sitka spruce,** p. 61
      6. Needles 4-sided, blue-green; western mountain region.
         7. Cones 1–2½ in. long, persistent 1 year; needles flexible, acute but not prickly to touch; twigs minutely hairy; buds ⅛–¼ in. long with scales usually appressed; bark on mature trees thin and scaly ....
            .... *P. engelmannii,* **Engelmann spruce,** p. 59
         7. Cones 2¼–4½ in. (mostly about 3½ in.) long, persistent 2 years; needles stiff, bristle-pointed; twigs glabrous; buds ¼–½ in. long with scales usually reflexed, bark on mature trees thick and furrowed; central Rocky Mountains .... *P. pungens,* **blue spruce,** p. 63

White Spruce

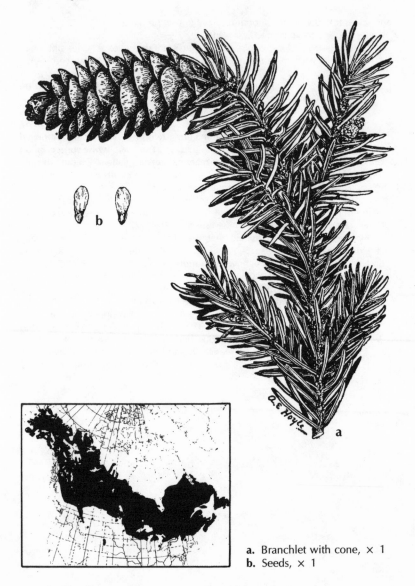

a. Branchlet with cone, × 1
b. Seeds, × 1

White Spruce

Picea glauca (Moench) Voss (*Picea canadensis* B.S.P.)

HABIT. A tree 60–70 ft high and 1½–2 ft in diameter (max. 120 by 4 ft); slender symmetrical bole; crown narrowly to broadly pyramidal with long, thick branches.

LEAVES. Tending to be crowded on upper side of branch by twisting of those on lower side; ⅓–¾ in. long; 4-angled; blue-green, occasionally with whitish tinge; rigid acute tips; odor pungent when crushed; 2 resin ducts in cross section.

FLOWERS. Male pale red to yellow; female with red or yellow-green scales.

FRUIT. 1–2½ in. long; oblong-cylindric; nearly sessile; cone scales flexible, rounded, and smooth at apex; light green or reddish before shedding seed and becoming light brown and falling soon after. Seeds: ⅛ in. long; pale brown; oblique wings ¼–⅜ in. long.

TWIGS. Glabrous, or in far Northwest downy; rather slender; orange-brown; skunklike odor when bruised. Winter buds: ⅛–¼ in. long; ovoid; obtuse; and chestnut-brown.

BARK. Thin, ¼–½ in. thick, ash-brown; silvery inner bark; separated into irregular thin plates or scales.

WOOD. Important in Northeast; used for pulp, construction lumber, boxes and crates, sounding boards, etc.

SILVICAL CHARACTERS. Tolerant of considerable shade, recovers from suppression well; slow-growing, but faster than black spruce; reaches age of 250–300 years; reproduction abundant on moist sites; shallow, spreading root system.

HABITAT. Hudsonian and Canadian zones; typical of low damp woods and banks of streams and lakes; altitudinal range from sea level to 5,000 ft; frequently gives way to black spruce or tamarack on wet sites and to lodgepole pine on dry sites; often forms pure, dense forests, but also in mixture with black spruce, fir, birch, poplars, and willows.

GENERAL. The western white spruce, *P. glauca* var. *albertiana* (S. Brown) Sarg., is the form found in the Rocky Mountain region and Black Hills. It is characterized by somewhat shorter and broader cones and a narrow crown.

Black Spruce

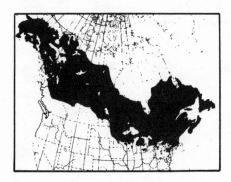

a. Branchlets with cones, × 1
b. Seeds, × 1

Black Spruce

Picea mariana (Mill.) B.S.P.

HABIT. A tree sometimes 40–80 ft high and ⅔–3 ft in diameter, but commonly much smaller; short, slender bole, usually pruning poorly; crown open, conical, more or less irregular.

LEAVES. Spreading in all directions; ¼–¾ in. long; 4-angled; pale blue-green and glaucous; blunt at apex; more or less incurved; hoary on upper surface from broad bands of stomata; lustrous and slightly stomatiferous below; 2 resin ducts in cross section.

FLOWERS. About ½ in. long; male red; female purple.

FRUIT. ½–1½ in. long; ovoid; on strongly incurved, short stalks; cone scales stiff, brittle, rigid, rounded, smooth or erose at apex, puberulous, and dull gray-brown; persistent many years. Seeds: ⅛ in. long; dark brown; pale brown oblique wings ¼–⅜ in. long.

TWIGS. Rusty-pubescent; rather slender; at first green, becoming dull red-brown. Winter buds: ⅛ in. long; ovoid; acute; light red-brown; puberulous.

BARK. Thin, ¼–½ in.; gray-brown; separated into thin, closely appressed scales or flakes; inner bark often olive-green.

WOOD. Not important except for pulp; used interchangeably with white spruce.

SILVICAL CHARACTERS. Very tolerant, recovering from suppression at an advanced age; slow-growing; rather short-lived, reaching age of 200 years; shallow, spreading root system; reproduction good on moist sites; lower branches often take root, forming clusters of small trees.

HABITAT. Hudsonian and Canadian zones; typical of cold sphagnum bogs and swamps but also found on dry slopes in Northwest; altitudinal range 100–3,500 ft; with white spruce and tamarack, reaches northern limit of tree growth; in dense, pure stands, or in mixture with tamarack, balsam fir, white spruce, white birch, aspen, etc.

Red Spruce

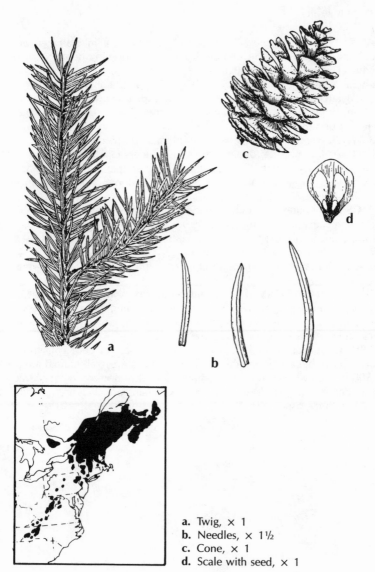

a. Twig, × 1
b. Needles, × 1½
c. Cone, × 1
d. Scale with seed, × 1

Red Spruce

Picea rubens Sarg. (*Picea rubra* Link)

HABIT. A tree 70–80 ft high and 1½–2 ft in diameter (max. 120 by 3½ ft); slender, symmetrical bole; crown narrow and conical with long branches.

LEAVES. Extending at nearly right angles from all sides of twig; ½–⅝ in. long; 4-angled; dark yellow-green; blunt or pointed at apex.

FLOWERS. Male bright red at maturity; female on different branches, red-green.

FRUIT. 1¼–2 in. long; ovoid-oblong; nearly sessile; cone scales rigid, rounded, and smooth at apex; light green or purplish before shedding seed, becoming red-brown and falling the first winter or following spring. Seeds: ⅛ in. long; dark brown; wings ¼ in. long.

TWIGS. More or less pubescent at first, becoming smooth second year; orange-brown. Winter buds: ¼–⅓ in. long; ovoid; acute; red-brown.

BARK. Thin, ¼–½ in. thick; gray-brown to red-brown, with red-brown inner bark; separating into irregular, close scales.

WOOD. Important; light; soft; even-grained; lustrous; used for lumber, pulp, musical instruments, containers, etc.

SILVICAL CHARACTERS. Very tolerant, though grows slowly under heavy shade; long-lived, reaching age of 400 years; good reproduction; spreading root system; susceptible to damage by fire and windthrow.

HABITAT. Varied, ranging from swamps and bogs where growth is slow to mountaintops; best growth on well-drained uplands and mountain slopes; in pure stands or mixed with yellow birch, beech, maple, white pine, and hemlock on better sites and with black spruce, balsam fir, tamarack, and red maple on swampy sites. This is the common spruce in the mountains of New York and New England and with white pine the most important timber species in this region.

Engelmann Spruce

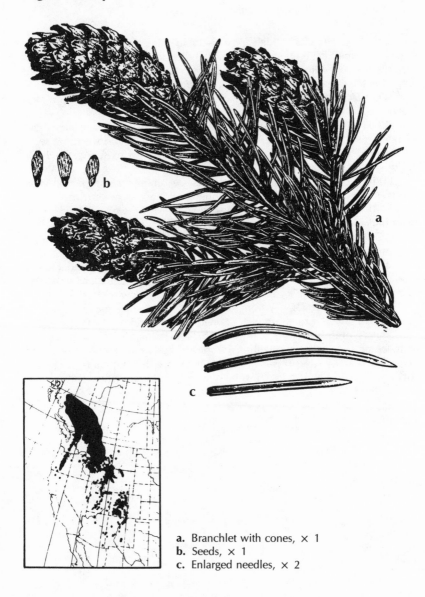

a. Branchlet with cones, × 1
b. Seeds, × 1
c. Enlarged needles, × 2

Engelmann Spruce

Picea engelmannii Parry

HABIT. A tree 60–120 ft high and 1½–3 ft in diameter (max. 165 by 5 ft); bole long but limby, cylindrical; crown compact, somewhat scraggly, narrowly pyramidal, with short, whorled branches. A prostrate shrub at high elevations.

LEAVES. Tending to be crowded on the upper side of the branch by the curving of those on the lower side; 1–1⅛ in. long; 4-angled; blue-green, occasionally with whitish, glaucous bloom; blunt or acute tips (not very sharp to touch); flexible; no resin ducts in cross section.

FLOWERS. Male dark purple; female bright scarlet.

FRUIT. 1–2½ in. long; oblong-cylindric; sessile or short-stalked; cone scales flexible, variable in outline and erose-dentate at apex; light chestnut-brown; falling during autumn or winter of first season. Seeds: ⅛ in. long; nearly black; broad, oblique wing ½ in. long.

TWIGS. Minutely pubescent (visible with hand lens); rather stout; orange-brown to gray-brown. Winter buds: ⅛–¼ in. long; broadly ovoid to conic; pale chestnut-brown; scales usually appressed.

BARK. Thin, ¼–½ in. thick; cinnamon-red to purple-brown; broken into large, thin, loosely attached scales.

WOOD. Properties similar to white spruce; this is the longest-fibered and lightest weight spruce, but at present not widely used because inaccessible; used for lumber, telephone poles, railroad ties, mine timbers, and fuel.

SILVICAL CHARACTERS. Tolerant and recovering well from prolonged suppression; generally rather slow-growing because of short summer season; long-lived, reaching age of 350–500 or more years; reproduction abundant and vigorous; shallow, spreading root system.

HABITAT. Hudsonian and Canadian zones; varying from 1,500–5,000 ft in the northern Rockies to 10,000–12,000 ft in the southern Rockies; rich, loamy soils with abundance of moisture; in pure stands or in mixture with alpine fir, lodgepole pine, and other conifers growing at high elevations.

Sitka Spruce

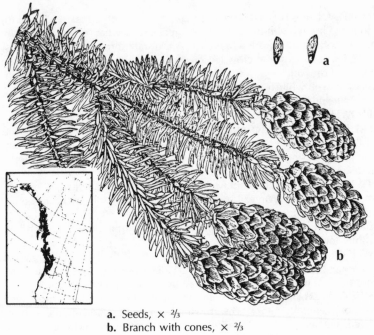

a. Seeds, × ⅔
b. Branch with cones, × ⅔

Brewer Spruce

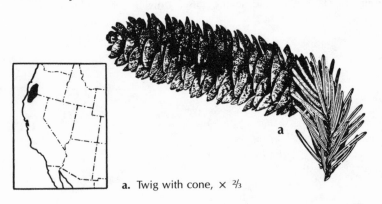

a. Twig with cone, × ⅔

Sitka Spruce

Picea sitchensis (Bong.) Carr.

HABIT. A large tree 180–200 ft high and 3–4½ ft in diameter (max. 300 by 16 ft); bole often clear for 100 ft, cylindrical; crown pyramidal, short, open.

LEAVES. Extending at nearly right angles from all sides of twig; ½–1⅛ in. long; flattened; bright yellow-green above, bluish-white, glaucous below; very sharp-pointed.

FLOWERS. Male dark red; female covered by elongated bracts.

FRUIT. 2–4 in. long; oblong-cylindric; short-stalked; cone scales thin, rough, papery, stiff, wedge-shaped at apex and erose-dentate at margin; chestnut-brown; falling first season. Seeds: ⅛ in. long; red-brown; wings ⅜ in. long.

TWIGS. Glabrous; slender; orange-brown to gray-brown. Winter buds: ¼–½ in. long; ovoid; red-brown.

BARK. Thin, ½–1 in. thick; red-brown to purple; broken into thin, loose, concave scales.

WOOD. Very important and much in demand for specialized uses such as wood aircraft; during World War II aircraft quality lumber reported to have sold for $600/mbf; soft, light, uniform grain.

SILVICAL CHARACTERS. Tolerant; fairly fast-growing, long-lived, reaching age of 700–800 years; reproduction vigorous; shallow roots.

HABITAT. A tidewater species; best development on deep, moist loams; in pure stands or mixed with hemlock, Douglas-fir, western redcedar, alder and maple.

Brewer Spruce

Picea breweriana S. Wats.

This is an uncommon timberline species restricted to the Siskiyou Mountains of southern Oregon and northern California. It is characterized by long, pendulous, weeping branches; flattened, blunt, dark green needles; rounded, entire-margined, purplish cone scales; and cones 2–4 in. long.

Blue Spruce

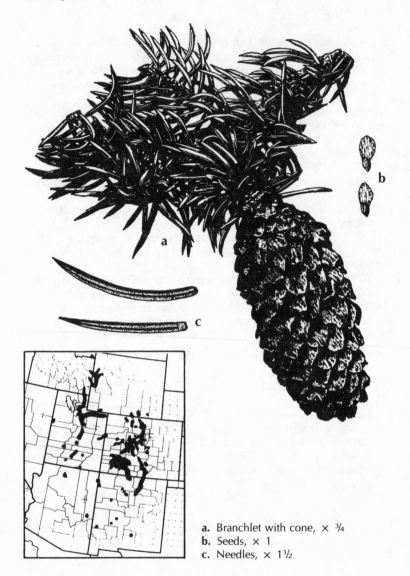

a. Branchlet with cone, × ¾
b. Seeds, × 1
c. Needles, × 1½

Blue Spruce • Colorado Blue Spruce

Picea pungens Engelm. (*Picea parryana* Parry)

HABIT. A tree 80–100 ft high and 1–2 ft in diameter (max. 150 by 4 ft); bole symmetrical, tapering, knotty; crown typically dense and conical when young; becoming thin, ragged, and pyramidal in age; and extending to the ground on open-grown species. The state tree of Colorado.

LEAVES. Extending at nearly right angles of all sides of twig; 1–1¼ in. long; 4-angled; blue-green, frequently with a silvery, glaucous bloom that persists for 3–4 years on young trees; rigid, tipped with long, bristle-sharp point; 1 resin duct in an angle of leaf in cross section.

FLOWERS. Male yellow, tinged with red; female pale green.

FRUIT. 2¼–4½ (mostly 3½) in. long; oblong-cylindric; sessile or short-stalked; cone scales tough, stiff, spreading, with erose margins; shiny, light chestnut-brown; not falling until fall of second season. Seeds: ⅛ in. long; dark chestnut-brown; broad oblique wings about ½ in. long.

TWIGS. Glabrous; stout and rigid; orange-brown to gray-brown. Winter buds: ¼–½ in. long; broadly ovoid and obtuse; light chocolate-brown; bud scales usually reflexed.

BARK. Pale to dark gray; thin and scaly on young trunks, becoming ¾–1½ in. thick and deeply furrowed with rounded ridges on old trunks.

WOOD. Rather similar to white spruce but brittle, knotty, and of little value. The chief use of this tree is for ornamental planting.

SILVICAL CHARACTERS. Moderately tolerant, but least so of spruces; slow-growing; long-lived; reproduction generally scanty because of dense ground cover; widespread, moderately deep root system, and decidedly windfirm.

HABITAT. Transition and Canadian zones, but mostly below the Engelmann spruce belt; varying from 6,000–9,000 ft in the north to 8,000–11,000 ft in the south; rich, moist soils, typically on stream banks; never abundant; in scattered pure groves or singly in mixture with ponderosa pine, Douglas-fir, alpine fir, Engelmann spruce, and hardwoods. Widely planted as an ornamental.

Douglas-fir

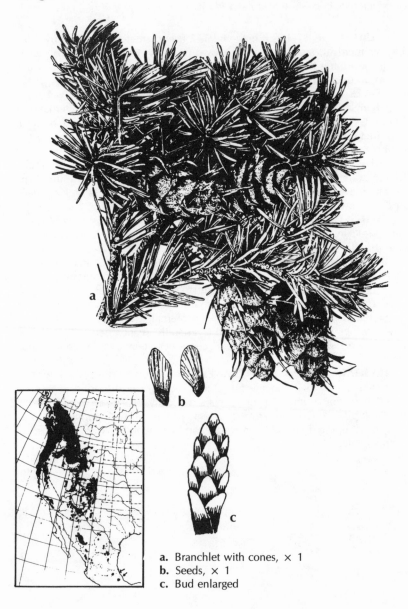

a. Branchlet with cones, × 1
b. Seeds, × 1
c. Bud enlarged

Douglas-fir

Pseudotsuga menziesii (Mirb.) Franco (*Pseudotsuga taxifolia* [Poir.] Britt.)

HABIT. A large evergreen tree attaining a height of over 300 ft on the West Coast and 130 ft in the Rocky Mountains; compact, pyramidal crown, with irregularly disposed branches.

LEAVES. Linear; single; more or less flattened; blunt to pointed; spirally arranged; petiolate; ¾–1¼ in. long; grooved above and stomatiferous below; persistent 5–8 years or longer.

FLOWERS. Monoecious; male orange-red; female red-green.

FRUIT. Pendent, woody cones; 2–4½ in. long; oblong-ovoid; maturing in one season; scales thin, rigid, rounded, much shorter than their long, exserted, 3-lobed bracts. Seeds: ¼ in. long; large, rounded, terminal wing.

TWIGS. Slender; pubescent; orange-brown, becoming gray-brown. Winter buds: ¼ in. long, characteristically long; conical; sharp-pointed; lustrous; brown.

BARK. Smooth; gray-brown; resin blisters on young trees; becoming very thick (6–24 in.); rough; red-brown ridges separated by deep furrows.

WOOD. Highly variable from yellowish, narrow-ringed, moderately light, and soft to red-brown, wide-ringed, with weak spring wood and very dense summer wood. This tree produces more timber than any other species.

SILVICAL CHARACTERS. Intermediate in tolerance; reproduction abundant and vigorous; well-developed, widespreading lateral root system; attaining great age.

HABITAT. Sea level to 11,000 ft; adapted to variety of soils but best on moist, deep, porous soils of northern exposure; will endure considerable drought; in pure stands or mixed with Rocky Mountain conifers.

GENERAL. European taxonomists have separated this species into 11 species; however, this view is not commonly accepted in North America. The Rocky Mountain form is recognized as the separate geographical variety *glauca* (Beissn.) Franco.

Bigcone Douglas-fir

Pseudotsuga macrocarpa (Vasey) Mayr.

This tree, found in the mountains of southern California, is distinguished by its larger fruit (4–6½ in. long), with bracts only slightly longer than the thick, stiff cone scales. The distribution shown on the map in southern California is for bigcone Douglas-fir.

The Hemlocks

Characteristics of the Genus *Tsuga* (Endl.) Carr.

HABIT. Tall, broadly pyramidal, evergreen trees; long, slightly tapering trunks; pyramidal or conical crown with scattered, slender, horizontal, and often pendulous branches; leading shoots characteristically drooping.

LEAVES. Spirally arranged, often appearing 2-ranked by a twist of the petioles; linear; single; abruptly petiolate; flattened or rounded; persistent 3–6 years and leaving conspicuous, woody, persistent bases (sterigmata) when they fall; deciduous in drying; usually grooved above, with 2 conspicuous bands of stomata below; 1 centrally located resin duct in cross section.

FLOWERS. Monoecious; single; on twigs of previous season; male, or pollen-bearing, axillary, globose, of numerous short stamens; female, or cone- and seed-bearing, terminal, erect, or numerous, circular scales of nearly the same length as their membranous bracts.

FRUIT. Woody, pendent cones; maturing in one season; scales thin, rounded, entire-margined, several times longer than bracts. Seeds: 2 under each scale; small, light, and widely disseminated; long, terminal, obovate wing; dotted with small resin vesicles.

TWIGS. Slender; round; usually roughened by persistent leaf bases. Winter buds: small; nonresinous; ovoid to globose.

BARK. Rough; hard; ridged; deeply furrowed; clear chocolate-red color when broken; containing tannin.

WOOD. Moderately soft; moderately strong; resin ducts normally absent; light to red-brown; considered inferior to pine and Douglas-fir.

SILVICAL CHARACTERS. Tolerant trees; requiring abundant moisture; seldom reaches age of more than 500 years; shallow, widespreading root system.

GENERAL. This genus contains 14 species widely scattered through North America and Asia. In North America there are 4 native species, 2 western and 2 eastern.

KEY TO THE SPECIES OF HEMLOCKS

1. Needles flat, obtuse, grooved above, with 2 whitish bands below; cones light brown, small (½–1½ in. long), ovoid.
   2. Needle margins finely toothed; needles mostly 2-ranked; cones ½–1 in. long.
      3. Needles tapering from base to apex, with well-defined, narrow white bands below; cones stalked, ½–¾ in. long, oblong-ovoid, with scale margins smooth; buds ovoid, pointed; eastern ....
      .... *T. canadensis*, **eastern hemlock,** p. 69
      3. Needles of uniform width from base to apex, with poorly defined bands below; cones sessile, ¾–1 in. long, ovoid, with scale margins undulate; buds globose; western .... *P. heterophylla*, **western hemlock,** p. 71
   2. Needle margins entire; needles spreading in all directions; cones 1–1½ in. long; Appalachian Mountains .... *P. caroliniana*, **Carolina hemlock,** p. 69
1. Needles rounded or keeled above, stomatiferous on all surfaces, spreading in all directions; bluntly pointed; cones yellow-green to purple, ¾–3½ in. long (mostly about 2 in. long), oblong-cylindric ..... *T. mertensiana*, **mountain hemlock,** p. 73

Eastern Hemlock

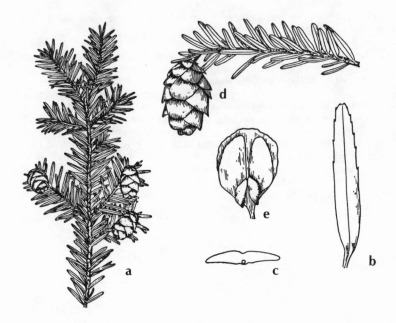

a. Fruiting branch viewed from beneath, × ½
b. Leaf, × 3
c. Cross section of leaf, enlarged
d. Branchlet with partly opened cone, × 1
e. Cone scale with seeds, × 3

Eastern Hemlock

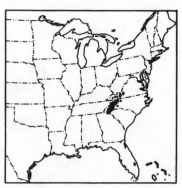

Carolina Hemlock

Eastern Hemlock

Tsuga canadensis (L.) Carr.

HABIT. A tree usually 60–70 ft high and 2–3 ft in diameter (max. 160 by 6 ft); dense, pyramidal crown with horizontal branches extending nearly to the ground in open-grown trees; typically flexible, drooping terminal leader.

LEAVES. Flattened; 1/3–2/3 in. long; tapering from base to apex; dark yellow-green and grooved above, 2 narrow, well-defined bands of stomata below; abrupt, slender petiole; appearing 2-ranked; rounded or notched at apex.

FLOWERS. Male yellow; female pale green, bracts shorter than scales.

FRUIT. 1/2–3/4 in. long; oblong-ovoid; light brown; scales suborbicular, smooth-margined. Seeds: 1/16 in. long; wings about 1/3 in. long; light brown.

TWIGS. Slender; light brown, and pubescent during first year, becoming gray-brown and glabrous. Winter buds: ovoid; 1/16 in. long.

BARK. Scaly on young trees, becoming deeply furrowed and ridged; red to gray with purple streaks on freshly cut surfaces; important source of tannin.

WOOD. Light, brash, coarse-grained, splintery; used for poorer grades of lumber and pulp; knotty as a result of persistent branches.

SILVICAL CHARACTERS. Tolerant; fast-growing; maximum age about 600 years; reproduction abundant and vigorous; shallow, widespreading root system.

HABITAT. Cool, moist sites; in small pure groves, or more commonly in mixed stands with white pine, red spruce, or hardwoods.

Carolina Hemlock

Tsuga caroliniana Engelm.

This handsome and somewhat rare tree is found on the upper slopes of the Appalachian Mountains from Virginia to northern Georgia. This tree, commonly planted as an ornamental, differs from eastern hemlock in having the needles extending from all sides of the twigs and larger cones that are 1–1½ in. long.

Western Hemlock

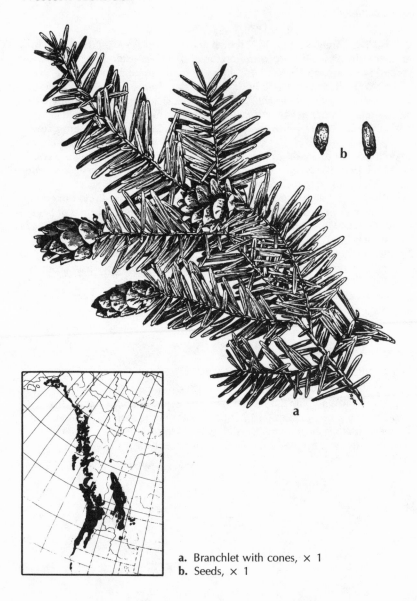

a. Branchlet with cones, × 1
b. Seeds, × 1

Western Hemlock

Tsuga heterophylla (Rafn.) Sarg.

HABIT. A tree 125–175 ft high and 2–4 ft in diameter (max. 259 by 9 ft); tall, clear trunk; short, open, pyramidal crown with typically flexible, drooping terminal leader.

LEAVES. Flattened; ¼–¾ in. long; dark, shiny green and grooved above, 2 broad bands of stomata below; abrupt, slender petiole; mostly 2-ranked; rounded or blunt at apex.

FLOWERS. Male yellow; female red or purple with rounded bracts shorter than scales.

FRUIT. ¾–1 in. long; ovoid; light brown; scales suborbicular; wavy-margined. Seeds: ¹⁄₁₆ in. long; ovoid; ⅓ as long as narrow; straw-colored wings.

TWIGS. Slender; pubescent for 5–6 years; pale yellow-brown becoming dark red-brown; drooping. Winter buds: ovoid; ¹⁄₁₆ in. long; blunt; bright chestnut-brown.

BARK. Thin (1–1½ in.) even on largest trees; young bark scaly, russet-brown; on old trunks hard, dark russet-brown, furrows separating wide flat ridges; inner bark dark red streaked with purple; used for its tannin content.

WOOD. Superior in quality to eastern hemlock; one of four major timber-producing species of Pacific Northwest; uniform texture, not very harsh or splintery; suitable for all uses but heavy construction; most important pulpwood species of region.

SILVICAL CHARACTERS. Tolerant throughout life; fast-growing, comparing favorably with Douglas-fir, seldom reaching age of over 500 years; reproduction very abundant and vigorous; shallow, widespreading root system; susceptible to fire injury; butt rot common in old trees.

HABITAT. Transition and Canadian zones; altitudinal range, sea level to 7,000 ft; prefers deep, moist, porous soils but hardy in drier situations; in pure, dense stands or mixed at lower levels with Douglas-fir, silver and grand firs, giant arborvitae, redwood, and hardwoods and at higher levels with noble fir, Alaska cedar, mountain hemlock, western white and lodgepole pines.

Mountain Hemlock

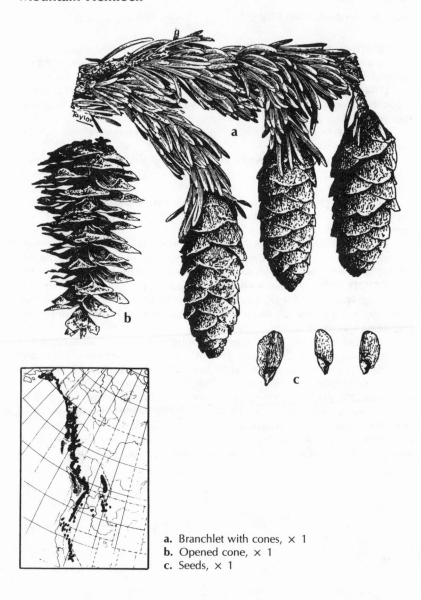

a. Branchlet with cones, × 1
b. Opened cone, × 1
c. Seeds, × 1

Mountain Hemlock • Black Hemlock

Tsuga mertensiana (Bong.) Carr.

HABIT. An alpine tree 75–100 ft high and 2½–3½ ft in diameter; trunk tapering, long and clear or knotty and malformed; crown open, pyramidal, with slender, drooping branches and drooping terminal leader; a sprawling shrub at timberline.

LEAVES. Semicircular in cross section; ½–1 in. long; pale bluish-green and stomatiferous on all surfaces; upper surface often keeled or grooved; abruptly narrowed into straight or twisted petiole; extending from all sides of twig or crowded toward upper side; bluntly pointed.

FLOWERS. Male purple on slender, drooping stems; female purple or green, slender-tipped bracts longer than scales.

FRUIT. ½–3½ in. long, (mostly 2 in.); oblong-cylindric; yellow-green to purple; scales oblong-obovate and spreading at right angles or reflexed when mature. Seeds: ⅛ in. long; ¼ as long as wings.

TWIGS. Thin or stout; dense; short; pale; pubescent for 2–3 years; light red-brown, becoming gray-brown and scaly. Winter buds: conical; ⅛ in. long; acute; red-brown; outer scales with awllike tip.

BARK. Rather thin on large trees (1–1½ in), early broken and rough on young trees; on old trunks hard, purplish to red-brown, with deep, narrow furrows separating narrow, rounded ridges; containing large quantities of tannin.

WOOD. Little used and inferior in quality to western hemlock; light; soft; not strong; close-grained.

SILVICAL CHARACTERS. Tolerant; growth slow; seldom over 500 years of age; reproduction generally abundant; shallow, widespreading root system.

HABITAT. Hudsonian and Canadian zones; altitudinal range, sea level (Alaska) to 11,000 ft but mostly near timberline; at its best on cool, moist, deep soils of northern exposure, moisture being essential; in pure stands or in mixture with alpine fir, alpine larch, Engelmann spruce, and whitebark, lodgepole, and western white pines.

The Firs

Characteristics of the Genus *Abies* Mill.

HABIT. Tall, pyramidal, evergreen trees; dense, spirelike crowns; slender, horizontal, whorled branches; straight, gradually tapering trunks.

LEAVES. Spirally arranged; linear; sessile; single; usually flat and blunt; extending from all sides of twig but mostly appearing 2-ranked by a twist near their base; persistent for 7–10 years; usually grooved above with stomatiferous lines below; 2 resin canals in cross section; when falling, leave a conspicuous, smooth, circular scar on twig.

FLOWERS. Monoecious, axillary, single; male (pollen-bearing) numerous on lower sides of lower crown branches, oval or cylindric, yellow to scarlet anthers; female (cone- and seed-bearing) on upper side of topmost branches, erect, globose to oblong, consisting of numerous, imbricated, 2-ovuled scales much shorter than their bracts.

FRUIT. Woody, erect cones; maturing in one season; scales thin, fan-shaped, and falling at maturity from the central, spikelike axis that persists many years. Seeds: 2 under each scale; large, thin wings; peculiar, conspicuous resin vesicles.

TWIGS. Smooth, glabrous, or pubescent. Winter buds: small; mostly sub-globose or ovoid; thin, loosely imbricated scales; usually thickly covered with resin.

BARK. Young bark thin, smooth, with numerous blisterlike resin pockets; old bark smooth or furrowed; Canada balsam obtained from the resin blisters of balsam fir.

WOOD. Light; soft; weak; color whitish to light brown, summer wood frequently with a purplish tinge; resin ducts absent; used for pulp, containers, and general construction.

SILVICAL CHARACTERS. Tolerant, moisture-loving trees of cool sites; slow- to fast-growing; moderately long-lived.

GENERAL. This genus contains about 40 species widely scattered through North and Central America, Europe, Asia, and northern Africa. There are 9 species native to Northern America.

KEY TO THE SPECIES OF FIRS

1. Winter buds subglobose, ⅛–⅓ in. long; needles not bristle-tipped; cones without spiny-tipped bracts.
   2. Needles crowded toward the upper side of the twigs; cones large and broad (3½–9 in. long); Pacific Coast region.
      3. Needles 4-sided, stomatiferous (covered with minute white dots) on all sides and usually glaucous; bark furrowed or scaly on mature trunks.
         4. Cones 4–6 in. long; bracts much longer than, and covering, cone scales; needles with sharply defined groove on upper surface; Washington, Oregon, northern California . . . . *A. procera,* **noble fir,** p. 89
         4. Cones 6–9 in. long; bracts never covering scales; needles ribbed above and below.
            5. Cones with bracts inserted . . . . *A magnifica,* **California red fir,** p. 87
            5. Cones with bracts exserted . . . .
               . . . . *A. magnifica shastensis,* **Shasta red fir,** p. 87
      3. Needles flattened, dark green, and lustrous above, with 2 distinct white bands (stomata) on lower surface; bark smooth and ashy gray on mature trunks; cones 3½–6 in. long with inserted bracts; British Columbia and Alaska to Washington and Oregon . . . . *A. amabilis,* **Pacific silver fir,** p. 85
   2. Needles flattened, on sterile branches spreading and not crowded, often 2-ranked; cones narrow, 2–5 in. long.
      5. Cones with bracts inserted.
         6. Needles on lower branches ¾–1¾ in. long; cones dark purple, scales slightly longer than broad.
            7. Needles dark green and lustrous above with 2 distinct white bands (stomata) below, 2-ranked on lower branches; northern United States to northwestern Canada . . . . *A. balsamea,* **balsam fir,** p. 77
            7. Needles stomatiferous on both surfaces, nearly erect on lower branches; western.
               8. Mature bark hard, smooth, gray; high western mountains . . . .
                  . . . . *A. lasiocarpa,* **subalpine fir,** p. 79
               8. Mature bark distinctly soft and corky, yellow-white; Colorado, Arizona, New Mexico . . . .
                  . . . . *A. lasiocarpa arizonica,* **corkbark fir,** p. 79
         6. Needles 1½–3 in. long; cones yellow to green-purple, scales slightly broader than long; western.
            9. Needles distinctly 2-ranked, 1½–2 in. long, dark green above with 2 white bands of stomata below; Montana to British Columbia and California . . . . *A. grandis,* **grand fir,** p. 83
            9. Needles spreading or obscurely 2-ranked, 2–3 in. long, stomatiferous and pale green on both surfaces; western United States . . . .
               . . . . *A. concolor,* **white fir,** p. 81
      5. Cones with bracts exserted; needles ½–1 in. long; Appalachian Mountains .
         . . . . *A. fraseri,* **Fraser fir,** p. 77
1. Winter buds ovoid, pointed, ¾–1 in. long; needles 1½–2¼ in. long, flat, rigid, bristle-tipped; cones 3–4 in. long with spiny bracts exserted ¾–1¾ in.; California (Monterey County) . . . . *A. bracteata,* **bristlecone fir,** p. 89

Balsam Fir

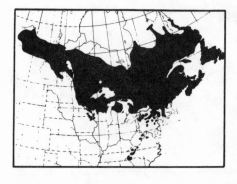

a. Lower crown branchlet
b. Branchlet with cone, × 1
c. Upper and lower sides
   of cone scale, × 1
d. Seed, × 1

Balsam Fir

Abies balsamea (L.) Mill.

HABIT. A medium-sized tree 40–60 ft high and 1–1½ ft in diameter (max. 85 by 2 ft); a dense, dark green, narrowly pyramidal crown with a slender spirelike tip.

LEAVES. On lower branches 2-ranked, ¾–1½ in. long, scattered, flattened, blunt, notched; on upper branches shorter, spreading, crowded; dark green above, two silvery bands of stomata below.

FLOWERS. Male of yellow anthers; female purple.

FRUIT. 2–4 in. long; oblong-cylindric; dark purple; scales longer than broad and twice as long as short, pointed bracts. Seeds: ¼ in. long; broad purple-brown wings.

TWIGS. Slender; finely pubescent; yellow-green; becoming smooth and gray to purple. Winter buds: subglobose; resin-covered; ⅛–¼ in. long; orange-green scales.

BARK. Thin; ash-gray; smooth except for numerous resin blisters on young trees; becoming ½ in. thick, red-brown, and broken into thin scales.

WOOD. Soft and brittle; used for pulp, boxes, etc.; resin in bark blisters is source of Canada balsam.

SILVICAL CHARACTERS. Tolerant (less so than spruce), recovering well from suppression; a short-lived tree, reaching age of 150 years, but generally defective before 90 years; reproduction plentiful and aggressive; shallow root system; lower branches sometimes take root, producing new trees.

HABITAT. Canadian and Hudsonian zones; demands abundant soil moisture and humid atmosphere; forms pure stands in swamps; on higher sites in mixture with spruce, hemlock, broad-leaved species; *A. balsamea* var. *phanerolephis* Fern. ranging north from northern Virginia has slightly exposed fruit bracts and appears to be intermediate between balsam and fraser fir.

Fraser Fir

Abies fraseri (Pursh) Poir.

This is a tree of the high mountains of Tennessee, North Carolina, and southwestern Virginia (shown in these areas on the map, where it grows with balsam fir). It is similar to balsam fir except for the long fruit bracts that extend beyond the scales and are strongly reflexed.

Subalpine Fir

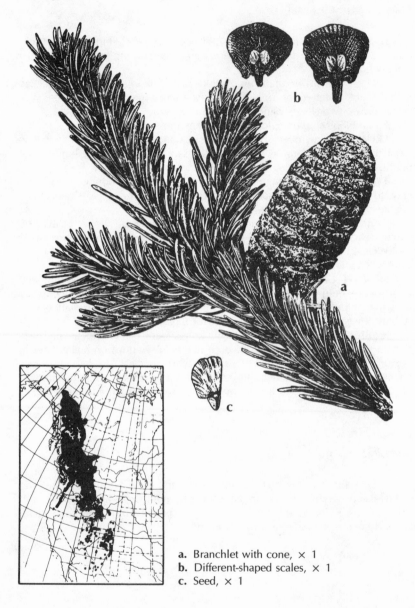

a. Branchlet with cone, × 1
b. Different-shaped scales, × 1
c. Seed, × 1

Subalpine Fir

Abies lasiocarpa (Hook.) Nutt.

HABIT. A tree 60–100 ft high and 1½–2 ft in diameter (max. 160 by 3 ft); a dense, narrowly pyramidal, spirelike crown often extending to the ground, with short, thick branches; a prostrate shrub at timberline.

LEAVES. On lower branches, 1–1¾ in. long (mostly about 1 in.), flattened, blunt, or notched; on upper branches ½ in. long and pointed; deep blue-green; crowded and nearly erect by a twist at their base; stomatiferous on both surfaces (less conspicuous above).

FLOWERS. Male dark indigo-blue; female dark purple.

FRUIT. 2–4 in. long; oblong-cylindric; dark purple; scales mostly longer than broad and 3 times longer than long-tipped bracts. Seeds: ¼ in. long; dark lustrous wings.

TWIGS. Stout, pubescent; pale orange-brown; becoming smooth and gray or silver-white. Winter buds: subglobose; resinous; ⅛–¼ in. long; light orange-brown scales.

BARK. Thin; gray; smooth except for numerous resin blisters on young trees; becoming shallowly fissured.

WOOD. Similar to balsam fir but little used except for fuel.

SILVICAL CHARACTERS. Tolerant (of its associates, only Engelmann spruce and mountain hemlock are more so); growth moderate; reproduction abundant and vigorous; shallow root system; lower branches sometimes taking root.

HABITAT. Canadian and Hudsonian zones; growing from 3,500 ft to timberline in the north and from 10,500 ft to timberline in the south; in cool, moist sites. Commonly with Engelmann spruce; lodgepole, whitebark, limber, or bristlecone pines; alpine larch; cork fir; and aspen.

GENERAL. Corkbark fir *A. lasiocarpa* var. *arizonica* (Merr.) Lemm. of New Mexico, Arizona, and southern Colorado, differs from alpine fir in having soft, corky, yellow-white to ash-gray trunk bark.

White Fir

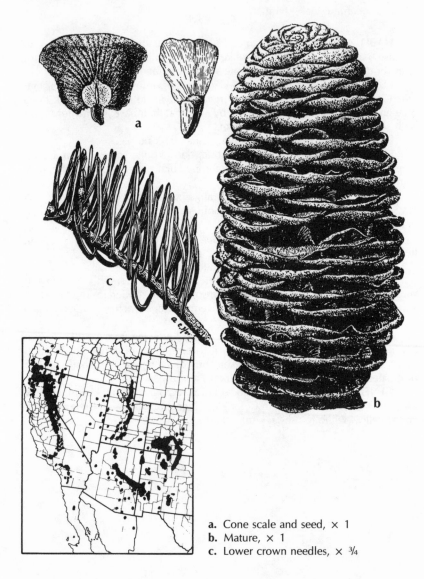

a. Cone scale and seed, × 1
b. Mature, × 1
c. Lower crown needles, × ¾

White Fir

Abies concolor (Gord. & Glend.) Lindl.

HABIT. A tree 120–150 ft high and 3–4 ft in diameter (max. 200 by 6 ft); a dense conelike crown with heavily foliaged, long-persisting, short branches.

LEAVES. On lower branches 2–3 in. long, flat, straight, and acute at apex; on fertile branches or on old trees, ¾–1½ in. long, thick, keeled above, usually curved, acute or rarely notched at apex; silver-blue to silver-green; crowded; more or less obscurely 2-ranked or extending from all sides of twig; stomatiferous above and below.

FLOWERS. Male rose to dark red; female greenish.

FRUIT. 3–5 in. long; oblong; bright yellow to olive-green or purple; scales much broader than long and twice as long as short-tipped bracts. Seeds: ⅓–½ in. long; yellow-brown; rose-tinted broad wings.

TWIGS. Moderately stout; smooth; yellow-green to brown-green, ultimately gray-brown. Winter buds: subglobose; resin-covered; ⅛–¼ in. long; yellow-brown.

BARK. Thin, gray, smooth except for numerous resin blisters on young trees; becoming 4–7 in. thick, ash-gray, hard and horny, with deep furrows and wide ridges.

WOOD. Similar to balsam fir; used for lumber, pulp, boxes, and novelties.

SILVICAL CHARACTERS. Tolerant, although less so than alpine fir; moderately fast-growing, reaching maturity in about 300 years; reproduction generally abundant and aggressive; root system normally shallow.

HABITAT. Transition and Canadian zones; altitudinal range 6,000–11,000 ft; requires less moisture than other western firs, existing surprisingly well on poor, dry sites; seldom in pure stands, usually with ponderosa and limber pine, Douglas-fir, alpine fir, Engelmann spruce, and aspen.

GENERAL. The California white fir (*A. concolor* var. *lowiana* [Gord.] Lemm.) of southwest Oregon and California differs from the species in having smaller buds and somewhat longer needles that are more pectinately arranged.

Grand Fir

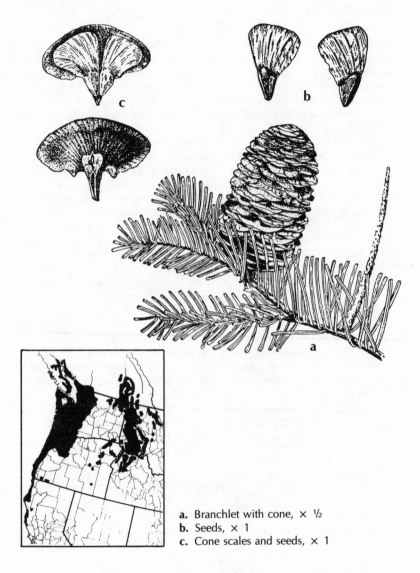

a. Branchlet with cone, × ½
b. Seeds, × 1
c. Cone scales and seeds, × 1

Grand Fir • Lowland White Fir

Abies grandis (Dougl.) Lindl.

HABIT. A tree 140–160 ft in height and 2–4 ft in diameter (max. 250 by 6 ft); rather open domelike crown, on old trees appearing wider in the middle because of the drooping of the lower branches.

LEAVES. On lower branches 1½–2 in. long, scattered, distinctly 2-ranked; on fertile branches 1–1½ in. long, more crowded, obscurely 2-ranked or nearly erect; blunt, flat, lustrous, dark yellow-green, and grooved above; white with 2 bands of stomata below.

FLOWERS. Male pale yellow; female light yellow-green.

FRUIT. 2–4½ in. long; cylindric; yellow-green to green-purple; scales ⅓ broader than long, 3–4 times longer than short-tipped bracts. Seeds: ⅜ in. long; light brown; straw-colored wings about ¾ in. long.

TWIGS. Slender; yellow-green to orange-brown; puberulous, becoming glabrous in second year. Winter buds: subglobose; ⅛–¼ in. long; resinous.

BARK. Thin, gray-brown, smooth except for resin blisters and chalky white blotches on young trees; becoming 2–3 in. thick, red-brown, plated or divided into flat ridges separated by deep furrows.

WOOD. Similar to balsam fir but with disagreeable odor, thus known as "stinking fir"; lumber, pulp, and boxes.

SILVICAL CHARACTERS. Moderately tolerant but less so than associated firs; growth moderate, reaching maturity in about 200 years; reproduction abundant if sufficient moisture and protection against frost present; windfirm with deep, spreading root system; subject to attack by spruce budworm and stringy brown-rot fungus.

HABITAT. Transition and Canadian zones; altitudinal range, sea level to 5,000 ft; on deep, moist, alluvial soils along streams or on mountain slopes. In limited pure stands, or more frequently in mixed hardwood and coniferous forests with Douglas-fir, western larch, alpine fir, Engelmann spruce, ponderosa, western white, and lodgepole pines, etc.

Pacific Silver Fir

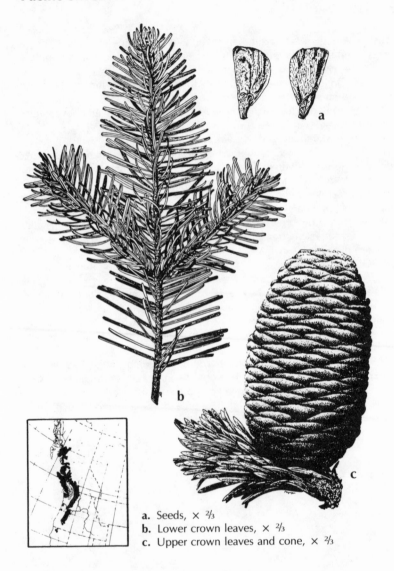

a. Seeds, × 2/3
b. Lower crown leaves, × 2/3
c. Upper crown leaves and cone, × 2/3

Pacific Silver Fir

Abies amabilis (Dougl.) Forb.

HABIT. A tree 140–160 ft in height and 2–4 ft in diameter (max. 200 by 6 ft); crown spirelike or pyramidal; bole clear in dense forest but clothed to the ground with rather short branches in open.

LEAVES. On lower branches ¾–1¼ in. long, crowded toward the upper side of the twig, flat, lustrous dark green and grooved above, silvery white with stomata below, notched or pointed at apex; on fertile branches often somewhat thickened and stomatiferous above at apex.

FLOWERS. Male red; female with broad scales and lustrous purple bracts.

FRUIT. 3½–6 in. long; cylindric–barrel-shaped; deep purple; scales slightly broader than long, longer than the spiny-tipped, inserted bracts. Seeds: ½ in. long; light yellow-brown; pale brown wings ¾ in. long.

TWIGS. Stout; orange-brown; puberulous the first year, becoming red-brown. Winter buds: subglobose; ¼ in. long; dark purple; resin-covered.

BARK. Thin; silver-white to ash-gray; chalk-colored blotches and resin blisters on trees at maturity; on overmature trunks, becoming scaly at the base.

WOOD. Similar to balsam fir; used in limited quantities for lumber and pulp.

SILVICAL CHARACTERS. Moderately tolerant; growth moderate, reaching maturity in about 250 years; reproduction abundant; often planted as ornamental because of handsome crown shape and dense foliage; the most abundant fir of the Northwest.

HABITAT. Transition and Canadian zones; altitudinal range from sea level to 6,000 ft; best on deep, moist soils with southern or western exposure; in pure stands or mixed with Sitka spruce, Douglas-fir, grand fir, western hemlock, and western redcedar.

California Red Fir

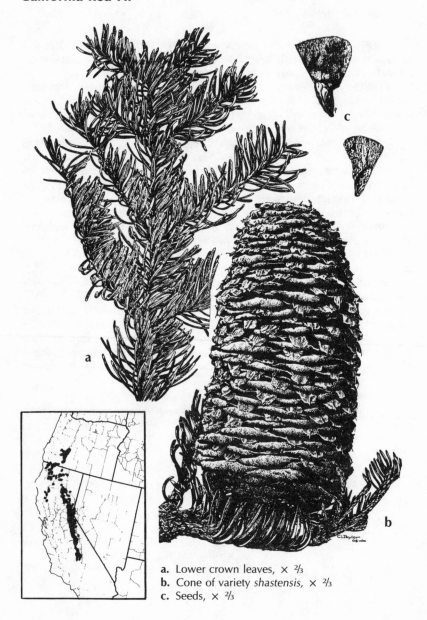

a. Lower crown leaves, × ²/₃
b. Cone of variety *shastensis*, × ²/₃
c. Seeds, × ²/₃

California Red Fir

Abies magnifica A. Murr.

HABIT. The largest of the firs, varying from 150–180 ft in height and 4–5 ft in diameter (max. 230 by 10 ft); crown narrow but round-topped; bole clear for much of its height, then with short, small branches.

LEAVES. On lower branches ¾–1½ in. long, somewhat flattened, rounded apex, and somewhat 2-ranked; on upper, fertile branches almost equally 4-sided, erect, crowded, and with short callous tips; glaucous during first year, becoming blue-green; stomatiferous on all sides.

FLOWERS. Male red-purple; female with green bracts much longer than rounded scales.

FRUIT. 6–9 in. long; cylindric–barrel-shaped; dark purplish brown; scales longer than broad and longer than the spiny-tipped, inserted bracts. Seeds: ½–¾ in. long; dark brown; large, broad, rose-colored wings.

TWIGS. Stout; yellow-green and slightly rusty-pubescent the first year, becoming smooth and light red-brown. Winter buds: ovoid; ¼ in. long; slightly resinous at the tip; dark brown.

BARK. Distinctly reddish-colored, thick (4–6 in.), furrowed on old trunks; smooth and chalky-gray on young trunks.

WOOD. Similar to and substituted for noble fir; light and soft; used for lumber.

SILVICAL CHARACTERS. Moderately intolerant at maturity; growth rather slow, reaching maturity in about 300 years; reproduction abundant on moist mineral soil; deep, spreading roots.

HABITAT. Transition zone to timberline in some places; altitudinal range 5,000–10,000 ft; in pure stands or mixed with Douglas-fir, sugar and ponderosa pine, and numerous other species.

GENERAL. A distinctive variety, the Shasta red fir, *A. magnifica* var. *shastensis* Lemm. (also regarded as a hybrid with *A. procera*), is occasionally found throughout the range of the species. It is characterized by cone bracts that are exserted and strongly reflexed and by winter buds almost free of resin.

Noble Fir

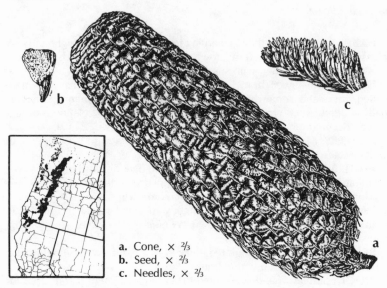

a. Cone, × ⅔
b. Seed, × ⅔
c. Needles, × ⅔

Bristlecone Fir

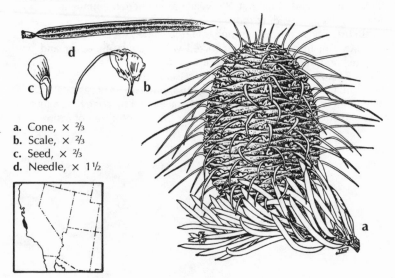

a. Cone, × ⅔
b. Scale, × ⅔
c. Seed, × ⅔
d. Needle, × 1½

Noble Fir

Abies procera Rehd. (*Abies nobilis* [Dougl.] Lindl.)

HABIT. A large tree 150–200 ft high and 4–6 ft in diameter (max. 250 by 8 ft); crown broad and rounded; bole clear for much of its length.

LEAVES. On lower branches 1–1½ in. long, flattened, rounded, and often notched at the apex, on upper, fertile branches almost equally 4-sided, with long, rigid, callous tips; marked on upper surface by sharply defined groove; glaucous during first year, becoming blue-green; stomatiferous on all sides.

FLOWERS. Male red-purple; female with orbicular bracts much longer than rounded scales.

FRUIT. Very distinctive; 4–6 in. long; cylindric; purple or olive-brown; scales wider than long, nearly or entirely covered by strongly reflexed, greenish bracts. Seeds: ½ in. long; red-brown; short, lustrous, light brown wings.

TWIGS. Slender; red-brown; rusty-pubescent. Winter buds: oblong-conic; ⅛ in. long; slightly resinous at tip; red-brown; blunt.

BARK. 1–2 in. thick, red-brown, and fissured on old trunks; smooth and gray for many years on younger trunks, with prominent resin blisters.

WOOD. Best quality of native true firs; used in aircraft; light; straight-grained; not durable.

SILVICAL CHARACTERS. Seedlings and trees both intolerant; growth rather rapid; reaches maturity in about 350 years; reproduction sparse; deep, spreading roots.

HABITAT. Transition zone; in stands of mixed conifers; altitudinal range 2,000–5,000 ft; on cool, deep, moist sites.

Bristlecone Fir

Abies bracteata D. Don (*Abies venusta* [Dougl.] K. Koch)

This curious species is native only to Monterey County, California. It is easily distinguished by its flat, bristle-pointed needles 1–2 in. long, its ovoid, nonresinous bud ¾–1 in. long, and its 3- to 4-in. cone with its spiny, long-exserted bracts.

Redwood

a. Fruiting branch, × ⅔
b. Seeds, × ⅔
c. Cone, × 1

TAXODIACEAE

Redwood

Sequoia sempervirens (D. Don) Endl.

HABIT. This tree reaches greater heights than any in the world, commonly rising 200–275 ft, and is 8–12 ft in diameter (max. 372 by 20 ft); crown short and narrowly conical; bole clear, straight; often tight circles of young trees found around old stumps due to sprouts.

LEAVES. Spirally arranged; flattened; decurrent; on lower branches ½–1 in. long, linear, appearing 2-ranked, acute tips, short petioles; on leaders and fertile branches ¼–½ in. long, awl- to needle-shaped, in several ranks; dark yellow-green above, two bands of stomata below; persistent several years, falling with twigs.

FLOWERS. Monoecious; solitary; male oblong, of several spirally arranged bracts containing stamens; female of 15–20 spirally arranged, peltate scales, each bearing 3–12 erect ovules; ovuliferous bract and scale partially fused.

FRUIT. Woody, ovoid, pendent cone; ¾–1 in. long; red-brown; wrinkled, peltate scales; maturing in one season. Seeds: ¹⁄₁₆ in. long; light brown; laterally 2-winged with wings as broad as seed; 2–9 seeds on each scale.

TWIGS. Slender; greenish; smooth. Winter buds: small; globose; covered by numerous, imbricated, acute scales.

BARK. 6–12 in. thick; fibrous; red-brown to cinnamon-brown; deeply furrowed.

WOOD. Important; light clear red weathering to dark red; soft and weak; very durable; used for lumber, dimension stock, tanks. A single tree has yielded 480,000 bd ft.

SILVICAL CHARACTERS. Very tolerant; fast-growing; reaches maturity in 400–1,800 years; reproduces vigorously by stump sprouts as well as seeds; deep, widespreading, lateral root system; remarkably free from enemies.

HABITAT. Restricted to the fog belt; the dominant species in this narrow belt; in pure stands or mixed with Douglas-fir, Sitka spruce, grand fir, western hemlock, and hardwoods.

Dawn Redwood

Metasequoia glyptostroboides Hu & Cheng

This species, long thought extinct, was found in China in 1941 and is now widely planted. The foliage resembles redwood but is deciduous; cones and needles are longer and narrower.

Giant Sequoia

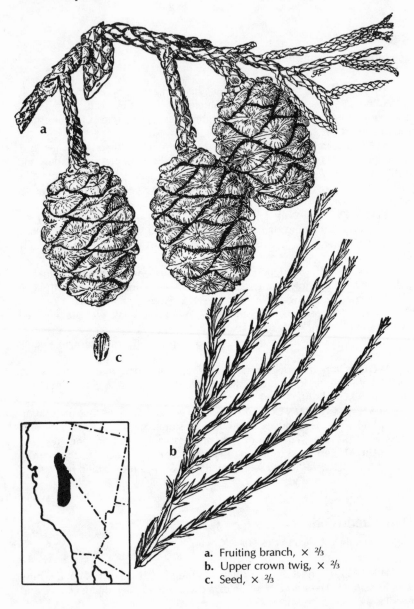

a. Fruiting branch, × ⅔
b. Upper crown twig, × ⅔
c. Seed, × ⅔

Giant Sequoia • Bigtree

Sequoiadendron giganteum (Lindl.) Buckholz (*Sequoia gigantea* [Lindl.] Decne.)

HABIT. This tree is the most massive and possibly the oldest of all living things, commonly reaching a height of 250–280 ft and a diameter of 10–15 ft (max. 293 by 37 ft); crown scraggly and open; bole clear with short thick branches.

LEAVES. Spirally arranged; ¼–½ in. long; ovate to lanceolate; appressed or spreading, but thickly clothing the twig; rigid; sharp-pointed; decurrent at base; blue-green; turning brown in 2–3 years but persisting for several years.

FLOWERS. Similar to redwood, but female with 25–40 scales.

FRUIT. Woody, ovoid-oblong, pendent cones; 2–3½ in. long; red-brown; peltate, wrinkled scales; reaching full size first year, but not maturing until second year; unique in that seeds may be retained in cones up to 20 years, while peduncles live and grow and cones look like young cones. Seeds: ¼ in. long; light brown; laterally 2-winged, with wings broader than seed; 2–9 seeds on each scale.

TWIGS. Slender; leaf-covered. Winter buds: small; naked.

BARK. 12–24 in. thick; fibrous; cinnamon-red; furrowed between broad, rounded ridges.

WOOD. Unimportant; similar to redwood but brittle; impractical to log because of size.

SILVICAL CHARACTERS. Intermediate in tolerance; fast-growing; reaches age of 4,000–5,000 years; reproduction sparse, mineral soil needed for seed germination; tree does not sprout; widespreading lateral root system; few natural enemies aside from lightning and fire; no tree known to have died from old age, insects, or fungal attack.

HABITAT. Native only in some 32 groves of varying extent found along the western middle slopes of the Sierra Nevada of California; in former geologic periods this genus was widely scattered through the forests of the Northern Hemisphere. Generally associated with sugar, ponderosa, and Jeffrey pines; white and red fir; and incense-cedar.

Baldcypress

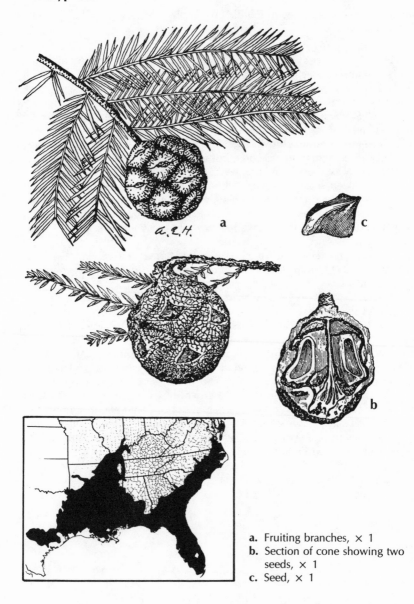

a. Fruiting branches, × 1
b. Section of cone showing two
   seeds, × 1
c. Seed, × 1

Baldcypress

Taxodium distichum (L.) Rich.

HABIT. A large and important tree, 100–120 ft high and 3–5 ft in diameter (max. 150 by 17 ft); young crown narrowly pyramidal, becoming irregular and flattened with age; bole tapered with fluted butt; peculiar conical structures known as knees arise from roots on wetter sites.

LEAVES. Spirally arranged; deciduous; lateral twigs falling with attached leaves; on lower branches ½–¾ in. long, linear, appearing 2-ranked; on fertile branches about ½ in. long, appressed, and nearly scalelike; yellow-green.

FLOWERS. Monoecious; male cones in drooping panicles, each composed of 6–8 stamens; female subglobose, of several spirally arranged, peltate scales each bearing 2 erect ovules.

FRUIT. Woody, subglobose, pendent cone; ¾–1 in. in diameter; brown; of several wrinkled, peltate scales; maturing in 1 year and usually disintegrating at maturity. Seeds: ¼ in. long; brown; irregularly 3-angled and 3-winged; 2 seeds to each scale.

TWIGS. Terminal twigs bearing axillary buds and persistent; lateral twigs deciduous, with needles still attached. Winter buds: small; subglobose; several imbricated scales.

BARK. Variable; thin and scaly to fibrous and 1½ in. thick; red-brown to ash-gray.

WOOD. Important; variegated from light to dark brown; moderately heavy, hard, and strong; very durable; used for construction lumber, siding, caskets, shingles, etc.

SILVICAL CHARACTERS. Intolerant; rather slow-growing, on wet sites; reaches age of 1,000–2,000 years; reproduces well from seed, and stump sprouts vigorously; shallow, widespreading roots; surprisingly windfirm even on wet, unstable soils; wood of old trees riddled with pecky rot.

HABITAT. Typical in swamps; in pure stands or with water tupelo, sweetgum, and other bottomland hardwoods.

Pondcypress

Taxodium distichum var. *nutans* (Ait.) Sweet

Closely related to the baldcypress, this unimportant, smaller tree differs from baldcypress in having smaller scalelike to needle-shaped leaves that are closely appressed. It is found in bogs and along ponds from southern Virginia to Louisiana.

Montezuma Baldcypress

Taxodium mucronatum Ten.

This tree grows in Mexico and enters southern Texas. It differs from other species in having persistent needles.

CUPRESSACEAE

The Cypresses and White-cedars

Characteristics of the Genera *Cupressus* L. and *Chamaecyparis* Spach

HABIT. Evergreen, resinous, pyramidal trees (sometimes shrubs); clear tapering trunks; dense crowns of stout, erect, or horizontal branches.

LEAVES. Small; scalelike (often awl-shaped on leading shoots); ovate; slender, spreading, or appressed tip; thickened, rounded, often glandular on the back; persistent 3–6 years; decussate (in pairs alternately crossing at right angles); becoming brown and woody before falling; margins smooth to finely serrate.

FLOWERS. Monoecious; minute; terminal; male oblong of numerous decussate stamens each bearing 2–6 subglobose anthers; female of 4–14 peltate decussate scales, each with 2–20 erect, basal ovules; bract and ovuliferous scale wholly fused.

FRUIT. Subglobose, leathery to woody, erect cone; maturing in 1–2 seasons; cone scales peltate, thick, often with a central boss or mucro that is a remnant of flower scales. Seeds: 1–20 in several rows on each scale; erect; lateral wings.

TWIGS. Slender; quadrangular or flattened; leaf-covered. Winter buds: minute; naked; inconspicuous.

WOOD. Strongly aromatic; light brown to yellow heartwood; pale yellow sapwood; very durable.

SILVICAL CHARACTERS. Tolerant; usually slow-growing.

GENERAL. The genus *Chamaecyparis* is considered by many authors to be but a section of the genus *Cupressus,* and because of their similarity they are described together here. The chief differences are described in the key on the next page. Six species of *Cupressus* and three of *Chamaecyparis* are native to the United States. Italian cypress and two Asiatic species of *Chamaecyparis* are commonly planted ornamentals and are included in the key.

KEY TO THE SPECIES OF *Cupressus* AND *Chamaecyparis*

1. Cones woody, 6–16-scaled, ½–1½ in. diameter, ripening second year, 6–20 seeds per scale; branchlets round or 4-angled; leaves fringed, narrow translucent border visible with lens .... *Cupressus*, the Cypress
   2. Leaves glaucous, pale blue to silvery gray-green; cones 6–8-scaled, ¾–1¼ in. in diameter.
      3. Leaves acute, glandular; twigs gray; Arizona to Texas and Mexico .... *Cupressus arizonica* Greene, **Arizona cypress,** p. 99
      3. Leaves obtuse; twigs bright red; southern and lower California, Mexico .... *Cupressus guadalupensis* S. Wats., **tecate cypress**
   2. Leaves dark or bright green.
      4. Leaves conspicuously glandular-pitted on back; cone 6–8-scaled, ½–1 in. in diameter.
         5. Cones with prominent hornlike umbos; rare; Oregon, California .... *Cupressus macnabiana* A. Murr., **McNab cypress**
         5. Cones with short, conical umbos; southern Oregon, northern California .... *C. bakeri* Jeps., **modoc cypress**
      4. Leaves without glands or obscurely glandular.
         6. Cones 6–8-scaled, ½–¾ in. diameter; California (Mendocino County) ... . *Cupressus goveniana* Gord., **Gowen cypress**
         6. Cones 8–14-scaled, ⅞–1½ in. diameter.
            7. Branchlets and boss of cone scales thick; California .... *Cupressus macrocarpa* Hartw., **Monterey cypress**
            7. Branchlets and boss of cone scales thin; planted ornamental .... *Cupressus sempervirens* L., **Italian cypress**
1. Cones leathery to semifleshy, 4–10-scaled, ¼–½ in. diameter, ripening in 1 or 2 years, 2 seeds (rarely 5) per scale; twigs somewhat flattened; leaves entire .... CHAMAECYPARIS, the White-cedar
   8. Branchlets not arranged in conspicuous horizontal planes; leaves green on both sides; bark on mature trees thin; cones with 4–6 scales; lateral and facial leaves nearly equal in size.
      9. Branchlets slender; leaves about 1/16 in. long, usually glandular; cones ¼ in. in diameter, maturing in 1 year, 1–2 seeds per scale; heartwood light brown; Atlantic Coast from Maine to Mississippi .... *Chamaecyparis thyoides* (L.) B.S.P., **Atlantic white-cedar,** p. 103
      9. Branchlets stout; leaves about ⅛ in. long, often without glands; cones ¼–½ in. in diameter, maturing in 2 years, 2–4 seeds per scale; heartwood clear yellow; Pacific Northwest .... *Chamaecyparis nootkatensis* (D. Don) Spach, **Alaska-cedar,** p. 103
   8. Branchlets arranged in conspicuous horizontal planes; cones with 10 scales; leaves with glaucous or whitish marks below; heartwood light brown.
      10. Bark on mature trees thick and furrowed; leaves conspicuously glandular on the back and indistinctly marked with white streaks below, lateral much larger than facial; Oregon and California, also widely planted .... *Chamaecyparis lawsoniana* (A. Murr.) Parl., **Port Orford-cedar,** p. 101
      10. Bark on mature trees thin; leaves without glands or glands indistinct, but with distinct white markings below; Japanese ornamentals widely planted in the United States.
         11. Leaves closely appressed, obtuse to acute, the lateral much larger than the facial, conspicuous Y-shaped white mark below; cone ⅓–½ in. diameter .... *Chamaecyparis obtusa* (S. & Z.) Endl., **hinoke white-cedar,** p. 101
         11. Leaves loosely appressed, acuminate, the lateral slightly larger than the facial, conspicuous white patches below; cone ¼ in. in diameter .... .. *Chamaecyparis pisifera* (S. & Z.) Endl., **sawara white-cedar,** p. 101

Arizona Cypress

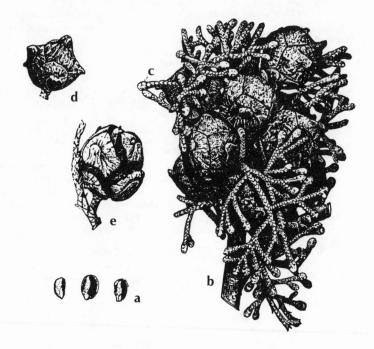

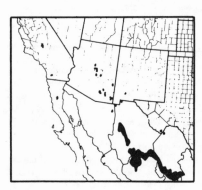

a. Seeds, × ¾
b. Branchlet with cones, × ¾
c. Male flower bud in autumn
d. Different form of cone, × ¾
e. Opened cone, × ¾

Arizona Cypress

Cupressus arizonica Greene

HABIT. Under favorable conditions a tree 50–60 ft high and 1–2½ ft in diameter (max. 80 by 4 ft); trunk short, limby, sharply tapering; crown dense, sharply conical.

LEAVES. Scalelike, pointed, ¹⁄₁₆ in. long; silvery gray-green; dying and turning red-brown the second year and falling about 4 years later; commonly without glands or pits on back; giving off a skunklike odor when bruised.

FLOWERS. Male oblong, yellow; female subglobose.

FRUIT. ¾–1 in. in diameter; subglobose; dark red-brown on stout stalks; of 6–8 peltate scales, each with stout, incurved, prominent boss; maturing during second summer and remaining on tree many years. Seeds: 6–20 on each scale; ¹⁄₁₆–⅛ in. long; oblong to triangular; deep red-brown; thin, narrow, lateral wings.

TWIGS. 4-angled; dark gray; loose-scaly bark, with smooth, reddish inner bark visible below. Winter buds: minute; inconspicuous; naked.

BARK. Loose-scaly on young trunks and branches, showing smooth reddish inner bark below; on old trunks 1¼ in. thick, fibrous, deeply furrowed, ridged, dark red-brown.

WOOD. Slightly aromatic; durable; heartwood light brown; sapwood straw-colored; soft and light, splitting easily; used locally for fence posts, mine timbers, etc.

SILVICAL CHARACTERS. Tolerant throughout life; slow-growing; trees seldom over 400 years old; reproduction generally scanty, although seed produced every year.

HABITAT. Transition zone; altitudinal range 4,500–8,000 ft; best growth on moist, gravelly, north slopes and benches but hardy on dry, sterile, rocky sites.

SIMILAR SPECIES. Five similar but unimportant species are native to the Pacific Coast. These are separated in the key to the species of *Cupressus*. The distinctions between these are minor, and it is often difficult to identify the species. These species as well as the Italian cypress, *C. sempervirens* L., with its distinctive, very narrow, columnar crown, are commonly planted as ornamentals in warmer sections of the United States.

Port Orford-cedar

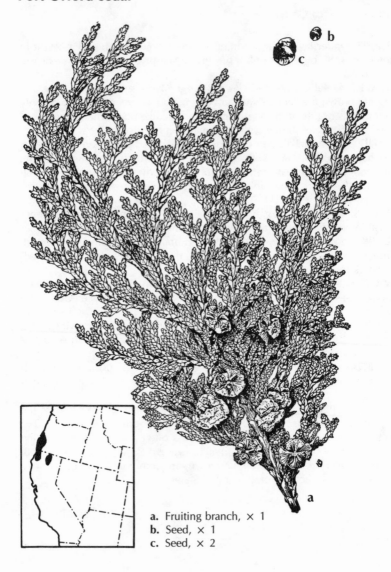

a. Fruiting branch, × 1
b. Seed, × 1
c. Seed, × 2

Port Orford-cedar

Chamaecyparis lawsoniana (A. Murr.) Parl.

HABIT. A large, handsome tree 140–180 ft high and 4–6 ft in diameter (max. 225 by 16 ft); bole clear and often buttressed; crown short-conical, with many branches.

LEAVES. Scalelike; blunt; ¹⁄₁₆ in. long; entire; yellow-green to blue-green; turning brown after 2–3 years, but persisting for several years; glandular; forming flat, horizontal, feathery sprays.

FLOWERS. Male oblong, bright red; female subglobose.

FRUIT. ⅓ in. in diameter; globose; red-brown; abundant; of 6–8 decussate, peltate scales, each with thin, acute, reflexed boss; maturing in 1–2 years; persistent on twig after seed released. Seeds: 2–5 on each scale; ⅛ in. long; ovoid; chestnut-brown; 2 broad lateral wings.

TWIGS. Slender; flattened; leaf-covered. Winter buds: minute; naked; inconspicuous.

BARK. 6–10 in. thick; red-brown to silver-brown; fibrous and furrowed on old trunks; young bark thin and scaly.

WOOD. Important; aromatic; very durable; pale brown; light; easily worked; used for battery separators, venetian blinds, boats, aircraft; cut far exceeds growth.

SILVICAL CHARACTERS. Moderately tolerant; growth moderate; reaches maturity in 300–350 years but often living for more than 500 years; reproduction aggressive; free from insect and fungal enemies, though damaged by fire.

HABITAT. Altitudinal range from sea level to 5,000 ft; requires abundant soil and atmospheric moisture; in pure stands or mixed with numerous conifers.

SIMILAR SPECIES. The following two Japanese species are widely planted as ornamentals.

Sawara White-cedar

Chamaecyparis pisifera (S. & Z.)

This is a narrow, pyramidal tree of fairly rapid growth, easily identified by its acuminate leaves that are obscurely glandular and dark green above and have conspicuous white lines below. The cones are ¼ in. or less in diameter and consist of 10–12 scales.

Hinoki White-cedar

Chamaecyparis obtusa (S. & Z.)

This is a tree with a broad, pyramidal crown, characterized by obtuse leaves that are dark green above and not glandular and with conspicuous white lines below. The cones are ⅓–½ in. in diameter and consist of 8–10 scales.

Alaska Yellow-cedar

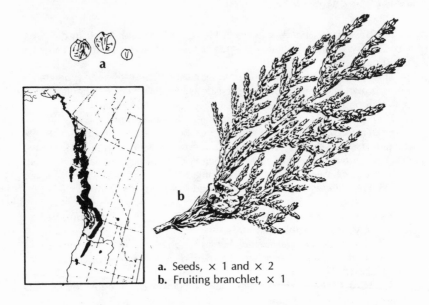

a. Seeds, × 1 and × 2
b. Fruiting branchlet, × 1

Atlantic White-cedar

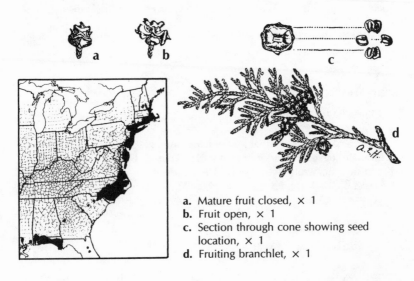

a. Mature fruit closed, × 1
b. Fruit open, × 1
c. Section through cone showing seed
   location, × 1
d. Fruiting branchlet, × 1

Alaska-cedar • Yellow-cedar

Chamaecyparis nootkatenis (D. Don) Spach

HABIT. A medium-sized tree 60–90 ft high and 2–3 ft in diameter (max. 130 by 6 ft); clear, buttressed; often fluted bole; crown conical, of drooping branches.

LEAVES. Scalelike; acute; ⅛ in. long; blue-green to gray-green; persistent 2–3 years; usually without glands; sprays appearing limp and wilted.

FLOWERS. Male bright yellow; female subglobose, brown.

FRUIT. ¼–½ in. in diameter; globose; purple to red-brown; of 4–6, decussate, peltate, bossed scales, maturing in 2 years. Seeds: 2–4 on each scale; ¼ in. long; broad wings.

TWIGS. Rather stout; pendulous. Winter buds: minute.

BARK. Thin; gray-brown; fibrous; furrowed on old trunks; young bark thin and scaly.

WOOD. Moderately important; durable; heartwood clear yellow; used for boats, trim, blinds, etc.

SILVICAL CHARACTERS. Intermediate in tolerance; slow-growing; reaches ages over 600 years; reproduction sparse; lateral roots.

HABITAT. Sea level (Alaska) to timberline; moist sites; pure stands or mixed with many conifers.

Atlantic White-cedar • Southern White-cedar

Chamaecyparis thyoides (L.) B.S.P.

This tree of the Atlantic seaboard differs from other native species by the following characters:

HABIT. Small- to medium-sized (max. 120 by 5 ft); bole clear, cylindrical; crown conical, with drooping branches.

LEAVES. ¹⁄₁₆–⅛ in. long; blue-green; keeled and glandular.

FRUIT. ¼ in. in diameter; globose; purple to red-brown; reflexed boss; somewhat fleshy; maturing in 1 year. Seeds: 1–2 on each scale; ⅛ in. long.

BARK. Thin; gray to red-brown; fibrous; furrowed.

WOOD. Similar to northern white-cedar; used for posts and poles.

SILVICAL CHARACTERS. Moderately tolerant; slow-growing; reproduction vigorous; shallow, lateral roots.

HABITAT. Swamps and bogs in the coastal plains; pure stands or mixed with many species.

Incense-cedar

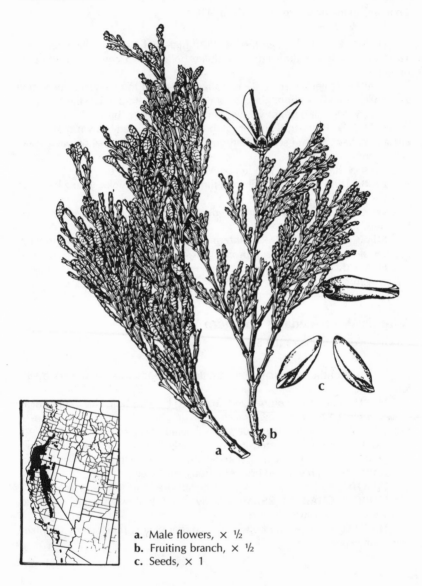

a. Male flowers, × ½
b. Fruiting branch, × ½
c. Seeds, × 1

Incense-cedar

Libocedrus decurrens Torr.

HABIT. A medium-sized tree 80–120 ft high and 3–4 ft in diameter (max. 186 by 8 ft); tapering, often fluted trunk covered for up to half its length with lustrous, irregular foliage.

LEAVES. Small; scalelike; whorled in 4's; facial leaves flattened; the lateral keeled and almost ensheathing facial leaves; oblong–ovate; ⅛–½ in. long; persistent 3–5 years; glandular; aromatic when crushed; fronds usually in a vertical plane.

FLOWERS. Monoecious; terminal; male oblong, golden, with 12–16 decussate 4-celled anthers; female oblong, yellow-green, 6-scaled, with the inner 2 each bearing 2 erect ovules.

FRUIT. Leathery, pendent cones; ¾–1½ in. long; oblong; 6-scaled, with 2 becoming greatly enlarged and spreading at maturity; maturing in 1 season. Seeds: ⅓–½ in. long; in pairs on fertile scales; unequally laterally winged; straw-colored.

TWIGS. Slender; flattened; leaf-covered; in long sprays that are more often in a vertical plane than in a horizontal plane. Winter buds: minute; naked; inconspicuous.

BARK. Thin; smooth to scaly; gray-green on young stems; becoming 3–8 in. thick, yellow-brown to cinnamon-red, fibrous, and deeply furrowed on old trees.

WOOD. Chief source of pencil stock; would be highly important for many uses except for prevalence of pecky rot; sapwood white; heartwood reddish, soft, and fragrant.

SILVICAL CHARACTERS. Tolerant; rather slow-growing; reaches maturity in about 300 years; reproduction abundant and vigorous; moderately deep, lateral root system; fire and pecky rot caused by *Polyporus amarus* cause extensive damage.

HABITAT. Transition zone; altitudinal range 1,000–9,000 ft; on cool, moist soils. In mixed stands with sugar, ponderosa, Jeffrey, and white pine; white fir; and Douglas-fir.

Western Redcedar and Northern White-cedar

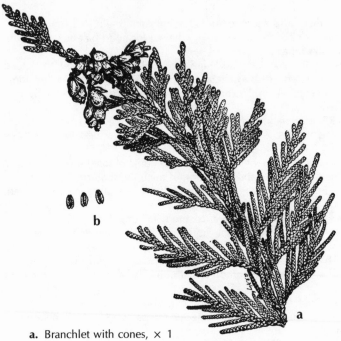

a. Branchlet with cones, × 1
b. Seeds, × 1

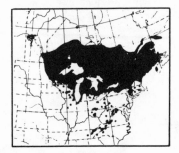

Western Redcedar   Northern White-cedar

Western Redcedar • Giant Arborvitae

Thuja plicata Donn

HABIT. A large tree, 150–200 ft high and 4–8 ft in diameter (max. 250 by 16 ft); tapering, fluted trunk; irregular crown of horizontal or drooping branches.

LEAVES. Small, scalelike; persistent 2–5 years; decussate; facial leaves flattened, grooved; lateral leaves rounded or keeled; lustrous, dark yellow-green.

FLOWERS. Monoecious; terminal; dark brown; male with 3–6 pairs of decussate stamens; female 8- to 12-scaled.

FRUIT. Leathery or subwoody erect cones; ½ in. long; ovoid-oblong; maturing in 1 season; 8–12 scales (only 7 being fertile), thin, spine-tipped. Seeds: ⅛ in. long; brown; lateral wings each about as wide as seed.

TWIGS. Slender; flattened; leaf-covered in long drooping sprays. Winter buds: minute; naked; inconspicuous.

BARK. Thin (½–1 in.); fibrous; narrow interlacing ridges; cinnamon-red to gray-brown on old trunks.

WOOD. Widely used where durability rather than strength is required; sapwood white; heartwood reddish, soft, fragrant; used for shingles, siding, interior trim, boats, poles, etc.

SILVICAL CHARACTERS. Tolerant; rather fast-growing; trees over 1,000 years old reported; reproduction generally plentiful; shallow, widespreading root system; fire and pecky heart rot cause serious damage.

HABITAT. Transition and Canadian zones; altitudinal range 2,000–7,000 ft in Rocky Mountains; on rich soils with abundant moisture; in mixed coniferous stands.

Northern White-cedar • Eastern Arborvitae

Thuja occidentalis L.

Aside from its eastern distrubution, this species differs from *Thuja plicata* by only minor characters, the cones having but 4 fertile scales and the leaves being dull green and usually glandular-pitted. This small tree grows on a variety of sites and is typical of swampy areas. It is not important, although used to some extent for posts and poles.

Oriental Arborvitae

Thuja orientalis L.

This tree is widely planted and perhaps naturalized. It is easily distinguished from the native species by the vertical disposition of the leaf sprays, the thick cone scales, and the wingless seed.

CUPRESSACEAE

The Junipers

Characteristics of the Genus *Juniperus* L.

HABIT. Evergreen, aromatic small trees or shrubs.

LEAVES. Persistent for several years; sessile; aromatic; needlelike or awl-shaped on young growth; of three types on older growth: (1) ternate, spreading, and entirely needlelike or subulate; (2) decussate, appressed, decurrent, and entirely scalelike; and (3) a combination of the types (1) and (2).

FLOWERS. Dioecious (rarely monoecious); minute and inconspicuous; male yellow, solitary, of numerous ternate or decussate stamens; female of 3–8 decussate or ternate pointed scales, some or all bearing 1 or 2 ovules.

FRUIT. Berrylike, succulent, indehiscent cones, formed by coalescence of flower scales; subtended by persistent flower bracts; maturing in 1–3 years. Seeds: 1–21 in cone; ovoid; unwinged; marked at base by a scar (hilum).

BUDS. Small; naked; covered by leaves (scaly in dwarf juniper).

BARK. Thin; soft; fibrous; shreddy (brittle, thick, and divided into nearly square plates in alligator juniper).

WOOD. Durable; weak; close-grained; aromatic; heartwood red-purple to brown; sapwood whitish.

SILVICAL CHARACTERS. Exceedingly variable; mostly intolerant; slow-growing; long-lived; seed disseminated by birds or mammals; deep lateral roots.

GENERAL. This genus contains 40–60 species widely scattered through the Northern Hemisphere, with 13 species native to the United States. Only *J. virginiana* is of any commercial importance, although several other species form conspicuous parts of the vegetation. Two appear as small shrubs, *J. communis* and *J. horizontalis* Moench.

The dwarf juniper, *Juniperus communis* L., while circumpolar and extending through most of the United States and Canada, attains tree size only in New England and southern Illinois. This species has ternate leaves ⅓–½ in. long that are all needlelike, scaly buds, and axillary flowers; the prostrate, high-mountain form has been designated *J. communis* var. *montana* Ait. (*J. communis* var. *sibirica* Rydb.).

The prostrate juniper, *J. horizontalis* Moench, entering the United States from the north, differs from dwarf juniper in having closely appressed, decussate leaves, ⅛–¼ in. long. This species often forms dense creeping mats.

KEY TO THE SPECIES OF JUNIPERS

1. Leaves all needlelike or awl-shaped, ⅓ to ½ in. long, ternate; bud scale, ⅛ in. long; usually a small shrub, rarely a small tree ....
.... *J. communis,* **common juniper,** p. 108
1. Leaves on mature branches usually scalelike, ⅛ in. long or less, opposite (on young or vigorous shoots often needlelike); buds indistinct, naked.
    2. Trunk bark in thick, squarish plates; fruit red-brown, ½ in. diameter, usually 4-seeded, ripening in 2 years; heartwood brown; Southwest ....
    .... *J. deppeana,* **alligator juniper,** p. 115
    2. Trunk bark fibrous and shreddy.
        3. Fruit bright red to red-brown beneath, whitish bloom; western.
            4. Fruit bright red (rarely copper-colored), ¼ in. diameter, 1-seeded; heartwood brown; southwestern.
                5. Seeds with large dark ridgeband and 3 concavities ....
                .... *J. erythrocarpa,* **redberry juniper,** p. 115
                5. Seeds without large dark ridgeband ....
                .... *J. pinchotii,* **Pinchot juniper,** p. 115
            4. Fruit dull red-brown or copper-colored; heartwood brown.
                6. 4–12 seeds per fruit; drooping branches; southern Texas, Mexico ....
                .... *J. flaccida,* **drooping juniper,** p. 115
                6. 1 (rarely 2) seeds per fruit; branches seldom drooping.
                    7. Fruit ¼–¾ in. diameter; seed completely enclosed; fruit maturing in 2 years; heartwood brown.
                        8. Leaves in whorls of 3's, rarely opposite; seed marked at base by light-colored hilum; California ....
                        .... *J. californica,* **California juniper,** p. 117
                        8. Leaves opposite, rarely in 3's; seed marked to middle by conspic-uous hilum; Rocky Mountains ....
                        .... *J. osteosperma,* **Utah juniper,** p. 115
                    7. Fruit ⅛–⅓ in. diameter; seed marked at base by hilum; fruit ma-turing in 1 year; Nevada to Colorado and south to Texas and Ari-zona .... *J. monosperma,* **one-seed juniper,** p. 113
        3. Fruit bluish to blue-black, 1- to 3-seeded.
            9. Leaf margin smooth; heartwood distinctly reddish.
                10. Fruit maturing in 2 years; western ....
                .... *J. scopulorum,* **Rocky Mountain juniper,** p. 113
                10. Fruit maturing in 1 year; eastern.
                    11. Fruit ¹⁄₂₄–¹⁄₁₂ in. diameter; drooping branches; South Carolina to eastern Texas .... *J. silicicola,* **southern redcedar,** p. 111
                    11. Fruit ¼–⅓ in. diameter; branches erect or spreading ....
                    .... *J. virginiana,* **eastern redcedar,** p. 111
            9. Leaf margin minutely fringe-toothed (under hand lens); heartwood brown-ish.
                12. Fruit with 2–3 thick-shelled seeds; maturing in 2 years; Northwest and Pacific Coast .... *J. occidentalis,* **western juniper,** p. 117
                12. Fruit with 1–2 thin-shelled seeds, maturing in 1 year.
                    13. 1 (rarely 2) seeds, pale brown; leaves gray-green; Nevada to Cali-fornia and south ....
                    .... *J. monosperma,* **one-seed juniper,** p. 113
                    13. 1–2 seeds; dark brown; leaves blue-green; Missouri to Texas and Mexico .... *J. ashei,* **Ashe juniper,** p. 115

Eastern Redcedar

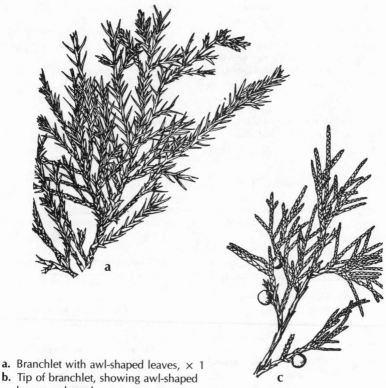

a. Branchlet with awl-shaped leaves, × 1
b. Tip of branchlet, showing awl-shaped
   leaves, enlarged
c. Fruiting branchlet with scalelike leaves, × 1
d. Tip of branchlet, showing scalelike
   leaves, enlarged

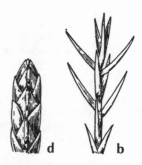

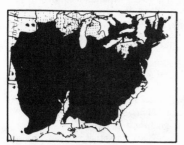

Eastern Redcedar • Eastern Juniper

Juniperus virginiana L.

HABIT. A small to medium-sized tree 30–40 ft high and 1–2 ft in diameter (max. 100 by 4 ft); crown dense, irregular, pyramidal; numerous ornamental varieties widely planted.

LEAVES. The scalelike leaves decussate, closely appressed, dark green, acute, 1/16 in. long, smooth-margined, glandular; the awl-shaped, juvenile leaves often ternate, sharp-pointed, 1/4–1/2 in. long.

FLOWERS. Dioecious; rarely monoecious.

FRUIT. Glaucous; dark blue; berrylike; 1/4–1/3 in. in diameter; subglobose; maturing in 1 year. Seeds: 1–2 (rarely 3–4) in each cone; angled and acute; requiring 2–3 years to germinate.

TWIGS. Slender; 4-angled. Winter buds: naked; minute; leaf-covered.

BARK. Thin (1/8–1/4 in.); red-brown; fibrous, exfoliating into long, narrow strips.

WOOD. Bright red, often streaked with white; aromatic; durable; easily worked; moderately heavy and hard; weak; used for chests, trim, pencils, posts.

SILVICAL CHARACTERS. Intermediate in tolerance; slow-growing; reaches maximum age of about 300 years; deep, lateral roots; reproduction abundant and vigorous; often disfigured by "cedar apples" caused by *Gymnosporangium juniperi.*

HABITAT. Adapted to a variety of sites but typical on poor, dry soils; in pure stands or mixed with hardwoods such as oaks and hickory.

Southern Redcedar

Juniper silicicola (Small) Bailey (*Juniperus lucayana* Britt.)

This species is very similar to eastern redcedar, but can be distinguished by its very small fruit (1/12–1/24 in. in diameter) and very slender, pendulous branches. It also differs from eastern redcedar in that it is found on wet, swampy, coastal plain sites from South Carolina to eastern Texas.

Rocky Mountain Juniper

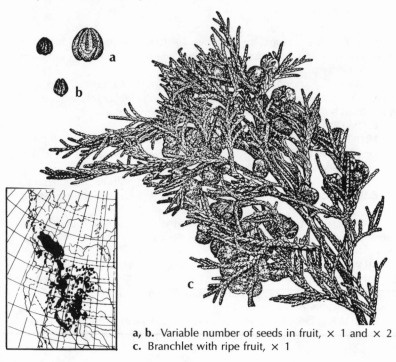

a, b. Variable number of seeds in fruit, × 1 and × 2
c. Branchlet with ripe fruit, × 1

One-seed Juniper

a. Seeds, × 1 and × 2
b. Branchlet with fruit, × 1

Rocky Mountain Juniper

Juniperus scopulorum Sarg.

HABIT. From a bushy shrub on exposed sites to a tree 40–55 ft high and 15–30 in. in diameter; trunk often dividing near the ground; crown typically irregular and rounded.

LEAVES. ⅛ in. long; acute or acuminate; pale to dark green; obscurely glandular on back; smooth margins.

FLOWERS. Dioecious.

FRUIT. Glaucous; blue; ¼–⅓ in. in diameter; maturing in 2 years. Seeds: 1–2 per cone; angled; acute; grooved.

WOOD. Heartwood dull red or bright red and streaked with white; sapwood thick and white; durable.

HABITAT. Upper Sonoran and transition zones; largest distribution of any western juniper; very drought-resistant; in pure stands or mixed with pinyon, ponderosa pine, etc.

One-seed Juniper

Juniperus monosperma (Engelm.) Sarg.

HABIT. A small tree, or shrubby as a result of large branches leaving trunk at or below root collar.

LEAVES. ⅛ in. long; acute; gray-green; denticulately fringed; usually glandular.

FLOWERS. Dioecious.

FRUIT. Glaucous; copper-colored (rarely blue); ⅛–¼ in. long; maturing in 1 year. Seeds: 1 (rarely 2) in each cone; ovoid.

WOOD. Heartwood yellow-brown to red-brown; sapwood white; durable; rather heavy and hard; used for posts and fuel.

HABITAT. Upper Sonoran zone; growing on dry, rocky slopes, in pure stands or with pinyon and ponderosa pines.

GENERAL. A related southwestern form with a single seed exposed at the apex and formerly given specific rank as open-seed juniper, *J. gymnocarpa* (Lemm.) Cory, is now considered a form of *J. monosperma*.

Utah Juniper

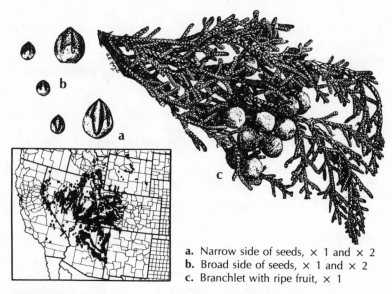

a. Narrow side of seeds, × 1 and × 2
b. Broad side of seeds, × 1 and × 2
c. Branchlet with ripe fruit, × 1

Alligator Juniper

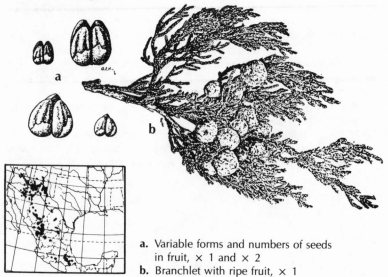

a. Variable forms and numbers of seeds
in fruit, × 1 and × 2
b. Branchlet with ripe fruit, × 1

Utah Juniper

Juniperus osteosperma (Torr.) Little (*Juniperus utahensis* [Eng.] Lemm.)

HABIT. A spreading shrub or small tree; trunk single, or many-stemmed just above the ground; crown rounded.

LEAVES. ⅛ in. long; acute; pale yellow-green; minutely toothed; usually glandular.

FLOWERS. Usually monoecious; sometimes dioecious.

FRUIT. Glaucous; red-brown; ¼–¾ in. long; maturing in 2 years. Seeds: 1 (rarely 2) in each cone; ovoid; sharply angled; acute; marked to the middle by a conspicuous hilum.

WOOD. Heartwood light yellow-brown; sapwood thick and white; very durable; used locally for fuel and fence posts.

HABITAT. Upper Sonoran zone; on dry, rocky slopes; in pure stands or with one-seed juniper, pinyon, and desert shrubs.

Alligator Juniper

Juniperus deppeana Steud. (*Juniperus pachyphloea* Torr.)

HABIT. A spreading shrub or small tree; crown broad.

LEAVES. ⅛ in. long; acute; blue-green; minutely toothed; conspicuously glandular.

FLOWERS. Monoecious.

FRUIT. Glaucous; dark red-brown; ⅓–½ in. long; maturing in 2 years. Seeds: 1–4 (usually 4) in each cone; distinctly grooved; conspicuously swollen on back.

BARK. Very characteristic; ½–4 in. thick; red-brown; deeply furrowed into square plates 1–2 in. across.

WOOD. Heartwood brown; durable; used locally.

HABITAT. Upper Sonoran and transition zones; drought-resisitant; commonly mixed with nut pines and oaks.

Other Junipers Distinguished in the Key

Ashe juniper, *J. ashei* Buch., is in Missouri, Arkansas, Oklahoma, and Texas.

Drooping juniper, *J. flaccida* Schl., is in southwestern Texas.

Pinchot juniper, *J. pinchotii* Sudw., is in southwest Oklahoma, Texas, and southeast New Mexico.

Redberry juniper, *J. erythrocarpa* Cory, ranges from southwest Texas to southern Arizona. It is similar to and possibly not distinct from *J. pinchotii*.

Western Juniper

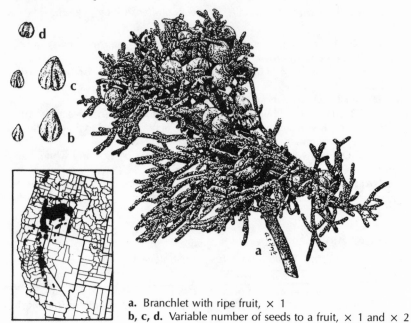

a. Branchlet with ripe fruit, × 1
b, c, d. Variable number of seeds to a fruit, × 1 and × 2

California Juniper

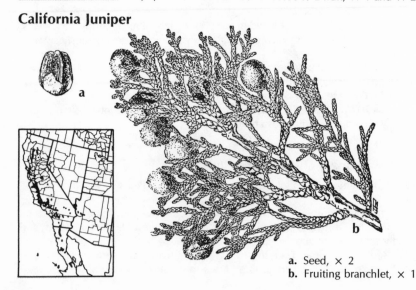

a. Seed, × 2
b. Fruiting branchlet, × 1

Western Juniper • Sierra Juniper

Juniperus occidentalis Hook.

HABIT. A bushy shrub or small tree; short, straight trunk; broad, rounded crown, extending nearly to ground.

LEAVES. ⅛ in. long; acute or acuminate; gray-green; conspicuously glandular-pitted on back; denticulately fringed.

FLOWERS. Dioecious.

FRUIT. Glaucous; blue-black; ¼–⅓ in. in diameter; maturing in 2 years. Seeds: 2–3 in each cone; ovoid; acute.

WOOD. Heartwood pale brown tinged with red; sapwood white and thick; exceedingly durable; used locally for posts.

HABITAT. Upper Sonoran to Hudsonian zones; on exposed, dry, rocky mountain slopes; usually in pure, open stands.

California Juniper

Juniperus californica Carr.

HABIT. A small tree, or shrubby as a result of large branches leaving the trunk near the ground.

LEAVES. ⅛ in. long; acute; yellow-green; conspicuously glandular on back; fringed on the margins.

FLOWERS. Dioecious.

FRUIT. Red-brown; glaucous; ⅜–¾ in. long; maturing in 2 years. Seeds: 1–2 in each cone; obtuse.

WOOD. Heartwood pale brown tinged with red; thin, white sapwood; durable; used locally for posts.

HABITAT. Upper Sonoran zone; on desert and mountain slopes; with pinyon and chaparral.

California Torreya

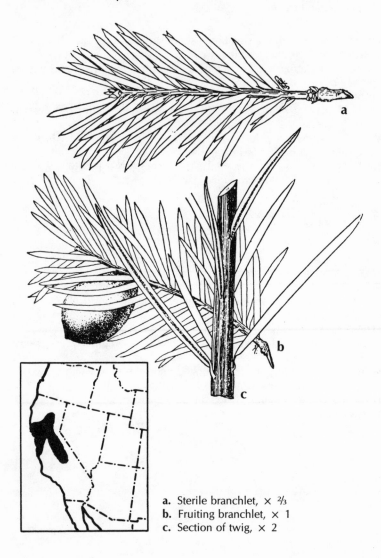

a. Sterile branchlet, × ⅔
b. Fruiting branchlet, × 1
c. Section of twig, × 2

TAXACEAE

California Torreya • California Nutmeg

Torreya californica Torr. (*Tumion californicum* [Torr.] Greene)

HABIT. A rare, small tree 15–70 ft high and 1–2 ft in diameter; clear, often malformed bole; crown pyramidal, with slender, spreading branches.

LEAVES. Persistent many years; linear-lanceolate; spirally arranged, appearing 2-ranked; 1–3½ in. long; acuminate and often bristle-tipped; flat; rigid; dark green and lustrous above; pale below, with 2 narrow, distinct bands of stomata; petioled; decurrent.

FLOWERS. Dioecious; male solitary, consisting of numerous stamens in whorls of 4; female in pairs, ¼ in. long, the ovule surrounded by and finally enclosed in a fleshy sac.

FRUIT. Drupelike; a single seed with a woody outer coat completely enclosed in a thin, fleshy, green to purple envelope; ellipsoidal; 1–1½ in. long; maturing in 2 years, but requiring additional year before germinating.

TWIGS. Slender; drooping. Winter buds: small; ovoid; acute; of few overlapping, shining, opposite scales.

BARK. Thin (⅓–½ in.); gray-brown; in narrow, scaly ridges.

WOOD. Unimportant; soft; light clear yellow.

SILVICAL CHARACTERS. Tolerant; slow-growing; long-lived; reproduction sparse, but stumps sprout vigorously; lateral roots.

HABITAT. Dependent on moist sites; in pure, dense thickets or mixed with hardwoods. In small, scattered, isolated areas within shaded portion on map.

Florida Torreya • Stinking-cedar

Torreya taxifolia Arn. (*Tumion taxifolium* [Arn.] Greene)

This is a rare, small, handsome tree found only along the bluffs of the Apalachicola River in Florida and southern Georgia. It differs from the western species in having needles slightly rounded on the back and about 1½ in. long and malodorous.

Pacific Yew

a. Branchlet with fruit, × 1

Pacific Yew • Western Yew

Taxus brevifolia Nutt.

HABIT. A small tree or large shrub, 20–50 ft high and 1–2 ft in diameter; limby, often fluted or malformed trunks; large, open, conical crown, with long, slender, drooping branches; a sprawling shrub near timberline.

LEAVES. Persistent 5–12 years; linear-lanceolate; spirally arranged, appearing 2-ranked; ½–1 in. long; sharp-pointed; petiolate; green above, paler beneath.

FLOWERS. Dioecious; solitary; axillary; surrounded by scales of bud; male in globose heads of 6–14 stamens, yellowish; female single, greenish, the apical scale bearing a solitary erect ovule with a basal disk.

FRUIT. A single, erect, ovoid-oblong seed with a hard, bony shell; ⅓ in. long; exposed at apex, but partially or entirely surrounded by, but free from, the thickened, scarlet, fleshy aril-like disk of the flower; maturing in one season.

TWIGS. Slender; drooping. Winter buds: small; ovoid; obtuse; of numerous overlapping scales.

BARK. Very thin (¼ in.); scaly; dark red-purple.

WOOD. Heavy; hard; strong; durable; heartwood bright orange to rose-red; sapwood thin, yellow; used for bows, canoe paddles, fence posts, turned articles.

SILVICAL CHARACTERS. Most tolerant forest tree of Northwest; slow-growing; reaches maturity in 250–350 years; reproduction scanty; deep, wide-spreading roots; stumps sprout.

HABITAT. Transition to Hudsonian zone; altitudinal range 2,000–8,000 ft; on deep, moist soils; in small groups or as an occasional understory tree in mixed forests.

Florida Yew

Taxus floridana Nutt.

This is a rare, small, bushy tree found only along the bluffs of the Apalachicola River in Florida. It differs from Pacific yew in having dark green, falcate needles, ¾–1 in. long.

SALICACEAE

The Poplars and Cottonwoods

Characteristics of the Genus *Populus* L.

HABIT. Mostly large, fast-growing, deciduous trees.

LEAVES. Alternate; simple; turning yellow before falling in autumn; petioles mostly long and often laterally compressed; stipules present, falling as leaves unfold.

FLOWERS. Regular; dioecious; both sexes in drooping aments; appearing from separate buds, before the leaves; individual flowers solitary, apetalous, inserted on broad, cup-shaped disk, subtended by dilated, lobed, and often laciniate scale or bract; staminate with 4 to many stamens; pistillate, a single, 1-celled, usually sessile ovary with 2–4 placentas and 2–4 stigmas.

FRUIT. A 1-celled, 2- to 4-valved capsule containing numerous seeds. Seeds: small; turfted with long silky hairs; extremely buoyant; vitality transient and must germinate within few days.

TWIGS. Pith homogeneous; angled or stellate in cross section. Winter buds: terminal present, covered by several scales.

BARK. Astringent; light-colored; deeply furrowed or smooth.

WOOD. Light; soft; weak; diffuse-porous; not durable; heartwood light brown; used for pulp, veneer, and lumber.

SILVICAL CHARACTERS. Intolerant; fast-growing; short-lived; reproduction widespread and abundant; stumps and roots sprout vigorously; extensive, widespreading root systems.

GENERAL. This genus contains about 35 species scattered over the Northern Hemisphere and in northern Africa; 8 species and several hybrids are native to North America; 3 European species have become naturalized and are included.

KEY TO THE SPECIES OF POPLARS AND COTTONWOODS

1. Twigs, buds, petioles, and lower surfaces of leaves white tomentose; widely planted and naturalized.
   2. Leaves irregularly sinuate-dentate or palmately 3- to 5-lobed, base usually rounded or flat .... *P. alba,* **white poplar,** p. 125
   2. Leaves toothed, not lobed, base heart-shaped ....
   .... *P.* X *canescens,* **gray poplar,** p. 125
1. Twigs, buds, petioles, and leaves hairy or glabrous at maturity.
   3. Leaf petiole round in cross section, leaf base round or heart-shaped.
      4. Leaves broadly ovate, 4–7 in. long and nearly as broad, densely hairy when they unfold, but becoming glabrous; wet sites; Atlantic Coast, southeastern and central states .... *P. heterophylla,* **swamp cottonwood,** p. 127
      4. Leaves ovate to lanceolate, ⅓ or more longer than broad.

5. Leaves lanceolate to ovate-lanceolate, 2–4 in. long; petioles short (less than ⅓ length of blade); buds ¼–¾ in. long, resinous; Rocky Mountains . . . . *P. angustifolia,* **narrowleaf cottonwood,** p. 131
5. Leaves ovate to ovate-lanceolate; petioles at least ½ as long as leaf blade.
  6. Leaves 3–6 in. long, margins finely toothed; buds ¾–1 in. long, very resinous and aromatic.
    7. Capsule 3-valved, hairy; stigmas 3; 40–60 purple stamens; Pacific region . . . . *P. trichocarpa,* **black cottonwood,** p. 129
    7. Capsule 2-valved, glabrous; stigmas 2; 20–30 pink stamens; northern North America . . . . *P. balsamifera,* **balsam poplar,** p. 129
  6. Leaves 2–4 in. long, margins coarsely toothed; buds ½–¾ in. long, slightly resinous, not aromatic; Rocky Mountains . . . . *P. X acuminata,* **lanceleaf cottonwood,** p. 131
3. Leaf petiole definitely flattened laterally.
  8. Leaves broadly ovate to suborbicular, 1–5 in. long, base rounded; buds almost nonresinous; capsules 2-valved, thin-walled; 6–12 stamens.
    9. Leaves finely toothed, glabrous; buds glabrous; Atlantic to Pacific . . . . *P. tremuloides,* **quaking aspen,** p. 125
    9. Leaves with few coarse teeth; buds hairy; eastern . . . . *P. grandidentata,* **bigtooth aspen,** p. 125
  8. Leaves deltoid to rhombic-ovate, 2–7 in. long; buds resinous; capsules 3- or 4-valved (2-valved in black and Lombardy poplars), thick-walled; 12–60 stamens.
    10. Leaves rhombic-ovate (rarely deltoid), long acuminate, base wedge-shaped or rounded, hybrids or naturalized trees widely planted through North America.
      11. Leaves longer than broad, 2–6 in. long, coarsely toothed . . . . *P. X canadensis,* **Carolina poplar,** p. 127
      11. Leaves about as long as broad, 2–4 in. long, finely toothed.
        12. Tree with widespreading, stout branches . . . . *P. nigra,* **black poplar,** p. 125
        12. Columnar tree; erect branches; narrow, spinelike crown . . . . *P. nigra italica,* **Lombardy poplar,** p. 125
    10. Leaves deltoid in shape, 3–6 in. long; native trees.
      13. Leaves with glands at point where petiole and blade meet; margins ciliate, with numerous teeth.
        14. Buds glabrous; leaves finely toothed, eastern . . . . *P. deltoides,* **eastern cottonwood,** p. 127
        14. Buds slightly hairy, leaves coarsely toothed; Great Plains to Rocky Mountains . . . . *P. deltoides* var. *occidentalis (P. sargentii),* **plains cottonwood,** p. 127
      13. Leaves without glands at point where petiole and blade meet; margins not ciliate, with usually less than 15 teeth on a side.
        15. Pedicels longer than capsules; leaves with no more than 10 teeth on a side; Colorado, New Mexico, west Texas, Mexico . . . . *P. fremontii wislizeni,* **Rio Grande cottonwood**
        15. Pedicels shorter than capsules; leaves, more than 10 teeth on a side; New Mexico west to California . . . . *P. fremontii,* **Fremont cottonwood,** p. 131

Quaking Aspen

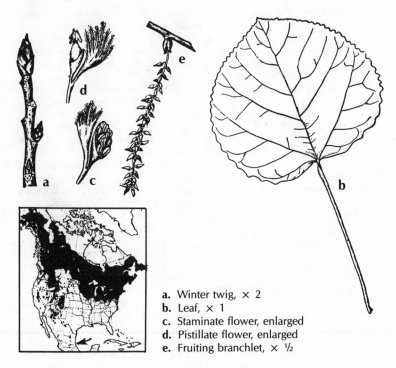

a. Winter twig, × 2
b. Leaf, × 1
c. Staminate flower, enlarged
d. Pistillate flower, enlarged
e. Fruiting branchlet, × ½

Bigtooth Aspen

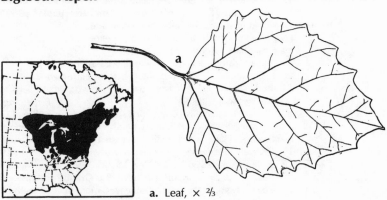

a. Leaf, × ⅔

Quaking Aspen • Poplar

Populus tremuloides Michx.

HABIT. A small tree 50–60 ft high and 1–2 ft in diameter; loose, rounded crown with slender branches.

LEAVES. Semiorbicular or broadly ovate; 1½–3 in. in diameter; yellow-green; apex acute; base rounded; finely crenate-serrate with glandular teeth; thin and firm; glabrous; petioles flattened, 1½–3 in. long.

FRUIT. Capsules narrowly conical; ¼ in. long; curved; 2-valved; gray-hairy. Seeds: light brown; 1/32 in. long.

TWIGS. Slender; round; bright red-brown and lustrous, becoming gray. Winter buds: terminal ¼–½ in. long; conical; sharp-pointed; red-brown; sometimes slightly resinous.

BARK. Smooth; green-white to cream-colored.

SILVICAL CHARACTERS. Canadian and Hudsonian zones; reproducing vigorously on cutover or burned-over areas and forming a protective canopy for more tolerant species.

Bigtooth Aspen

Populus grandidentata Michx.

This medium-sized tree differs from quaking aspen in having coarsely sinuate-toothed leaves 2–5 in. long, stout twigs, and puberulous, dusty-gray buds ⅛ in. long.

Naturalized European Species

The following European forms have become naturalized in parts of the United States; their distinguishing features appear in the key:

White poplar, *P. alba* L., is a large, widely planted tree with distinctive white hairy leaves.

Gray poplar, *P.* X *canescens* (Ait.) Sm., is a hybrid of *alba* X *tremula*.

Black poplar, *P. nigra* L., is a widespreading tree.

Lombardy poplar, *P. nigra* var. *italica* Muenchh., a hybrid clone with a narrow columnar crown and ascending branches, is widely planted.

Eastern Cottonwood

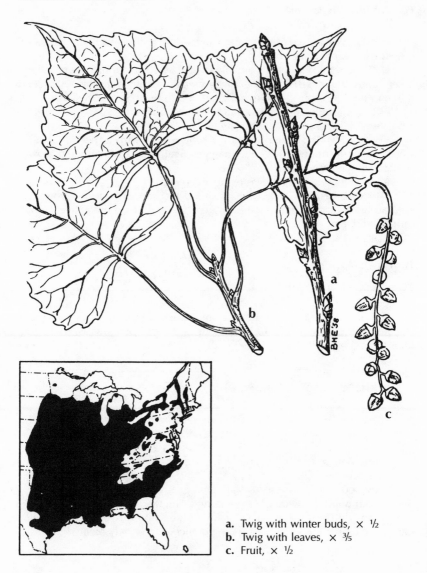

a. Twig with winter buds, × ½
b. Twig with leaves, × ⅗
c. Fruit, × ½

Eastern Cottonwood
Populus deltoides Bartr.

HABIT. This important eastern species is a large tree 60–100 ft high and 3–5 ft in diameter (max. 175 by 11 ft); broad, open crown; large, spreading branches.

LEAVES. Broadly deltoid; 3–6 in. long; apex acuminate; coarsely crenate-serrate, teeth glandular; glabrous; petiole flattened, 1½–3 in. long, with 2 glands at apex.

FRUIT. Capsules ovoid, ⅓ in. long; in catkins 8–12 in. long. Seeds: light brown; hairy; about 1/16 in. long.

TWIGS. Stout; yellow-brown; angular; glabrous. Winter buds: ¾ in. long; conical; acute; shiny-brown; resinous.

BARK. Yellow-green and smooth on young trunks, becoming thick ash-gray, and furrowed.

GENERAL. The western variety, plains cottonwood, *P. deltoides* var. *occidentalis* Rydb. (*P. sargentii* Dode) is not shown on the map but extends from Texas and New Mexico north to Alberta and Saskatchewan. The widely planted Carolina poplar, *P.* X *canadensis* Moench., includes hybrid clones of *P. deltoides* X *nigra*.

Swamp Cottonwood
Populus heterophylla L.

This species of the coastal plain from Connecticut to Louisiana and north in the Mississippi valley to Ohio and southern Michigan differs from eastern cottonwood in having the leaf petiole round in cross section and the leaf base round or heart-shaped. It is characteristic of river bottoms and swamps, usually mixed with other hardwood species.

Black Cottonwood

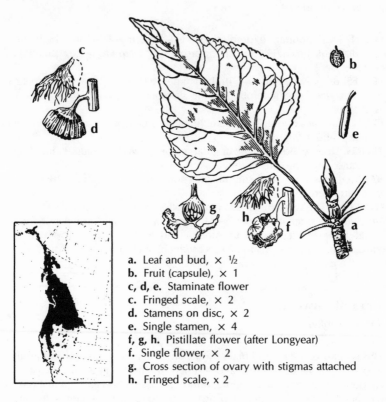

a. Leaf and bud, × ½
b. Fruit (capsule), × 1
c, d, e. Staminate flower
c. Fringed scale, × 2
d. Stamens on disc, × 2
e. Single stamen, × 4
f, g, h. Pistillate flower (after Longyear)
f. Single flower, × 2
g. Cross section of ovary with stigmas attached
h. Fringed scale, x 2

Balsam Poplar

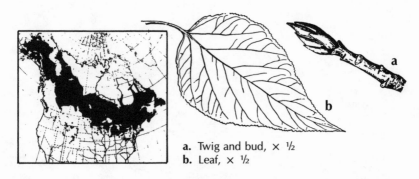

a. Twig and bud, × ½
b. Leaf, × ½

Black Cottonwood

Populus trichocarpa Torr. & Gray

HABIT. The largest of American poplars and the largest broad-leaved tree in the Pacific Northwest, reaching 200 ft in height and 7–8 ft in diameter; long, clear, cylindrical trunk; crown open, rounded.

LEAVES. Ovate to ovate-lanceolate; 5–6 in. long and 3–4 in. wide; apex acute to long-acuminate; base rounded or slightly cordate; margin finely crenate; leathery; dark green above, silver-white to pale green below; petioles round, long.

FRUIT. Capsules subglobose, 1/3 in. long; 3-valved; hairy.

TWIGS. Moderately slender; round or slightly angled; red-brown at first, becoming glabrous and dark gray. Winter buds: terminal 3/4 in. long; ovoid; orange-brown; covered by fragrant, yellow-brown resin.

BARK. Smooth and greenish on young stems; becoming pale gray, 1–2 1/2 in. thick, deeply and sharply furrowed.

Balsam Poplar

Populus balsamifera L. (*Populus tacamahacca* Mill.)

HABIT. A medium-sized tree seldom over 60–80 ft high and 1–3 ft in diameter; open, narrow crown.

LEAVES. Broadly ovate to ovate-lanceolate; 3–6 in. long and 2–4 in. broad; apex acute to acuminate; base rounded or cordate; finely crenate-serrate; thin and firm; dark green above, much paler below; petioles round, slender, long.

FRUIT. Capsules ovoid; 1/4–1/3 in. long; 2-valved; glabrous; short-stalked. Seeds: light brown; 1/12 in. long.

TWIGS. Moderately stout; round; red-brown. Winter buds: terminal 1 in. long; ovoid; chestnut-brown; saturated by fragrant, amber-colored resin.

BARK. On young trunks smooth and green-brown; on large trunks deeply furrowed and gray-black.

GENERAL. Balm-of-Gilead, a widely planted ornamental tree in the Northeast, is a clone or hybrid of this species.

Narrowleaf Cottonwood

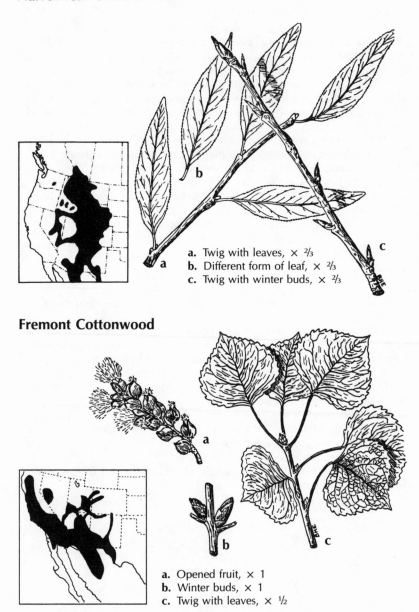

a. Twig with leaves, × ⅔
b. Different form of leaf, × ⅔
c. Twig with winter buds, × ⅔

Fremont Cottonwood

a. Opened fruit, × 1
b. Winter buds, × 1
c. Twig with leaves, × ½

Narrowleaf Cottonwood

Populus angustifolia James

HABIT. A medium-sized tree 50–70 ft high and 12–20 in. in diameter; crown pyramidal with slender, erect branches.

LEAVES. Lanceolate to ovate-lanceolate; 2–4 in. long and ½–1½ in. wide; apex long-tapering; finely to coarsely serrate; thin and firm; bright yellow-green above, paler below; petioles short (less than ⅓ length of blade), slender, somewhat flattened on upper side.

FRUIT. Capsules broadly ovoid; ¼ in. long; 2-valved.

TWIGS. Slender; round; yellow-green, becoming ash-gray. Winter buds: terminal ¼–¾ in. long; slender; long-pointed; chestnut-brown; very resinous and somewhat aromatic.

BARK. Light yellow-green; ¾–1 in. thick; smooth except near base of old trees where it is divided by shallow furrows.

GENERAL. Lanceleaf cottonwood, *P.* X *acuminata* Rydb., is considered a hybrid between *P. angustifolia* and *P. deltoides.*

Fremont Cottonwood

Populus fremontii Wats.

HABIT. A medium-sized to large tree rarely 4–6 ft in diameter and 100 ft tall; wide, open crown.

LEAVES. Deltoid to reniform, apex short-pointed, coarsely serrate; petiole flattened, without glands where blade and petiole meet.

FRUIT. Capsules ovoid, ⅓–½ in. long; thick-walled. Seeds: light brown, hairy, ⅛ in. long.

TWIGS. Stout, yellow-gray. Winter buds: ⅓–½ in. long, ovoid, acute, greenish.

BARK. Gray-brown and smooth on young trunks, becoming thick, dark, and deeply furrowed.

GENERAL. Two varieties are recognized:

P. fremontii var. *mesetae* (Eck.) Little (*P. arizonica* Sarg.) on the Mexican border from Texas to Arizona.

P. fremontii var. *wislizeni* Wats. from southern Colorado and Utah to New Mexico and Texas.

Hinckley Cottonwood

P. fremontii X *angustifolia*

This is a rare and local hybrid in the Davis Mountains in Texas.

SALICACEAE

The Willows

Characteristics of the Genus *Salix* L.

HABIT. Shrubs or less frequently trees; latter often with several trunks from greatly extended rootstalk.

LEAVES. Alternate; simple; commonly lanceolate; margins entire or toothed; pinnately veined; sessile or short-petioled; stipules small and soon falling, except on vigorous shoots where they are leaflike and persistent.

FLOWERS. Regular; dioecious; in terminal and axillary aments, appearing with or before the leaves; individual flowers solitary, apetalous, on glandlike disk, subtended by pubescent, entire to dentate, deciduous, or persistent scale or bract; staminate with 1–2 or 3–12 stamens inserted on base of bract; pistillate a single, 1-celled, sessile or stalked ovary, containing 4–8 ovules on each of 2 placentas, style short, terminating in 2 short, 2-part stigmas.

FRUIT. A 1-celled, 2-valved, acuminate capsule. Seeds: small; dark brown; tufted with long, silky hairs; buoyant; of transient vitality.

TWIGS. Slender to stout; round; tough; often easily separated at junction with branch; marked by elevated leaf scars; pith homogeneous, terete. Winter buds: terminal absent; lateral covered by single caplike scale.

BARK. Astringent; scaly; variously colored.

WOOD. Light; soft; weak; usually brittle; durable in some species; heartwood pale brown, often tinged with red; used to small extent for athletic goods and charcoal.

SILVICAL CHARACTERS. Intolerant; fast-growing; remarkable vitality, sprouting vigorously from stumps or cuttings; usually swamp or moisture-loving plants.

GENERAL. This genus contains about 170 species scattered over the Northern Hemisphere, with about 90 species native to North America. Twenty-seven native species have been listed as occasionally reaching tree size, but only 12 of these are commonly trees. Identification of the species is difficult, even for experts.

KEY TO THE SPECIES OF WILLOW FREQUENTLY REACHING TREE SIZE

1. Stamens 3–12, filaments free; flower bracts deciduous.
   2. Typically a tree; leaves green below; petioles without glands at base . . . .
   . . . . *S. nigra* Marsh., **black willow,** p. 135
   2. Commonly shrubby; leaves pale or bluish below.
      3. Petioles without glands at base of leaf.
         4. Twigs easily separable from branch; flower bracts entire.
            5. Leaves 4–5 in. long, narrowly lanceolate to lanceolate; petioles under
            ½ in.; southeastern and central . . . .
           . . . . *S. caroliniana* Michx., **coastal plain willow**
            5. Leaves 2½–4 in. long, lanceolate to ovate-lanceolate; petioles ½–¾ in.
            long; northern and central . . . .
           . . . . *S. amygdaloides* And., **peachleaf willow,** p. 137
         4. Twigs firmly attached; flower bracts toothed; southwestern . . . .
         . . . . *S. bonplandiana* H.B.K., **Bonpland willow**
      3. Petioles glandular; twigs separable; flower bracts toothed; Alaska to California,
      east to Black Hills and New Mexico . . . .
      . . . . *S. lasiandra* Benth., **Pacific willow**
1. Stamens 2.
   6. Widely planted, naturalized oranamentals; usually trees
      7. Distinctive "weeping" habit; leaves glabrous; capsule sessile . . . .
      . . . . *S. babylonica* L., **weeping willow,** p. 135
      7. Branches not drooping; capsule short-stalked.
         8. Leaves white with silky hairs on both sides; twigs green to bright yellow
         . . . . *S. alba* L., **white willow,** p. 135
         8. Leaves nearly glabrous; twigs brownish . . . .
         . . . . *S. fragilis* L., **crack willow**
   6. Native, usually shrubby species; seldom planted.
      9. Bracts deciduous, yellowish; filaments free, somewhat hairy.
         10. Leaves ⅓–1⅓ in. long, linear; Mexican border from west Texas to Arizona
         . . . . *S. taxifolia* H.B.K., **yewleaf willow**
         10. Leaves over 2 in. long, mostly linear-lanceolate; ranges over most of
         North America . . . . *S. exigua* Nutt., **sandbar willow**
      9. Bracts persistent, darker; filaments glabrous.
         11. Ovary and capsule glabrous; bracts dark brown.
             12. Leaves acute or rounded, thin; filaments united at base; Washington
            to California and east on border to Texas . . . .
           . . . . *S. lasiolepis* Benth., **arroyo willow**
            12. Leaves acuminate, thick and leathery; filaments free; Yukon to Cali-
            fornia, east to Wyoming . . . .
           . . . . *S. mackenzieana* Bar., **Mackenzie willow**
         11. Ovary and capsule hairy.
             13. Stipe of ovary longer than light, hairy flower bracts; ranges over most
            of North America . . . . *S. bebbiana* Sarg., **Bebb willow**
             13. Stipe shorter than brown, hairy flower bracts; Alaska and Yukon to
            California, east to Black Hills . . . .
           . . . . *S. scouleriana* Bar., **Scouler willow**

Black Willow

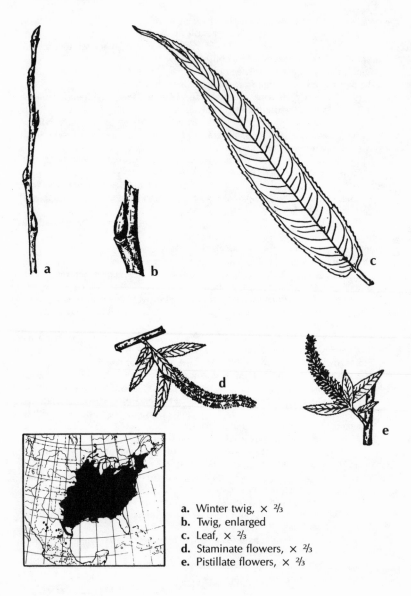

a. Winter twig, × ⅔
b. Twig, enlarged
c. Leaf, × ⅔
d. Staminate flowers, × ⅔
e. Pistillate flowers, × ⅔

Black Willow

Salix nigra Marsh.

HABIT. A small to large tree (max. 120 by 4 ft); trunk often divided; crown broad and open with stout branches.

LEAVES. Lanceolate; 3–6 in. long; acuminate; finely serrate; thin; bright green above, paler beneath; petiole short.

FRUIT. Capsules ovoid-conic; ¼ in. long; short-stalked; glabrous. Seeds: minute; hairy-tufted.

BARK. Nearly black; thick; deeply divided into furrows separating thick, scaly ridges.

SILVICAL CHARACTERS. Intolerant; fast-growing; stream banks and lake shores; with mixed hardwoods.

GENERAL. This is the largest American willow and the only one important for its wood products. It is used for lumber, veneer, pulp, charcoal, and artificial limbs.

White Willow

Salix alba L.

HABIT. A medium-sized European ornamental with a rounded crown and distinctive whitish foliage.

LEAVES. Lanceolate; 2–4 in. long; acuminate; finely toothed; white with silky hairs below.

BARK. Gray; thick; furrowed.

SILVICAL CHARACTERS. Intolerant; fast-growing; adapted to a variety of sites.

GENERAL. Widely planted in moist, temperate areas of the United States and Canada, where it has become naturalized. A variety, golden willow, *S. alba vitellina* (L.) Stokes is one of the basket willows.

Weeping Willow

Salix babylonica L.

HABIT. A medium-sized Chinese ornamental with characteristic long, slender, drooping branches.

LEAVES. Narrowly lanceolate; 2–6 in. long; acuminate; finely toothed; glabrous; dark green above and paler below.

BARK. Gray-brown; rough; fissured.

SILVICAL CHARACTERS. Intolerant; fast-growing; short-lived; moist sites.

GENERAL. Widely planted as a lawn or landscape ornamental and naturalized.

Peachleaf Willow

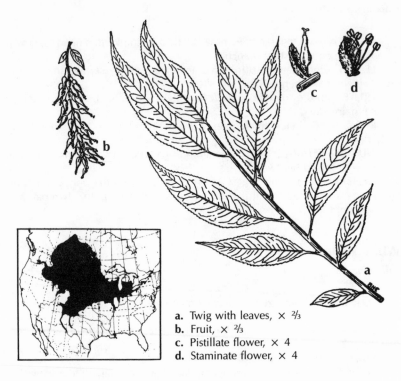

a. Twig with leaves, × ⅔
b. Fruit, × ⅔
c. Pistillate flower, × 4
d. Staminate flower, × 4

Waxmyrtle

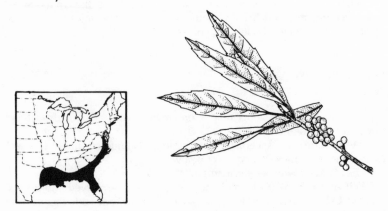

Peachleaf Willow

Salix amygdaloides Anderss.

HABIT. A tree rarely 60–70 ft high and 2 ft in diameter; trunk single.

LEAVES. Lanceolate to ovate-lanceolate; 2–5 in. long; acuminate; finely serrate; thin and firm; light green above, pale and glaucous below.

FRUIT. Capsules globose-conic; ¼ in. long; long-stalked; glabrous; light yellow-red. Seeds: minute; hairy-tufted.

BARK. Brown, often tinged with red; ½–¾ in. thick; divided by irregular furrows into broad, flat, connecting ridges.

SILVICAL CHARACTERS. Intolerant; moist sites along banks of streams.

GENERAL. This willow is the only species native to the Rocky Mountain region that is typically a tree.

MYRICACEAE

KEY TO THE SPECIES OF WAXMYRTLES AND BAYBERRIES

Five species very rarely form trees.

1. Southeastern species; flowers dioecious.
   2. Leaves oblanceolate, coarsely toothed, yellow-green with conspicuous orange glands; fruit ⅛ in. in diameter, coated with thick, blue wax; coastal plain from New Jersey to Florida, west to Arkansas and Texas . . . . *M. cerifera* L., **southern waxmyrtle**
   2. Leaves oblong-obovate, dark green.
      3. Leaves entire, glabrous; fruit ⅓–½ in. in diameter thinly coated with white wax; Florida to Mississippi and eastern Louisiana . . . . *M. inodora* Bartr., **odorless bayberry**
      3. Leaves toothed, glabrous or pubescent below; fruit ⅛ in. in diameter, thickly coated with whitish wax; coastal plain New Jersey to Louisiana . . . . *M. heterophylla* Raf., **evergreen bayberry**
1. Northeastern species; leaves entire or nearly so, fruits heavily covered with wax; grows chiefly near the coast from Newfoundland to North Carolina and locally through Pennsylvania to Ohio . . . . *M. pensylvanica* hoisel, **northern bayberry**
1. Pacific Coast species; flowers monoecious; leaves 2–4 in. long, oblanceolate to oblong-lanceolate, remotely toothed, with minute black glands below; fruit ¼ in. in diameter, purple, thinly coated with gray wax . . . . *M. californica* Cham., **Pacific waxmyrtle**

Waxmyrtle • Bayberry

Myrica cerifera L.

HABIT. Usually shrubby, occasionally forming a small tree.

FLOWERS. Dioecious or monoecious; in aments.

FRUIT. A small, globose drupe; ⅛ in. in diameter; covered with a bluish wax; often persistent until spring. Seeds: A small, thick-walled nut.

BARK. Thin; smooth; whitish to gray; with gray patches.

SILVICAL CHARACTERS. Intolerant; in sandy soils near the seacoast.

GENERAL. The fruit wax is used in making candles.

JUGLANDACEAE

The Walnuts

Characteristics of the Genus *Juglans* L.

HABIT. Small to large handsome trees; crowns broad and open; stout, ascending branches.

LEAVES. Alternate; pinnately compound; deciduous; native species with 9–23 nearly sessile, oblong-lanceolate, finely serrate, acute to acuminate leaflets; stipules absent.

FLOWERS. Monoecious; apetalous; appearing with or after the leaves; staminate in preformed unbranched aments, with 8–40 stamens; pistillate in spikes of 2–8 flowers, each with a 2-celled ovary and 2 divergent, plumose stigmas.

FRUIT. A drupelike nut encased in a semifleshy, indehiscent husk; maturing in 1 year; nut thick-shelled, containing solitary, 2- to 4-lobed, sweet, oily, edible seed.

TWIGS. Stout; round; with characteristic chambered pith. Winter buds: terminal present; few-scaled. Leaf scars: conspicuous; three groups of U-shaped bundle scars.

WOOD. Dark-colored; durable; diffuse-porous; valuable.

SILVICAL CHARACTERS. Intolerant; deep taproot; nuts disseminated largely by rodents or streams.

GENERAL. Of the 6 native species only 2 eastern ones are of commercial importance and treated separately. The 4 southwestern species (listed below) are distinguished in the key:

California walnut, *Juglans californica* S. Wats.

Hinds walnut, *Juglans hindsii* Jeps.

Arizona walnut, *Juglans major* (Torr.) Heller.

Little walnut, *Juglans microcarpa* Berl. (*J. rupestris* Engelm.)

The Persian or English walnut, *Juglans regia* L., is widely planted in warmer parts of the country and is included in the key. The variety with thin-shelled nuts is commonly marketed and the wood is widely used under the name of Circassian walnut.

KEY TO THE SPECIES OF WALNUTS

1. Leaves with 9–29 toothed leaflets; nut with thick, bony partitions; native species.
  2. Fruit ovoid-oblong in clusters of 3–5; band of pale hair separating leaf scar from bud; leaflets 11–17, oblong-lanceolate . . . . *J. cinerea,* **butternut,** p. 141
  2. Fruit globose, solitary or in pairs; buds not separated by hairy band from leaf scar; heartwood dark brown, hard.
    3. Fruit 1½–2 in. in diameter.
      4. Nut deeply ridged; 15–23 leaflets; eastern . . . .
      . . . . *J. nigra,* **black walnut,** p. 141
      4. Nut smooth or faintly grooved; 15–19 leaflets; California . . . .
      . . . . *J. hindsii,* **Hinds walnut,** p. 138
    3. Fruit 1–1½ in. long; nut grooved; leaflets 9–13 (rarely to 19), oblong-lanceolate; Colorado, New Mexico, and Arizona . . . .
    . . . . *J. major,* **Arizona walnut,** p. 138
    3. Fruit ½–¾ in. long; nut grooved.
      5. Leaflets 17–23, narrow-lanceolate; Oklahoma, Texas, and New Mexico
      . . . . *J. microcarpa,* **little walnut,** p. 138
      5. Leaflts 11–15 (rarely to 19), oblong-lanceolate; California . . . .
      . . . . *J. californica,* **California walnut,** p. 138
1. Leaves with 5–9 (rarely to 13), entire or nearly entire leaflets; fruit globose, 1½–2 in. in diameter; nut wrinkled . . . . *J. regia,* **English walnut,** p. 138

Black Walnut

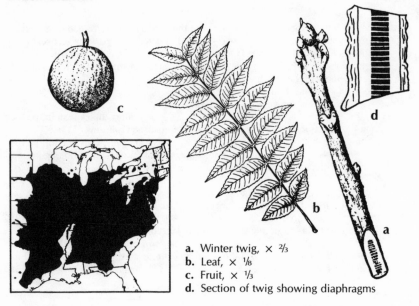

a. Winter twig, × ⅔
b. Leaf, × ⅛
c. Fruit, × ⅓
d. Section of twig showing diaphragms

Butternut

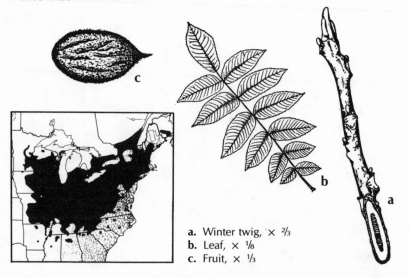

a. Winter twig, × ⅔
b. Leaf, × ⅛
c. Fruit, × ⅓

Black Walnut

Juglans nigra L.

HABIT. A tree 60–90 ft high and 2–3 ft in diameter (max. 150 by 6 ft); trunk straight and clear; crown broad and open.

LEAVES. 1–2 ft long, 15–23 leaflets (terminal leaflet often suppressed); leaflets 3–4 in. long, ovate-lanceolate, finely serrate, yellow-green, glabrous above and hairy below.

FRUIT. Globose; 1½–2 in. in diameter; solitary or in clusters of 2–3; husk thick, yellow-green, pubescent; nut shell corrugated.

TWIGS. Stout; light brown; leaf scar obcordate, without downy pad at top; chambered pith, buff-colored with thin diaphragms. Winter buds: terminal ⅓ in. long, ovoid, blunt, hairy; lateral buds smaller, often superposed.

BARK. Thick; dark brown to nearly black; deep, narrow, interlacing furrows.

WOOD. Heavy; hard; strong; very valuable and important.

SILVICAL CHARACTERS. Fast-growing; long-lived; on fertile, moist soils; in mixed stands; reproduction depends largely on rodents.

Butternut

Juglans cinerea L.

HABIT. A tree 30–60 ft high and 1–2 ft in diameter (max. 110 by 3 ft); trunk short; crown broad and open.

LEAVES. 1–2½ ft long with 11–17 leaflets; leaflets 2–4 in. long, oblong-lanceolate, serrate, yellow-green, rugose above and hairy below.

FRUIT. Oblong-ovoid; 1½–2½ in. long; solitary or in clusters of 2–5; husk green-brown, sticky, glandular-hairy; nut shell deeply corrugated.

TWIGS. Stout; green to red-brown; leaf scar straight across top with dense hairy pad at top; chambered pith, dark chocolate-brown with thick diaphragms. Winter buds: terminal ½–¾ in. long, conical, flattened, hairy; lateral buds smaller, rusty-tomentose.

BARK. Rather thick; light gray; smooth on young trunks, becoming shallowly furrowed with broad ridges.

WOOD. Rather light and soft; light brown; substitute for walnut.

SILVICAL CHARACTERS. Fast-growing; short-lived; varied sites; mixed stands; becoming rare in South.

The Hickories

Characteristics of the Genus *Carya* Nutt.

HABIT. Medium-sized trees with clear straight trunks and open spreading crowns.

LEAVES. Alternate; pinnately compound; deciduous; 3–17 leaflets, short-stalked to nearly sessile, ovate to obovate or lanceolate, finely serrate, tips acute to acuminate, bases inequilateral, stipules absent.

FLOWERS. Monoecious; apetalous; appearing after the leaves; staminate in 3-branched aments, with 3–10 stamens; pistillate in spikes of 2–10 flowers, each with a 1-celled ovary and 2 sessile stigmas.

FRUIT. Nut enclosed in a semiwoody, partly dehiscent, 4-valved husk; maturing in 1 year; nut shell thin to thick, hard, ribbed, smooth to rugose; sweet to bitter.

TWIGS. Mostly rather stout; round; leaf scars large, heart-shaped, or 3-lobed, with numerous bundle scars; pith solid, angular to star-shaped. Winter buds: terminal present, much larger than laterals, with imbricated or valvate scales.

BARK. Smooth and gray on young trunks, becoming scaly or rough; very hard and compact.

WOOD. Highly important; very heavy; hard; strong; light colored; not durable; semi-ring-porous; used for handles, tools, etc.

SILVICAL CHARACTERS. Moderately intolerant; slow-growing; long-lived; taproot system; varied moist sites.

GENERAL. Eleven species are recognized in the United States (some authors recognize 19 species); several, together with numerous varieties and hybrids, are difficult to identify. Seven species come under the group known as "true hickories," characterized by numerous, imbricated bud scales, 3–9 leaflets, and essentially unwinged fruit husks; and 4 species are classified as "pecan hickories," characterized by 4–6 valvate bud scales, 5–17 (mostly more than 7) often falcate leaflets, and fruit husks that are typically broadly winged at the sutures.

KEY TO THE SPECIES OF HICKORIES

1. Bud naked or with 4–6 valvate scales; leaflets 7–17, usually lanceolate, often falcate, about of same size; fruit husk winged . . . . **pecan hickories**
   2. Nuts about twice as long as broad, sweet, thin-shelled; buds brown, covered with yellow hairs; leaflets 9–17; bark thick, furrowed; Illinois to Alabama, Texas . . . . *C. illinoensis,* **pecan,** p. 145
   2. Nuts about as long as broad; leaflets 7–13; bark scaly.
      3. Leaflets 7–9 (rarely 5–11), ovate-lanceolate to obovate, silvery white below; buds brown, hairy; nut sweet, with thick, hard shell; South Carolina to Arkansas and south . . . . *C. myristiciformis,* **nutmeg hickory,** p. 145
      3. Leaflets lanceolate to ovate-lanceolate, pale green below; nut bitter.
         4. Leaflets 7–13 (usually 9–11); buds red-brown; Virginia to Illinois and south . . . . *C. aquatica,* **water hickory,** p. 145
         4. Leaflets 7–9 (usually 7); buds bright yellow; Quebec to Minnesota and south . . . . *C. cordiformis,* **bitternut hickory,** p. 145
1. Bud with more than 6 overlapping scales; leaflets 3–9, the uppermost largest; husk usually without wings; nut thick-shelled, sweet . . . . **true hickories**
   5. Terminal buds ½–1 in. long; twigs thick; fruit 1–2½ in. long.
      6. Bark on old trunks shaggy with loose plates; fruit husk ¼–½ in. thick; upper 3 leaflets conspicuously larger than others; twigs and petioles glabrous to hairy.
         7. Leaflets usually 7 (rarely 5–9), hairy below; twigs pale orange, hairy; shell very thick; New York to Kansas and south . . . . *C. laciniosa,* **shellbark hickory,** p. 149
         7. Leaflets usually 5 (rarely 7), glabrous or slightly hairy below; twigs red-brown, usually glabrous; Quebec to Minnesota and south . . . . *C. ovata,* **shagbark hickory,** p. 149
      6. Bark on old trunks close; fruit husk ⅛–¼ in. thick; leaflets 5–9, of about same size; twigs and petioles often woolly; Massachusetts to Nebraska and south . . . . *C. tomentosa,* **mockernut hickory,** p. 147
   5. Terminal buds ¼–½ in. long; twigs moderately thick to slender; fruit ¾–1½ in. long; bark on old trunks close; fruit husk ¹⁄₁₂–¼ in. thick.
      8. Winter buds and leaves glabrous or pale hairy.
         9. Buds, leaves, and petioles essentially glabrous; husk of fruit very thin (¹⁄₁₂– ⅛ in.); leaflets 5 (rarely 3–7); fruit obovoid, pyriform or oval; Maine to Missouri and south . . . . *C. glabra,* **pignut hickory,** p. 147
         9. Winter buds and leaves with silvery or pale hairs; husk of fruit ⅛–¼ in. thick; leaflets 7 (rarely 5–9), Coastal Plain from New Jersey to Florida, west to Louisiana and north in Mississippi valley to Indiana . . . . *C. pallida,* **sand hickory,** p. 147
      8. Buds, twigs, and leaves red-hairy; leaflets 5–7.
         11. Fruit obovoid; Florida . . . . *C. floridana,* **scrub hickory,** p. 147
         11. Fruit subglobose, obovoid, or pyriform; Indiana to Kansas, Texas, Louisiana . . . . *C. texana,* **black hickory,** p. 147

Bitternut Hickory

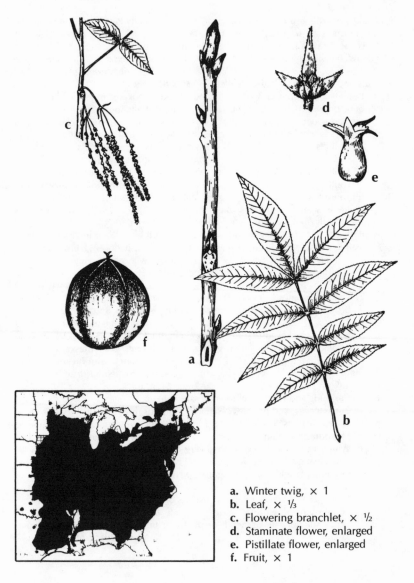

a. Winter twig, × 1
b. Leaf, × ⅓
c. Flowering branchlet, × ½
d. Staminate flower, enlarged
e. Pistillate flower, enlarged
f. Fruit, × 1

Bitternut Hickory

Carya cordiformis (Wang.) K. Koch (*Hicoria cordiformis* [Wang.] Britt.)

HABIT. A tree 50–75 ft. high and 1–2 ft in diameter (max. 100 by 3 ft); broad, open crown with slender ascending branches.

LEAVES. 6–10 in. long with 7–11 leaflets; leaflets lanceolate to oblong-lanceolate, the terminal 3–6 in., slightly larger than lateral, finely to coarsely serrate margins, bright green and glabrous above, paler below.

FRUIT. Subglobose; about 1 in. long; husk thin (less than ⅛ in.) with yellow-green, scurfy pubescence, splitting halfway to base; 4-winged above middle; nut smooth, thin-shelled, bitter.

TWIGS. Rather stout; green to gray-brown. Winter buds: terminal ⅓–¾ in. long, flattish, long-pointed, sulfur-yellow, scurfy-pubescent, valvate scales.

BARK. Thick; firm; gray; shallow furrows and ridges.

SILVICAL CHARACTERS. Adapted to variety of sites; most abundant and uniformly distributed of the hickories; with mixed hardwoods.

Other "Pecan Hickories"

There are three other native species of "pecan hickories":

Pecan, *Carya illinoensis* (Wang.) K. Koch (*Carya pecan* Engl. & Graebn.), famed for its nuts, is the largest of the hickories (max. 180 by 6 ft). This species is characterized by having 9–17 lanceolate, usually falcate leaflets; fruit ellipsoidal, 1–2½ in. long, with thin dark brown husk, splitting from apex to base; nut nearly smooth with sweet seed; buds ¼–½ in. long, yellow-brown, and scurfy. Mississippi valley from southern Wisconsin to Texas, Oklahoma, and Alabama and widely planted through the South.

Water hickory, *Carya aquatica* (Michx.) Nutt., is similar to pecan but differs in having a smaller (1½ in. long) fruit, with a thin nearly black, husk that splits halfway to the base and an obovoid, 4-ribbed nut with a bitter seed. In coastal plain swamps from Virginia to Texas and north to Illinois.

Nutmeg hickory, *Carya myristiciformis* (Michx.) Nutt., is a rather rare tree with 5–9 ovate-lanceolate leaflets silvery white below and an ellipsoidal, 4-winged fruit 1½ in. long, with a very thin husk that splits to the base. In swamps or moist sites from South Carolina to Alabama and Texas and north to Arkansas.

Mockernut Hickory

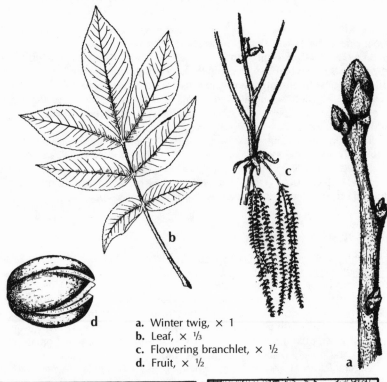

a. Winter twig, × 1
b. Leaf, × ⅓
c. Flowering branchlet, × ½
d. Fruit, × ½

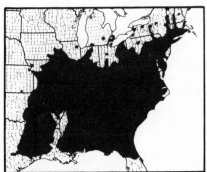

Mockernut Hickory   Pignut Hickory

Mockernut Hickory

Carya tomentosa Nutt. (*Hicoria alba* [L.] Britt.) (*Carya alba* [L.] Nutt.)

HABIT. A tree 50–70 ft high and 1–2½ ft in diameter (max. 100 by 4 ft); broad, open crown with large branches.

LEAVES. 8–12 in. long with 7–9 (rarely 5) leaflets; leaflets lanceolate to obovate-oblanceolate, the terminal 4–7 in. long and somewhat larger than the lateral; finely to coarsely serrate margins; thick; dark yellow-green and glabrous above, paler and hairy below; glandular, resinous, and fragrant.

FRUIT. Globose to ovoid; 1½–2 in. long; husk ⅛–¼ in. thick, splitting nearly to the base; thick shell; sweet seed.

TWIGS. Stout; gray to red-brown; hairy. Winter buds: terminal ½–¾ in. long; subglobose; red-brown; hairy.

BARK. Thick; firm; dark gray; shallow furrows and low, interlacing ridges on mature trunks.

SILVICAL CHARACTERS. Typical of well-drained upland slopes; associated with oak and other hardwoods.

Pignut Hickory

Carya glabra (Mill.) Sweet (*Carya ovalis* [Wang.] Sarg.)

Pignut hickory differs from mockernut in having 5 (rarely 7) essentially glabrous leaflets; glabrous terminal buds ¼–½ in. long; fruit usually about 1 in. long, oval, pyriform, or obovoid, with a thin husk (under ⅛ in.) often splitting only part way to the base.

Other Hickories

Three other unimportant species of "true hickories" have furrowed and firm to scaly bark and are distinguished in the key:

Scrub hickory, *Carya floridana* Sarg., on dry central Florida hills.

Sand hickory, *Carya pallida* (Ashe) Engl. & Graebn., on dry coastal plain sites from New Jersey to Florida and Louisiana and north in Mississippi valley to Indiana.

Black hickory, *Carya texana* Buckl., on dry uplands from Indiana to Kansas to Louisiana and Texas.

Shagbark Hickory

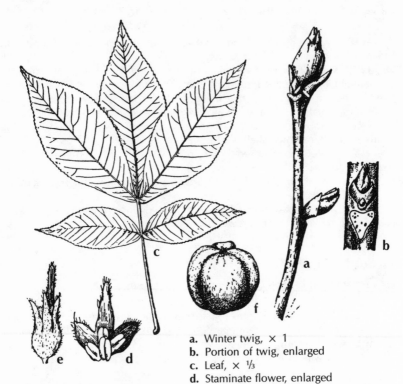

a. Winter twig, × 1
b. Portion of twig, enlarged
c. Leaf, × ⅓
d. Staminate flower, enlarged
e. Pistillate flower, enlarged
f. Fruit, × ½

Shagbark Hickory

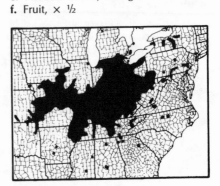

Shellbark Hickory

Shagbark Hickory

Carya ovata (Mill.) K. Koch (*Hicoria ovata* [Mill.] Britt.) (*Carya carolinae-septentrionalis* [Ashe] E. & G.)

HABIT. A tree 60–80 ft high and 1–2 ft in diameter (max. 120 by 4 ft); narrow, open crown and large branches.

LEAVES. 8–14 in. long with 5 (rarely 7) leaflets; leaflets obovate to ovate-lanceolate, the terminal 5–7 in. long and usually much longer than the lateral; finely serrate margins; thick, dark green and glabrous above, yellow-green and usually glabrous below.

FRUIT. Globose to ellipsoidal; 1–2½ in. long (mostly about 1½ in.); husk ¼–½ in. thick, completely dehiscent; nut 4-ribbed with thick shell and sweet seed.

TWIGS. Stout, gray to red-brown, more or less hairy. Winter buds: terminal ½–¾ in. long; broadly ovoid; 3–4 visible, overlapping, brown, pubescent, loosely fitting scales.

BARK. Very characteristic on mature trunks; ¾–1 in. thick; gray; breaking into thin plates 1–3 ft long free at one or both ends, giving tree typical shaggy appearance.

SILVICAL CHARACTERS. This important tree has a varied habitat, being typically mixed with oak on upland slopes in the north, while in the south it is commonly on moist alluvial soils with several hardwoods.

Shellbark Hickory

Carya laciniosa (Michx.) Loud. (*Hicoria laciniosa* [Michx.] Sarg.)

This species has similar shaggy bark and differs from shagbark hickory in having larger leaves 15–22 in. long, with usually 7 leaflets that are velvety below; orange twigs; and somewhat larger fruit (1¾–2½ in. long) with a 4–6 ribbed nut.

LEITNERIACEAE

Corkwood

Leitneria floridana Chapm.

This shrub or small tree with extremely soft wood is the only species in the family. It is rare and local in the coastal plain of southeastern Georgia, western Florida, and southeastern Texas; also in eastern Arkansas and southeastern Missouri. Simple, alternate, deciduous leaves are 4–6 in. long, lanceolate and entire. Fruit is an oval, pointed, dry drupe ¾ in. long with conspicuously netted veins. Twigs are stout with scaly buds; marked by conspicuous circular lenticles and elevated leaf scars.

BETULACEAE

The Birches

Characteristics of the Genus *Betula* L.

HABIT. Small to medium-sized graceful trees and shrubs; crown on young trees narrow, pyramidal, symmetrical; branches short and slender, more or less erect on young trees and becoming horizontal or pendulous on older trees.

LEAVES. Alternate; simple; deciduous; mostly ovate to triangular; acute to acuminate; serrate, dentate, or lobulate; deciduous; petioled; stipules fugacious; scarious.

FLOWERS. Regular; monoecious; apelatous; appearing before or with leaves; staminate in 1- to 3-clustered long, pendulous aments produced early the previous season, every bract with 3 individual flowers, each of 4 stamens adnate to a 4-part calyx; pistillate in solitary, small, slender aments on ends of spurlike lateral branches below staminate flowers, individual flowers naked, clusters of 3, subtended by 3-lobed bract.

FRUIT. Small, compressed, laterally winged nutlet; erect or pendent strobiles; scales shaped like a fleur-de-lis, decidous from persistent cone axis at maturity, releasing nutlets; maturing in fall of first year (1 species in spring).

TWIGS. Slender; round; horizontal lenticels and small leaf scars having 3-bundle scars; spur shoots with paired leaves commonly present on old growth; pith small, round, homogeneous. Winter buds: terminal absent; lateral, acute, 3 (rarely 4) visible scales; twig lengthening by one of upper lateral buds.

BARK. Smooth, papery (or in sweet birch furrowed); resinous; marked by horizontally elongated lenticels; often peeling off in thin, papery layers.

WOOD. Strong; heavy; hard; diffuse-porous; light-colored; some species highly valued for timber.

SILVICAL CHARACTERS. Mostly fast-growing and short-lived; adapted to planting on poor, sandy, or boggy soil; many used for ornamental planting because of handsome foliage and showy bark; lateral root systems.

GENERAL. This genus contains about 50 species of trees and shrubs scattered through the Northern Hemisphere; the European white birch (*Betula pendula* Roth.) and especially its cut-leaf, weeping variety (*B. dalecarlica* Schn.) are often planted in this country; 11 species are native to North America, 7 of which form trees. *B. uber* (Ashe) Fern., very rare in Smyth County, Virginia, may be a hybrid.

KEY TO THE SPECIES OF BIRCHES

1. Leaves with 9–12 pairs of veins; fruit erect, sessile, or nearly so, oblong-ovoid; wing about as broad as nutlet; twigs with wintergreen flavor; important eastern timber species
     2. Bark dark, furrowed, not separating into papery layers; bracts of fruit glabrous
     . . . . *B. lenta,* **sweet birch,** p. 157
     2. Bark dirty-yellow, scaly, separating into thin, papery layers; bracts of fruit hairy
     . . . . *B. alleghaniensis,* **yellow birch,** p. 155
1. Leaves, 8 or less pairs of veins (7–9 in river birch); fruit penduncled, oblong or cylindric; twigs, no wintergreen flavor.
     3. Bark red-brown to chestnut-brown.
          4. Bark separating into papery layers; fruit erect; wing narrower than nutlet; eastern . . . . *B. nigra,* **river birch,** p. 155
          4. Bark not separating into papery layers; fruit pendent; wing broader than nutlet; western.
               5. Fruit ½–¾ in.; leaves wedge-shaped at base; west Canada, Alaska . . . . .
               . . . . *B. X eastwoodiae,* **Yukon birch,** p. 159
               5. Fruit 1–1¼ in. long; leaves usually rounded at base; western United States and southwestern Canada . . . . *B. occidentalis,* **water birch,** p. 159
     3. Bark distinctly white in color.
          6. Bark, chalky-white, not separating freely into papery layers; leaves triangular, bright green; Delaware, Pennsylvania to eastern Canada . . . .
          . . . . *B. populifolia,* **gray birch,** p. 157
          6. Bark lustrous, pink-white, separating freely into papery layers; leaves usually ovate to oval.
               7. Young twigs hairy, nearly nonglandular; bracts of fruit with middle lobe much longer than lateral; northern transcontinental . . . .
               . . . . *B. papyrifera,* **paper birch,** p. 153
               7. Young twigs glabrous and resinous-glandular; bracts of fruit with middle lobe not longer than lateral lobes.
                    8. Leaves hairy along veins on lower surface; small tree from Vermont north to east Canada . . . .
                    . . . . *B. X caerulea-grandis,* **blueleaf birch,** p. 153
                    8. Leaves strictly glabrous; a handsome, widely cultivated, Eurasian tree; often with pendulous branches and lobed leaves . . . .
                    . . . . *B. pendula,* **European birch,** p. 150

Paper Birch

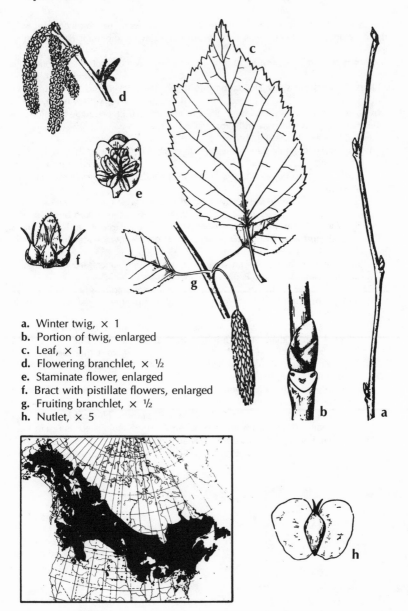

a. Winter twig, × 1
b. Portion of twig, enlarged
c. Leaf, × 1
d. Flowering branchlet, × ½
e. Staminate flower, enlarged
f. Bract with pistillate flowers, enlarged
g. Fruiting branchlet, × ½
h. Nutlet, × 5

Paper Birch

Betula papyrifera Marsh.

HABIT. A tree 60–70 ft high and 2–3 ft in diameter (max. 120 by 4 ft); old trees with open crowns and short, pendulous branches.

LEAVES. Ovate; 2–5 in. long; coarsely, irregularly, and usually doubly serrate; dull dark green and glabrous above; light yellow-green, black-glandular, glabrous or puberulous below.

FRUIT. Strobiles cylindrical, pendent, on slender penduncles, 1–1½ in. long; scales about as long as broad, puberulous; nutlet narrower than wings.

TWIGS. At first green, hairy, and marked by scattered, orange-colored, oblong lenticels; becoming dark orange-brown and lustrous; not aromatic. Winter buds: ¼ in. long; obovoid; acute; dark chestnut-brown; glabrous.

BARK. Cream-white; separating into thin, papery layers; marked by long, narrow, raised lenticels; inner bark orange.

WOOD. Moderately important; used for pulp, lumber, turned articles, fuel.

SILVICAL CHARACTERS. Canadian zone; intolerant; short-lived; spreading roots; reproduction vigorous, taking over extensive areas following fire; rich or sandy soils.

GENERAL. Six varieties have been differentiated and are included in the distribution map:

commutata (Reg.) Fern. from Labrador to Alaska and northern United States.

cordifolia (Reg.) Fern. from Labrador to Ontario and southern New York to Iowa; in mountains to North Carolina.

kenaica (Evans) Henry in Alaska.

neoalaskana (Sarg.) Raup near tree limits in Yukon and Alaska to British Columbia and Saskatchewan.

papyrifera Marsh with distribution shown on map.

subcordata (Rydb.) Sarg. from Idaho to Oregon and western Canada.

Blueleaf Birch

Betula X *caerulea-grandis* Blanchard

This is a small tree found in Nova Scotia, Maine, and Vermont. It is characterized by ovate, blue-green leaves and pink-white bark that is not papery, or is exfoliating but slightly. It is considered to be a hybrid of *B. populifolia* and *B. papyrifera*.

Yellow Birch

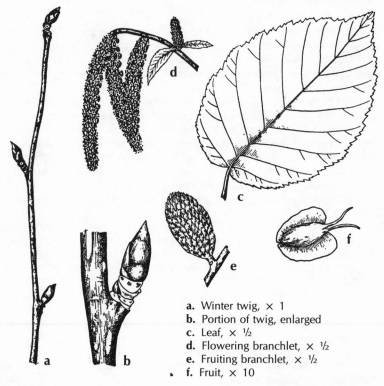

a. Winter twig, × 1
b. Portion of twig, enlarged
c. Leaf, × ½
d. Flowering branchlet, × ½
e. Fruiting branchlet, × ½
f. Fruit, × 10

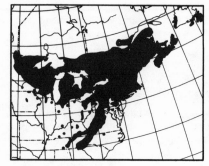

Yellow Birch

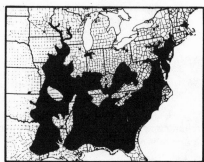

River Birch

Yellow Birch

Betula alleghaniensis Britt. (*Betula lutea* Michx.)

HABIT. A tree 60–80 ft high and 1–2 ft in diameter (max. 100 by 4 ft); rounded, open crown and pendulous branches.

LEAVES. Ovate to oblong-ovate; 3–5 in. long; sharply doubly serrate; rounded, unequal at base; dull, dark green and glabrous above, paler below; slightly aromatic; 9–11 pairs of veins.

FRUIT. Strobiles ovoid, erect, nearly sessile, 1–1½ in. long; scales hairy, longer than broad, wide lateral lobes, tardily deciduous; nutlet about as broad as wing.

TWIGS. Smooth; lustrous; yellow-brown to dark brown; slight wintergreen taste (one source of oil of wintergreen). Winter buds: lateral ¼ in. long; ovate; acute; chestnut-brown; ciliate on scale margins.

BARK. Thin; dirty yellow to bronze-colored; separating horizontally into thin, papery, curled strips.

WOOD. Very important, supplying about 75% of birch lumber; used for furniture, flooring, veneer, etc.

SILVICAL CHARACTERS. Intermediate in tolerance; reaches maturity in about 150 years; rather fast-growing; reproduction vigorous; shallow roots; restricted to cool, moist sites; in mixtures with conifers and hardwoods.

River Birch

Betula nigra L.

This unimportant species is a medium-sized tree typical of stream banks. It is quite similar to yellow birch in appearance and silvical characters and differs from it in the following ways:

HABIT. Rhombic-ovate, often lobed; base wedge-shaped; more or less hairy below; 5–9 pairs of veins.

FRUIT. Unique in that it matures in May or June; strobiles oblong, erect, on stout peduncles; scales with narrow, hairy, erect lobes.

TWIGS. Red-brown; hairy at first; not aromatic. Winter buds: ¼ in. long; woolly through summer.

BARK. Thin; salmon-pink to red-brown; separating into thin, papery, curled strips; furrowed and scaly at base of old trees.

Sweet Birch

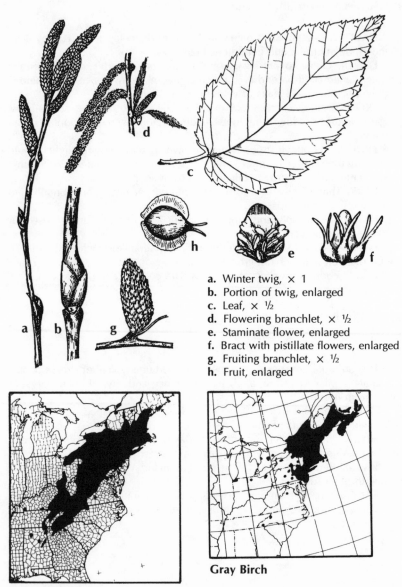

a. Winter twig, × 1
b. Portion of twig, enlarged
c. Leaf, × ½
d. Flowering branchlet, × ½
e. Staminate flower, enlarged
f. Bract with pistillate flowers, enlarged
g. Fruiting branchlet, × ½
h. Fruit, enlarged

Sweet Birch

Gray Birch

Sweet Birch

Betula lenta L.

HABIT. A medium-sized tree 50–75 ft high and 1–2 ft in diameter (max. 80 by 4½ ft); rounded, open crown with pendulous branches.

LEAVES. Ovate to oblong-ovate; 2½–4 in. long; usually singly serrate; heart-shaped or unequally rounded at base; dull, dark green, and glabrous above, paler below; strongly aromatic; 9–11 pairs of veins.

FRUIT. Strobiles oblong-ovoid, erect, nearly sessile, 1–1½ in. long; scales glabrous, longer than broad, wide lateral lobes; nutlet about as broad as wing.

TWIGS. Smooth; lustrous; light red-brown; strong wintergreen taste (one source of oil of wintergreen). Winter buds: ¼ in. long; conical; acute; red-brown; mostly glabrous.

BARK. ½–¾ in. thick; nearly black; not papery; breaking into irregular, thin, scaly plates; smooth on young trees.

WOOD. Important and similar to yellow birch.

SILVICAL CHARACTERS. Intermediate in tolerance; reaches maturity in about 150 years; rather slow-growing; reproduction not abundant; typical on moist sites, but hardy on poor, dry soils; a scattered tree with mixed hardwoods.

Gray Birch

Betula populifolia Marsh.

This unimportant, small tree is typical on poor sites in the Northeast. In its silvical characters it is similar to paper birch.

HABIT. Triangular to rhombic; long-pointed; doubly serrate; 5–9 pairs of veins; petioles slender, elongated.

FRUIT. Strobiles cylindrical, pendent, on slender peduncles; scales about as long as broad with recurved lateral lobes; nutlet slightly narrower than wing.

TWIGS. Resinous-glandular; red-yellow; not aromatic. Winter buds: ¼ in. long; ovoid; chestnut-brown; gummy.

BARK. Thin; gray-white; close and firm; not papery, or exfoliating very slightly; black, triangular patches below branches.

Water Birch

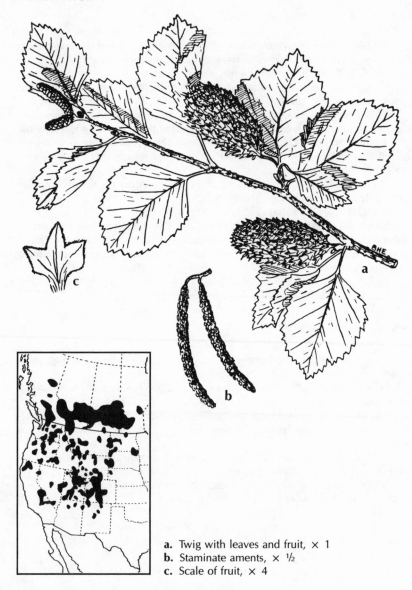

a. Twig with leaves and fruit, × 1
b. Staminate aments, × ½
c. Scale of fruit, × 4

Water Birch • Red Birch

Betula occidentalis Hook. (*Betula fontinalis* Sarg.)

HABIT. A shrub or small tree 20–25 ft high and 12–14 in. in diameter; broad, open crown with ascending branches; frequently in crowded, dense thickets.

LEAVES. Ovate; 1–2 in. long and ¾–1 in. wide; acute or acuminate; sharply and often doubly serrate; sometimes slightly lobed; thin and firm; glabrous; dark dull green above, pale yellow-green and minutely glandular below; turning dull yellow in autumn; petioles stout, ⅓–½ in. long, light yellow, glandular-dotted; stipules bright green, slightly ciliate.

FRUIT. Strobiles cylindrical, pendent (rarely erect), long-stalked, 1–1¼ in. long; scales ciliate; nutlet slightly narrower than wing.

TWIGS. At first light green and glandular, becoming dark red-brown; marked by horizontal lenticels. Winter buds: ¼ in. long; ovoid; acute; very resinous; chestnut-brown.

BARK. Thin (¼ in.); smooth; lustrous dark bronze; marked by pale horizontal lenticels, becoming 6–8 in. long and ¼ in. wide on old trunks.

WOOD. Rather light and soft; strong; heartwood light brown; sapwood thick, light-colored; not important; used locally for fencing and fuel.

SILVICAL CHARACTERS. Upper Sonoran and transition zones; intolerant; shallow root system; reproduction abundant in moist, mineral soil; generally along borders of streams in moist mountain valleys and canyons.

Yukon Birch

Betula X *eastwoodiae* Sarg.

Yukon birch, a hybrid of *B. glandulosa* and *B. papyrifera* is a small tree or shrub found in swampy sites in northern Alberta and the Yukon. It is characterized by broadly ovate to elliptic leaves 1–1½ in. long; pendulous, cylindric strobiles ¾ in. long, with glabrous scales longer than broad; and close, chestnut-brown bark not readily separating into papery scales. The bog or resin birch, *B. glandulosa* Michx., is a shrubby circumpolar form of cold sites.

The Alders

Characteristics of the Genus *Alnus* Mill.

HABIT. Deciduous shrubs or small to medium-sized trees.

LEAVES. Alternate; simple; usually serrate or dentate; pinnately veined; falling without change of color; petioled; stipules fugacious, ovate, acute, scarious.

FLOWERS. Regular; monoecious; apetalous; mostly appearing before or with leaves (rarely opening in autumn); in 1- to 3-flowered cymes; formed during previous season; staminate in long, pendulous aments, every scale bearing 3–6 flowers, each flower subtended by 3–5 bractlets and composed of a 4-part calyx and 4 (rarely 1–3) stamens; pistillate in erect, stalked, ovoid or oblong aments, appearing below staminate flowers, individual flowers in pairs, composed of a naked ovary surmounted by 2 stigmas and subtended by 2–4 bractlets.

FRUIT. Small, flat, chestnut-brown, wingless or laterally winged nutlet, bearing remnants of style at apex; in persistent, semiwoody strobiles, each scale bearing 2–4 nutlets.

TWIGS. Slender to moderately stout; round; reddish or tinged with red; marked by raised leaf scars with 3-bundle scars and lenticels; pith homogeneous, triangular in cross section. Winter buds: terminal absent; lateral typically stalked and 2- to 3-scaled; usually red; twig lengthening by one of upper lateral buds.

BARK. Astringent; mostly gray; smooth, except at the base of trunks of large trees.

WOOD. Light; soft; straight-grained; diffuse-porous; durable in water; heartwood red-brown; sapwood very thick and whitish.

SILVICAL CHARACTERS. Tolerant to intolerant; rather short-lived; shallow, spreading roots; on moist or wet sites, commonly along streams or on mountain slopes.

GENERAL. This genus contains about 30 species scattered through the cooler portions of the Northern Hemisphere and extending into the mountains of South America; 8 species attaining tree size are native to North America, although 7 of these are typically shrubs and only *Almus rubra* is of commercial importance. The European alder, *Almus glutinosa* (L.) Gaertn., has become naturalized in the eastern United States.

KEY TO THE SPECIES OF ALDERS

1. Buds sessile, 3- to 6-scaled, dark purple; pistillate ament enclosed in bud during winter; leaves ovate, lobulate, usually irregulary singly toothed; Alaska and Yukon, south to California and east to Montana ....
.... *Alnus sinuata* (Reg.) Rydb., **Sitka alder,** p. 165
1. Buds stalked, 2- to 3-scaled; pistillate ament appearing in fall (sometimes enclosed during winter in red alder).
   2. Leaves with 8–15 pairs of veins.
      3. Leaves lobulate, doubly toothed; buds reddish.
         4. Wing of nut broad; leaves ovate to elliptic, often red-hairy below, slightly revolute; important tree; Alaska to California and east to Idaho ....
.... *Alnus rubra* Bong., **red alder,** p. 163
         4. Wing of nut reduced to narrow border; leaves neither red-hairy nor revolute; shrubs or rarely small trees to 30 ft.
            5. Twigs marked with orange lenticels; Rocky Mountains and Pacific Coast from Yukon and Alaska to California and New Mexico ....
.... *Alnus tenuifolia* Nutt., **thinleaf alder,** p. 165
            5. Twigs marked with white lenticels; Newfoundland to Yukon, south to British Columbia and east to Iowa and New Jersey, also in Europe and Asia .... *Alnus rugosa* (D.R.) Spr., **speckled alder,** p. 165
      3. Leaves finely to coarsely toothed.
         6. Western shrubs or small trees; leaves coarsely toothed.
            7. Leaves oval or ovate; Idaho to Washington and south to Nevada and southern California .... *Alnus rhombifolia* Nutt., **white alder**
            7. Leaves oblong-lanceolate; New Mexico, Arizona, south into Mexico .... *Alnus oblongifolia* Torr., **Arizona alder**
         6. Eastern shrubs, rarely small trees; leaves finely toothed.
            8. Leaves with straight veins; several pistillate catkins per bud; New Brunswick west to Kansas and south to Florida and Texas ....
.... *Alnus serrulata* (Alt) Willd., **hazel alder**
            8. Leaves with arching veins; 1–3 pistillate catkins per bud; local in Delaware, eastern Maryland, and reported in southern Oklahoma ....
.... *Alnus maritima* (Marsh.) Muhl., **Seaside alder**
   2. Leaves with 5–6 pairs of veins, oval to orbicular, coarsely and doubly toothed; native to Eurasia but naturalized in the northeastern United States ....
.... *Alnus glutinosa* (L.) Gaertn., **European alder**

Red Alder

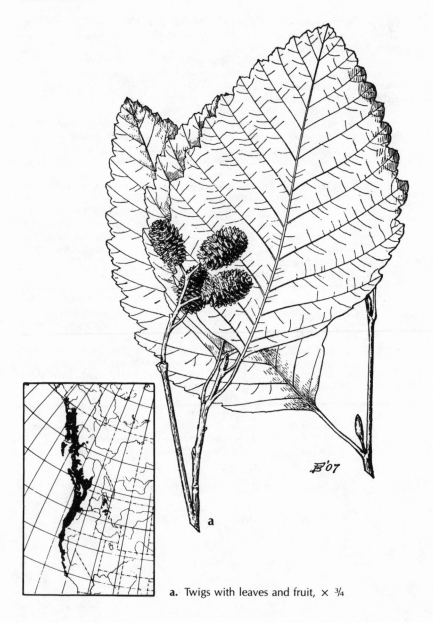

a. Twigs with leaves and fruit, × ¾

Red Alder

Alnus rubra Bong.

HABIT. A medium-sized tree 80–100 ft high and 1–3 ft in diameter (max. 130 by 5 ft); clear trunk; crown narrow and rounded with pendulous branches.

LEAVES. Ovate to elliptic; 3–6 in. long and 1½–3 in. wide; obtuse or rounded at base; apex acute; margins slightly crenately lobed with doubly dentate gland-tipped teeth; thick and firm; dark green and glabrous above, paler and rusty-pubescent below; petiole orange, round, grooved, ¼–¾ in. long.

FLOWERS. Preformed; staminate aments 1¼ in. long, becoming 4–6 in. long, orange; pistillate opening in spring, ⅓–½ in. long with dark red scales and bright red style.

FRUIT. Strobiles ½–1¼ in. long; woody; persistent; ovoid to oblong; on orange peduncles or rarely sessile; truncate scales with much thickened, rugose tips; nutlet nearly circular with encircling membranous wing or 2 lateral wings.

TWIGS. Slender to rather stout; light green and tomentose at first, becoming bright red and lustrous during second year. Winter buds: lateral ⅓–⅔ in. long; stalked; dark red; pale, scurfy pubescence.

BARK. Thin; smooth; nearly white to blue-gray outer bark and bright red-brown inner bark; sometimes roughened by small, warty excrescences; breaking into large, flat plates on old trees.

WOOD. Important (probably the most important hard wood on the Pacific Coast); light; soft; prominent rays; used for furniture, veneer, and novelties.

SILVICAL CHARACTERS. Intermediate in tolerance; fast-growing; short-lived, maturity being reached in 60–90 years; lateral roots; aggressive reproduction, often taking over burned or logged areas; on varied sites, but typical of stream banks; in pure or mixed stands.

Thinleaf Alder

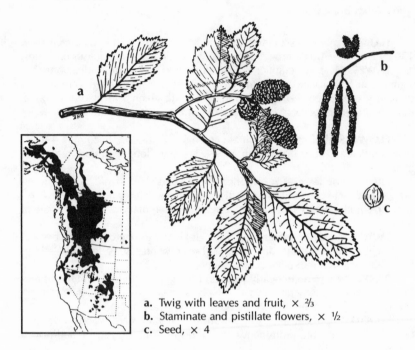

a. Twig with leaves and fruit, × ⅔
b. Staminate and pistillate flowers, × ½
c. Seed, × 4

Sitka Alder

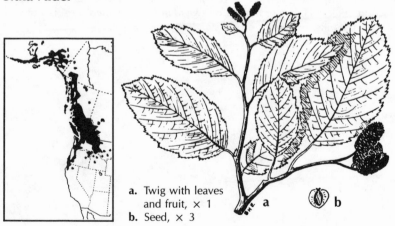

a. Twig with leaves
   and fruit, × 1
b. Seed, × 3

Thinleaf Alder • Mountain Alder

Alnus tenuifolia Nutt.

HABIT. A shrub or small tree occasionally 30 ft high and 6–8 in. in diameter; crown narrow and round-topped.

LEAVES. Ovate-oblong; 2–4 in. long; slightly, acutely, and lacinately lobed; doubly serrate; thin and firm; dark green and glabrous above, pale yellow-green below.

FRUIT. Nut nearly circular; wing reduced to thin, membranaceous border; strobiles ⅓–½ in. long, obovoid-oblong; scales truncate, much thickened, 3-lobed at apex.

TWIGS. Slender; marked by few, large orange-colored lenticels. Winter buds: stalked; ¼–⅓ in. long; bright red; puberulous.

BARK. Thin; smooth; red-brown.

SILVICAL CHARACTERS. Tolerant when young, becoming intolerant with age; on banks of mountain streams; the common alder of the Rocky Mountain region; closely related and considered by some authors to be a synonym of the eastern speckled alder, *Alnus rugosa*, or of the Eurasian white alder, *A. incana* L.

Sitka Alder

Alnus sinuata (Reg.) Rydb. (*Alnus sitchensis* Sarg.)

HABIT. A shrub or small tree rarely 40 ft high and 7–8 in. in diameter; crown narrow and open.

LEAVES. Ovate; 3–6 in. long; acute; usually divided into numerous, short, lateral lobes; sharply and doubly serrate; membranaceous; yellow-green above, pale below.

FRUIT. Nut oval, about as wide as its wings; strobiles ½–¾ in. long and about ⅓ in. wide; truncate scales thickened at apex; on slender peduncles; in elongated, leafly panicles.

TWIGS. Slender; large, pale lenticels. Winter buds: sessile, ½ in. long; acuminate; dark purple; finely pubescent.

BARK. Thin; blue-gray; bright red inner bark.

SILVICAL CHARACTERS. Tolerant when young, becoming intolerant with age; in moist flats and along stream borders.

Eastern Hophornbeam

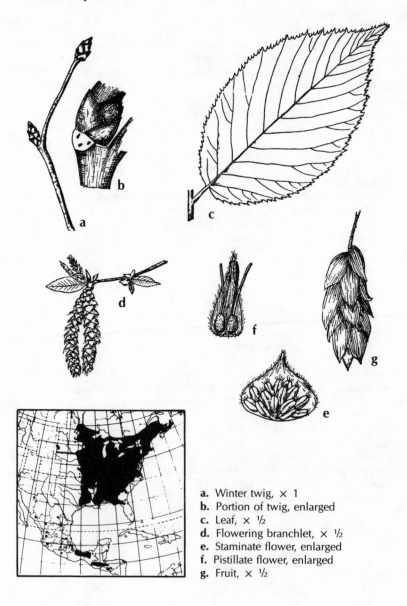

a. Winter twig, × 1
b. Portion of twig, enlarged
c. Leaf, × ½
d. Flowering branchlet, × ½
e. Staminate flower, enlarged
f. Pistillate flower, enlarged
g. Fruit, × ½

Eastern Hophornbeam

Ostrya virginiana (Mill.) K. Koch

HABIT. A small tree 20–40 ft high and 8–18 in. in diameter (max. 65 by 3 ft); rounded crown and slender, pendulous, often contorted branches.

LEAVES. Alternate; simple; oblong-ovate; 3–5 in. long with 11–15 pairs of veins; deciduous; acuminate; sharply doubly serrate margins; thin and tough; dull dark green above, paler and somewhat hairy below; stipules fugacious.

FLOWERS. Regular; monoecious; perianth absent; appearing with leaves; staminate in long, drooping, cylindrical aments in clusters of 3, each flower containing 3–14 stamens crowded on a hairy receptacle; pistillate in erect, loose, paired aments, each flower enclosed in a hairy, saclike involucre.

FRUIT. Small (¼ in.), 1-celled, 1-seeded, ovoid, flat, unwinged nut; enclosed in enlarged (1 in.), pale, membranaceous, involucre of flower; in loose, suspended strobiles 1–1½ in. long, resembling clusters of hops.

TWIGS. Slender; round; red-brown becoming dark brown; leaf scars with 3 bundle scars. Winter buds: terminal absent; lateral ⅛–¼ in. long; ovoid; acute; bud scales with greenish base and brown tips and characteristic striations.

BARK. Thin; gray-brown; broken into small, shaggy plates that give it characteristic shreddy appearance.

WOOD. Very heavy; hard; strong; unimportant; resembling hickory and known as ironwood; little used.

SILVICAL CHARACTERS. Tolerant; slow-growing; lateral roots; varied sites, but typical on dry slopes.

Knowlton Hophornbeam

Ostrya knowltonii Cov.

This rare, local tree is found in mountains and canyons of western Texas, southeastern New Mexico, northern Arizona, and southeastern Utah. It differs from *O. virginiana* in having leaves 1–2 in. long with 5–8 pairs of veins. Chisos hophornbeam, *O. chisosensis* Correl, is rare and local in the Chisos mountains of Texas.

American Hornbeam

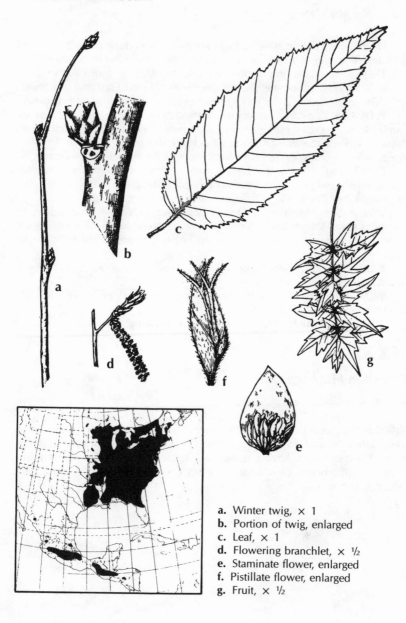

a. Winter twig, × 1
b. Portion of twig, enlarged
c. Leaf, × 1
d. Flowering branchlet, × ½
e. Staminate flower, enlarged
f. Pistillate flower, enlarged
g. Fruit, × ½

American Hornbeam • Bluebeech

Carpinus caroliniana Walt.

HABIT. A large shrub or small bushy tree rarely 40 ft high and 1 ft in diameter; trunk characteristically fluted; crown close and flat-topped with slender, zigzag branches.

LEAVES. Alternate; simple; ovate to oval; 2–4 in. long; 2 distinct sizes; deciduous; acuminate; sharply doubly serrate; thin and tough; dull dark green above, paler below.

FLOWERS. Regular; monoecious; perianth absent; appearing with leaves; staminate in aments 1½ in. long, with green, hairy scales, each flower with 3–20 stamens; pistillate in loose aments ½–¾ in. long, each bearing 2 pistils with scarlet styles.

FRUIT. Small (⅓ in.), 1-seeded, ovoid, flat, brown, unwinged nut; attached to base of halberd-shaped, leafy involucre; in loose strobiles.

TWIGS. Slender; round; pale green at first, becoming lustrous and red-brown; leaf scars with 3 bundle scars. Winter buds: terminal absent; lateral ⅛ in. long; rusty brown; acute; scaly; usually 4-sided in cross section.

BARK. Thin; smooth; blue-gray; often mottled with light or dark patches; fluted trunk an unmistakable character.

WOOD. Heavy; hard; strong; unimportant.

SILVICAL CHARACTERS. Tolerant; slow-growing; lateral roots; on varied sites but prefers moist soil.

Hazelnut

Corylus L.

Three shrubby species are native to North America and one of these, *Corylus cornuta* var. *californica* (A. OC.) Sharp, may occasionally reach tree size in California. The other two species are small eastern shrubs known for their edible nuts, American hazelnut (*C. americana* Walt.) and beaked hazelnut (*C. cornuta* Marsh. var. *cornuta*). The giant filbert, *Corylus maxima* Mill., of southern Europe is planted in warm parts of the United States. The hazelnuts are characterized by deciduous, alternate, simple, oval to ovate, doubly serrate leaves; scaly lateral buds; and an ovoid nut surrounded by a leafy, toothed involucre.

American Beech

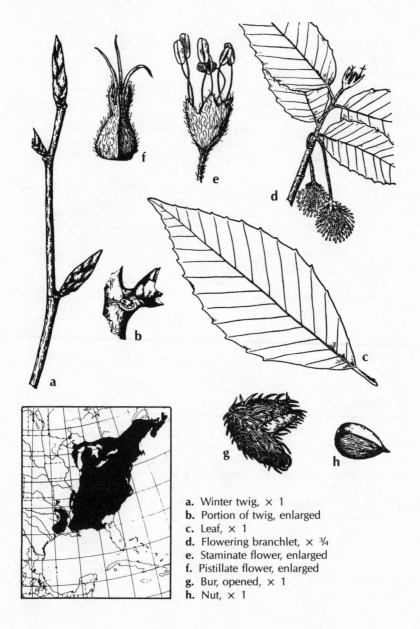

a. Winter twig, × 1
b. Portion of twig, enlarged
c. Leaf, × 1
d. Flowering branchlet, × ¾
e. Staminate flower, enlarged
f. Pistillate flower, enlarged
g. Bur, opened, × 1
h. Nut, × 1

FAGACEAE

American Beech

Fagus grandifolia Ehrh.

HABIT. A beautiful, medium-sized tree 60–80 ft high and 2–3 ft in diameter (max. 120 by 5½ ft); clear straight trunk; compact, rounded crown with slender, spreading branches.

LEAVES. Alternate; simple; deciduous; elliptical to oblong-ovate; 2½–6 in. long; penniveined; coarsely serrate with sharp teeth; acuminate; thin; dark blue-green above and yellow-green and lustrous below; short-petioled; stipules small.

FLOWERS. Monoecious; apetalous; appearing after the leaves open; staminate in globose heads 1 in. in diameter, each with a 4- to 8-lobed calyx and 8–16 stamens; pistillate in 2- to 4-flowered spikes, each with a 4- to 5-lobed calyx, a 3-celled ovary, and 3 styles.

FRUIT. A triangular, edible nut ½–¾ in. long; 2–3 completely enclosed in a woody, 4-part bur or involucre covered with weak, unbranched spines; maturing in 1 year.

TWIGS. Slender; round; lustrous; olive green, becoming ash-gray; occasionally zigzag; pith round; leaf scars small with many bundle scars. Winter buds: terminal present; ¾–1 in. long; slender; lance-shaped; numerous scales.

BARK. Thin; close; smooth; light blue-gray; often mottled; similar in appearance on old and young trunks.

WOOD. Important; strong; heavy; hard; diffuse-porous; light color; not durable; used for flooring, handles, furniture.

SILVICAL CHARACTERS. Very tolerant; rather fast-growing; long-lived, reaching age of about 400 years; shallow, lateral roots; reproduction good; roots sprout vigorously; on moist sites; in mixture with numerous hardwoods.

GENERAL. This genus contains about 10 species scattered through the Northern Hemisphere, with only 1 native to North America. The important, commonly planted, European beech, *Fagus sylvatica* L. has darker bark and smaller leaves 2–4 in. long, with smaller rounded teeth and hairy margins and veins on the lower surface; 3 common varieties of European beech are *atropunicea* West., with dark bronze-purple leaves; *pendula* Loud., with the weeping habit of drooping branches; and *laciniata* Vig., with deeply cut leaves.

American Chestnut

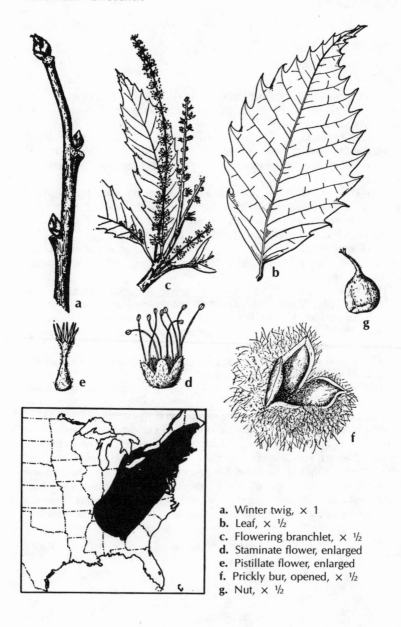

a. Winter twig, × 1
b. Leaf, × ½
c. Flowering branchlet, × ½
d. Staminate flower, enlarged
e. Pistillate flower, enlarged
f. Prickly bur, opened, × ½
g. Nut, × ½

American Chestnut

Castanea dentata (Marsh.) Borkh.

HABIT. A handsome tree 60–90 ft high and 2–4 ft in diameter (max. 120 by 10 ft); frequently divided trunk; broad, open crown with large, horizontal branches.

LEAVES. Alternate; simple; deciduous; oblong-lanceolate; 5½–8 in. long; penniveined; coarsely serrate with sharp, glandular teeth; acuminate; thin; yellow-green; glabrous.

FLOWERS. Monoecious; apetalous; appearing after leaves; staminate and bisexual aments; staminate in 3- to 7-flowered cymes; pistillate flowers solitary or clusters of 2–3.

FRUIT. Rounded, flattened, chestnut-brown, edible nut ½–1 in. long; 2–3 nuts completely enclosed in a 2- to 4-valved, globose bur, 2–2½ in. in diameter and covered with prickly, sharp, branched spines; maturing in 1 year.

TWIGS. Rather stout; round; lustrous; chestnut-brown; glabrous; oval leaf scars with many bundle scars; pith stellate. Winter buds: terminal absent; lateral ovoid, acute, brown, ¼ in. long, 2–3 visible scales.

BARK. Thick; gray-brown; furrowed, with broad, flat ridges.

WOOD. Formerly important; soft; very durable; ring-porous; used for furniture, poles, posts, ties, tannin.

SILVICAL CHARACTERS. Intermediate in tolerance; long-lived; taproot; stump sprouts vigorously; threatened with extinction by chestnut blight, a fungal bark disease; varied sites; with mixed hardwoods.

The Chinkapins

Three other native species of *Castanea*, known as Chinkapins, form small trees or shrubs in the southern states:

Florida chinkapin, *C. alnifolia* Nutt., with leaves 3–4 in. long, thin and lustrous; spines on bur short and scattered; coastal plain from Florida to Louisiana.

Ozark chinkapin, *C. ozarkensis* Ashe, with large leaves 5–9 in. long, bristle-tipped, and brown or tawny hairy below; burs spiny and 1 in. in diameter; local in the Ozark plateau and the mountains of southern Missouri, Arkansas, and eastern Oklahoma.

Allegheny chinkapin, *C. pumila* Mill., with leaves 3–5 in. long, with short, rigid teeth, woolly to hairy below; burs about 2 in. in diameter with needle-sharp spines; New Jersey to Arkansas and south to east Texas and central Florida.

Golden Chinkapin

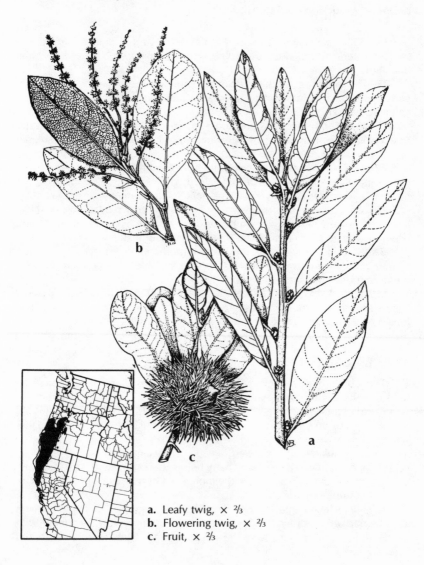

a. Leafy twig, × ⅔
b. Flowering twig, × ⅔
c. Fruit, × ⅔

Golden Chinkapin

Castanopsis chrysophylla (Dougl.) A. DC.

HABIT. A small to medium-sized tree 60–80 ft high and 12 ft in diameter (max. 125 by 3½ ft), often a large shrub in Washington; trunk clear and straight; dense, rounded crown with stout, spreading branches.

LEAVES. Alternate; simple; persistent 2–3 years; lanceolate to oblong-ovate; 2–6 in. long; penniveined; entire and often revolute; usually acuminate; thick and leathery; dark green and lustrous above; covered with small golden-yellow scales below; stipules fugacious.

FLOWERS. Monoecious; apetalous; appearing after the leaves; in staminate and bisexual aments; the staminate aments in 3-flowered cymes, each flower with 10–12 stamens; the pistillate flowers solitary or in clusters of 2–3, with 3-celled ovaries.

FRUIT. A rounded, broadly ovoid, yellow-brown nut ½ in. long; 1–2 nuts enclosed in a 4-valved, globose bur 1–1½ in. in diameter and covered with prickly, dense, unbranched spines; maturing in 2 years.

TWIGS. Rather slender; rigid; round; covered at first with golden-yellow scales, becoming scurfy and red-brown; pith stellate. Winter buds: terminal present; ovoid; ¼ in. long; light brown; numerous overlapping scales.

BARK. Thick; dark red-brown; deeply furrowed.

WOOD. Unimportant; intermediate in strength and hardness; ring-porous; occasionally used for lumber.

SILVICAL CHARACTERS. Tolerant; growth rather rapid; long-lived, reaching 500 years; taproot in early life, giving way to deep lateral system; often in pure stands on poor, dry sites and as an understory tree in redwood and Douglas-fir stands.

GENERAL. There are about 100 Asiatic species of this genus, with only 2 species native to the West Coast of the United States. *Castanopsis sempervirens* Dudl. is a small alpine shrub in California and southern Oregon.

Tanoak

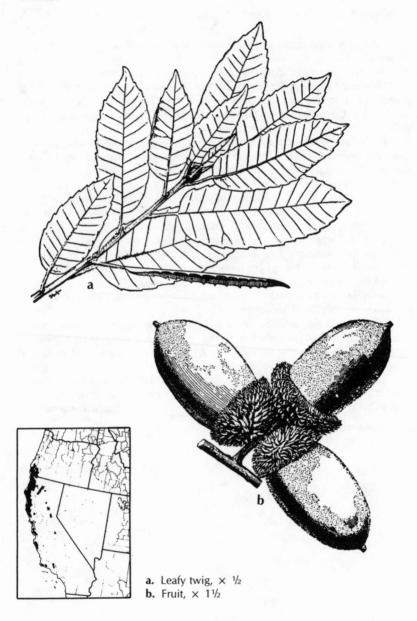

a. Leafy twig, × ½
b. Fruit, × 1½

Tanoak • Tanbark-oak

Lithocarpus densiflorus (Hook. & Arn.) Rehd.

HABIT. A medium-sized tree 70–90 ft high and 2–3 ft in diameter (max. 150 by 8 ft); trunk clear; crown rounded with ascending branches.

LEAVES. Alternate; simple; persistent 3–4 years; oblong to oblong-lanceolate; 3–5 in. long; penniveined; repand or dentate to entire-revolute; acute or rounded; thick; pale green and usually glabrous above; brown, woolly pubescent below in spring, becoming blue-white and nearly glabrous; stipules persistent on upper leaves.

FLOWERS. Monoecious; apetalous; appearing after the leaves; in staminate and bisexual aments; staminate flowers crowded, each with 10 stamens; the pistillate flowers solitary with 3-celled ovary.

FRUIT. Oval, bitter, yellow-brown nut (acorn) ¾–1 in. long; enclosed at base in a shallow, tomentose, spiny, cuplike involucre, lined with a lustrous red pubescence; maturing in 2 years.

TWIGS. Stout; round; covered for 1–3 years with a thick tomentum of fascicled hairs, becoming red-brown, often with a glaucous bloom. Winter buds: terminal present; ovoid; obtuse; ¼ in. long; covered by a few tomentose scales.

BARK. Thick; red-brown; deeply furrowed with broad, rounded, scaly ridges; high in tannin content.

WOOD. Unimportant; hard and strong; ring-porous; little used.

SILVICAL CHARACTERS. Tolerant; growth moderate; maturity reached in 200–300 years; deep taproot system; typical on moist well-drained sites; in mixture with conifers and hardwoods; coppices vigorously and reproduces well by seed.

GENERAL. There are about 100 Asiatic species of this genus found in warm climates. Only the one species is native to North America.

The Oaks

Characteristics of the Genus *Quercus* L.

HABIT. Deciduous or evergreen trees or shrubs; with astringent properties; pubescence of fascicled hairs.

LEAVES. Alternate; simple; deciduous or persistent; shape and size often variable on same tree; stipulate.

FLOWERS. Regular; monoecious; vernal; staminate in clustered aments, individual flowers with a 4- to 7-lobed calyx enclosing 6 (rarely 2–12) stamens; pistillate solitary or in 2 to many-flowered spikes, individual flowers with a 6-lobed calyx surrounding a 3-celled (rarely 4- to 5-celled) ovary, 1–2 ovules in each cell, the whole partly enclosed in involucre.

FRUIT. Acorn; 1-seeded by abortion; maturing in 1–2 years; partially enclosed by scaly cup (modified involucre).

TWIGS. Slender to stout; pith homogeneous, stellate; marked by pale lenticels, semicircular leaf scars, many bundle scars. Winter buds: clustered at end of twig; terminal present; many chestnut-brown scales imbricated in 5 ranks.

BARK. Scaly or dark and furrowed.

WOOD. Heavy; hard; strong; prominent rays.

SILVICAL CHARACTERS. From intermediate in tolerance (many white oaks) to intolerant (most red and live oaks); long-lived; generally with deep taproot systems; hybridizes frequently.

GENERAL. This is a variable genus containing about 500 species, and it is often difficult to distinguish between the species. Fifty-eight native species are recognized as reaching tree size; in addition there are numerous hybrids and varieties as well as many shrubby species. Six shrubby southwestern forms reported to become small trees in Texas, New Mexico, or Arizona are not keyed out. These are *Q. glaucoides* M. & G., *Q. graciliformis* Mull., *Q. gravesii* Sudw., *Q. grisea* Liebm., *Q. harvardii* Rydb., and *Q. turbinella* Greene. The key distinguishes between the other tree species, and all oaks of importance are described and pictured in more detail. The native oaks logically break themselves down into 2 subgenera, the white oaks and the red oaks, each of which is further subdivided into 2 or 3 groups. A recent study indicates that all the live oaks should be placed under the red oak group on the basis of wood structure.

The English oak, *Quercus robur* L. is commonly planted and has leaves that resemble white oak but are smaller (2½–5 in. long). It is further characterized by fruit borne on peduncles 1–3 in. long.

KEY TO THE SPECIES OF OAKS

I. Leaves turning brown in the fall of the first year, neither thick and leathery nor spiny-toothed
- II. Leaves or leaf lobes not bristle-tipped; acorn maturing in 1 year, usually sweet; nut shell smooth inside . . . . **white oaks**
  - III. Leaves deeply lobed or rarely entire . . . . **true white oaks,** p. 179
  - III. Leaves coarsely toothed or shallowly lobed . . . . **chestnut oaks,** p. 180
- II. Leaves or leaf lobes commonly bristle-tipped; acorn maturing in 2 years, usually bitter; nut shell woolly inside . . . . **red oaks**
  - IV. Leaves lobed, rarely broadly ovate and entire . . . . **true red oaks,** p. 180
  - IV. Leaves entire and mostly narrow . . . . **willow oaks,** p. 181
I. Leaves remaining green on the tree at least until the new leaves appear the following spring, usually thick and leathery, margins entire or spiny-toothed . **live oaks,** p. 181

TRUE WHITE OAKS

1. Eastern species (east of the Rocky Mountains).
    2. Leaves entire or slightly lobed.
        3. Acorns enclosed only at base by thin cup.
            4. Acorn ¾–1 in. long; leaves mostly blue-green; shrubby; Oklahoma to central Texas . . . . *Q. durandii* var. *breviloba* (Torr.) Palmer, **Bigelow oak**
            4. Acorn ½–⅔ in. long; leaves yellow-green; large tree; coastal plain from North Carolina to Florida, west to Texas and north to Arkansas and Oklahoma . . . . *Q. durandii* Buckl., **Durand oak**
        3. Acorns enclosed ¼–⅔ of length in thick cup.
            5. Acorn ⅓–½ in. long; leaves blue-green; western Oklahoma to Texas and northeastern New Mexico . . . . *Q. mohriana* Buckl., **Mohr oak**
            5. Acorn ½–¾ in. long; southeast.
                6. Leaves silvery green or white below; coastal plain from South Carolina to Florida and Alabama . . . . *Q. chapmanii* Sarg., **Chapman oak**
                6. Leaves yellow-hairy below; local in South Carolina and northeast Georgia . . . . *Q. oglethorpensis* Duncan, **Oglethorpe oak**
    2. Leaves more or less deeply lobed.
        7. Acorn enclosed in cup, or cup fringed.
            8. Acorn cup conspicuously fringed on margin; leaves nearly divided in two by deep sinuses . . . . *Q. macrocarpa,* **bur oak,** p. 185
            8. Acorn cup not fringed and nearly covering acorn; leaves irregularly lobed . . . . *Q. lyrata,* **overcup oak,** p. 187
        7. Acorn enclosed ¼–½ of length in unfringed cup.
            9. Leaves regularly, usually deeply, 7- to 9-lobed, glabrous below; buds nearly glabrous . . . . *Q. alba,* **white oak,** p. 185
            9. Leaves typically cross-shaped, 5-lobed, woolly below; buds hairy . . . . *Q. stellata,* **post oak,** p. 187
1. Western species (Rocky Mountains and Pacific Coast)
    10. Leaves undulately lobed and spiny toothed with acute lobes or entire, blue-green, 1–1½ in. long; acorn enclosed only at base in cup; Texas to Arizona . . . . *Q. pungens* Liebm., **sandpaper oak**
    10. Leaves pinnately and usually deeply lobed, lobes rounded.
        11. Acorn under ¾ in. long, enclosed in cup for ½ or more of length; leaves yellow-green, 3–7 in. long; usually shrubby; Rocky Mountains, Wyoming to Nevada, south to Texas and Arizona . . . . *Q. gambelii* Nutt., **Gambel oak,** p. 189
        11. Acorn ¾ in. long or longer, enclosed in cup for less than ½ of length; Pacific Coast.

    12. Acorns 1–2¼ in. long, slender; deep, cuplike bowl; leaves 2½–3 in.
        long; California . . . . *Q. lobata,* **valley oak,** p. 191
    12. Acorns ¾–1½ in. long, ovoid; very shallow cup.
        13. Leaves dark yellow-green, 3–6 in. long; petioles hairy, ½–1 in.
            long; British Columbia to California . . . .
            . . . . *Q. garryana,* **Oregon white oak,** p. 191
        13. Leaves blue-green, 2–4 in. long; shallowly lobed to sinuately
            toothed to entire; petioles woolly, ¼–½ in. long; California . . . .
            . . . . *Q. douglasii,* **blue oak,** p. 189

CHESTNUT OAKS (Eastern Trees)

1. Fruit long-stalked (1–4 in.); leaves coarsely sinuate-toothed to shallowly lobed, usually with 6–8 pairs of veins . . . . *Q. bicolor,* **swamp white oak,** p. 195
1. Fruit short-stalked or sessile; leaves coarsely toothed.
   2. Leaves 4–9 in. long with 9–17 pairs of veins; large trees.
      3. Leaves obovate, white-hairy below and dark green above; acorn 1–1½ in. long
         in thick, subsessile cup with wedge-shaped scales . . . .
         . . . . *Q. michauxii,* **swamp chestnut oak,** p. 193
      3. Leaves mostly elliptical, slightly hairy below and yellow-green above; acorn in
         thin cup with partially fused scales.
         4. Leaves with rounded teeth, acorn 1–1½ in. long; cup on short stalk (¼–½
            in. long), buds ¼ in. long . . . . *Q. prinus,* **chestnut oak,** p. 193
         4. Leaves with sharp teeth; acorn ½–¾ in. long; cup subsessile; buds ⅛ in.
            long . . . . *Q. muehlenbergii,* **chinkapin oak,** p. 195
   2. Leaves 2½–5 in. long with 3–8 pairs of veins and usually sharp teeth; acorn ⅖–⅗
      in. long, thick cup; shrubby or rarely a small tree; Massachusetts to North Caro-
      lina, west to Nebraska, Texas . . . . . . *Q. prinoides* Willd., **dwarf chinkapin oak**

TRUE RED OAKS

1. California and Oregon species; leaves usually 7-lobed; scales of fruit cup loosely
   imbricated . . . . *Q. kelloggii,* **California black oak,** p. 205
1. Eastern species (not reaching the Rocky Mountains).
   2. Leaves deeply lobed.
      3. Leaves white- to red-woolly below.
         4. Leaves usually 5-lobed, 2–5 in. long; shrub to small tree; Maine to North
            Carolina . . . . *Q. ilicifolia* Wang., **bear oak**
         4. Leaves of 2 forms, either 3-lobed at apex or deeply 5- to 11-lobed, 6–8 in.
            long . . . . *Q. falcata,* **southern red oak,** p. 199
      3. Leaves green below, often with hairy tufts in axils.
         5. Leaves dull, 7- to 11-lobed, nearly glabrous, sinuses extending about ½
            way to midrib; acorn enclosed at base or to ⅓ length in thick cup . . . . .
            . . . . *Q. rubra,* **northern red oak,** p. 197
         5. Leaves lustrous, mostly 5- to 7-lobed, sinuses extending more than ½ way
           to midrib.
           6. Acorn cup shallow, covering basal ⅓ or less of acorn; acorn cup scales
             tightly imbricated.
             7. Leaves 6–8 in. long, many-toothed; acorns ¾–1¼ in., oblong-ovoid
               . . . . *Q. shumardii,* **Shumard oak,** p. 199
             7. Leaves 2½–6 in. long; acorn not over ½ in.
               8. Leaves 5- to 7-lobed, 4–6 in. long; acorn hemispheric, ½ in.
                 . . . . *Q. palustris,* **pin oak,** p. 203
               8. Leaves 3- to 5-lobed, 2½ in. long; acorn ellipsoidal to globose,
                 ⅓–½ in. long; rare in Georgia, South Carolina, and Alabama
                 . . . . *Q. georgiana* Curtis, **Georgia oak**

6. Acorn cup covering at least the basal ⅓ of acorn.
  9. Acorn cup with loosely imbricated scales, forming a free margin on rim; winter buds woolly or red-hairy.
    10. Leaves usually 7-lobed; petioles 1–2 in. long; winter buds gray, tomentose . . . . *Q. velutina,* **black oak,** p. 197
    10. Leaves 3- to 5-lobed; petioles ¼–¾ in. long; winter buds rusty-pubescent . . . . *Q. laevis,* **turkey oak,** p. 205
  9. Acorn cup with tightly imbricated scales; winter buds not woolly or red-hairy.
    11. Buds white-hairy; acorn, rings near apex, ½–1 in. long . . . . .
    . . . . *Q. coccinea,* **scarlet oak,** p. 201
    11. Buds not white-hairy; acorn without rings.
      12. Acorn ellipsoidal, ½–¾ in.; Lake states . . . .
      . . . . *Q. ellipsoidalis,* **northern pin oak,** p. 203
      12. Acorn oblong, ¾–1¼ in. long; lower Mississippi Valley
      . . . . *Q. nuttallii,* **Nuttall oak,** p. 203
2. Leaves 3-lobed at apex or entire.
  13. Mature leaves distinctly hairy below.
    14. Leaves gray to rusty-woolly below, of two types; acorn ½ in. long, enclosed in thin cup for ⅓ or less of length . . . .
    . . . . *Q. falcata,* **southern red oak,** p. 199
    14. Leaves tawny-hairy below and scurfy; acorn ¾ in. long, enclosed in thick cup for ⅓–½ its length . . . .
    . . . . *Q. marilandica,* **blackjack oak,** p. 201
  13. Mature leaves nearly glabrous and green below; acorn enclosed in thin cup for ⅓ or less of length.
    15. Leaves rounded at base; acorn ¼–⅓ in. long; Georgia, Florida, Alabama, Arkansas . . . . *Q. arkansana* Sarg., **Arkansas oak**
    15. Leaves wedge-shaped at base, lobing variable; acorn ⅓–⅔ in. long
    . . . . *Q. nigra,* **water oak,** p. 207

WILLOW OAKS (Eastern Species)

1. Leaves mostly linear-lanceolate, glabrous to woolly below; acorn ⅓–½ in. long, green-brown . . . . *Q. phellos,* **willow oak,** p. 207
1. Leaves mostly oblong-lanceolate to oblong-obovate.
  2. Leaves white-woolly below; North Carolina to Florida, west to Texas . . . .
  . . . . *Q. incana,* **bluejack oak,** p. 209
  2. Leaves glabrous to hairy below.
    3. Leaves hairy below; acorn dark chestnut-brown, ½–¾ in. long . . . .
    . . . . *Q. imbricaria,* **shingle oak,** p. 209
    3. Leaves essentially glabrous below; acorn nearly black, ½ in. long.
      4. Leaves elliptical to oblong-ovate, nearly evergreen . . . .
      . . . . *Q. X laurifolia,* **laurel oak,** p. 209
      4. Leaves variable, spatulate to obovate to linear, sometimes lobed, deciduous
      . . . . *Q. nigra,* **water oak,** p. 207

LIVE OAKS

1. Southeastern live oaks.
  2. Shell of nut glabrous inside, acorn maturing in 1 year, on long stalks; leaves 2–5 in., elliptical to ovate . . . . *Q. virginiana,* **live oak,** p. 211
  2. Shell of nut woolly inside, acorn maturing in 2 years, short-stalked; leaves obovate, revolute, ½–2 in. long; South Carolina to Florida, west to Mississippi
  . . . . *Q. myrtifolia* Willd., **myrtle oak**

1. Western live oaks.
   3. California live oaks.
      4. Shell of nut glabrous on inside, acorn maturing in 1 year.
         5. Leaves about ¾ in. long; usually a shrub; through California . . . .
            . . . . *Q. dumosa* Nutt., **California scrub oak**
         5. Leaves 1–3 in. long; southwestern California . . . .
            . . . . *Q. engelmannii* Greene, **Engelmann oak**
      4. Shell of nut woolly inside, acorn maturing in 2 years (except coast live oak).
         6. Acorn ¾–1½ in. long, narrow; more than ½ covered by thin cup . . . . . .
            . . . . *Q. wislizeni,* **interior live oak,** p. 215
         6. Acorn less than ½ covered by cup.
            7. Acorn ¾–1½ in. long, narrow; leaves glabrous to hairy below . . . . . .
               . . . . *Q. agrifolia,* **coast live oak,** p. 215
            7. Acorn ½–2 in. long, oblong to ovoid; leaves woolly below.
               8. Leaves oblong-lanceolate; restricted to islands off coast of southern
                  California . . . . *Q. tomentalla* Engelm., **island live oak**
               8. Leaves oblong-ovate; Washington to California, Arizona . . . .
                  . . . . *Q. chrysolepis,* **canyon live oak,** p. 217
   3. Southwestern live oaks (Mexican border region with only *Q. turbinella* extending
      north to Nevada, Utah, Colorado).
      9. Acorn shell glabrous inside, light brown outside, nut maturing in 1 year.
         10. Fruit in long-stalked clusters of 2 or more; leaves broadly obovate, yellow-
             hairy below . . . . *Q. rugosa* Née, **netleaf oak**
         10. Fruit sessile or nearly so, single or paired; leaves oblong to ovate.
             11. Leaves with many spiny teeth, ½–1¼ in. long . . . .
                 . . . . *Q. turbinella* Greene, **shrub live oak**
             11. Leaves entire or with few short teeth.
                 12. Leaves glabrous below, 1–2 in. long; acorn enclosed about ⅓ of
                     length in cup slightly fringed at rim . . . .
                     . . . . *Q. oblongifolia,* **Mexican blue oak,** p. 211
                 12. Leaves hairy below; acorn enclosed in unfringed cup about ½ of
                     length.
                     13. Leaves ½–1 in. long; acorn ½–⅔ in. long; Arizona . . . . .
                         . . . . *Q. toumeyi* Sarg., **Toumey oak**
                     13. Leaves 1–4 in. long; acorn ¾–1 in. long; Arizona, New
                         Mexico . . . . *Q. arizonica,* **Arizona white oak,** p. 213
      9. Acorn shell woolly on inner surface.
         14. Acorn maturing in 1 year, dark brown to nearly black; leaves nearly gla-
             brous below . . . . *Q. emoryi,* **Emory oak,** p. 213
         14. Acorn maturing in 2 years, light brown; leaves woolly below.
             15. Leaves lanceolate to elliptic, persistent until second spring . . . .
                 . . . . *Q. hypoleucoides,* **silverleaf oak,** p. 217
             15. Leaves oblong-ovate to elliptic, persistent 3–4 years . . . .
                 . . . . *Q. chrysolepis,* **canyon live oak,** p. 217

Leaf Types

White Oak Group

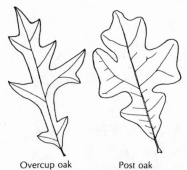

Chestnut oak
Generally similar:
  Swamp chestnut oak
  Swamp white oak
  Chinkapin oak

Overcup oak

Post oak
Generally similar:
  Bur oak

White oak
Generally similar:
  Gambel oak
  Calif. white oak
  Oregon white oak

Red Oak Group

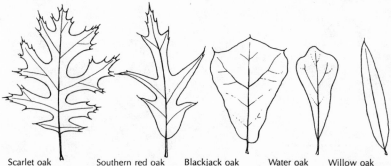

Scarlet oak
Generally similar:
  Nuttall oak
  Shumard oak
  Pin oak
  Northern red oak
  Black oak
  California black oak

Southern red oak
Generally similar:
  Turkey oak
  Bear oak

Blackjack oak
Generally similar:
  Some leaves of
  southern red oak

Water oak
(also with
several or
no lobes)

Willow oak
Generally similar:
  Shingle oak
  Bluejack oak
  Laurel oak

White Oak

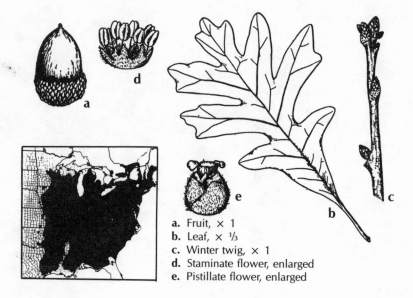

a. Fruit, × 1
b. Leaf, × ⅓
c. Winter twig, × 1
d. Staminate flower, enlarged
e. Pistillate flower, enlarged

Bur Oak

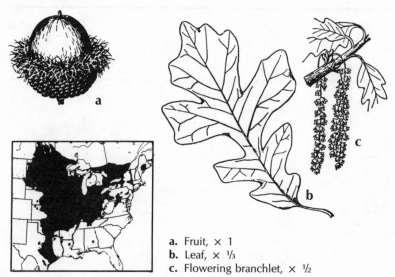

a. Fruit, × 1
b. Leaf, × ⅓
c. Flowering branchlet, × ½

White Oak

Quercus alba L.

HABIT. A medium-sized tree 80–100 ft high and 3–4 ft in diameter (max. 150 by 9 ft); crown rounded, heavy branches.

LEAVES. Deciduous; oblong to obovate; 5–9 in. long; 7- to 9-lobed (rarely 5-lobed), lobes either broad with shallow sinuses or narrow with deep sinuses extending nearly to the midrib; apex of lobes rounded; thin and firm; bright green and glabrous above, paler below.

FRUIT. Maturing in first year; sessile or short-stalked; acorn ½–¾ in. long, light brown, oblong, enclosed for about ¼ of length in bowllike cup with thickened warty scales; kernel sweet.

TWIGS. Rather stout; reddish. Winter buds: terminal ⅛–³/₁₆ in. long; ovoid to globose; obtuse; red-brown; nearly glabrous.

BARK. Light ashy gray; typically irregularly plated with loose plates, but sometimes furrowed with narrow ridges.

WOOD. The most important species of oak; heavy; hard; strong; heartwood light brown, quite durable; used for furniture, cooperage, finish, ties, etc.

SILVICAL CHARACTERS. Intermediate in tolerance; rather slow-growing; dry to moist sites; long-lived, attaining ages of 600 years; hybridizes with many species.

Bur Oak

Quercus macrocarpa Michx.

HABIT. A handsome medium-sized tree 60-80 ft high and 2–3 ft in diameter (max. 170 by 7 ft); crown rounded with large, heavy branches.

LEAVES. Deciduous; oblong to obovate; 6–10 in. long; characteristically 5- to 9-lobed, rounded lobes, the 2 center sinuses nearly dividing the leaf into 2 halves; thick; dark green and lustrous above, paler and hairy below.

FRUIT. Maturing in 1 year; sessile or long-stalked; acorn ⅗–2 in. long, ellipsoidal, brown, enclosed for ⅓ to all of length in characteristic fringe-margined cup; kernel sweet.

TWIGS. Stout; yellow-brown to gray; often with characteristic corky wings. Winter buds: ⅛–¼ in. long; hairy.

BARK. Thick; gray-brown; deeply furrowed and ridges.

WOOD. Important; similar to *Q. alba*.

SILVICAL CHARACTERS. Similar to *Q. alba*; moist bottomlands to dry hills in northwest; extending farthest west of eastern oaks; hybridizes with many species.

Post Oak

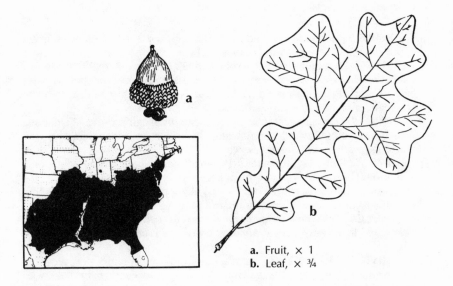

a. Fruit, × 1
b. Leaf, × ¾

Overcup Oak

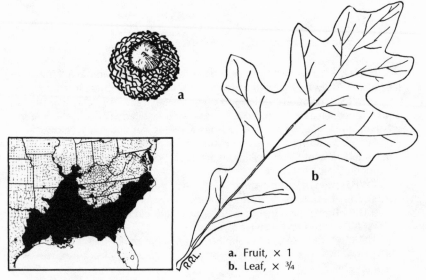

a. Fruit, × 1
b. Leaf, × ¾

Post Oak

Quercus stellata Wang.

HABIT. A small to medium-sized tree 40–50 ft high and 1–2 ft in diameter (max. 100 by 4½ ft), on poor sites a shrub; crown rounded, few large branches.

LEAVES. Deciduous; oblong to obovate; 4–6 in. long; variable but typically deeply 5-lobed, rounded middle lobes opposite giving a crosslike appearance; thick; dark green above, tawny-tomentose below.

FRUIT. Maturing in 1 year; sessile or nearly so; acorn ½–⅔ in. long, red-brown, oval, enclosed for ⅓–½ of length in usually thin-scaled, bowl-shaped cup; kernel sweet.

TWIGS. Stout; more or less tomentose. Winter buds: ⅛–¼ in. long; hairy; chestnut-brown.

BARK. Gray-brown; furrowed; without loose plates of *Q. alba*.

WOOD. Important; similar to *Q. alba;* often poor quality.

SILVICAL CHARACTERS. Similar to *Q. alba;* site varies from dry sandy plains to moist river bottoms; a variable species with several varieties and hybrids.

Overcup Oak

Quercus lyrata Walt.

HABIT. A tree 40–60 ft high and 2–3 ft in diameter (max. 100 by 5 ft); crown open and rounded with large, crooked branches.

LEAVES. Deciduous; oblong to obovate; 6–10 in. long; deeply 5- to 9-lobed, broad irregular sinuses and rounded lobes, giving the leaf an irregular, deeply cut appearance; dark green above, paler below; glabrous or white-hairy.

FRUIT. Maturing in 1 year; sessile or nearly so; acorn ½–1 in. long, chestnut-brown, subglobose; nearly enclosed in deep, thin cup with unfringed margin; kernel sweet.

TWIGS. Rather stout; gray-brown; usually glabrous. Winter buds: ⅛ in. long; mostly woolly; rounded; red-brown.

BARK. Similar to *Q. alba*.

WOOD. Important; similar to *Q. alba;* poor quality.

SILVICAL CHARACTERS. Similar to *Q. alba;* typical of wet, poorly drained clay soils; hybridizes with many species.

Gambel Oak

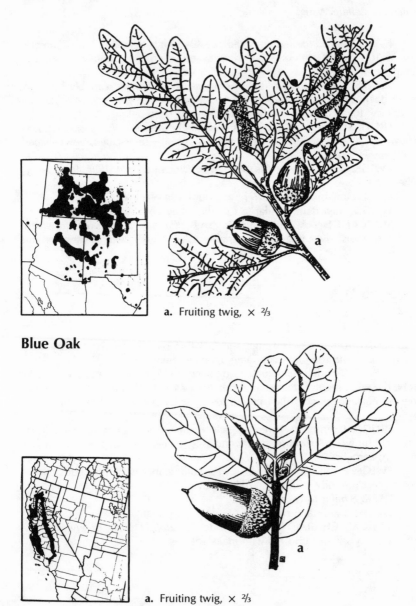

a. Fruiting twig, × ⅔

Blue Oak

a. Fruiting twig, × ⅔

Gambel Oak

Quercus gambelii Nutt. (*Quercus utahensis* Rydb.)

HABIT. A shrub or small tree 25–35 ft high and 1 ft in diameter (max. 60 by 5 ft); crown open with thick, erect branches.

LEAVES. Deciduous; oblong to obovate; 2½–7 in. long; deeply 7- to 9-lobed, rounded lobes; thick; dark green above, paler and hairy below.

FRUIT. Maturing in 1 year; sessile or nearly so; acorn ⅗–¾ in. long; brown; ovoid; enclosed for about ¼–½ of length in thick-scaled, hairy cup.

TWIGS. Stout; orange-brown to red-brown; hairy. Winter buds: ⅛–¼ in. long; brown; hairy.

BARK. Similar to *Q. alba.*

WOOD. Unimportant; similar to *Q. alba;* used for fuel.

SILVICAL CHARACTERS. Similar to *Q. alba;* on dry foothills and canyon walls; the only abundant deciduous oak in the low Rocky Mountain forests; has been subdivided into several species by some authors; hybridizes with *Q. douglasii, Q. dumosa,* and *Q. durata.*

Blue Oak

Quercus douglasii Hook. & Arn.

HABIT. A shrub to medium-sized tree 50–80 ft high and 2–3 ft in diameter; dense rounded crown.

LEAVES. Deciduous; oblong to obovate; 2–5 in. long; entire to sinuate-toothed to shallowly and irregularly 4- to 5-lobed; lobes and teeth rounded but often mucronate; dark blue-green above, paler and hairy below.

FRUIT. Maturing in 1 year; sessile or nearly so; acorn ¾–1¼ in. long, chestnut-brown, ellipsoidal; enclosed at base in thin, shallow, hairy cup; kernel sweet.

TWIGS. Stout; red-brown. Winter buds: ⅛–¼ in. long; bright red.

BARK. Thin; gray; scaly; similar to *Q. alba.*

WOOD. Unimportant; similar to the red oaks and placed in that group by some authors.

SILVICAL CHARACTERS. Intolerant; on dry foothill sites; hybridizes with *Q. garryana, Q. lobata,* and *Q. turbinella.*

Valley Oak

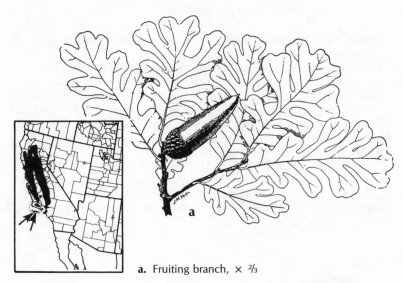

a. Fruiting branch, × ⅔

Oregon White Oak

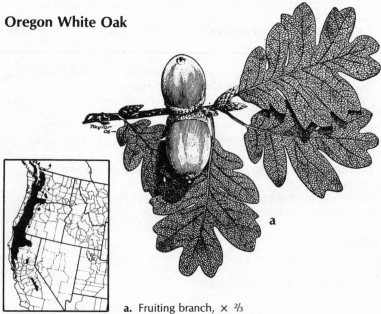

a. Fruiting branch, × ⅔

Valley Oak • California White Oak

Quercus lobata Née

HABIT. The largest western oak, commonly 60–80 ft high and 3–5 ft in diameter (max. 125 by 9 ft); massive trunk dividing near the ground into large, spreading limbs; widespreading, drooping crown.

LEAVES. Deciduous; oblong to obovate; 2½–3½ in. long; deeply 7- to 11-lobed, rounded lobes; dark green and hairy above, pale and hairy below.

FRUIT. Maturing in 1 year; sessile or nearly so; acorn characteristic, 1¼–2¼ in. long, elongate-conic, green becoming brown; enclosed for ⅓ of length in hairy cup with scales free at tip; kernel sweet.

TWIGS. Slender; gray to red-brown; hairy. Winter buds: ¼ in. long; orange-brown; ovoid; hairy.

BARK. Thick; light gray; scaly or broken into square plates.

WOOD. Unimportant; similar to *Q. alba*.

SILVICAL CHARACTERS. Similar to *Q. alba;* fast-growing; fertile loams to poor dry soils; hybridizes with *Q. douglasii, Q. dumosa,* and *Q. turbinella*.

Oregon White Oak

Quercus garryana Dougl.

HABIT. A tree 50–70 ft high and 2–3 ft in diameter (max. 120 by 8 ft); broad, compact crown with large branches.

LEAVES. Deciduous; oblong to obovate; 3–6 in. long; deeply 5- to 9-lobed with rounded lobes; thick and leathery; dark green above, paler and somewhat hairy below.

FRUIT. Maturing in 1 year; sessile or nearly so; acorn 1–1¼ in. long, ovoid; enclosed at base or to ⅓ of length in shallow cup with hairy, thickened scales; glabrous; kernel sweet.

TWIGS. Stout; hairy and orange at first, becoming red-brown and glabrous. Winter buds: ⅓–½ in. long; densely woolly.

BARK. Similar to *Q. alba*.

WOOD. Unimportant; similar to *Q. alba*.

SILVICAL CHARACTERS. Similar to *Q. alba;* moist to dry sites; a low shrub in north and at higher altitudes; hybridizes with *Q. douglasii, Q. dumosa,* and Q. durata.

Chestnut Oak

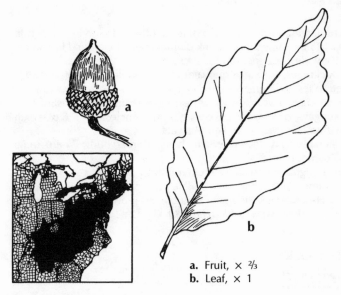

a. Fruit, × ⅔
b. Leaf, × 1

Swamp Chestnut Oak

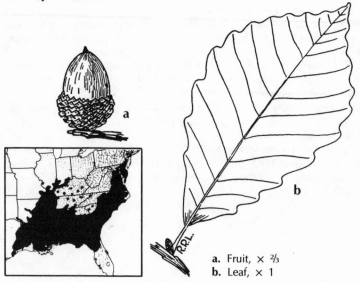

a. Fruit, × ⅔
b. Leaf, × 1

Chestnut Oak

Quercus prinus L. (*Quercus montana* Willd.)

HABIT. Medium-sized tree 50–70 ft high, 2–3 ft in diameter (max. 100 by 6½ ft); trunk often forking shortly above ground into large ascending limbs; crown broad, open.

LEAVES. Deciduous; elliptical to obovate; 4–9 in. long; 1½–3 in. wide; coarsely serrate or crenate; yellow-green and lustrous above, paler, finely hairy below; petioles 1 in.

FRUIT. Maturing in 1 year; short stalk; acorn 1–1½ in., oval to ovoid, chestnut-brown, lustrous; enclosed for ½ or less of length (sometimes only at base) in thin cup with scales more or less fused; kernel sweet.

TWIGS. Stout; orange to red-brown. Winter buds: ¼–½ in.; conical; acute; bright chestnut-brown; soft-hairy; ciliate.

BARK. Thick; dark gray-brown to black; deeply furrowed with broad, rounded, scaly ridges; important source of tannin.

WOOD. Important; similar to *Q. alba*.

SILVICAL CHARACTERS. Similar to *Q. alba;* on poor, dry sites; in pure or mixed stands; hybridizes with *Q. alba, Q. bicolor, Q. robur,* and *Q. stellata*.

Swamp Chestnut Oak

Quercus michauxii Nutt. (*Quercus prinus* L.)

HABIT. A medium-sized tree 60–80 ft high and 2–3 ft in diameter (max. 120 by 10 ft); straight, clear trunk; crown narrow, rounded, compact.

LEAVES. Deciduous; obovate; 5–8 in. long; 3–4½ in. wide; coarsely dentate or crenate, often with gland-tipped teeth; dark green and lustrous above, pale green and hairy below, petioles ¾ in. long.

FRUIT. Maturing in 1 year; sessile or nearly so; acorn 1–1½ in., ovoid, bright brown; enclosed ⅓ or less of length in thick cup with distinct wedge-shaped scales; kernel sweet.

TWIGS. Stout; green to red-brown. Winter buds: ¼ in. long; ovoid; acute; red; thin, hairy scales with pale margins.

BARK. Rather thick; ash-gray; scaly or irregularly furrowed with scaly, narrow ridges.

WOOD. Important; similar to *Q. alba*.

SILVICAL CHARACTERS. Similar to *Q. alba;* on moist to wet, often inundated sites; in mixed stands; hybridizes with *Q. alba, Q. lyrata,* and *Q. macrocarpa*.

Swamp White Oak

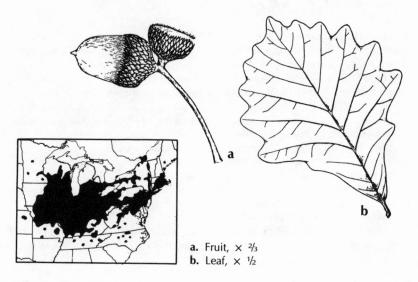

a. Fruit, × ⅔
b. Leaf, × ½

Chinkapin Oak

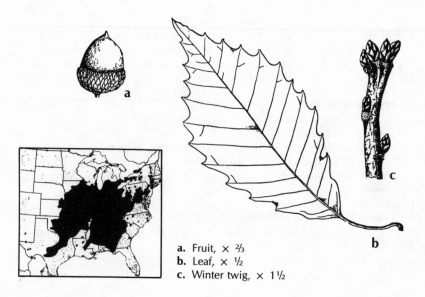

a. Fruit, × ⅔
b. Leaf, × ½
c. Winter twig, × 1½

Swamp White Oak

Quercus bicolor Willd.

HABIT. A medium-sized tree 50–70 ft high and 2–3 ft in diameter (max. 100 by 5½ ft); trunk often limby; crown irregular, open.

LEAVES. Deciduous; obovate to oblong-obovate; 5–7 in. long; 2–4 in. wide; coarsely sinuate-crenate or dentate with glandular teeth or often shallowly, irregularly lobed; dark green and lustrous above, paler and slightly hairy to woolly below.

FRUIT. Maturing in 1 year; characteristic stalks 1–4 in. long; acorn ¾–1¼ in. long, ovoid, light brown; enclosed for about ⅓ of length in thick, light brown, slightly fringed, hairy cup; kernel sweet.

TWIGS. Slender to rather stout; dark brown. Winter buds: 1/16–⅛ in. long; orange-brown; globose; nearly glabrous.

BARK. Thick; dark brown; deeply furrowed into blocky or long, scaly ridges; on younger parts separated into curly, papery scales.

WOOD. Moderately important; similar to *Q. alba*.

SILVICAL CHARACTERS. Similar to *Q. alba;* moist to wet sites; hybridizes with many species.

Chinkapin Oak

Quercus muehlenbergii Engelm.

HABIT. A medium-sized tree 50–70 ft high and 1–3 ft in diameter (max. 160 by 4½ ft); narrow, rounded crown with rather short, ascending branches.

LEAVES. Deciduous; obovate to oblong-lanceolate; 4–7 in. long; coarsely serrate with sharp, gland-tipped teeth; thick; lustrous yellow-green above, paler and hairy below.

FRUIT. Maturing in 1 year; sessile or nearly so; acorn ½–¾ in., chestnut-brown to black, ovoid; enclosed about ½ of length in thin, hairy cup with small scales; kernel sweet.

TWIGS. Slender; orange to gray-brown; glabrous. Winter buds: ⅛ in. long; orange-brown; acute; conical.

BARK. Thin; ash-gray; roughly shallowly furrowed or scaly.

WOOD. Moderately important; similar to *Q. alba*.

SILVICAL CHARACTERS. Similar to *Q. alba;* often on dry sites. Intergrades or hybridizes with shrubby dwarf chinkapin, *Q. prinoides* Willd.; also hybridizes with *Q. alba, Q. bicolor, Q. gambelli,* and *Q. macrocarpa*.

Northern Red Oak

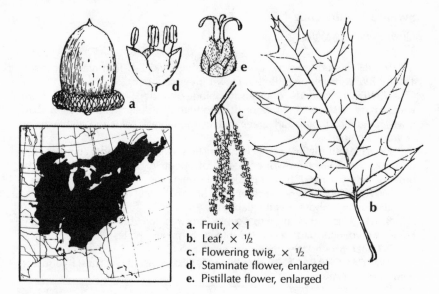

a. Fruit, × 1
b. Leaf, × ½
c. Flowering twig, × ½
d. Staminate flower, enlarged
e. Pistillate flower, enlarged

Black Oak

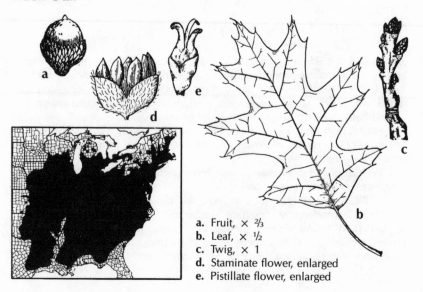

a. Fruit, × ⅔
b. Leaf, × ½
c. Twig, × 1
d. Staminate flower, enlarged
e. Pistillate flower, enlarged

Northern Red Oak

Quercus rubra L. (*Quercus borealis* Michx.)

HABIT. A medium-sized tree 60–80 ft high and 2–4 ft in diameter (max. 150 by 6 ft); broad, rounded crown.

LEAVES. Deciduous; oblong to obovate; 5–9 in. long; 7- to 11-lobed with narrow sinuses extending halfway to midrib; lobes pointing forward, toothed, and bristle-tipped; dull green above, paler and nearly glabrous below except for axillary tufts.

FRUIT. Maturing in 2 years; sessile or nearly so; acorn ⅝–1 in. long, pale brown, oblong to ovoid; enclosed at base or to ⅓ of length in thick cup with closely appressed scales (shallow cup form known as var. *maxima*); inner surface of nut shell woolly; kernel bitter, white.

TWIGS. Stout; red-brown; lustrous. Winter buds: ¼–⅜ in. long; not strongly angled; lustrous; red; hairy toward tip of scales.

BARK. Thick; nearly black; shallow furrows with wide, smooth, light, flat ridges; inner bark light red.

WOOD. Important; less strong and durable than *Q. alba*.

SILVICAL CHARACTERS. Moderately intolerant; sprouts vigorously; on moist sites; rather fast-growing; in mixed stands; hybridizes with many species.

Black Oak

Quercus velutina Lam.

HABIT. A medium-sized tree 50–70 ft high and 2–3 ft in diameter (max. 150 by 8 ft); irregular, rounded crown.

LEAVES. Deciduous; obovate to oblong; 5–9 in. long; 5- to 7-lobed with broad sinuses extending ⅔–⅞ of way to midrib; lobes toothed and bristle-tipped; lustrous and dark green above, paler or coppery below with more or less scurfy pubescence and prominent axillary tufts.

FRUIT. Maturing in 2 years; sessile or nearly so; acorn ½–¾ in. long, red-brown, often striate, ovoid; enclosed for ⅓ to ½ of length in bowl-shaped cup of thin, loose, dull, woolly scales with free tips; kernal bitter, yellow.

TWIGS. Stout; red-brown; glabrous. Winter buds: ¼–½ in. long; sharp-pointed; angled with gray-woolly scales.

BARK. Thick; nearly black; deeply furrowed with narrow, scaly ridges; inner bark thick, orange-yellow, very bitter.

WOOD. Important; similar to *Q. rubra*.

SILVICAL CHARACTERS. Moderately intolerant; similar to *Q. rubra;* on dry to good, moist sites; hybridizes with many species.

Southern Red Oak

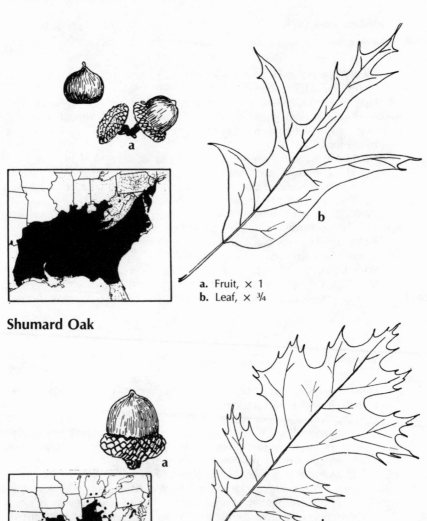

a. Fruit, × 1
b. Leaf, × ¾

Shumard Oak

a. Fruit, × 1
b. Leaf, × ¾

Southern Red Oak

Quercus falcata Michx. (*Quercus rubra* L. in part)

HABIT. A medium-sized tree 70–80 ft high and 2–3 ft in diameter (max. 120 by 7½ ft); large, rounded crown.

LEAVES. Deciduous; obovate to ovate; 5–10 in. long; lobed in 2 ways often on same tree: (1) shallowly 3-lobed at apex and (2) deeply and irregularly 5- to 7-lobed with falcate lobes; lobes bristle-tipped; dark green above, gray-green and white- or red-woolly below; petioles 1–1½ in. long, slender.

FRUIT. Maturing in 2 years; sessile or nearly so; acorn ½ in. long; orange-brown, subglobose; enclosed at base or to ⅓ of length in thin, shallow cup with red-brown, appressed, pale, hairy scales; kernel bitter, yellow.

TWIGS. Stout; red-brown; nearly glabrous. Winter buds: ⅛–¼ in. long; ovoid; blood-red; hairy; not strongly angled.

BARK. Thick; nearly black; deeply furrowed with broad, scaly ridges; inner bark slightly yellow.

WOOD. Important (especially varieties); similar to *Q. rubra.*

SILVICAL CHARACTERS. Similar to *Q. velutina;* dry to wet sites. The economically important cherrybark oak, *Q. falcata* var. *pagodifolia* Ell., is widely distributed on well-drained bottomlands and is easily distinguished by more uniformly, 6- to 11-lobed leaves with angular bases and gray-black flaky or scaly ridged bark.

Shumard Oak

Quercus shumardii Buckl.

HABIT. A large tree 80–100 ft high and 3–5 ft in diameter (max. 180 by 8 ft); open, widespreading crown.

LEAVES. Deciduous; obovate to oblong; 6–8 in. long; 5- to 9-lobed with sinuses extending more than halfway to midrib; lobes many-toothed and bristled-tipped; dark green above, paler below and glabrous except for tufts; petiole slender.

FRUIT. Maturing in 2 years; sessile or nearly so; acorn ¾–1¼ in. long, red-brown, oblong-ovoid; enclosed at base in thick, shallow cup with appressed scales; kernel bitter, whitish.

TWIGS. Slender to stout; gray; glabrous. Winter buds: ¼ in. long; straw-colored; often angled; downy to glabrous.

WOOD. Important; similar to *Q. rubra.*

SILVICAL CHARACTERS. Similar to *Q. velutina;* moist sites. Passing into the variety *texana* (Buckl.) Ashe in southern Oklahoma and central Texas; hybridizes with many species.

Scarlet Oak

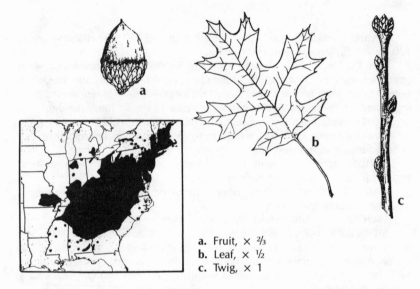

a. Fruit, × ⅔
b. Leaf, × ½
c. Twig, × 1

Blackjack Oak

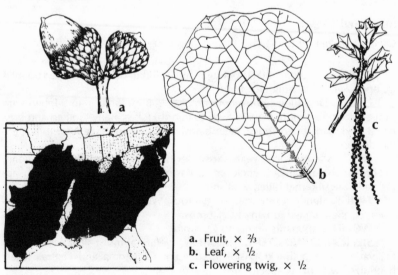

a. Fruit, × ⅔
b. Leaf, × ½
c. Flowering twig, × ½

Scarlet Oak

Quercus coccinea Muenchh.

HABIT. A medium-sized tree 60–80 ft high and 1–3 ft in diameter (max. 100 by 4 ft); open, rounded crown.

LEAVES. Deciduous; obovate to oval; 3–7 in. long; deeply 5- to 9-lobed with wide circular sinuses; lobes toothed and bristle-tipped; bright, shiny green above, paler and glabrous below except axillary tufts; turning brilliant scarlet in autumn; petioles 1½–2½ in. long, slender.

FRUIT. Maturing in 2 years; sessile or nearly so; acorn ½–1 in. long, red-brown, subglobose, usually with distinctive concentric rings near apex; enclosed for ½ or less of length in thick cup with lustrous scales; kernel bitter, white.

TWIGS. Slender; smooth; red-brown. Winter buds: ⅛–¼ in. long; not strongly angled; red-brown; silky hairs on upper half of scales.

BARK. Similar to *Q. velutina,* but inner bark red, not bitter.

WOOD. Important; similar but inferior to *Q. rubra.*

SILVICAL CHARACTERS. Similar to *Q. velutina;* dry, sandy sites; hybridizes with *Q. ilicifolia, Q. palustris,* and *Q. velutina.*

Blackjack Oak

Quercus marilandica Muenchh.

HABIT. A small, shrubby tree 20–30 ft high and ½–1 ft in diameter (max. 50 by 2½ ft); rounded, contorted crown.

LEAVES. Deciduous; thick; variable, but typically obovate, more or less 3-lobed at apex; 5–7 in. long; lobes entire or toothed, bristle-tipped; dark-green, lustrous above, paler, tawny, scurfy-pubescent below; petioles ½–2 in. long, stout.

FRUIT. Maturing in 2 years; sessile or nearly so; acorn ¾ in. long, yellow-brown, subglobose; enclosed for ½ of length in bowl-shaped cup with large, loose, red-brown, hairy scales; kernel yellow, bitter.

TWIGS. Stout; green to red-brown. Winter buds: ¼–½ in. long; angled; hairy; rusty-brown; conical.

BARK. Thick; nearly black; divided into rough, square blocks.

WOOD. Unimportant; similar to *Q. rubra.*

SILVICAL CHARACTERS. Similar to *Q. velutina;* poor, dry sites; hybridizes with many species.

Pin Oak

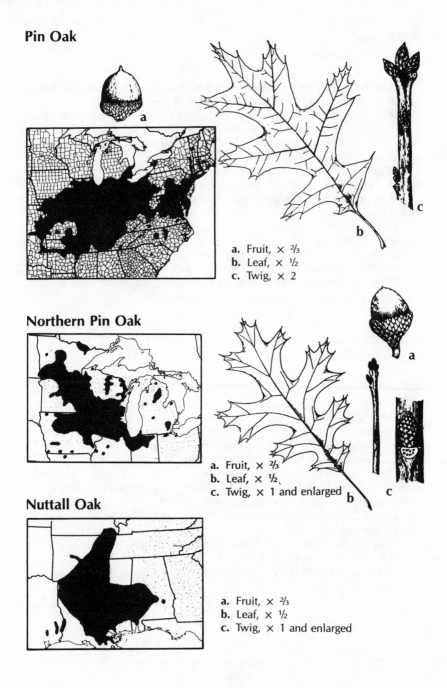

a. Fruit, × ⅔
b. Leaf, × ½
c. Twig, × 2

Northern Pin Oak

a. Fruit, × ⅔
b. Leaf, × ½
c. Twig, × 1 and enlarged

Nuttall Oak

a. Fruit, × ⅔
b. Leaf, × ½
c. Twig, × 1 and enlarged

Pin Oak

Quercus palustris Muenchh.

HABIT. A medium-sized tree 60–80 ft high and 1–3 ft in diameter (max. 120 by 6 ft); pyramidal crown with drooping lower branches that prune poorly.

LEAVES. Deciduous; obovate; 3–6 in. long; deeply 5- to 7-lobed with wide, rounded sinuses; lobes toothed and bristle-tipped; bright green and lustrous above, paler and glabrous below except axillary tufts; petioles slender.

FRUIT. Maturing in 2 years; sessile or nearly so; acorn ½ in. long, hemispherical, light brown; often striate; enclosed at base in thin cup with red-brown, appressed, free-tipped scales; kernel bitter, yellow.

TWIGS. Slender; smooth; green to red-brown; many short pinlike branches. Winter buds: ⅛ in. long; red-brown; shiny; sharp-pointed; angled; ciliate.

BARK. Thick; gray-brown; long, smooth, finally scaly ridged.

WOOD. Important; similar to *Q. rubra.*

SILVICAL CHARACTERS. Similar to *Q. velutina;* on moist sites; a common ornamental; easily transplanted; hybridizes with many species.

Northern Pin Oak

Quercus ellipsoidalis E. J. Hill

This species is similar to pin oak except for the ellipsoidal acorn ½–¾ in. long enclosed for ⅓–½ of length in bowl-shaped cup. Hybridizes with *Q. rubra* and *Q. velutina.*

Nuttall Oak

Quercus nuttallii Palmer (*Quercus palustris* f. *nuttallii* Muller)

This species is similar to pin oak except for its oblong-ovoid acorn ¾–1¼ in. long enclosed for about ⅓ of length in a bowl-shaped cup and for yellow axillary hairs on lower surface of the leaf. Bottomlands. Hybridizes with *Q. shumardii.*

204

California Black Oak

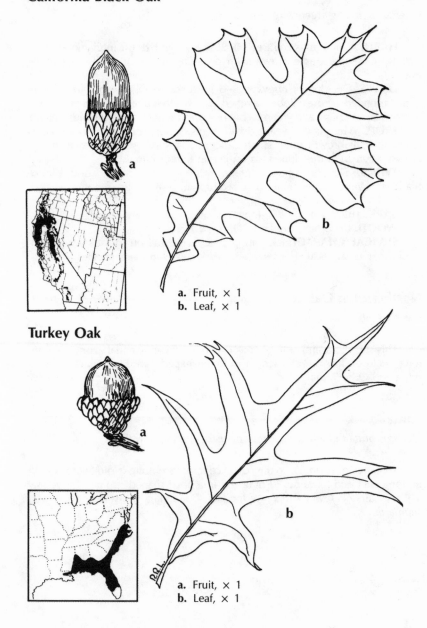

a. Fruit, × 1
b. Leaf, × 1

Turkey Oak

a. Fruit, × 1
b. Leaf, × 1

California Black Oak

Quercus kelloggii Newb.

HABIT. A medium-sized tree 60–90 ft high and 2–4 ft in diameter (max. 130 by 9 ft); large, open, globose crown.

LEAVES. Deciduous; obovate; 3–8 in. long; deeply 5- to 7-lobed, rounded usually narrow sinuses; lobes usually toothed, bristle-tipped; dark yellow-green above, paler below; usually hairy.

FRUIT. Maturing in 2 years; short-stalked; acorn 1–1½ in. long, ellipsoidal, light chestnut-brown; enclosed for ⅓ to ¾ of length in bowl-shaped cup with thin, chestnut-brown, erose-margined scales; inner surface of nut shell woolly.

TWIGS. Slender to rather stout; red-brown. Winter buds: ¼ in. long; ovoid; chestnut-brown; ciliate on margins.

BARK. Thick; nearly black; divided by deep furrows into wide ridges; light brown and smooth on young stems.

WOOD. Unimportant; similar to *Q. rubra.*

SILVICAL CHARACTERS. Similar to *Q. velutina;* on dry, sandy soils; hybridizes with *Q. agrifolia* and *Q. wislizeni.*

Turkey Oak

Quercus laevis Walt. (*Quercus catesbaei* Michx.)

HABIT. A small tree 20–30 ft high and 1–2 ft in diameter (max. 60 by 2½ ft); open, irregular crown.

LEAVES. Deciduous; variable; distinctive; 3–12 in. (usually about 5); deeply 3- to 5-lobed; lobes spreading, falcate, bristle-tipped; lustrous yellow-green above, paler below; glabrous except tufts of red hairs in axils of veins; persisting on tree into winter; petioles ¼–¾ in., stout.

FRUIT. Maturing in 2 years; short-stalked; acorn 1 in. long, oval, light brown; enclosed for ⅓ to ½ of length in bowl-shaped, hairy cup of loosely imbricated scales; kernel bitter, yellow.

TWIGS. Stout; red-brown; glabrous. Winter buds: ½ in. long; narrow; tapering; chestnut-brown; red-hairy.

BARK. Rather thick; nearly black; deeply furrowed with rough, scaly ridges.

WOOD. Unimportant; similar to *Q. rubra.*

SILVICAL CHARACTERS. Similar to *Q. velutina;* dry, sandy soils; hybridizes with *Q. falcata, Q. incana, Q. laurifolia,* and *Q. nigra.*

Willow Oak

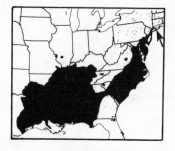

a. Fruit, × 1
b. Leaf, × 1

Water Oak

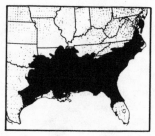

a. Fruit, × 1
b. Leaf, × 1

Willow Oak

Quercus phellos L.

HABIT. A medium-sized tree 70–100 ft high and 2–4 ft in diameter (max. 130 by 7 ft); dense, rounded crown.

LEAVES. Deciduous; typically linear-lanceolate to ovate-lanceolate; 2–5 in. long; entire or wavy; acute with bristle tip; bright green above, paler and glabrous to hairy below.

FRUIT. Maturing in 2 years; sessile or nearly so; acorn not over ½ in. long, green-brown to yellow-brown, hemispherical; enclosed at base by shallow cup with thin, hairy, red-brown scales; kernel bitter, yellow.

TWIGS. Slender; red-brown; glabrous. Winter buds: ⅛–¼ in. long; sharp-pointed; chestnut-brown; smooth.

BARK. Rather thick; nearly black; broken by deep furrows into rough ridges on old trunks; smooth and red-gray when young.

WOOD. Moderately important; similar to *Q. rubra*.

SILVICAL CHARACTERS. Similar to *Q. velutina;* wet sites; fast-growing; commonly planted as ornamental; hybridizes with many species.

Water Oak

Quercus nigra L.

HABIT. A medium-sized tree 50–70 ft high and 2–3 ft in diameter (max. 125 by 6 ft); rounded, even crown.

LEAVES. Deciduous, though tardily so, as many remain green until late winter; extremely variable in shape, size, margin; commonly spatulate, also obovate to narrow-oblong; margin entire to shallowly 3-lobed at apex at deeply 5- to 7-lobed; 2–6 in. long; dull blue-green above, paler below; mostly glabrous.

FRUIT. Maturing in 2 years; sessile or nearly so; acorn ⅓–⅔ in. long, nearly black, subglobose; enclosed at base by shallow cup with thin, hairy scales; kernel bitter, bright orange.

TWIGS. Slender; red-brown; glabrous. Winter buds: ⅛–¼ in. long; angled; sharp; loose, red-brown, hairy scales.

BARK. Rather thin; gray-black; broken by shallow furrows into wide, scaly ridges; smooth when young.

WOOD. Moderately important; similar to *Q. rubra*.

SILVICAL CHARACTERS. Similar to *Q. velutina;* moist to wet sites; reproduces aggressively; common ornamental; hybridizes with many species.

Laurel Oak

a

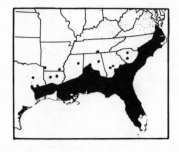

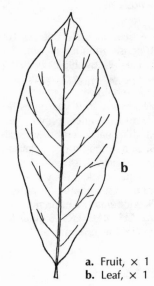

b

a. Fruit, × 1
b. Leaf, × 1

Shingle Oak

a

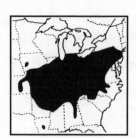

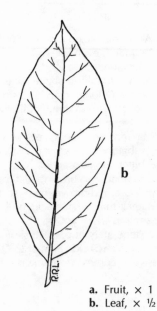

b

a. Fruit, × 1
b. Leaf, × ½

Laurel Oak

Quercus laurifolia Michx.

HABIT. A medium-sized tree 50–70 ft high and 2–3 ft in diameter (max. 100 by 8 ft); dense, rounded crown.

LEAVES. Nearly evergreen, falling in early spring just before new leaves appear; elliptical to oblong-lanceolate; 2–4 in. long; entire or wavy, occasionally 3-lobed at apex; bristle-tipped or rounded at apex; bright green above, paler below; glabrous.

FRUIT. Maturing in 2 years; sessile or nearly so; acorn ⅓–½ in. long, nearly black, hemispherical; base enclosed by shallow cup with thin, red-brown, hairy scales; kernel bitter.

TWIGS. Slender; red-brown; glabrous. Winter buds: ⅒–³⁄₁₆ in. long; ovoid; pointed; tight, bright red scales.

BARK. Thick; nearly black; deeply furrowed with broad, flat ridges; dark brown and smooth or scaly when young.

SILVICAL CHARACTERS. Recent study indicates laurel oak may be a hybrid of *Q. phellos* and *Q. nigra*. It hybridizes with *Q. falcata, Q. incana, Q. laevis,* and *Q. marilandica.*

Shingle Oak

Quercus imbricaria Michx.

HABIT. A medium-sized tree 50–60 ft high and 2–3 ft in diameter (max. 4 ft); narrow, rounded crown.

LEAVES. Deciduous; elliptical to oblong-obovate; 4–6 in. long; dark green, lustrous above, paler and white-hairy below with many slender yellow veins.

FRUIT. Maturing in 2 years; usually short-stalked; acorn ½–¾ in. long, chestnut-brown, ovoid; enclosed for ⅓ to ½ of length in bowl-shaped cup lustrous within with thin, red-brown, appressed, hairy scales; kernel bitter.

TWIGS. Slender; green-brown. Winter buds: ⅛–³⁄₁₆ in. long; conical; chestnut-brown; pubescent.

BARK. Thick; gray-brown; long, smooth, becoming shallowly furrowed and ridged.

SILVICAL CHARACTERS. Similar to *Q. velutina;* moist sites; hybridizes with many species.

Similar Species

The bluejack oak, *Q. incana* Bartr., is a similar small tree of dry, sandy coastal plain sites extending from Virginia to Florida west to Texas and north to Arkansas and Oklahoma. Characterized by small 2- to 5- in. elliptical leaves, blue-green above and white-woolly below, with obscure, remote veins and shallow acorn cups hairy on inner surface and thick, dark, blocky bark.

Live Oak

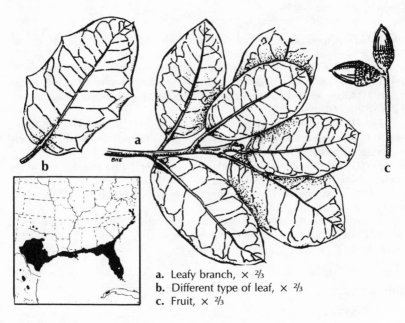

a. Leafy branch, × ⅔
b. Different type of leaf, × ⅔
c. Fruit, × ⅔

Mexican Blue Oak

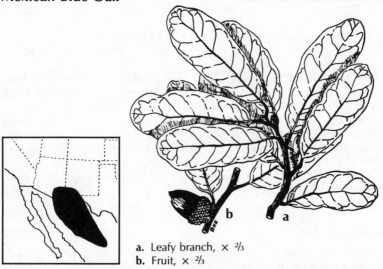

a. Leafy branch, × ⅔
b. Fruit, × ⅔

Live Oak

Quercus virginiana Mill.

HABIT. A medium-sized tree 40–50 ft high and 3–4 ft in diameter (max. 80 by 11½ ft); trunk usually dividing near the ground into several large, horizontal limbs; crown dense, rounded with span of 100–150 ft (max. 168 ft).

LEAVES. Persistent until new leaves appear; elliptical to oblong-obovate; 2–5 in. long; entire and wavy margin (rarely with few teeth); rounded tip; dark green above, paler and somewhat hairy below.

FRUIT. Maturing in 1 year; stalks 1–5 in. long; acorn ¾–1 in. long, dark brown, ellipsoidal; enclosed for ⅓ to ½ of length in bowl-shaped cup with thin, red-brown, woolly scales; inner surface of nut shell glabrous; kernel sweet.

TWIGS. Slender; gray-brown; hairy. Winter buds: ¹⁄₁₆ in. long.

BARK. Rather thick; dark red-brown; shallowly furrowed with flat, scaly ridges.

WOOD. The only important live oak; diffuse porous; very heavy, hard, and strong; durable; used for ships, posts, etc.

SILVICAL CHARACTERS. Intolerant; typical of dry sites; long-lived; 3 varieties reach tree size.

GENERAL. Intergrades or hybridizes with dwarf live oak, *Q. minima* (Sarg.). Small.

Mexican Blue Oak

Quercus oblongifolia Torr.

HABIT. A shrub or small tree rarely 30 ft high and 18–30 in. in diameter; handsome, rounded crown.

LEAVES. Persistent until new leaves appear; ovate to elliptic; 1–2 in. long; entire or wavy with revolute margins (rarely coarsely toothed); blue-green above, paler and glabrous below.

FRUIT. Maturing in 1 year; sessile or rarely stalked; acorn ½–¾ in. long, chestnut-brown, ovoid to obovoid; enclosed for ⅓ of length in bowllike cup with thin, red-tipped, woolly scales; inner surface of nut shell glabrous; kernel sweet.

TWIGS. Slender; red-gray. Winter buds: ¹⁄₁₆–⅛ in. long; brown.

BARK. Thick; ash-gray; broken into nearly square, platelike scales on old trunks.

SILVICAL CHARACTERS. Intolerant; on dry foothills.

Arizona White Oak

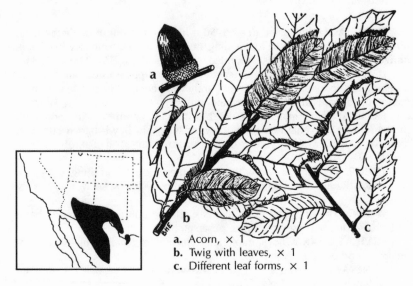

a. Acorn, × 1
b. Twig with leaves, × 1
c. Different leaf forms, × 1

Emory Oak

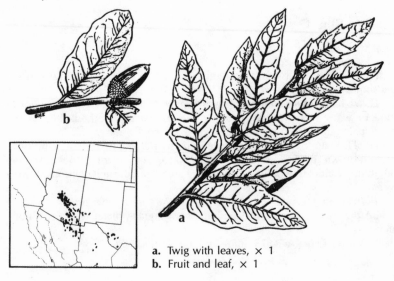

a. Twig with leaves, × 1
b. Fruit and leaf, × 1

Arizona White Oak

Quercus arizonica Sarg.

HABIT. A shrub or small tree rarely 60 ft high and 3 ft in diameter; handsome, round-topped crown with massive, contorted, nearly horizontal branches.

LEAVES. Persistent until appearance of new leaves; oblong-lanceolate to broadly ovate; 1–4 in. long (most about 2½ in.); entire or with wavy, spiny teeth; revolute margin; dark blue-green above, paler and densely hairy below.

FRUIT. Maturing in 1 year; sessile or short-stalked; acorn ¾–1 in. long, chestnut-brown, oblong to obovoid, enclosed for ½ of length in deep cup with thick, corky, woolly, red-tipped scales; inner surface of nut shell glabrous; kernel sweet.

TWIGS. Stout; red-brown; red and hairy at first, becoming glabrous. Winter buds: ¹⁄₁₆ in. long; subglobose, brown; ciliate.

BARK. Rather thick; ash-gray; furrowed and scaly-ridged.

SILVICAL CHARACTERS. Intolerant; on dry mountain slopes; most common live oak in the Southwest; hybridizes with *Q. gambelii* and *Q. grisea*.

Emory Oak

Quercus emoryi Torr.

HABIT. A shrub or small tree rarely 60 ft high and 2–5 ft in diameter; round-topped, even crown with stout, drooping branches.

LEAVES. Persistent until appearance of new leaves; oblong-lanceolate; 1–2½ in. long; entire or remotely wavy toothed; leathery; dark green above, paler below; glabrous or slightly hairy.

FRUIT. Maturing in 1 year; sessile or nearly so; acorn ½–¾ in. long, nearly black, oblong to ovoid; enclosed for ⅓ to ½ of length in bowl-shaped cup with brown, hairy scales; inner surface of nut shell woolly; kernel sweet.

TWIGS. Slender; red and hairy at first, becoming dark brown and glabrous.

BARK. Thick; nearly black; deeply furrowed and scaly-plated.

SILVICAL CHARACTERS. Intolerant; on dry foothills and mountains; very abundant; in pure or mixed stands; coppices freely; acorns important source of human and animal food; hybridizes with *Q. graciliformis* and *Q. gravesii*.

Interior Live Oak

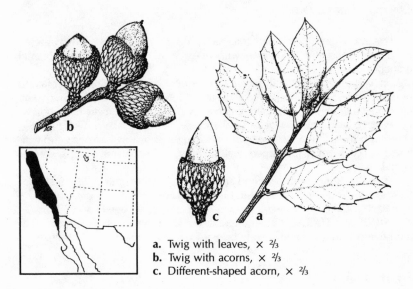

a. Twig with leaves, × ²⁄₃
b. Twig with acorns, × ²⁄₃
c. Different-shaped acorn, × ²⁄₃

Coast Live Oak

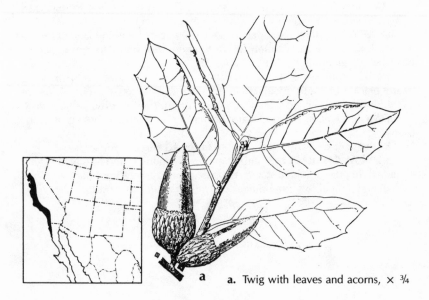

a. Twig with leaves and acorns, × ³⁄₄

Interior Live Oak

Quercus wislizeni A. DC.

HABIT. Commonly shrubby though becoming a medium-sized tree 60–80 ft high and 2–4 ft in diameter (max. 100 by 6½ ft); wide, rounded crown with large, spreading branches.

LEAVES. Persistent 2 years; lanceolate to broadly elliptic; 1–3 in. long (mostly about 1¼ in.); entire or with spiny teeth; leathery; glabrous; lustrous dark green above, paler below.

FRUIT. Maturing in 2 years; sessile or short-stalked; acorn 1–1½ in. long, chestnut-brown, slender-oblong, pointed; enclosed for ½ or less of length in bowl-shaped cup with thin, closely imbricated, ciliate scales; inner surface of nut shell woolly; kernel bitter.

TWIGS. Slender; dark brown. Winter buds: ⅛–¼ in. long; ovoid.

BARK. Thick; nearly black; deeply furrowed with scaly ridges.

SILVICAL CHARACTERS. Intolerant; slow-growing; dry sites; hybridizes with *Q. agrifolia* and *Q. kelloggii*.

Coast Live Oak • California Live Oak

Quercus agrifolia Née

HABIT. A medium-sized tree 50–75 ft high and 2–4 ft in diameter (max. 90 by 12½ ft); trunk dividing shortly above ground into several large, horizontal limbs that often rest on the ground; broad crown often 150 ft across.

LEAVES. Persistent until new leaves appear; oval or oblong to suborbicular; 1–3 in. long; margins entire to spiny-toothed, revolute; leathery; lustrous dark green above, paler below; glabrous to hairy.

FRUIT. Maturing in 1 year; sessile or nearly so; acorn ¾–1½ in. long, chestnut-brown, slender-conic, pointed; enclosed for ⅓ of length or only at base in bowl-shaped cup with thin, closely imbricated scales; inner surface of nut shell woolly; kernel bitter.

TWIGS. Slender; gray-brown. Winter buds: 1/16 in. long; globose.

BARK. Thick; nearly black; deeply furrowed with scaly ridges.

SILVICAL CHARACTERS. Intolerant; slow-growing; dry sites.

Canyon Live Oak

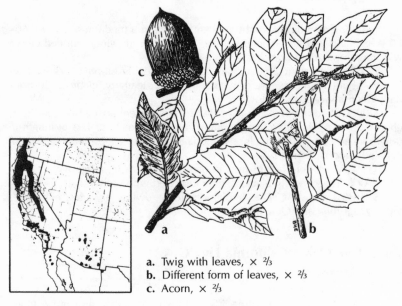

a. Twig with leaves, × ²/₃
b. Different form of leaves, × ²/₃
c. Acorn, × ²/₃

Silverleaf Oak

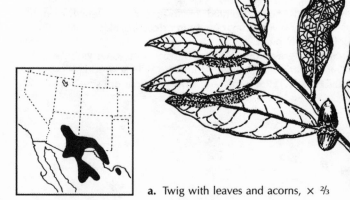

a. Twig with leaves and acorns, × ²/₃

Canyon Live Oak

Quercus chrysolepis Liebm.

HABIT. A shrub to medium-sized tree 60–80 ft high and 1–5 ft in diameter (max. 100 by 12 ft); usually dividing above ground into large, horizontal branches; large spreading crown; forming dense thickets on dry slopes.

LEAVES. Persistent 3–4 years; oblong-ovate to elliptic; 1–4 in. long; mostly entire on old trees and sinuate-dentate on young trees, or both forms appearing together; revolute margins; leathery; bright yellow-green and glabrous above; tawny-tomentose, becoming glabrous and blue-green below.

FRUIT. Maturing in 2 years; sessile or nearly so; acorn ½–2 in. long, chestnut-brown, ellipsoidal to ovate; enclosed at base in thick, shallow cup with hairy to golden-woolly scales; inner surface of nut shell woolly; kernel bitter.

TWIGS. Slender; brown to gray; woolly, sometimes becoming smooth. Winter buds: ⅛ in. long; ovoid; acute; chestnut-brown.

BARK. Rather thick (¾–1½ in.); gray-brown, tinged with red; smooth except for small scales on old trunks.

SILVICAL CHARACTERS. Tolerant when young; long-lived; canyon walls to dry mountain slopes; closely related to the shrubby *Q. dunnii* Kell. of the Mexican border and *Q. vaccinifolia* Kell. in California and Oregon.

Silverleaf Oak

Quercus hypoleucoides A. Camus (*Quercus hypoleuca* Engelm.)

HABIT. A shrub or small tree 20–30 ft high (rarely 60 ft) and 10–15 in. in diameter; narrow, rounded crown.

LEAVES. Persistent until appearance of new leaves; lanceolate to elliptic; 2–4 in. long; entire or with few coarse teeth near apex; revolute margins; leathery; dark yellow-green and lustrous above, woolly below.

FRUIT. Maturing in 2 years; sessile or short-stalked; acorn ½–⅔ in. long, chestnut-brown, ovoid; enclosed for ⅓ of length in thick cup with thin, brown, silvery-hairy scales; inner surface of nut shell woolly; kernel bitter.

TWIGS. Stout; red-brown. Winter buds: ⅛ in. long; brown.

BARK. Rather thick (¾–1 in.); nearly black; deeply furrowed into broad, thick-scaled ridges.

SILVICAL CHARACTERS. Intolerant; on dry, low mountain sites; hybridizes with *Q. gravesii* and *Q. shumardii*.

ULMACEAE

The Elms

Characteristics of the Genus *Ulmus* L.

HABIT. Handsome trees often planted for shade or ornamental purposes; irregularly pinnate branching.

LEAVES. Alternate; simple; deciduous; lanceolate to obovate; stipulate; penniveined; simply or more commonly doubly serrate; 2-ranked; mostly unequal and oblique at the base and acuminate at the apex; petioles short.

FLOWERS. Regular; perfect; small; in fascicles or cymes; appearing before the leaves (in a few species not appearing until autumn); on slender, drooping pedicels; calyx 5- to 9-lobed; corolla absent; 4–6 stamens; ovary usually 1-celled by abortion 1-ovuled, flattened, deeply 2-lobed style.

FRUIT. A distinctive oblong to suborbicular samara; maturing in spring or autumn of first year; surrounded at base by calyx remnants; seed cavity compressed, surrounded by a thin papery wing commonly notched at the apex and tipped with the remnants of the persistent style.

TWIGS. Slender to stout; somewhat zigzag; corky wings on some species; pith solid, round, leaf scars with 3 somewhat depressed bundle scars. Winter buds: terminal absent; lateral with overlapping scales.

BARK. Thick and furrowed; often with layers of two colors.

WOOD. Moderately important; heavy; hard; strong; tough; ring-porous; not durable; difficult to split; specialized uses.

SILVICAL CHARACTERS. Rather tolerant trees; fast-growing; widespreading, lateral roots.

GENERAL. This genus contains about 45 species of trees scattered through the Northern Hemisphere; many are among our most important shade and ornamental trees. Six species are native to eastern North America. Five exotic species commonly planted in this country are included in the key; of these *U. pumila*, widely grown in the central and western states, has been naturalized from Kansas to Minnesota, in Utah, and probably elsewhere.

KEY TO THE SPECIES OF ELMS

1. Leaves doubly serrate, unequal at base.
    2. Some of twigs with corky wings; fruit hairy, at least on margins; leaves not over 4 in. long.
        3. Buds, young twigs pale-hairy; spring fruit, ovoid to suborbicular, hairy and ciliate, seed cavity not pronounced; leaves smooth above, hairy below .... *U. thomasii,* **rock elm,** p. 223
        3. Buds and young twigs glabrous or nearly so; fruit oblong, seed cavity pronounced; southern.
            4. Leaves 2–4 in., acuminate, glabrous above, slightly hairy along veins below; fall fruit, fringed margin with long white hairs; Kentucky, Illinois to Georgia, west to Oklahoma . . . . *U. serotina,* **September elm,** p. 221
            4. Leaves 1–2½ in.; fruit covered, long white hairs.
                5. Leaves acuminate, coarsely doubly toothed, smooth above, hairy below; spring fruit; Illinois, Virginia to Oklahoma, south . . . . *U. alata,* **winged elm,** p. 221
                5. Leaves rounded or acute at apex, unequally doubly toothed, almost singly toothed; roughened above, hairy below; fall fruit; Arkansas to Mississippi, west to Louisiana, Oklahoma, Texas . . . . *U. crassifolia,* **cedar elm,** p. 221
    2. Twigs without corky ridges; fruit appearing in spring; seed cavity distinct.
        6. Fruit hairy or ciliate; buds glabrous or with rusty hairs; leaves usually 4–7 in. long, rough on top.
            7. Buds with rusty hairs; fruit hairy over seed cavity; leaves rough on both surfaces; bark of trunk dark red-brown . . . . *U. rubra,* **slippery elm,** p. 223
            7. Buds nearly glabrous; fruit hairy only on margins; leaves rough above; bark of trunk with alternating gray and brown layers . . . . *U. americana,* **American elm,** p. 221
        6. Fruit glabrous; buds pale-hairy or glabrous; European ornamentals.
            8. Twigs hairy; leaves rough above; petioles ⅛–¼ in.
                9. Leaves 2–3 in.; petioles ⅙–¼ in.; bark gray, furrowed; seed near apex of deeply notched fruit . . . . *U. procera* Salisb., **English elm**
                9. Leaves 3–6½ in. long; petioles ⅛ in.; bark dark, remaining smooth many years; seed near center of slightly notched fruit . . . . *U. glabra* Huds., **Wych elm**
            8. Twigs glabrous; leaves 2–3 in.; smooth above; petioles ¼–½ in. . . . . *U. carpinifolia* Gled., **smooth-leaved elm**
1. Leaves singly or nearly singly serrate, nearly equal at base, ¾–3 in. long; fruit glabrous; Asiatic ornamentals.
    10. Leaves ¾–2 in. long, predominantly rounded to acute at apex; fall fruit, ovate, notched at apex . . . . *U. parvifolia* Jacq., **Chinese elm**
    10. Leaves 1–3 in. long, predominantly acuminate to acute at apex; spring fruit, suborbicular, closed notch . . . . *U. pumila* L., **Siberian elm**

American Elm

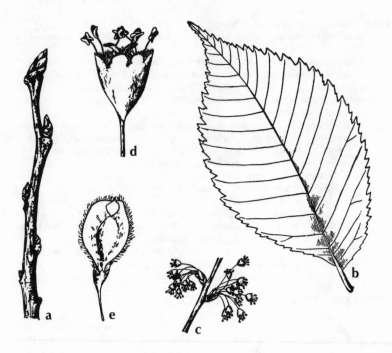

a. Winter twig, × 2
b. Leaf, × ½
c. Flowering branchlet, × ½
d. Flower, enlarged
e. Fruit, × 2

American Elm • White Elm

Ulmus americana L.

HABIT. A handsome tree 75–100 ft high and 3–6 ft in diameter (max. 120 by 10 ft); open-grown trees commonly dividing near ground into several ascending limbs forming a vase-shaped crown; perhaps our most common ornamental species.

LEAVES. Oblong-obovate to oval; 4–6 in. long; coarsely doubly serrate; thick and firm; base conspicuously oblique; dark green and more or less rough above, paler below.

FRUIT. A smooth, oval to ovate samara ½ in. long, hairy on margins and deeply notched at apex; seed cavity distinct; long-stalked fascicles maturing in late spring.

TWIGS. Slender; round; red-brown; hairy at first, becoming glabrous. Winter buds: lateral ¼ in. long; chestnut-brown; acute; glabrous or with scales hairy-fringed.

BARK. Thick; ash-gray; variable, but typically diamond-shaped by furrows; alternate light and dark layers in outer bark.

WOOD. The most important of the elms.

SILVICAL CHARACTERS. Moderately tolerant; shallow-rooted; typical of moist sites, but hardy and widely planted as a shade tree; seriously threatened by Dutch Elm disease; with mixed hardwoods.

Other Native Elms

Three unimportant elms are found in the eastern United States, all characterized by corky wings on some twigs and by small leaves; they are distinguished in the key:

Winged elm, *Ulmus alata* Michx., a common small tree that flowers and fruits in spring; characterized by doubly serrate leaves 1–2½ in. long and hair-covered fruit ⅓ in. long with a distinct seed cavity.

Cedar elm *Ulmus crassifolia* Nutt., flowers and fruits in the fall; characterized by nearly singly-toothed leaves 1–2½ in. long with rounded to acute apex and hair-covered fruit ⅓–½ in. long with a distinct seed cavity.

September elm, *Ulmus serotina* Sarg., flowers and fruits in the fall; characterized by acuminate leaves 2–4 in. long and fruit ciliate with white hairs.

Slippery Elm

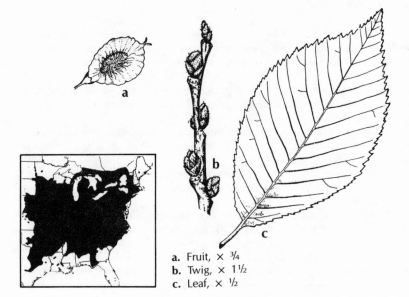

a. Fruit, × ¾
b. Twig, × 1½
c. Leaf, × ½

Rock Elm

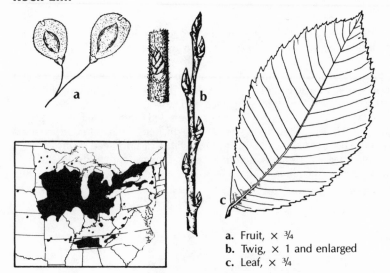

a. Fruit, × ¾
b. Twig, × 1 and enlarged
c. Leaf, × ¾

Slippery Elm

Ulmus rubra Muhl. (*Ulmus fulva* Michx.)

HABIT. A medium-sized tree 40–70 ft high and 1–2 ft in diameter (max. 5 ft); clear trunk; rounded, open crown with spreading branches and ascending twigs.

LEAVES. Oblong-obovate to oval; 4–7 in. long; coarsely doubly serrate; thick and firm; base conspicuously oblique; dark green and rough above; paler and rough below.

FRUIT. A suborbicular samara about ¾ in. long; seed cavity distinct, brown-woolly; wings and margins smooth; apex entire or nearly so; in short-stalked fascicles; maturing in spring.

TWIGS. Rather stout; ash-gray; rough. Winter buds: lateral ¼ in. long; nearly black, hairy.

BARK. Thick; dark red-brown; nearly parallel furrows; without alternate light and dark layers; inner bark mucilaginous.

SILVICAL CHARACTERS. Moderately tolerant; wide lateral roots; with mixed hardwoods; varied sites.

Rock Elm • Cork Elm

Ulmus thomasii Sarg. (*Ulmus racemosa* Thomas)

HABIT. A handsome medium-sized tree 60–80 ft high and 2–3 ft in diameter (max. 100 by 5½ ft); trunk persisting into crown; narrow crown with drooping lower branches.

LEAVES. Obovate to oval; 2½–5 in. long; coarsely doubly serrate; thick and firm; base nearly equal; dark green and usually glabrous above, paler and slightly hairy below.

FRUIT. An obovate to oval samara ¾–1 in. long, hairy all over; seed cavity indistinct; apex shallowly notched; margins ciliate; in racemose cymes on long slender stalks; maturing in spring.

TWIGS. Rather stout; red-brown; usually developing corky wings. Winter buds: lateral ¼ in. long; brown; acute; downy-ciliate.

BARK. Thick; dark gray-brown; deeply and irregularly furrowed; alternate light and dark layers in outer bark.

SILVICAL CHARACTERS. Intermediate in tolerance; wide lateral roots; with mixed hardwoods; varied sites; poor reproduction.

The Hackberries

Characteristics of the Genus *Celtis* L.

HABIT. Shrubs or trees often planted for shade or ornamentals; irregularly pinnate branching.

LEAVES. Alternate; simple; lanceolate to ovate; acute or acuminate at apex; often oblique at base; serrate or entire margins; membranaceous or subcoriaceous; deciduous; mostly long-petiolate; 2-ranked; stipules thin, caducous, fugacious, enclosing leaf in bud.

FLOWERS. Regular; polygamo-monoecious or rarely monoecious; minute; staminate in fascicles toward base of twig; above these the pistillate or perfect, solitary or in few-flowered fascicles; pedicellate; appearing soon after unfolding of leaves; calyx 4- to 5-lobed, green-yellow, deciduous; corolla absent; stamens as many as calyx lobes and opposite them; ovary 1-celled, ovoid, sessile, green, and lustrous.

FRUIT. Subglobose or ovoid drupe; tipped with remnants of style; thick firm skin; thin, pulpy flesh; nutlet bony, thick-walled, reticulate-pitted; ripening in autumn, often remaining long after leaves fall. Seeds: filling cavity in nutlet.

TWIGS. Slender; round; unarmed or spinose; pith round and usually finely chambered at nodes. Winter buds: terminal absent; lateral small, appressed, scaly; branchlets prolonged by an upper lateral bud.

BARK. Usually gray and smooth, sometimes with conspicuous, corky, warty excrescences.

WOOD. Rather heavy; fairly hard; not strong; odorless; ring-porous; moderately important; often sold as elm.

GENERAL. This genus consists of about 70 species scattered through the north temperate and tropical regions; 5 tree species and several varieties have been listed for the United States; native species often disfigured by gall-making insects distorting the buds and producing broomlike clusters of branchlets; this genus is in a confused state and needs revision; distributions have not been accurately determined.

KEY TO THE SPECIES OF HACKBERRIES

1. Fruit dark purple, on pedicels somewhat longer than leaf petioles; leaves 2½–4 in. long, usually sharply serrate with numerous teeth, green on both surfaces, without conspicuous reticulate veinlets on lower surface . . . .
. . . . *C. occidentalis,* **hackberry,** p. 227
1. Fruit orange to red-brown to yellow; leaves entire or sparingly toothed.
   2. Fruit on pedicels much longer than leaf petioles; leaves 1½–3 in. long, conspicuous reticulate veinlets below.
      3. Leaves broadly ovate, green below; fruit yellow to orange-red . . . .
      . . . . *C. reticulata,* **netleaf hackberry,** p. 229
      3. Leaves oblong-ovate, pale below; fruit dark red-brown; Texas . . . .
      . . . . *C. lindheimeri,* **Lindheimer hackberry,** p. 227
   2. Fruit on pedicels shorter or but little longer than leaf petioles; leaves without conspicuous reticulate veinlets below.
      4. Leaves mostly oblong-lanceolate, long-acuminate, 2–5 in. long; fruit yellow to orange-red . . . . *C. laevigata,* **sugarberry,** p. 229
      4. Leaves ovate-lanceolate, short-acuminate, 1½–2½ in. long; fruit dark orange-red to red-purple . . . . *C. tenuifolia,* **Georgia hackberry,** p. 227

Planertree • Waterelm

Planera aquatica Gmel.

A small, monotypic tree growing in swampy sites on the coastal plain from North Carolina to northern Florida west to Texas and north in the Mississippi River valley to southern Illinois. Characterized by elmlike leaves, 2–3 in. long, but crenate-serrate with gland-tipped teeth and a peculiar prickly drupe ⅓ in. long, covered with odd plates and processes.

Florida Trema

Trema micrantha (L.) Blume

A small tree growing from central Florida to Central and South America. Characterized by 2-ranked, ovate, cordate, finely serrate, persistent leaves 3–4 in. long, dark green above and pale tomentose below; stout, hoary, tomentose twigs; fruit a yellow-brown drupe ⅙–⅕ in. long crowned with persistent style. West Indies trema, *T. lamarckiana* (R. & S.) Blume, reaches southern Florida.

Hackberry

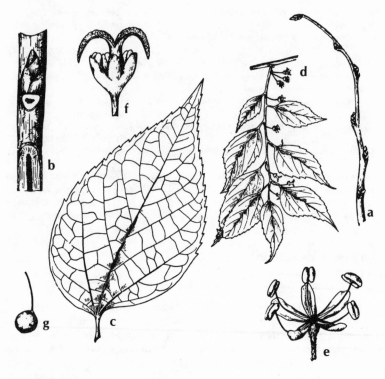

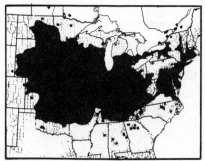

a. Winter twig, × 1
b. Portion of twig, enlarged
c. Leaf, × ¾
d. Flowering branchlet, × ½
e. Staminate flower, enlarged
f. Pistillate flower, enlarged
g. Fruit, × 1

Hackberry

Celtis occidentalis L.

HABIT. Occasionally shrubby, but often rather large tree 100–120 ft high and 1–2 ft in diameter (max. 130 by 5 ft); crown rounded, large, spreading branches.

LEAVES. Ovate to ovate-lanceolate; 2½–4 in. long; long-acuminate apex; obliquely rounded base; coarsely serrate or rarely almost entire; rather thin; light, dull green and rough above, slightly paler and pilose along veins below; turning light yellow in autumn; petioles ¼–½ in. long.

FRUIT. ⅓ in. in diameter; subglobose; ovoid, or obovoid; dark purple; stems ½–¾ in. long; thick, tough skin; dark orange-colored flesh; oblong, pointed, light brown nutlet with prominently reticulated pit.

TWIGS. Slender; ridged; light brown, becoming darker; pubescent or glabrous; marked by pale, oblong lenticels; pith often finely chambered at nodes. Winter buds: ¼ in. long; ovoid; pointed; pubescent; chestnut-brown.

BARK. Rather thick (1–1½ in.); dark brown; smooth, or more or less roughened by irregular wartlike excrescences or by long ridges.

SILVICAL CHARACTERS. Intermediate in tolerance; fast-growing; lateral roots; the largest and handsomest of the genus; frequently planted in West because of drought resistance; adapted to variety of sites, doing best on moist, rich soils, stunted and scraggly on poor, dry sites.

Lindheimer Hackberry

Celtis lindheimeri Engelm.

A small tree native only to Texas and quite similar to netleaf hackberry. Identifying characters are included in the key.

Georgia Hackberry

Celtis tenuifolia Nutt. (*Celtis pumila* var. *georgiana* [Small] Sarg.)

A shrub or small tree found on hills from Pennsylvania to Indiana, Missouri, eastern Kansas and south to Oklahoma, Louisiana, northern Florida. Identifying characters are included in the key.

Sugarberry

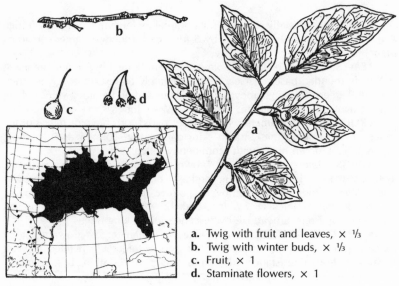

a. Twig with fruit and leaves, × ⅓
b. Twig with winter buds, × ⅓
c. Fruit, × 1
d. Staminate flowers, × 1

Netleaf Hackberry

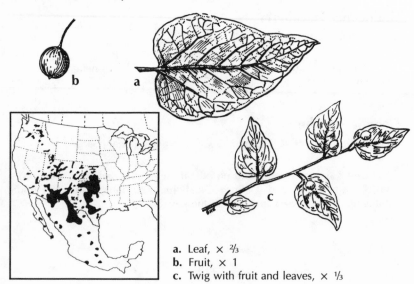

a. Leaf, × ⅔
b. Fruit, × 1
c. Twig with fruit and leaves, × ⅓

Sugarberry • Sugar Hackberry

Celtis laevigata Willd. (*Celtis mississippiensis* Bose)

HABIT. A medium-sized tree 60–80 ft high and 2–3 ft in diameter (max. 5 ft); crown rounded, spreading branches.

LEAVES. Oblong-lanceolate; 2–5 in. long; acuminate apex; obliquely rounded or cordate at base; entire or irregularly and sparingly toothed; thin; light green and smooth or slightly rough above, smooth below, with veinlets not conspicuous; petioles ¼–½ in. long.

FRUIT. ¼ in. long; subglobose; dark orange-red; on pedicels shorter or slightly longer than leaf petioles.

BARK. Rather thin (⅓–⅔ in. thick); pale gray; covered with prominent wartlike excrescences.

SILVICAL CHARACTERS. Intermediate in tolerance; fast-growing; lateral roots; site varies from moist stream banks to the variety *texana* (Scheele) Sarg. on dry rocky bluffs in West.

Netleaf Hackberry

Celtis reticulata Torr. (*Celtis douglasii* Planch.) (*Celtis laevigata* var. *brevipes* Sarg.)

HABIT. A shrub or small tree rarely 30 ft high and 1 ft in diameter; crown open with stout, ascending branches.

LEAVES. Broadly ovate; 1¼–3 in. long; acute or acuminate tips; obliquely rounded at base; margins entire or with a few coarse teeth; thick; dark green and rough or smooth above, paler below with conspicuous reticulate veinlets; petioles ⅛–½ in. long.

FRUIT. ¼ in. long; subglobose; orange-red to yellow; on pedicels longer but not twice as long as leaf petioles.

BARK. Thick; red-brown to ash-gray; rough with prominent, short, projecting ridges.

SILVICAL CHARACTERS. Moderately intolerant; on dry, rocky hillsides; a confused species including many forms previously considered distinct.

Red Mulberry

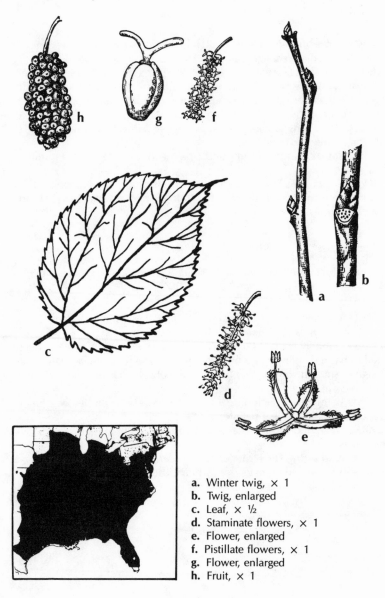

a. Winter twig, × 1
b. Twig, enlarged
c. Leaf, × ½
d. Staminate flowers, × 1
e. Flower, enlarged
f. Pistillate flowers, × 1
g. Flower, enlarged
h. Fruit, × 1

MORACEAE

The Mulberries, *Morus* L.

There are 2 native and 3 naturalized mulberries.

KEY TO THE SPECIES OF MULBERRIES

1. Fruits ovoid to cylindric; buds with 3–6 outer scales .... *Morus*
  2. Leaves usually rough above, hairy below, usually undivided on old shoots, 2½–6 in. long.
    3. Leaves truncate or slightly heart-shaped at base; fruit dark purple at maturity; native .... *M. rubra* L., **red mulberry**
    3. Leaves deeply heart-shaped at base, rarely lobed; fruit dark red; Asiatic ....
    .... *M. nigra* L., **black mulberry**
  2. Leaves smooth above, nearly glabrous below, variously lobed.
    3. Leaves 2½–7 in. long, lustrous; fruit white, pink, or violet; Chinese ....
    .... *M. alba* L., **white mulberry**
    3. Leaves 1–2 in. long; fruit nearly black; Arizona to west Texas and southern Oklahoma .... *M. microphylla* Buckl., **Texas mulberry**
1. Fruits globose, orange-red; buds with 2–3 outer scales; leaves 0- to 3-lobed, 3–8 in. long, velvety-hairy below; Asiatic ....
.... *Broussonetia papyrifera* (L.) Vent., **paper-mulberry**

Red Mulberry

Morus rubra L.

HABIT. A small tree with milky juice 20–40 ft high and 8–15 in. in diameter (max. 70 by 3½ ft); dense, round-topped crown.

LEAVES. Alternate; simple; suborbicular; 3–5 in. long; unlobed or deeply 1- to 3-lobed; margins coarsely serrate; thin; deciduous; dark blue-green, smooth, or rough above, and paler, more or less hairy below, with all veinlets hairy; stipulate.

FLOWERS. Monoecious or dioecious; minute; appearing with leaves; dense spikes; calyx 4-lobed, green; corolla absent.

FRUIT. Drupaceous; juicy; enclosed in thickened, berrylike calyx and united into a multiple fruit (syncarp) resembling a blackberry; 1–1¼ in. long; purple; oblong; edible.

TWIGS. Slender; brown; smooth; leaf scars with many bundle scars. Winter buds: terminal absent; lateral ovoid; acute; lustrous; ¼ in. long; light brown.

BARK. Thin; dark brown tinged with red; scaly and furrowed, bark of roots yellow.

WOOD. Rather heavy and hard; ring-porous; dark; unimportant.

SILVICAL CHARACTERS. Tolerant; rich, moist sites; taproot. White mulberry, extensively cultivated in United States in the past as food for silkworms, has become naturalized.

Osage-orange

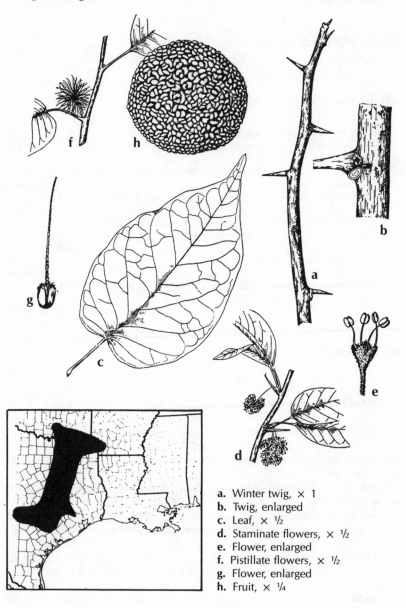

a. Winter twig, × 1
b. Twig, enlarged
c. Leaf, × ½
d. Staminate flowers, × ½
e. Flower, enlarged
f. Pistillate flowers, × ½
g. Flower, enlarged
h. Fruit, × ¼

Osage-orange

Maclura pomifera (Raf.) Schneid. (*Toxylon pomiferum* Raf.)

HABIT. A small tree with milky juice, 20–30 ft high and 1–2 ft in diameter (max. 65 by 6 ft); rounded open crown with few large, curving branches; extensively planted.

LEAVES. Alternate; simple; ovate to oblong-lanceolate; 3–5 in. long; long-pointed apex; entire; thick and firm; deciduous; dark green and shining above; paler and smooth below.

FLOWERS. Dioecious or monoecious; minute; appearing after the leaves; male in dense racemes; female in dense, globose heads; calyx 4-lobed, hairy; corolla absent.

FRUIT. Drupaceous; numerous small drupes crowded and grown together into a multiple fruit resembling an orange; 4–5 in. in diameter; pale green; containing a bitter, milky juice; becoming woody.

TWIGS. Stout; orange-brown; armed with straight, stout, axillary thorns about ½ in. long and with spurlike lateral branchlets. Winter buds: terminal absent; lateral small, globular, brown, depressed, and partially embedded in the bark.

BARK. Thin; dark orange-brown; furrowed; flat ridges.

WOOD. Hard and heavy; tough; durable; ring-porous; bright orange; used for bows; a yellow dye is extracted from the roots.

SILVICAL CHARACTERS. Intolerant; a monotypic genus with a small natural distribution, but now widely planted throughout much of the United States.

Fig

Ficus L.

Two species of fig are native to southern Florida, *Ficus aurea* Nutt., the Florida strangler fig, and *Ficus citrifolia* Mill. Vahl, the shortleaf fig. *Ficus carica* L. of western Asia is often cultivated for fruit and sometimes found as an escape in the southern states. India-rubber fig, *Ficus elastica* Roxb., is a commonly planted ornamental and possibly naturalized in south Florida. This tree has large, showy, elliptical leaves 4–12 in. long, leathery, shiny smooth, and sharp-pointed. It is the rubber-plant commonly grown indoors. The milky latex has been a source of rubber.

MAGNOLIACEAE

The Magnolias

Characteristics of the Genus *Magnolia* L.

HABIT. Handsome trees with straight stems and round-topped, pyramidal crowns; frequently planted as ornamentals.

LEAVES. Simple; alternate; deciduous or persistent; margins entire; unlobed; sometimes auriculate at base; mostly large and thin and very conspicuous.

FLOWERS. Perfect; appearing after the leaves; large and usually showy; terminal and solitary; sepals 3; petals 6–15, in series of 3, white or yellow to greenish; stamens and pistils spirally arranged, numerous.

FRUIT. A large, conelike aggregate of spirally arranged follicles; each follicle 1- to 2-seeded, the seed drupelike with a scarlet, fleshy outer coat and suspended from the cone by a long slender thread at maturity.

TWIGS. Stout; round; aromatic and somewhat bitter tasting; pith homogeneous or diaphragmed between nodes; round; conspicuously marked by large leaf scars with numerous bundle scars and narrow encircling stipular rings. Winter buds: terminal present, large, single outer scale; bud scales large, membranaceous stipules adnate to the base of the petiole and deciduous with the unfolding of each successive leaf.

BARK. Ash-gray or brown; smooth or scaly.

WOOD. Rather light and soft; diffuse-porous; light, yellow-brown heartwood; unimportant except for cucumbertree, the wood of which is often sold as yellow-poplar.

SILVICAL CHARACTERS. Intolerant; fairly fast-growing; short-lived; deep, wide root systems; typical of moist forest sites; in mixture with other hardwoods.

GENERAL. About 80 species of magnolia are native to Asia and South and North America, with 8 species native to the United States. Numerous native and Asiatic species are commonly planted through the southern part of the United States as ornamentals for their showy flowers, which in some species appear before the leaves.

KEY TO THE SPECIES OF MAGNOLIA

1. Leaves evergreen, persistent 2 years, thick and leathery, 5–8 in. long, densely red-hairy below; fruit buds, and twigs densely red or white-hairy; flowers white, fragrant, 7–8 in. across . . . . *M. grandiflora* L., **southern magnolia, p.** 237
1. Leaves deciduous (in Sweetbay semievergreen in the South); parts not densely red-hairy.
  2. Leaves 4–10 in. long; flowers 2–4 in. across.
    3. Leaves obovate-spatulate, auriculate at base; buds, twigs, and lower leaf surface glabrous; flowers creamy white; rare; coastal plain; South Carolina, Georgia, and Florida west to Louisiana and Texas . . . . *M. pyramidata* Bartr., **pyramid magnolia**
    3. Leaves elliptic to oblong-obovate; buds and lower leaf surfaces usually white-hairy.
      4. Leaves oblong-ovate to elliptic, 6–10 in. long; flowers greenish or yellow; styles deciduous from follicles of fruit . . . . *M. acuminata* L., **cucumbertree, p.** 237
      4. Leaves oblong-lanceolate to elliptic, 4–6 in. long, nearly evergreen; coastal swamps from Massachusetts to Pennsylvania, south to southern Florida and west to Texas; north in river valleys to Tennessee and Arkansas . . . . *M. virginiana* L., **sweetbay**
  2. Leaves 10–30 in. long; flowers 5 or more in. across; styles persistent on follicles of fruit.
    5. Leaves, buds, and fruit glabrous.
      6. Leaves obovate-lanceolate, wedge-shaped at base, 18–20 in. long; petioles 1–1½ in. long; terminal bud about 1 in., covered with glaucous bloom; flowers white, ill-scented; Pennsylvania to Ohio, Missouri, Oklahoma, and south . . . . *M. tripetala* L., **umbrella magnolia**
      6. Leaves obovate-spatulate, auriculate at base, 10–12 in. long; flowers pale yellow, fragrant; mountains, Virginia and Kentucky to Tennessee and Georgia . . . . *M. fraseri* Walt., **Fraser magnolia**
    5. Leaves, buds, and fruit hairy; flowers white, fragrant; petioles 3–4 in. long; buds 1¾–2 in. long, covered with thick, white tomentum.
      7. Leaves silvery-hairy on lower surface, obovate, heart-shaped at base, 20–30 in. long; fruit ovoid to globose; rare and local, North Carolina to Kentucky and Arkansas, south to Georgia and Louisiana . . . . *M. macrophylla* Michx., **bigleaf magnolia**
      7. Leaves hairy on midrib of lower surface, obovate-spatulate, 16–22 in. long; fruit ovoid-cylindric; western Florida . . . . *M. ashei* Weatherby, **ash magnolia**

Florida Anise-Tree

Illicium floridanum Ellis

An ornamental shrub or small tree with persistent, entire elliptical, long, acuminate leaves; showy, perfect flowers; distinctive, buttonlike fruit that is a flattened aggregate of follicles. Coastal plain from northwest Florida to southeastern Louisiana. Yellow anise-tree, *I. parviflorum* Michx., is local and rare in central Florida and central Alabama.

Cucumbertree

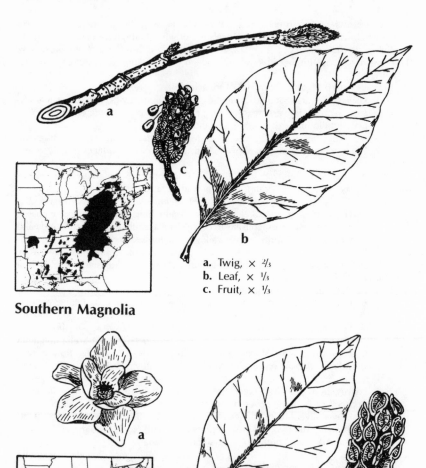

a. Twig, × ⅔
b. Leaf, × ⅓
c. Fruit, × ⅓

Southern Magnolia

a. Flower, × ⅙
b. Leaf, × ½
c. Fruit, × ⅓

Cucumbertree • Cucumber Magnolia

Magnolia acuminata L.

HABIT. A medium-sized tree 70–90 ft high and 3–4 ft in diameter (max. 100 by 6 ft); clear, straight bole; pyramidal crown with small branches.

LEAVES. Deciduous; broadly elliptical to ovate; 6–10 in. long; acute to acuminate at apex; rounded to broadly wedge-shaped at base; margin entire or slightly repand; thin; bright yellow-green and glabrous above; paler and glabrous to hairy below.

FLOWERS. Yellow-green; 2–3 in. long; not showy.

FRUIT. Conelike aggregate of follicles; cylindric to ovoid; 2–3 in. long; glabrous. Seeds: ½ in. long; red; suspended on slender, white thread.

TWIGS. Moderately stout; lustrous. Winter buds: terminal ½–¾ in. long, with white silvery hairs; lateral smaller.

BARK. Thin; dark brown; shallowly furrowed with narrow, scaly ridges.

GENERAL. The rare and local *M. cordata* (Michx.) Sarg., with yellow flowers and hairy twigs, ranges from central North Carolina to central Georgia.

Southern Magnolia • Evergreen Magnolia

Magnolia grandiflora L.

HABIT. A medium-sized tree 60–80 ft high and 2–3 ft in diameter (max. 135 by 4½ ft); clear, straight bole; pyramidal crown with small spreading branches.

LEAVES. Persistent 2 years; narrowly oval to ovate; 5–8 in. long; acute to acuminate at apex; wedge-shaped at base; margin entire; thick and leathery; bright green and lustrous above; at maturity red-woolly below.

FLOWERS. White; showy and fragrant; 6–8 in. in diameter; 6–12 large petals.

FRUIT. Conelike aggregate of follicles; ovoid; 3–4 in. long; red-woolly. Seeds: ½ in. long; red; suspended on slender, white thread.

TWIGS. Stout; red-woolly. Winter buds: terminal 1–1½ in. long, white- or red-woolly; lateral smaller.

BARK. Thin; gray to light brown; on old stems scaly with small scales rarely over 1 in. in length.

Yellow-poplar

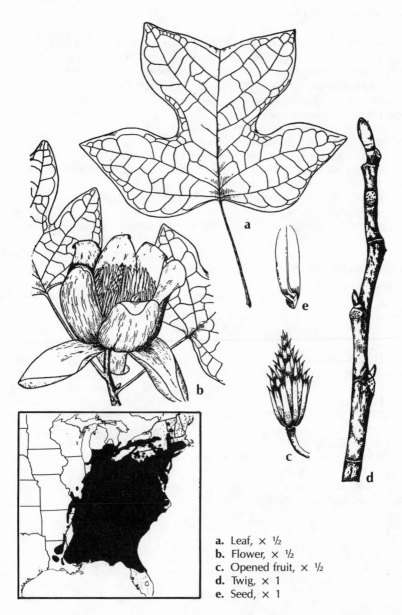

a. Leaf, × ½
b. Flower, × ½
c. Opened fruit, × ½
d. Twig, × 1
e. Seed, × 1

Yellow-poplar • Tuliptree

Liriodendron tulipifera L.

HABIT. A large, handsome tree 80–100 ft high and 4–6 ft in diameter (max. 198 by 12 ft); clear, straight bole; open, oblong, or conical crown with small branches.

LEAVES. Simple; alternate; deciduous; suborbicular; 4–6 in. long; characteristically 4-lobed, resembling a tulip in outline; lobes entire-margined; truncate at base and truncate or notched at apex; glabrous; lustrous dark green above; paler below; petioles slender; 5–6 in. long; stipules large, conspicuous.

FLOWERS. Perfect; appearing after the leaves; yellow-green; cup-shaped; 1½–2 in. long; 3 sepals; 6 petals in 2 rows; stamens and pistils numerous and spirally arranged around a central axis.

FRUIT. A large (2½–3 in. long) erect, conelike aggregate of spirally arranged samaras; each samara 1½ in. long, 4-angled, terminally winged, deciduous from the slender, more or less persistent, central axis.

TWIGS. Rather stout; lustrous red-brown; stipular scars encircling twig; bitter; pith round, diaphragmed; leaf scars round, with several bundle scars. Winter buds: terminal present, about ½ in. long, flattened, dark red or green; valvate stipular scales; only 2 outer scales visible, the entire bud resembling a duck's bill.

BARK. Smooth and dark green on young stems; becoming thick, ash-gray, furrowed, with rough, rounded ridges; inner bark bitter.

WOOD. Highly important, valuable hardwood species; rather light and soft; light yellow to dark brown heartwood; easily worked; used for plywood, furniture, interior finish, and construction work.

SILVICAL CHARACTERS. Very intolerant; fast-growing; reaches maturity at 200–250 years; deep, widespreading roots; in mixture with other hardwoods; typical of moist forest sites.

GENERAL. Only 2 species of this genus are now in existence, one a native of central China, *L. chinense* Sarg. The native species attains the greatest height of any of our broadleaf species and perhaps the greatest diameter.

California-laurel

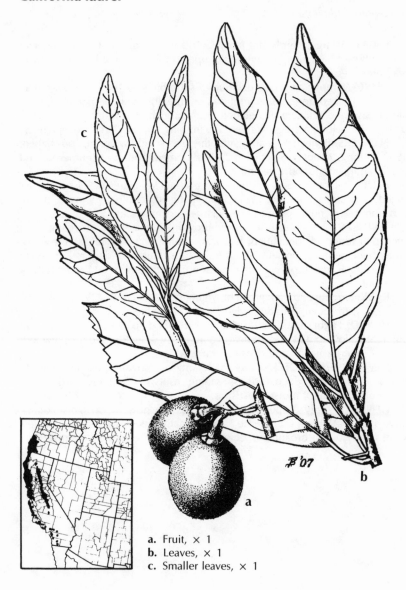

a. Fruit, × 1
b. Leaves, × 1
c. Smaller leaves, × 1

LAURACEAE

California-laurel • Oregon-myrtle

Umbellularia californica (Hook. and Arn.) Nutt.

HABIT. A small to medium-sized tree 20–80 ft high and 1–3 ft in diameter (max. 175 by 12 ft); broad, rounded, dense crown; trunk often divided; shrubby on dry sites.

LEAVES. Alternate; simple; lanceolate to elliptical; 2–5 in. long; thick and leathery; entire; glabrous; persistent 2–6 years; spicy-scented; dark green and lustrous above; paler below.

FLOWERS. Perfect; small; in umbels; appearing before the new leaves; calyx yellow-green, 6-part; corolla absent.

FRUIT. An olivelike, acrid, yellow-green, drupelike berry about 1 in. in diameter; maturing in 1 year; surrounded at base by enlarged lobes of calyx; seed ovoid, light brown.

TWIGS. Slender; yellow-green; glabrous; aromatic. Winter buds: terminal present, minute, naked.

BARK. Rather thin; dark brown; tight scales; smooth and gray-green on branches.

WOOD. Rather hard and heavy; diffuse-porous; fine-textured; lustrous light brown; expensive and highly valued for furniture, finish, and novelties; sold as myrtle wood.

SILVICAL CHARACTERS. Moderately tolerant; deep, widespreading, fleshy roots; on varied sites, but best growth on moist bottomlands; a monotypic genus.

Camphor-tree

Cinnamonum camphora (L.) Presl.

This is a widely planted Asiatic tree that has become naturalized from Florida to southern Texas. It is easily recognized by the distinctive odor of the crushed, entire, lustrous evergreen leaves and the black, lustrous, long-peduncled drupes.

Sassafras

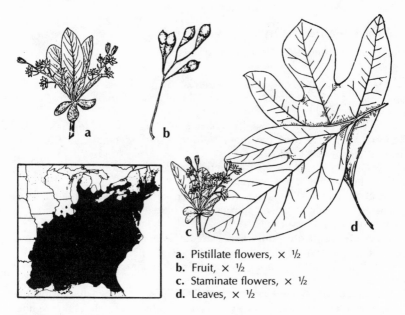

a. Pistillate flowers, × ½
b. Fruit, × ½
c. Staminate flowers, × ½
d. Leaves, × ½

Redbay

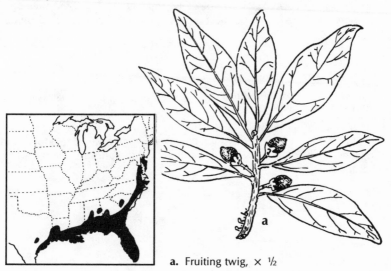

a. Fruiting twig, × ½

Sassafras

Sassafras albidum (Nutt.) Nees

HABIT. A shrub to medium-sized tree 20–50 ft high and 1–2 ft in diameter (max. 90 by 5 ft); flat, open crown.

LEAVES. Alternate; simple; deciduous; oval to obovate; aromatic; three forms on same tree, entire, 1-lobed or 3-lobed; 3–6 in. long; thin; bright green above; glabrous and glaucous below.

FLOWERS. Dioecious; small; in racemes; yellow-green; with the leaves; corolla absent.

FRUIT. Subglobose, lustrous, blue drupelike berry, ⅓ in. long; borne on bright red, club-shaped pedicel 1½–2 in. long; maturing in 1 year.

TWIGS. Rather stout; glabrous; glaucous; yellow-green; aromatic. Winter buds: terminal present, ⅓ in. long; green, 3- to 4-scaled.

BARK. Thick; red-brown; furrowed on old trunks.

SILVICAL CHARACTERS. Very intolerant; fast-growing; short-lived; indicator of poor sites; oil of sassafras distilled from roots and bark.

Redbay

Persea borbonia (L.) Spreng.

HABIT. A small to medium-sized tree, rarely 60 ft high; rounded, dense crown with stout, erect branches.

LEAVES. Alternate; simple; persistent; elliptic to lanceolate; 2–4 in. long; entire; thick; aromatic; nearly glabrous; bright green and lustrous above; paler and glaucous below.

FLOWERS. Perfect; small; yellow; panicles; no corolla.

FRUIT. Oblong, dark blue, lustrous drupelike berry, ½ in. long; on glabrous red peduncles, ½–1 in. long; calyx persistent.

TWIGS. Slender; glabrous; dark green. Winter buds: terminal present, naked, ¼ in. long, red-woolly.

BARK. Thin; dark red; furrowed and scaly.

SILVICAL CHARACTERS. Intermediate in tolerance; wet swampy sites.

GENERAL. The swampbay, *P. borbonia* var. *pubescens* (Pursh.) Little, is considered a form of redbay but differs in having lower leaf surfaces and twigs brown-woolly, peduncles 1½–2 in. long, and fruit about ¾ in. Silkbay, *P. borbonia* var. *humilis* (Nash) Kopp, is a shrubby species in central Florida. The avocado, *P. americana* Mill, is naturalized in southern Florida.

Sweetgum

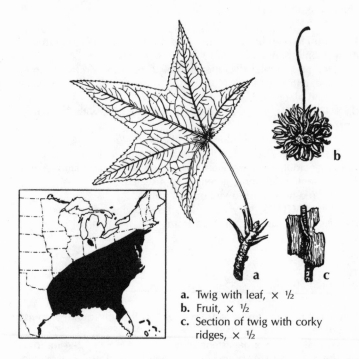

a. Twig with leaf, × ½
b. Fruit, × ½
c. Section of twig with corky ridges, × ½

Witch-hazel

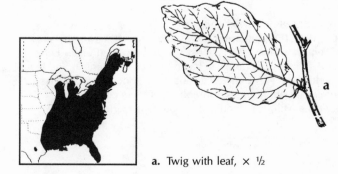

a. Twig with leaf, × ½

HAMAMELIDACEAE

Sweetgum • Redgum

Liquidambar styraciflua L.

HABIT. A medium-sized to large tree 80–120 ft high and 2–4 ft in diameter (max. 200 by 7 ft); small, oblong crown with small branches; long, clear, frequently buttressed bole.

LEAVES. Alternate; simple; deciduous; star-shaped; deeply and palmately 5- to 7-lobed; 4–7 in. long; lobes toothed and acuminate; lustrous and bright green above; paler below and glabrous except for axillary tufts of hairs; stipulate.

FLOWERS. Monoecious; both male and female in heads; male in terminal racemes 2–3 in. long without calyx or corolla; female in solitary, long-stalked heads, minute calyx, and 2-celled ovary; appearing with leaves.

FRUIT. A multiple, globose fruit 1–1½ in. in diameter, of woody, 2-celled, beaked capsules; maturing in 1 year but persistent through the winter; 2 seeds in each capsule, each about ⅜ in. long with a short terminal wing.

TWIGS. Slender to stout; round or slightly angled; frequently developing corky wings during the second year; green to red-brown; pith angled and homogeneous. Winter buds: terminal present, ¼–½ in. long, ovate, orange-brown, scaly.

BARK. Thick; gray-brown; deeply furrowed, with narrow, rounded, and somewhat scaly ridges.

WOOD. Very important, exceeded only among hardwoods by oaks in volume of timber cut; diffuse-porous; fairly hard and heavy; heartwood dark red-brown and often figured; used for veneer, lumber, furniture, and containers.

SILVICAL CHARACTERS. Very intolerant; on rich moist bottomlands or swampy sites; wide, shallow, lateral roots; reproduction aggressive; storax gum, for drugs and soaps, obtained from bark. This genus is composed of 4 species, 2 in Asia and 1 in Central America.

Witch-hazel

Hamamelis virginiana L.

Witch-hazel is a distinctive shrub or small tree found through the eastern United States. It is characterized by conspicuous, perfect, yellow, autumnal flowers; woody, 2-valved capsules from which the black seeds are forcibly ejected; simple, alternate, deciduous, oval leaves, 4–6 in. long, which are crenately toothed or lobed and smooth; and naked buds, ¼–½ in. long.

American Sycamore

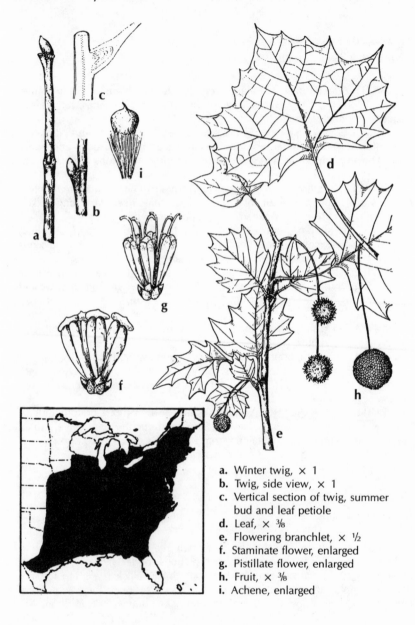

a. Winter twig, × 1
b. Twig, side view, × 1
c. Vertical section of twig, summer bud and leaf petiole
d. Leaf, × ⅜
e. Flowering branchlet, × ½
f. Staminate flower, enlarged
g. Pistillate flower, enlarged
h. Fruit, × ⅜
i. Achene, enlarged

PLATANACEAE

The Sycamores, *Platanus* L.

This is a monotypic family with a single genus and 8 or 9 species. The following key distinguishes between 3 native and 2 widely planted species.

KEY TO THE SPECIES OF SYCAMORES

1. Heads of fruit solitary or in pairs; leaves not deeply lobed.
   2. Leaf lobes broader than long; fruit heads usually single; bark creamy-white to brown .... *P. occidentalis* L., **American sycamore**
   2. Leaf lobes about as long as broad; 2 (rarely 3) fruit heads per stem; bark olive-green .... *P.* X *acerifolia* Willd., **London planetree**
1. Heads of fruit usually 3 or more; leaves deeply lobed.
   2. Leaves mostly 5- to 7-lobed, glabrous to hairy below; Eurasian .... *P. orientalis* L., **oriental planetree**
   2. Leaves woolly below; native and western.
      3. Arizona and New Mexico; leaves 5- to 7-lobed .... *P. wrightii* S. Wats., **Arizona sycamore**
      3. California; leaves 3- to 5-lobed .... *P. racemosa* Nutt., **California sycamore**

American Sycamore • Planetree

Platanus occidentalis L.

HABIT. A large tree 70–100 ft high and 3–8 ft in diameter (max. 175 by 14 ft); with yellow-poplar the largest of eastern hardwoods; long, clear bole.

LEAVES. Alternate; simple; deciduous; broadly ovate; 3- to 5-lobed; 4–7 in. long; lobe margins coarsely toothed; thin and firm; bright green and smooth above; paler and hairy along the veins below; petioles 2–3 in. long; stipules leaflike.

FLOWERS. Monoecious; both male and female in heads with minute individual flowers, each containing 3–8 sepals and petals; appearing with the leaves.

FRUIT. A multiple, globose fruit 1–1¼ in. in diameter; of elongated, obovoid achenes with spur at apex and ring of erect hairs around base; maturing in 1 year; borne singly on stems 3–6 in. long.

TWIGS. Stout; round; orange-brown; lustrous; encircled by stipular scars; pith round, homogeneous. Winter buds: terminal absent; lateral ¼–⅜ in., conical, brown, single visible scale, formed in petiole base.

BARK. Red-brown and scaly near base; thin and characteristically mottled on upper trunk by exfoliating outer layers that expose lighter colored inner layers.

WOOD. Intermediate in importance; diffuse-porous with broad rays; fairly hard and heavy; heartwood light red-brown; used for boxes, cooperage, vehicles, furniture, ties, and fuel.

SILVICAL CHARACTERS. Very intolerant; fast-growing; on moist sites; shallow, lateral roots; withstands smoke.

ROSACEAE

The Apples

Characteristics of the Genus *Malus* Mill.

HABIT. Shrubs to medium-sized trees, the native species having little or no importance; broad, rounded, open crowns.

LEAVES. Alternate; simple; deciduous, or rarely half-evergreen; toothed and in native species more or less lobed; stipules free from the petioles, early deciduous; petiolate.

FLOWERS. Regular; perfect; in short terminal racemes; on spurlike, sometimes spinescent branches; appearing with or after the leaves; calyx 5-lobed, sometimes persistent and erect on fruit; petals white to red, showy; stamens 15–50; ovary inferior, usually with 5 carpels.

FRUIT. A fleshy pome with papery carpels joined at their apex; indehiscent; important as food in some species. Seeds: 1–2 in each cell; ovoid; acute; chestnut-brown.

TWIGS. Slender to stout; round; frequently spiny or with spinescent spur shoots; fruit spurs roughened by leaf scars with 3 bundle scars. Winter buds: terminal present, small, scaly, obtuse.

BARK. Thin; scaly; gray to red-brown; often fissured.

WOOD. Heavy; hard; fine-textured; diffuse-porous; heartwood red-brown; used to some extent for tool handles.

GENERAL. This taxonomically difficult genus contains about 25 species scattered through the Northern Hemisphere. The 6 species native to North America are unimportant; however, several Eurasian species are widely cultivated for their fruits or flowers. The common apple, *M. sylvestris* (L.) Mill. (*M. pumila* Mill.), was introduced in colonial times and has escaped and become naturalized. Many authors combine *Malus* with *Pyrus*, the name for apple becoming *Pyrus malus* L.

KEY TO THE SPECIES OF APPLE

1. Leaves never lobed, rolled up in bud; naturalized.
   2. Calyx persistent on fruit; leaves hairy below; fruit 1 in. or more in diameter . . .
      . . . . *M. sylvestris* (L.) Mill., **apple,** p. 251
   2. Calyx deciduous from fruit; leaves glabrous; fruit ⅓–½ in. in diameter; introduced
      from Asia . . . . *M. baccata* (L.) Borkh., **Siberian crab apple**
1. Leaves more or less lobed, at least on vigorous shoots, folded in bud; native.
   3. Eastern; calyx persistent on green (rarely yellow) waxy fruit.
      4. Leaves and calyx woolly; Great Plains, Wisconsin, and Minnesota to Louisiana
         and Texas . . . . *M. ioensis* (Wood) Britt., **prairie crab apple**
      4. Mature leaves and calyx not woolly.
         5. Leaves on vigorous shoots distinctly and deeply lobed . . . .
            . . . . *M. coronaria* (L.) Mill., **sweet crab apple,** p. 251
         5. Leaves on vigorous shoots, slightly lobed; Virginia to Arkansas, Illinois,
            south to Florida and Louisiana . . . .
            . . . . *M. angustifolia* (Ait.) Michx., **southern crab apple**
   3. West Coast; calyx deciduous on yellow to red nonwaxy fruit; Alaska to northwest
      California . . . . *M. fusca* (Raf.) Schneid., **Oregon crab apple**

Torrey Vauquelinia

Vauquelinia californica (Torr.) Sarg.

This is a shrub or small tree rarely 20 ft high, native to southern Arizona, southwestern New Mexico, and northern Mexico. It is characterized by simple, persistent, lanceolate leaves 1½–3 in. long, with remote, small, glandular teeth; small, regular, perfect, white flowers borne in leafy, woolly panicles; and a woody, ovoid, capsular, 5-celled fruit about ¼ in. long, which is woolly, subtended by the remnants of the flower, and long persistent on the branches.

The similar fewflower vauquelinia, *V. pauciflora* Standl., is reported from southeast Arizona and southwest New Mexico.

Sweet Crab Apple

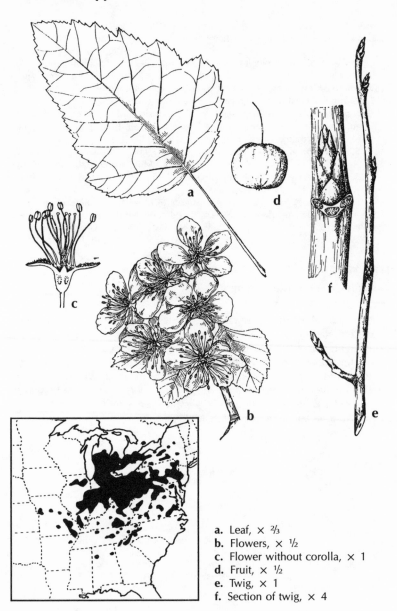

a. Leaf, × ²/₃
b. Flowers, × ½
c. Flower without corolla, × 1
d. Fruit, × ½
e. Twig, × 1
f. Section of twig, × 4

Sweet Crab Apple

Malus coronaria (L.) Mill. (*Pyrus coronaria* L.)

HABIT. A bushy shrub or small tree 15–30 ft high and ½-1 ft in diameter; crown broad, rounded, and bushy.

LEAVES. Ovate to ovate-oblong; 3–4 in. long; 3-lobed on vigorous shoots; sharply and deeply toothed; thin and smooth; dark green above; paler below; petioles long and slender.

FLOWERS. Handsome; fragrant; 1¼–2 in. across; white to rose-colored; in 5- to 6-flowered umbel-like racemes; appearing after the leaves.

FRUIT. Pome depressed-globose; 1–1½ in. in diameter; pale to yellow-green; waxy; fragrant; flesh very tart; ripening in late autumn, often remaining on tree until spring.

TWIGS. Rather stout; developing short, stout, often spinelike spurs; red-brown. Winter buds: terminal ⅛–¼ in. long, scaly, bright red.

BARK. Thin; red-brown; divided by shallow fissures into broad, scaly ridges.

SILVICAL CHARACTERS. Intolerant; rich, moist sites along streams or in thickets along roads and fences; fibrous roots; planted as an ornamental for its showy flowers.

Apple

Malus sylvestris (L.) Mill. (*Malus pumila* Mill.) (*Pyrus malus* L.)

This species, native to Eurasia, is the parent of most of our cultivated apples and has escaped in many parts of North America. It is stated that over 3,000 varieties of this species have been developed by pomologists. The apple is a small to medium-sized tree that can be identified from its unlobed, cre-nate-serrate to entire, thick leaves that are hairy below and rolled up in the bud.

Common Pear

Pyrus communis L.

This Eurasian species is widely cultivated for its fruit and is a common escape in North America. In addition to its distinctive "pear-shaped" poma-ceous fruit, it differs from the closely related apple in having more lustrous, thinner, and less hairy leaves.

American Mountain-ash

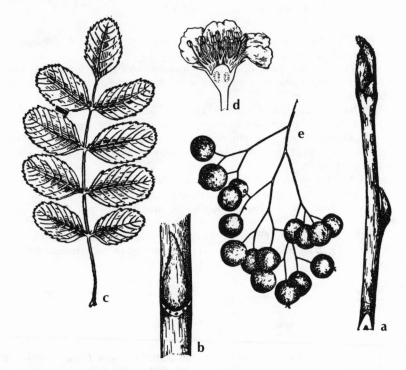

a. Winter twig, × 1
b. Portion of twig, enlarged
c. Leaf, × ½
d. Vertical section of flower, enlarged
e. Portion of a fruiting cyme, × 1

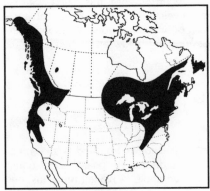

Eastern: *S. americana*
Western: *S. sitchensis*

The Mountain-ashes, *Sorbus* L.

There are about 80 species of trees and shrubs in North America and Eurasia, with 4 native and 1 naturalized species reaching tree size in North America. The taxonomy in this genus is confused. The related western species, *S. sitchenis* Roem., is usually a shrub; its distribution is included in the map.

KEY TO THE SPECIES OF MOUNTAIN-ASHES

1. Winter buds densely covered with long white hairs; leaflets 1–2 in. long, oblong; widely planted and naturalized through the northern United States and Canada . . . . *S. aucuparia* L., **European mountain-ash**
1. Winter buds glabrous or slightly hairy; leaflets 1½–4 in. long; native.
    2. Eastern and far northern.
        3. Winter buds glabrous or slightly white-hairy; leaflets usually lanceolate and acuminate . . . . *S. americana* Marsh., **American mountain-ash**
        3. Winter buds slightly red-hairy; leaflets oblong, short-pointed; distribution similar to *S. americana* but extending to Greenland and not in Appalachian Mountains . . . . *S. decora* Schneid., **showy mountain-ash**
    2. Western and far northern, seldom reaching tree size.
        4. Leaflets with rounded or blunt points, serrate above middle . . . . *S. sitchensis* Roem., **Sitka mountain-ash**
        4. Leaflets very sharp-pointed, serrate nearly to base; widely distributed from Alaska to California and east to South Dakota . . . . *S. scopulina* Greene, **Greene mountain-ash**

American Mountain-ash

Sorbus americana Marsh. (*Pyrus americana* DC.)

HABIT. A shrub or small tree, seldom 30 ft high and 12 in. in diameter; crown round-topped, handsome; spreading.

LEAVES. Alternate; pinnately compound in native species; 6–8 in. long; 7–17 mostly sessile leaflets; oblong-oval to lanceolate; 2–4 in. long and ½–1 in. wide; serrate; glabrous; dark green above; pale below; deciduous.

FLOWERS. Regular; perfect; small; in broad, flat cymes 3–5 in. across; on short, stout pedicels; appearing after leaves; 5 petals, cream-white, ¼ in.

FRUIT. Berrylike pome; subglobose; ¼–½ in. in diameter; bright orange-red; thin, acrid flesh; papery carpels. Seeds: 1 or 2 in each cell; ⅛ in. long; ovoid; brown.

TWIGS. Stout; round; red-brown and pubescent, becoming dark brown and glabrous; marked by large pith, large leaf scars, and oblong lenticels. Winter buds: terminal ¼–¾ in. long, acute, dark red, pilose, sticky with a gummy exudation.

BARK. Thin (⅛ in.); light gray; smooth or slightly roughened by scales; inner bark fragrant.

WOOD. Light; soft; weak; close-grained; diffuse-porous; heartwood pale brown; sapwood thick and lighter colored.

SILVICAL CHARACTERS. Intolerant; slow-growing; short-lived, abundant seeder; fibrous roots; prefers moist sites, but grows well on rocky hillsides; often cultivated.

Downy Serviceberry

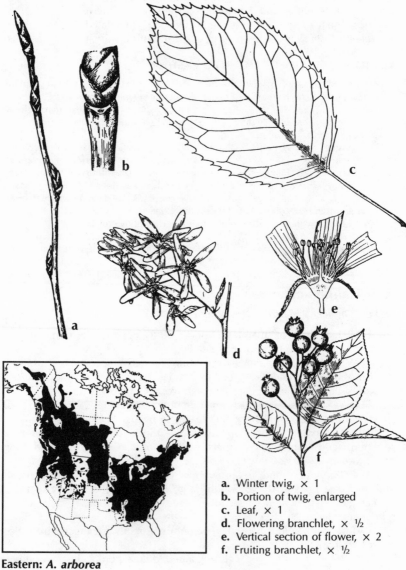

a. Winter twig, × 1
b. Portion of twig, enlarged
c. Leaf, × 1
d. Flowering branchlet, × ½
e. Vertical section of flower, × 2
f. Fruiting branchlet, × ½

Eastern: *A. arborea*
Western: *A. alnifolia*

Downy Serviceberry • Shad Bush

Amelanchier arborea (Michx.) Fern. (*Amelanchier laevis* Wieg.)

HABIT. A shrub or small tree 25–40 ft high and 8–14 in. in diameter (max. 70 by 2 ft); crown open.

LEAVES. Alternate; simple; oblong-ovate to oval or ovate; 2–4 in. long; acute at apex; finely serrate; dark green and glabrous above; pale below; deciduous; petioles slender.

FLOWERS. Regular; perfect; in erect, crowded racemes; appearing with leaves; calyx tube persistent on fruit; corolla white, ½–¾ in. long, of 5 strap-shaped petals.

FRUIT. Berrylike pome; globose; ¼–½ in. in diameter; dark red to purple; more or less covered with glaucous bloom; flesh sweet; open at summit. Seeds: 5–10; dark chestnut-brown.

TWIGS. Slender; round; red-brown to dark gray; narrow leaf scars, 3 bundle scars. Winter buds: terminal ¼–½ in. long, conical, acute or acuminate, chestnut-brown.

BARK. Thin (⅛ in.); light brown, tinged with red; smooth or slightly furrowed with scaly ridges.

WOOD. Heavy; hard; close-grained; diffuse-porous; heartwood light brown; sapwood thick, light; unimportant.

SILVICAL CHARACTERS. Tolerant when young; abundant seeder; deep fibrous roots; capable of sprouting repeatedly; moist valleys and borders of streams to dry mountain slopes.

GENERAL. The taxonomy within this genus is confused, relatively minor characters being used to separate species, with hybrids and intermediates common. The western serviceberry, *A. alnifolia* Nutt., is included on the map. Two other shrubby species have been reported to reach tree size: *A. sanguinea* (Pursh) DC. in the East and *A. utahensis* Koehne in the mountains of the West.

Black Hawthorn

a. Twig with leaves and flowers, × 1
b. Twig with fruit, × 1
c. Diagram of flower, × 2

The Hawthorns

Characteristics of the Genus *Crataegus* L.

HABIT. Deciduous shrubs or small trees; usually spiny; crown generally rounded, widespreading.

LEAVES. Alternate; simple; deciduous; usually serrate and often more or less lobed; membranaceous to coriaceous; stipules persistent until autumn or deciduous in spring, small to leaflike, often bright-colored; petiolate.

FLOWERS. Regular; perfect, in few- or many-flowered terminal corymbs; pedicellate; calyx 5-lobed, tubular, persistent on fruit or deciduous; corolla 5-petaled, white, inserted on edge of disk lining calyx tube; stamens 5–25; ovary inferior, of 1–5 carpels connate at base, with 2 ovules in each cell; styles as many as carpels.

FRUIT. Small, variously colored pome with 1–5 bony, 1-seeded nutlets; flesh usually dry and mealy; generally open or concave at apex.

TWIGS. Round; rigid; more or less zigzag; generally armed with stiff, sharp thorns; marked by oblong lenticels and small leaf scars. Winter buds: terminal usually present, small, globose, scaly, lustrous brown.

BARK. Dark red to gray; scaly or shallowly furrowed.

WOOD. Heavy; hard; tough; close-grained; diffuse-porous; heartwood red-brown; sapwood thick, light-colored; unimportant; used for tool handles, canes, turned articles.

SILVICAL CHARACTERS. Intolerant; reproduction aggressive; slow-growing.

GENERAL. An extremely large, unstable, and complex genus; various authors have named over 1,000 species; the identification to species presents great difficulty even to the specialist; hybridizing is common. In the 1979 USDA checklist the number of species reaching tree size has been reduced to 35. The black hawthorn, *C. douglasii* Lindl., which is common through the West, has been pictured on the opposite page as being typical of the genus. Many species are found in the East.

Curlleaf Mountain-mahogany

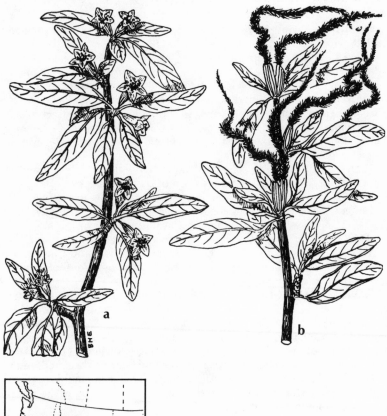

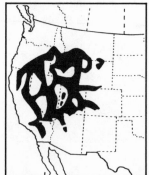

a. Twig with leaves and flowers, × 1
b. Twig with fruit, × 1

The Mountain-mahoganies, *Cercocarpus* H. B. K.

Five species of this shrubby western genus occasionally reach tree size. Three are keyed out below. In addition, *C. traskige* Eastw. is very rare on Santa Catalina Island, California. *C. montanus* Raf. is scattered through the Rocky Mountain region, rarely becoming a small tree in Utah.

KEY TO THE SPECIES OF MOUNTAIN-MAHOGANY, *CERCOCARPUS*

1. Leaves entire, lanceolate, leathery, persistent; flowers solitary or in 2's or 3's . . . . .
   . . . . *C. ledifolius* Nutt., **curlleaf mountain-mahogany**
1. Leaves usually somewhat toothed, elliptic to broadly obovate, deciduous.
   2. Leaves entire or slightly toothed near apex; flowers solitary or in 2's or 3's; Texas to Arizona and south . . . . *C. breviflorus* Gray., **hairy mountain-mahogany**
   2. Leaves with numerous teeth above the middle; flowers in many-flowered racemes; Oregon and California to Arizona and Mexico . . . .
   . . . . *C. betuloides* Nutt., **birchleaf mountain-mahogany**

Curlleaf Mountain-mahogany

Cercocarpus ledifolius Nutt.

HABIT. A shrub or small tree rarely 40 ft high and 12 in. in diameter; trunk short and crooked; crown round and compact with stout, more or less crooked, spreading branches.

LEAVES. Alternate; simple; lanceolate to lanceolate-elliptic; ½–1 in. long; acute; entire; coriaceous; revolute margins; dark green and lustrous above; pale and tomentulose below; resinous; persistent for 2 years; short-petiolate.

FLOWERS. Regular; perfect; solitary; inconspicuous; sessile in axils of leaves; calyx tube long, hoary-tomentose, whitish; corolla absent; stamens 15–30, in 2–3 rows; free; ovary inferior.

FRUIT. Linear-oblong, coriaceous achene ¼ in. long, enclosed in persistent calyx tube ½ in. long; chestnut-brown; covered with long hairs; tipped with persistent, hairy, elongated style 2–3 in. long. Seeds: solitary; linear; acute.

TWIGS. Stout; round; rigid; red-brown and pubescent at first, becoming dark brown or silver-gray and glabrous; spurlike lateral branches. Winter buds: minute, scaly, pubescent.

BARK. Thick on old trunks (1 in.); red-brown; hard; firm.

WOOD. Exceedingly heavy and hard; brittle; close-grained; diffuse-porous; heartwood red or dark brown; unimportant.

SILVICAL CHARACTERS. Intolerant; rather long-lived; slow-growing; on dry, gravelly, windswept slopes.

The Cherries, Plums, and Peaches

Characteristics of the Genus *Prunus* L.

HABIT. Shrubs or usually small trees, only a few species reaching sizes of commerical importance.

LEAVES. Alternate; simple; deciduous or persistent; usually serrate, rarely entire; stipules free from petiole, early deciduous; petiolate.

FLOWERS. Regular; perfect or rarely dioecious; solitary or in terminal or axillary racemes, corymbs, or umbels; appearing from separate buds with, before, or after leaves; calyx 5-lobed, tubular; corolla 5-petaled, usually white, deciduous, stamens usually 15–20; ovary inserted in bottom of calyx tube, inferior or superior, 1-celled, 2-ovuled.

FRUIT. Thin dry, or thick fleshy, 1-seeded drupe; stone bony, smooth or rugose; indehiscent; important as food in several species. Seeds: filling cavity of nut; suspended; thin-coated, pale brown.

TWIGS. Slender or stout; round; astringent; often with spinescent spur branches; red to brown; marked by lenticels, stipular scars, usually by small, elevated, horizontal leaf scars with 3 bundle scars. Winter buds: terminal present or absent; lateral nearly equal in size; scales imbricated, the inner accrescent and often colored.

BARK. Astringent; gray to dark brown; plated or scaly.

WOOD. From light to heavy and hard; fine-textured; diffuse-porous; durable; heartwood light or dark brown, often reddish; sapwood lighter colored; a few species important for timber.

GENERAL. About 30 species of *Prunus* are native to North America, 18 being arborescent at times. Seven introduced species, 4 of which are highly important fruit trees, have become naturalized in parts of the United States and Canada. These species are included in the key: *P. avium* (L.) L., Mazzard cherry; *P. cerasus* L., sour cherry; *P. domestica* L., garden plum; *P. insititia* L., Damson plum; *P. mahaleb* L., Mahaleb cherry; *P. persica* (L.) Batsch, peach; and *P. spinosa* L., sloe or blackthorn. The almond, *P. amygdalus* Batsch, and the apricot, *P. armeniaca* L., while not nauturalized, are commonly planted in warmer regions. As with other cultivated fruits, these have been improved until there are numerous forms or varieties. The commonly planted ornamental flowering almond, *P. triloba* Lindl., is a shrub or small tree.

KEY TO THE SPECIES OF CHERRIES, PLUMS, AND PEACHES

1. Fruit usually over ½ in. in diameter and usually slightly 2-lobed by ventral groove.
  2. Terminal bud present; fruit and ovary hairy; naturalized . . . .
  . . . . *P. persica*, **peach,** p. 263
  2. Terminal bud absent; fruit and ovary glabrous . . . . **plums**
    3. Leaves rolled up in bud; flowers 1 or 2; naturalized.
      4. Twigs glabrous; fruit 1 in. across . . . . *P. domestica,* **garden plum,** p. 269
      4. Twigs hairy or woolly; fruit about ½ in. across.
        5. Flowers single; buds round . . . . *P. spinosa* L., **sloe**
        5. Flowers in 2's; buds ovate . . . . *P. insititia,* **Damson plum,** p. 269
    3. Leaves folded in bud (except Klamath plum); flowers 3 to many; native.
      6. Oregon and California; leaves round-ovate, rolled in bud . . . .
      . . . . *P. subcordata* Benth., **Klamath plum**
      6. East of Pacific Coast; leaves ovate to lanceolate.
        7. Leaves with sharp teeth, dull dark green above.
          8. Leaves lanceolate to elliptic; fruit purple, glaucous.
            9. Fruit stone turgid; calyx hairy; Connecticut to Tennessee . . . . .
            . . . . *P. alleghanensis* Port., **Allegheny plum**
            9. Fruit stone flattened; calyx glabrous; North Carolina to Florida,
            Texas and Arkansas . . . . *P. umbellata* Ell., **flatwoods plum**
          8. Leaves oblong to obovate; fruit red to yellow; stone flattened.
            10. Leaves hairy below; twigs hairy; central and southern in to
            Mexico . . . . *P. mexicana* Wats., **Mexican plum**
            10. Leaves nearly glabrous below; twigs glabrous; Canada to
            Florida, west to the Rocky Mountains . . . .
            . . . . *P. americana,* **American plum,** p. 269
        7. Leaves with dull, rounded teeth.
          11. Leaves dull green, elliptic to obovate, coarsely or doubly toothed;
          stone flattened . . . . *P. nigra,* **Canada plum,** p. 269
          11. Leaves lustrous, thin, ovate to lanceolate, finely toothed; stones
          turgid; eastern and midwestern.
            12. Leaves 2½–6 in. long; fruit ¼–1 in.; calyx glandular.
              13. Leaves oblong to obovate . . . .
              . . . . *P. hortulana* Bail, **hortulan plum**
              13. Leaves elliptic to lanceolate . . . .
              . . . . *P. munsoniana* W. & H., **wildgoose plum**
            12. Leaves 1–2 in. long; fruit ½ in.; calyx lobes without glands
            . . . . *P. angustifolia* Marsh., **Chickasaw plum**
1. Fruit seldom ½ in. across, not lobed; leaves folded in bud; terminal bud present . .
. . . . **cherries**
  14. Flowers solitary or few, in umbels or corymbs.
    15. Calyx persistnet on fruit; naturalized.
      16. Leaves thin, 2½–5 in. long, hairy below at least along veins; fruit sweet
      . . . . *P. avium,* **Mazzard cherry,** p. 263
      16. Leaves semileathery, 2–3 in. long, glabrous; fruit sour . . . .
      . . . . *P. cerasus* L., **sour cherry,** p. 263
    15. Calyx deciduous from fruit.
      17. Leaves orbicular to broad-ovate; naturalized . . . .
      . . . . *P. mahaleb* L., **Mahaleb cherry**
      17. Leaves narrower; native.
        18. Leaves oblong-obovate; Montana and British Columbia to Arizona
        and New Mexico . . . . *P. emarginata,* **bitter cherry,** p. 267

        18. Leaves oblong-lanceolate; Newfoundland to British Columbia, south to Georgia, Iowa, Colorado . . . .
. . . . *P. pensylvanica,* **pin cherry,** p. 267

14. Flowers 12 or more in elongated racemes.
    19. Leaves deciduous; flowers in terminal, usually leafy racemes.
        20. Calyx deciduous from fruit; leaves oblong-oval to obovate, with spreading teeth; entire area . . . *P. virginiana,* **common chokecherry,** p. 265
        20 Calyx persistent on fruit; leaves oblong-lanceolate with incurved teeth
. . . . *P. serotina,* **black cherry,** p. 265
    19. Leaves persistent; flowers in axillary, leafless racemes.
        21. Southeast; leaves entire or rarely with a few small spiny teeth.
            22. Leaves elliptic to ovate; southern Florida . . . .
. . . . *P. myrtifolia* Urb., **West Indies cherry**
            22. Leaves oblong-lanceolate; North Carolina to Texas in coastal plain
. . . . *P. caroliniana* Ait., **Carolina laurelcherry**
        21. California.
            23. Leaves spiny toothed . . . . *P. ilicifolia* Dietr., **hollyleaf cherry**
            23. Leaves entire or minutely toothed . . . .
. . . . *P. lyonii* Sarg., **Catalina cherry**

Peach

Prunus persica (L.) Batsch (*Amygdalus persica* L.)

This small Asiatic tree with its many improved varieties produces the peaches of commerce. It has escaped from cultivation, mostly along roads or fences. The peach differs from other subgenera of *Prunus* in having large, grooved, hairy fruits; 1–2 sessile flowers with hairy ovaries; and scaly buds with the terminal present and separate lateral flower buds.

Almond

Prunus amygdalus Batsch

A small Asiatic tree cultivated for the edible kernels of the stone in the drupaceous fruit. This species is restricted to warm climates. This tree closely resembles the peach, differing from it in that the fruit becomes dry and splits open at maturity. The commonly planted flowering almond, *P. triloba* Lindl., is a handsome, pink-flowered shrub or small tree native to China. The desert almond, *P. fasciculata* Gray, is a shrub or rarely a small tree native to the Southwest.

Sour Cherry

Prunus cerasus L.

This native of southeastern Europe and Asia is widely naturalized as an escape through much of North America. It is important as the source of numerous varieties of canning cherries.

Mazzard • Sweet Cherry

Prunus avium (L.) L.

Native to Europe and Asia, but widely naturalized through North America, this species is widely cultivated for its garden cherries.

Apricot

Prunus armeniaca L.

This small to medium-sized tree, native to western Asia, is widely planted for its distinctive fruits. It closely resembles the peach in its hairy, grooved fruit, but differs from it in having no terminal bud and solitary axillary buds, and in having broad-ovate leaves rolled up in the bud. The native desert apricot, *P. fremontii* Wats., is restricted to southern and Baja California.

Black Cherry

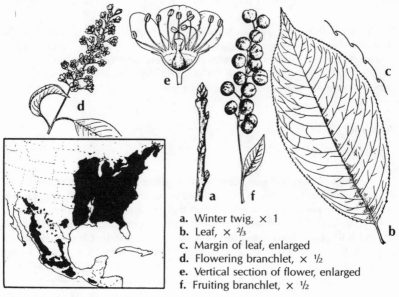

a. Winter twig, × 1
b. Leaf, × ⅔
c. Margin of leaf, enlarged
d. Flowering branchlet, × ½
e. Vertical section of flower, enlarged
f. Fruiting branchlet, × ½

Common Chokecherry

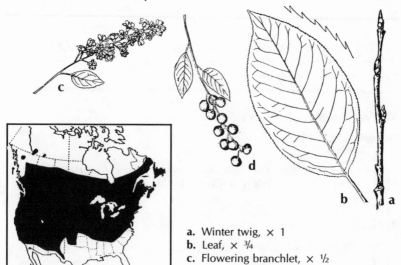

a. Winter twig, × 1
b. Leaf, × ¾
c. Flowering branchlet, × ½
d. Fruiting branchlet, × ½

Black Cherry

Prunus serotina Ehrh.

HABIT. A medium-sized tree 40–60 ft high and 1–3 ft in diameter (max. 100 by 5 ft); clear bole and narrow, oblong crown.

LEAVES. Oval to oblong-lanceolate; thick; acuminate or acute at apex; finely serrate with incurved callous teeth; dark green and lustrous above; paler, with red-brown hairs along base of midrib below; 2–6 in. long; petioles short, usually with 2 glands near blade.

FLOWERS. In many-flowered, loose racemes, 4–5 in. long; appearing with the leaves; calyx cup-shaped, persistent on fruit; petals 5, white, about ⅛ in. long.

FRUIT. Globose; in racemes; ⅓–½ in. in diameter; nearly black when ripe; flesh juicy, edible, slightly bitter.

TWIGS. Slender; round; glabrous; red-brown; bitter and aromatic; short spur shoots common on old growth. Winter buds: terminal ¼ in. long; ovoid, scaly, light brown.

BARK. Thin; smooth and red-brown with horizontal lenticels on young stems; nearly black and exfoliating into distinctive, persistent scales with up-turned edges on old trunks.

WOOD. Moderately important; rather heavy and hard; diffuse-porous; heartwood red-brown; a prized and valuable furniture wood.

SILVICAL CHARACTERS. Intermediate in tolerance; typical of rich, moist sites; usually in mixed stands; long taproot.

Common Chokecherry

Prunus virginiana L.

This shrub or small tree is one of the most widely distributed in North America. It closely resembles black cherry, but can be distinguished by usually red fruit without persistent calyx; thin leaves, with sharply serrate, spreading teeth; and smooth or slightly fissured bark. The western forms are designated as either western chokecherry, *P. virginiana* var. *demissa* (Nutt.) Torr., or black chokecherry, *P. virginiana* var. *melanocarpa* (A. Nels.) Sarg.

Pin Cherry

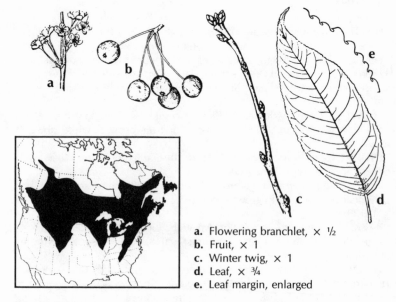

a. Flowering branchlet, × ½
b. Fruit, × 1
c. Winter twig, × 1
d. Leaf, × ¾
e. Leaf margin, enlarged

Bitter Cherry

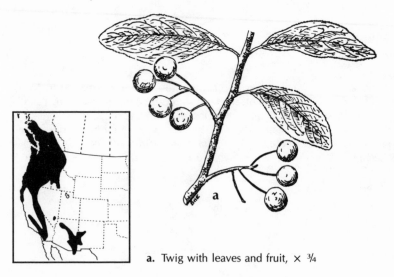

a. Twig with leaves and fruit, × ¾

Pin Cherry • Wild Red Cherry

Prunus pensylvanica L.

HABIT. A shrub or small tree rarely 30–40 ft high and 18–20 in. in diameter; short trunk; crown narrow, rounded or flat-topped, with slender, horizontal branches.

LEAVES. Obovate to oblong-lanceolate; acuminate or acute at apex; sharply and coarsely serrate, with incurved teeth; glabrous; bright green and lustrous above, paler below; 3–4 in. long and 1–2 in. broad; turning bright yellow in autumn; petiole slender; glabrous, or pilose.

FLOWERS. In 2- to 5-flowered, sessile umbels; on slender pedicels nearly 1 in. long; appearing when leaves half grown; calyx tube glabrous, marked by conspicuous orange band in mouth of throat; corolla cream-white, ½ in. in diameter.

FRUIT. Globose; in 2- to 5-fruited umbels; ¼–⅓ in. in diameter; on slender pedicels; light red; thick-skinned; flesh thin, quite sour; occasionally made into jelly; stone oblong, thin-walled, pointed, ³⁄₁₆ in. long, ridged.

TWIGS. Slender; round; puberulous and light red at first, becoming glabrous and bright to dull red; marked by orange-colored, raised lenticels; bark easily separable from green inner bark; lateral branchlets short, spurlike. Winter buds: terminal ⅛ in. long, acute, ovoid, bright red-brown.

BARK. Thin (⅓–½ in.); red-brown, marked by orange-colored bands of lenticels; smooth or scaly.

WOOD. Light; soft; close-grained; heartwood light brown; sapwood thin, yellow; unimportant.

SILVICAL CHARACTERS. Intolerant; fast-growing; short-lived; the abundant reproduction often completely taking over burned areas.

Bitter Cherry

Prunus emarginata Dougl.

This cherry closely resembles pin cherry in its flowers and fruit; it can be distinguished by its oblong-obovate, obtuse leaves and its more western distribution where it extends from British Columbia to Montana and south to California, Arizona, and New Mexico.

American Plum

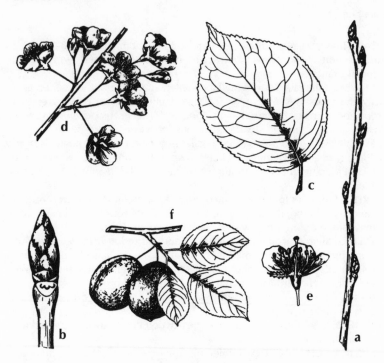

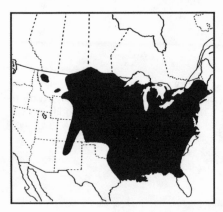

a. Winter twig, × 1
b. Portion of twig, enlarged
c. Leaf, × ½
d. Flowering branchlet, × ½
e. Vertical section of flower, × 1
f. Fruiting branchlet, × ½

American Plum

Prunus americana Marsh.

HABIT. A shrub or small tree 25–30 ft high and rarely 12 in. in diameter; trunk short, usually dividing near the ground; crown broad, with many spreading branches; usually spreading by shoots from the roots into dense thickets.

LEAVES. Oval to slightly oblong-oval, or sometimes obovate; acuminate at apex; sharply and often doubly serrate; thick and firm; dark green above, pale and glabrous below; 3–4 in. long and 1½–1¾ in. wide; petiole slender, ½–¾ in. long.

FLOWERS. In 2- to 5-flowered umbels; on slender, glabrous pedicels ½–⅔ in. long; appearing before or with leaves; ill-scented; calyx tube narrow, bright red without, green and pubescent within; corolla white, 1 in. in diameter.

FRUIT. Subglose; about 1 in. in diameter; red and often spotted at maturity; thick-skinned; nearly free from bloom; flesh bright yellow, juicy, acid; used for jellies; stone oval, rounded at apex, ¾–1 in. long.

TWIGS. Slender; glabrous; bright green at first, becoming orange-brown and marked by minute, circular, raised lenticels; sometimes spiny-tipped. Winter buds: terminal absent; lateral ⅛–¼ in. long; acute, chestnut-brown.

BARK. Up to ½ in. thick; dark brown, tinged with red; outer layer forming persistent plates.

WOOD. Heavy; hard; close-grained; strong; heartwood dark brown, tinged with red; sapwood thin, lighter colored.

SILVICAL CHARACTERS. Intolerant; on moist bottomlands to banks of intermittent streams on dry uplands and mountain slopes.

Canada Plum

Prunus nigra Ait.

The Canada plum is very similar to the American plum and often classed as a variety of it. It differs in having leaves with small, rounded teeth and biglandular petioles. Canada plum ranges from New Brunswick to southern Manitoba and south to New York, Indiana, Iowa, and Illinois. The garden plum, *P. domestica* L., while native to Europe and Asia, has escaped through much of North America, as has the Bullace or Damson plum, *P. domestica* var. *insititia* (L.) F. & P.

Toyon

Cliffrose

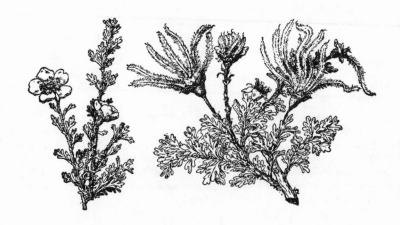

Toyon • Christmasberry

Heteromeles arbutifolia (Lindl.) Roem. (*Photinia abutifolia* Lindl.)

HABIT. A small tree or large shrub with erect branches and a handsome narrow crown.

LEAVES. Alternate; simple; thick; glossy; oblong to elliptical, serrate; persistent; 3–4 in. long.

FLOWERS. Small; white; perfect; in terminal leafy panicles 4–6 in. across.

FRUIT. Red to yellow pome; ⅓ in. long; remaining on branches until late winter.

TWIGS. Covered when young with pale hairs, becoming dark red and glabrous. Winter buds: ¼ in. long; acute; with loose scales.

BARK. Generally smooth; light gray; ½–⅔ in. thick.

WOOD. Hard; heavy; close-grained, dark red-brown; unimportant.

SILVICAL CHARACTERS. Intolerant; reproduction vigorous, often forming groves.

GENERAL. Fruit-covered branches widely used for Christmas decorations. Native to islands, coast ranges, and Sierra Nevada foothills from northern California to lower California.

Cliffrose • Quininebush

Cowania mexicana D. Don

HABIT. Usually a shrub, rarely a small tree reaching 25 ft in height.

LEAVES. Alternate; simple; thick; glandular dotted above; persistent or tardily deciduous; 3- to 5-lobed; dark green above and hoary-tomentose below; ⅓–½ in. long.

FLOWERS. Perfect; solitary; 1 in. in diameter; persistent calyx tube with rigid, glandular hairs; pale yellow to white.

FRUIT. 5–12 achenes included in calyx tube and tipped with elongated, white, hairy, persistent styles.

TWIGS. Slender; rigid; glandular during first year; reddish.

BARK. Thin; gray; separating into long, thin, loosely attached plates.

SILVICAL CHARACTERS. Intolerant; on dry, rocky slopes.

GENERAL. Range, from southwest Colorado into Utah and Nevada, west to eastern California and through Arizona and western New Mexico into Mexico.

FABACEAE (LEGUMINOSAE)

The Pea Family

Characteristics of the Pea Family

This important family contains about 500 genera and over 15,000 species, among them many of our important food plants. The family is characterized by its distinctive fruit, known as a legume, as well as by alternate, usually compound leaves and regular or distinctive papilionaceous flowers.

The genera growing in North America and reaching tree size are in the following key; important, common, or distinctive species are then described. The several unimportant forms occasionally reaching tree size in the southern fringe of the United States are briefly described below:

Smokethorn, *Dalea spinosa* A. Gray, in Arizona and southeastern California is a desert shrub with minute or no leaves, green, spiny twigs, and a small 1-seeded legume.

Southwestern coralbean, *Erythrina flabelliformis* Kearney, in southern Arizona and New Mexico is characterized by 3 foliolate leaves and showy red flowers. The eastern coralbean, *E. herbacea* L., from North Carolina to Texas is usually a perennial herb but becomes a tree in Florida. The South American *E. crista-galli* L. is cultivated and escaped in the Gulf states.

Kidneywood, *Eysenhardtia polystachya* (Ortega) Sarg., is a shrubby Mexican border form in Arizona characterized by small leaflets and a legume only ½ in. long. *E. texana* Scheele is a small tree in Texas.

Littleleaf leadtree, *Leucaena retusa* Benth., of southern Texas and New Mexico differs from lysiloma in having a linear legume 6–10 in. long on a peduncle 3–5 in. long. *L. pulverulenta* Benth. forms a small tree in southern Texas and Mexico.

Lysiloma, *Lysiloma microphyllum* Benth., is a rare shrub or small tree in southern Arizona characterized by bipinnately compound, persistent leaves and a linear-oblong, compressed legume 5–8 in. long. *L. latisiliquum* (L.) Benth. is found in southern Florida.

Tesota, *Olneya tesota* A. Gray, is a beautiful spiny small tree of the Arizona-California desert, with purple flowers and a compressed, glandular-hairy legume 2–2½ in. long.

Paradise poinciana, *Caesalpinia gilliesii* (Hook.) Dietr., is an ill-scented shrub or small tree native to South America but naturalized in southern Texas, New Mexico, Arizona, and California. It is characterized by large, showy, flowers with long-exserted red stamens and pistil. *C. mexicana* Gray is found in southern Texas and Mexico.

KEY TO THE GENERA OF THE PEA FAMILY REACHING TREE SIZE

1. Leaves bipinnately compound (3–4 pinnate in some genera and sometimes only pinnate in *Gleditsia*); flowers regular or nearly so.
    2. Flowers in globose heads or cylindrical spikes; leaflets mostly less than ½ in. long; shrubby; south Florida or Mexican border.
        3. Twigs armed with spines; legumes terete or compressed.
            4. Legumes dehiscent; stamens 10, united filaments . . . .
            . . . . *Pithecellobium* Mart., **Blackbead**, p. 287

4. Legumes indehiscent; filaments free except at base.
    5. Flowers in heads or spikes, yellow or white, stamens more than 10; petioles not spiny or glandular at apex. . . *Acacia* Mill., **acacia,** p. 275
    5. Flowers in cylindric spikes, greenish-white, stamens 10; petioles minutely glandular at apex and tipped with small spinescent rachis. . . . .
    . . . . *Prosopis* L., **mesquite,** p. 277
3. Twigs unarmed; legumes compressed, dehiscent; flowers in heads, whitish, or pink.
    6. Stamens numerous, long-exserted; flowers pink; planted in Southeast. . . .
    . . . . *Albizia* Dur., **mimosa,** p. 277
    6. Stamens 10–20; flowers white; western.
        7. Stamens 12–20, exserted, filaments united into a tube; legume broad
        . . . . *Lysiloma* Benth., **lysiloma,** p. 272
        7. Stamens 10, inserted, filaments free; legume linear . . . .
        . . . . *Leucaena* Benth., **leadtree,** p. 272
2. Flowers in racemes; stamens 10 or less, filaments free.
    8. Flowers large and showy, yellow, perfect; leaflets less than ½ in. long; southwestern shrubs, rarely small trees.
        9. Stamens red and long-exserted; legume broad and flat; naturalized . . . . .
        . . . . *Caesalpinia* L., **poinciana,** p. 272
        9. Stamens inserted; native.
            10. Legumes linear, terete; rachis of leaf spinscent . . . .
            . . . . *Parkinsonia* L., **Jerusalem-thorn,** p. 285
            10. Legumes oblong, compressed; rachis of leaf not spinescent . . . .
            . . . . *Cercidium* Tulasne, **paloverde,** p. 285
    8. Flowers not showy, greenish-white, polygamous or dioecious; leaflets over ½ in. long; eastern trees, but widely planted.
        11. Leaves 1–3 ft long with leaflets 2–2½ in. long; legume thick and woody, seeds ¾ in. . . . . *Gymnocladus* Lam., **coffeetree,** p. 281
        11. Leaves ½–1 ft long with leaflets ½–1½ in. long; legume leathery with seeds ⅓ in. long . . . . *Gleditsia* L., **honeylocust,** p. 283
1. Leaves simple or pinnately compound; flowers papilionaceous.
    12. Leaves simple.
        13. Leaves heart-shaped; flowers in fascicles, red with free stamens; spineless
        . . . . *Cercis* L., **redbud,** p. 279
        13. Leaves oblong or absent; flowers in racemes, blue, stamens, 9 united anthers; twigs reduced to spines; Ariz., Calif. . . . . *Dalea* Juss., **dalea,** p. 272
    12. Leaves pinnately compound.
        14. Leaflets 1–4 in. long.
            15. Leaves 3-foliate; flowers red . . . . *Erythrina* L., **coralbean,** p. 272
            15. Leaves many-foliate; flowers white, yellow, or blue.
                16. Leaflets 3–4 in. long; flowers white, in panicles; legumes compressed . . . . *Cladrastis* Raf., **yellowwood,** p. 281
                16. Leaflets 1–2½ in. long.
                      17. Twigs with stipular spines; legumes compressed, not constricted . . . . *Robinia* L., **locust,** p. 289
                    17. Twigs unarmed; legumes terete, constricted . . . .
                    . . . . *Sophora* L., **sophora,** p. 287
        14. Leaflets less than 1 in. long.
            18. Leaves with glandular dots . . . .
            . . . . *Eysenhardtia* H.B.K., **kidneywood,** p. 272
            18. Leaves without glandular dots.
                19. Flowers fascicled, yellow . . . . . *Caragana* Lam., **pea tree,** p. 287
                19. Flowers racemose, purple . . . . *Olneya* Gray, **tesota,** p. 272

Catclaw Acacia

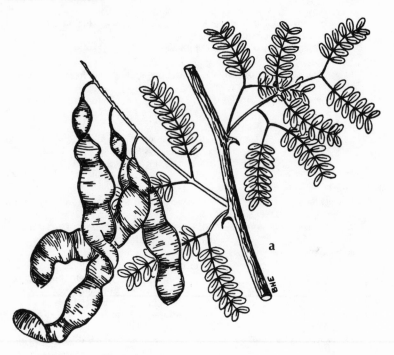

a. Twig with leaves and fruit, × 1

Catclaw Acacia • Paradise Flower

Acacia greggii Gray

HABIT. A spiny shrub or small tree rarely 30 ft high and 10–12 in. in diameter; trunk short; crown irregular.

LEAVES. Alternate; evenly doubly pinnate; 1–3 pairs of pinnae, each with 4–5 pairs of oblong, obtuse, thick, pubescent leaflets ¹⁄₁₆–¼ in. long; persistent; petiole short, glandular.

FLOWERS. Nearly regular; perfect or polygamous; fragrant; in dense, pubescent spikes; calyx 5-lobed, puberulous; corolla 5-petaled, bright yellow, ⅛ in. long; stamens numerous, exserted, ¼ in. long; ovary stalked and hairy.

FRUIT. Linear-oblong, flat, much curved and contorted, indehiscent, light brown legume 2–6 in. long and ½–¾ in. wide; contracted between the seeds; valves thin and membranaceous. Seeds: dark brown; lustrous; ¼ in. long.

TWIGS. Slender; angled; puberulous or glabrous; red-brown; armed with stout, broad, recurved, infrastipular spines ¼ in. long, giving tree its common name.

BARK. Thin (⅛ in.); furrowed and scaly; light gray-brown; astringent.

WOOD. Very heavy; hard; strong; close-grained; durable; ring-porous; heartwood red-brown; sapwood thin, light yellow.

SILVICAL CHARACTERS. Lower Sonoran zone; intolerant; vigorous reproducer; thrives in driest and poorest soils; on dry mesas, plains, and in low canyons.

GENERAL. Acacia, with more than 600 species, is widely distributed throughout the warmer regions of the world. Many species are used as ornamentals. Nine species are native, 2 being very rare on the Florida Keys and the 7 listed below reaching tree size along the Mexican border:

A. berlandieri Benth., with short spines; flowers in short spikes; and flat hairy legume with thickened sutures; Texas.

A. farnesiana (L.) Willd., with spines; yellow flowers in capitate heads; and a terete legume; Texas, rare in Arizona and California.

A. greggii Gray, described above.

A. rigidula Benth., a small tree in Texas.

A. roemeriana Scheele, a small tree in Texas and New Mexico.

A. tortuosa Willd., with slender or no spines and flat legume; Texas.

A. wrightii Benth., with short spines and yellow flowers on spikes; Texas.

Honey Mesquite

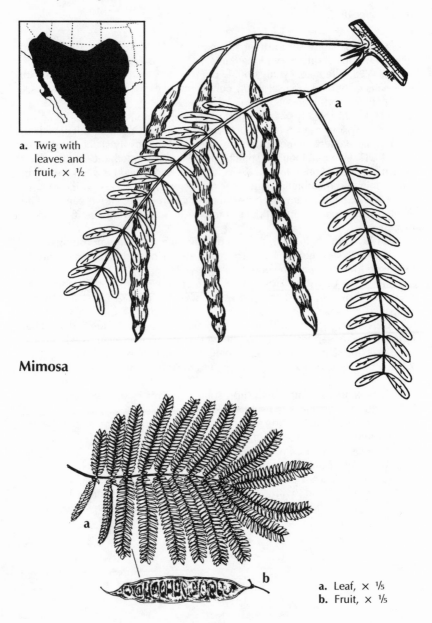

a. Twig with
leaves and
fruit, × ½

Mimosa

a. Leaf, × ⅕
b. Fruit, × ⅕

Honey Mesquite

Prosopis glandulosa Torr. (*Prosopis juliflora* [Sw.] DC.)

HABIT. A spiny shrub or small tree rarely 20–50 ft high and 1–4 ft in diameter; crown loose and straggling.

LEAVES. Alternate; evenly, doubly (rarely 3–4) pinnate; pinnae with 12–30 linear to linear-oblong, small, deciduous, glabrous leaflets ½–2 in. long; petioles spine-tipped.

FLOWERS. Nearly regular; perfect; fragrant; minute.

FRUIT. Linear, flat to subterete, indehiscent, yellowish, straight or falcate legume 4–9 in. long and ¼–½ in. wide; edible. Seeds: oblong; compressed; light brown; ¼ in. long.

TWIGS. Slender; smooth; usually with spines ½–2 in. long. Winter buds: terminal absent; lateral small, brown.

BARK. Thick; dark red-brown; furrowed and scaly.

WOOD. Very heavy; hard; close-grained; durable; ring-porous; heartwood dark brown or red; sapwood yellow.

SILVICAL CHARACTERS. Intolerant; long-lived; adapted to desert sites by huge taproot descending 40–50 ft.

GENERAL. Two other species reach tree size. Screwbean mesquite, *P. pubescens* Benth., ranging from Texas to California north into Nevada and Utah, is readily distinguished by its thick, linear, indehiscent, pale yellow legume 1–2 in. long, twisted by 12–20 turns into a narrow, straight spiral. Velvet mesquite, *P. pubescens* Woot., in southwest New Mexico to central Arizona has smaller leaflets (¼–½ in. long) and is hairy throughout.

Mimosa • Silktree

Albizia julibrissin Durazz.

A handsome ornamental, widely planted, escaped and naturalized from Maryland to Indiana and south. The powder puff appearance of the pink flowers in crowded heads and the bipinnate leaves with many tiny leaflets (10–25 pinnae, each with 40–60 leaflets) are distinctive, as are the flat, light-colored legumes 4–6 in. long and the stout twigs with large lenticels and 3-lobed leaf scars.

Eastern Redbud

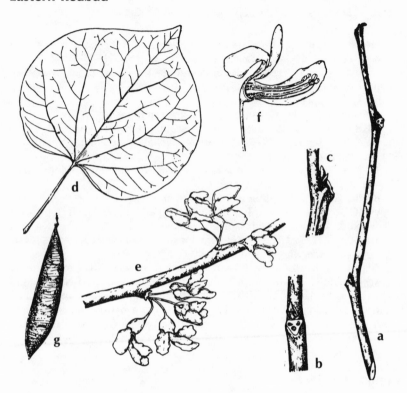

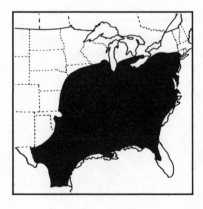

a. Winter twig, × 1
b. Portion of twig, front view, enlarged
c. Portion of twig, side view, enlarged
d. Leaf, × ⅔
e. Flowering branchlet, × 1
f. Vertical section of flower, enlarged
g. Fruit, × ½

Eastern Redbud

Cercis canadensis L.

HABIT. Usually a shrub, but not infrequently a small tree up to 40 ft high and 2½ ft in diameter; frequently planted as an ornamental.

LEAVES. Alternate; simple; broad-ovate to reniform; 3–5 in. in diameter; apex acute; base cordate; margins entire; glabrous; deciduous; petioles long, slender; stipules small, membranaceous.

FLOWERS. Irregular (subpapilionaceous); perfect; in simple fascicles; appearing before the leaves; calyx short, top-shaped, purple, 5-toothed, persistent; corolla 5-petaled, rose-colored; stamens 10, free, inserted in 2 rows on margin of thin disk, persistent; ovary short-stalked; ovules numerous in 2 ranks.

FRUIT. Stalked, flat, oblong, russet-brown legume 2–3½ in. long; tipped with remnant of style. Seeds: ¼ in. long; ovoid or oblong; compressed; red-brown.

TWIGS. Slender; round; unarmed; marked by numerous pale lenticels and elevated, often fringed leaf scars with 3 bundle scars. Winter buds: terminal absent; axillary small, scaly, obtuse, chestnut-brown.

BARK. Thin; gray; smooth or becoming scaly on old trunks.

WOOD. Heavy; hard; not strong; ring-porous; heartwood dark red-brown; sapwood white, thin; unimportant.

SILVICAL CHARACTERS. Tolerant; reproduction vigorous; typical of bottomlands and stream borders; a variety recognized in the Southwest is *texensis* (S. Wats.) Hopkins, the Texas redbud.

California Redbud

Cercis occidentalis Torr.

This similar species is usually shrubby but has been reported as a tree in California and in the Grand Canyon. Its range is from southern Utah and Nevada to California and Arizona, and it differs from the eastern redbud in having leaves 2–3 in. long that are obtuse or emarginate at the apex.

Kentucky Coffeetree

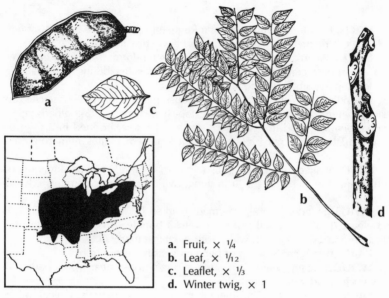

a. Fruit, × ¼
b. Leaf, × ¹/₁₂
c. Leaflet, × ⅓
d. Winter twig, × 1

Yellowwood

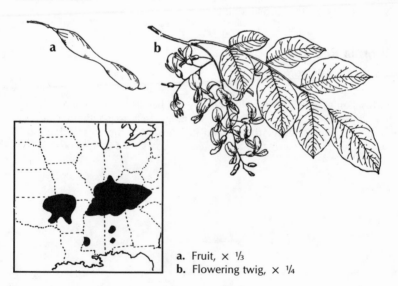

a. Fruit, × ⅓
b. Flowering twig, × ¼

Kentucky Coffeetree

Gymnocladus dioicus (L.) K. Koch

HABIT. A medium-sized to large tree 50–75 ft high and 2–3 ft in diameter (max. 110 by 4 ft); open, pyramidal crown.

LEAVES. Alternate; doubly pinnate with 40 or more leaflets; 1–3 ft long; leaflets 2–2½ in. long, ovate, acute, entire, short-stalked, glabrous, dark green above and paler below; appearing late in the spring; deciduous.

FLOWERS. Nearly regular; dioecious; in racemes; calyx tubular, hairy; petals 5, greenish-white; stamens 10; ovary hairy; appearing after the leaves.

FRUIT. A turgid, woody, short-stalked, red-brown legume 4–10 in. long and 1½–2 in. wide; containing sugary pulp between the 6–9 seeds. Seeds: ovoid, ¾ in. long, with thick bony coat, used as substitute for coffee in early days.

TWIGS. Very stout; unarmed; coated at first with short, dense, red hairs; roughened by large, pale, conspicuous leaf scars. Winter buds: terminal absent; lateral small, depressed in craters, brown, silky-hairy, with 2 in the axil of each leaf.

BARK. Smooth and brown to gray on limbs; becoming ¾–1 in. thick; gray; fissured; distinctive reflexed scales.

WOOD. Unimportant; heavy and hard; ring-porous; reddish and closely resembling honey locust; sapwood very thin, white.

SILVICAL CHARACTERS. Intolerant; fast-growing; rare throughout its range; a handsome tree often planted as an ornamental.

Yellowwood

Cladrastis kentukea (Dum.-Cours.) Rudd (*Cladrastis lutea* [Michx.] K. Koch)

This medium-sized tree is rare and unimportant except for occasional use as an ornamental. It is characterized by alternate, deciduous, pinnately compound leaves with 5–11 leaflets, each 3–4 in. long, obovate, entire, acute, and yellow-green; by perfect, showy, white, papilionaceous flowers; by a glabrous, flat, short-stalked, linear legume 3–4 in. long containing 4–6 flat, brown seeds; by slender, glabrous twigs containing naked lateral buds enclosed in the hollow base of the petiole; and by smooth, thin, gray bark.

Honeylocust

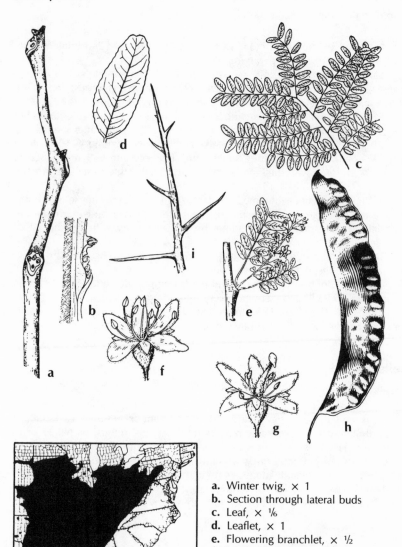

a. Winter twig, × 1
b. Section through lateral buds
c. Leaf, × 1/6
d. Leaflet, × 1
e. Flowering branchlet, × 1/2
f. Staminate flower, enlarged
g. Pistillate flower, enlarged
h. Fruit, × 1/4
i. Spine from trunk, × 1/2

Honeylocust

Gleditsia triacanthos L.

HABIT. A medium-sized tree 50–75 ft high and 2–3 ft in diameter (max. 140 by 5 ft); open, spreading crown; trunk and branches usually armed with clusters of straight or branched spines several inches long.

LEAVES. Alternate; pinnately or bipinnately compound with both types often on the same tree; 6–12 in. long; leaflets ½–1½ in. long, lanceolate-oblong, remotely crenulate, thin, glabrous, lustrous dark green above and yellow-green below; deciduous.

FLOWERS. Regular; polygamous; small; in axillary racemes; calyx 3- to 5-lobed; petals 3–5, greenish-white; stamens 3–10; ovary 1-celled, woolly; appearing after the leaves.

FRUIT. A strap-shaped, red-brown, usually twisted legume 12–18 in. long and 1 in. wide; containing 12–14 dark brown, oval seeds, each about ⅓ in. long.

TWIGS. Slender to rather stout; usually with straight or 3-branched spines 2–8 in. long; green to red-brown. Winter buds: terminal absent; lateral minute, nearly submerged in leaf scar, brownish, 3 or more superposed.

BARK. Smooth and gray on limbs; becoming ½–¾ in. thick, gray to nearly black, and broken by longitudinal fissures into plates or scaly ridges.

WOOD. Of slight importance; heavy and hard; durable; red-brown; ring-porous; used for veneer and fuel.

SILVICAL CHARACTERS. Intolerant; fast-growing; hardy; prefers rich, moist sites, but hardy on arid, sandy locations; the thornless variety *inermis* (Pursh) Schneid., is commonly planted in cities.

Waterlocust

Gleditsia aquatica Marsh.

This similar species is native to the coastal region from South Carolina to Texas and up the Mississippi valley to southern Indiana. It is readily distinguished by its oval, oblique, 1- to 3-seeded legume, which is 1–2 in. long. The Texas honeylocust, *Gleditsia* X *texana* Sarg., is a hybrid between waterlocust and honeylocust and is characterized by a legume 4–5 in. long. It has been reported from Indiana to Texas.

Blue Paloverde

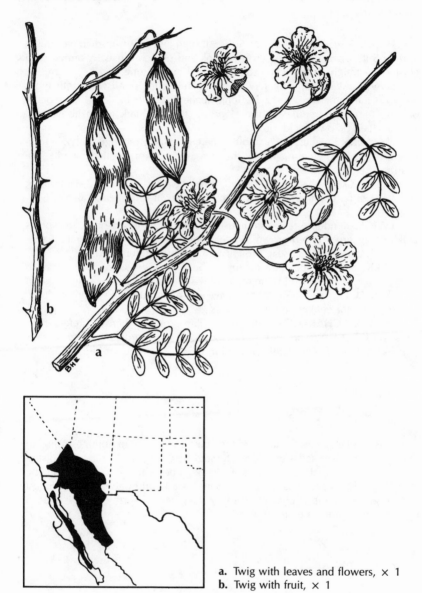

a. Twig with leaves and flowers, × 1
b. Twig with fruit, × 1

Blue Paloverde • Greenbarked-acacia

Cercidium floridum Benth. (*Cercidium torreyanum* [S. Wats.] Sarg.)

HABIT. A thorny shrub or small tree 15–30 ft high; wide, irregular, open crown with stout, tortuous branches.

LEAVES. Alternate; doubly and evenly pinnate with 2–3 pairs of oblong, obtuse, glaucous leaflets 1/12–1/6 in. long; few and totaling less area than green twigs; falling soon, but frequently bearing a second crop during the rainy season.

FLOWERS. Nearly regular; perfect; in conspicuous 4- to 5-flowered, axillary racemes; on slender pedicels 3/4–1 in. long; calyx 5-lobed, reflexed; corolla of 5, clawed, bright yellow petals, 3/4 in. in diameter; stamens 10, free, exserted.

FRUIT. Oblong, compressed or somewhat turgid legume 3–4 in. long and 1/4–1/3 in. wide; straight or somewhat contracted between the 2–8 seeds. Seeds: ovoid, compressed.

TWIGS. Stout; glabrous and glaucous; light yellow or pale olive-green; armed with thin spines 1/4 in. long.

BARK. Thin (1/8 in.); smooth and pale olive-green on young trunks, becoming furrowed, scaly, and red-brown.

WOOD. Unimportant; soft; weak; close-grained; ring-porous; heartwood light brown; sapwood yellow; used as fuel.

SILVICAL CHARACTERS. Lower Sonoran zone; intolerant; abundant seeder; typical of arid, desert sinks, canyons, and depressions; in sandy or gravelly soil.

GENERAL. Two other species may reach tree size in the Southwest:

Yellow paloverde, *C. microphyllum* (Torr.) R. & J., in extreme southeastern California and Arizona has leaves with 4–6 pairs of leaflets, a 1- to 2-seeded legume, and twigs terminating in spines.

Border paloverde, *C. texanum* Gray, in southeastern Texas has slightly glandular leaflets 1/16 in. long and a 2- to 3-seeded legume.

Jerusalem-thorn

Parkinsonia aculeata L.

Jerusalem-thorn is a widely planted similar small tree ranging from southern Arizona and Texas to South America. It differs from paloverde in having a linear, terete legume and leaves with 25–30 pairs of small leaflets and a spinescent rachis.

Mescalbean

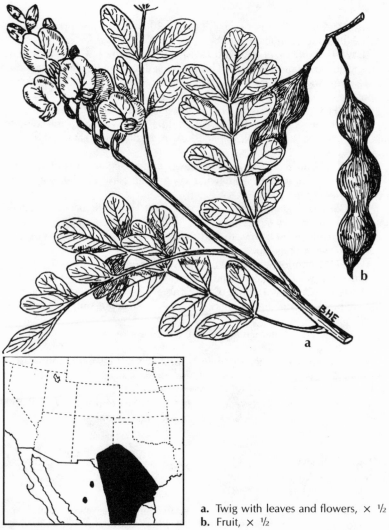

a. Twig with leaves and flowers, × ½
b. Fruit, × ½

Mescalbean • Frijolito

Sophora secundiflora (Ortega) Lag.

HABIT. A shrub or rarely a small tree 20 ft high and 6–8 in. in diameter; commonly thicket-forming.

LEAVES. Alternate; persistent; unequally pinnate with 7–13 elliptical, coriaceous, glabrous, entire leaflets ¾–2 in. long; rounded; lustrous above, paler below.

FLOWERS. Irregular (papilionaceous); perfect; fragrant; showy; appearing with leaves; in terminal racemes; corolla blue or white.

FRUIT. Oblong, terete, indehiscent legume 1–7 in. long; thick woody valves; much contracted between seeds; covered with dense tomentum; tipped with remnant of style. Seeds: bright scarlet; very poisonous.

TWIGS. Slender; round; unarmed; lateral buds minute.

WOOD. Heavy; hard; close-grained; orange-yellow; unimportant.

GENERAL. The Texas sophora, *S. affinis* Torr. & Gray, of Texas, Arkansas, Oklahoma, and Louisiana differs in having thin deciduous leaves, a fleshy legume, and white flowers in axillary racemes. The Chinese scholartree, *S. japonica* L., a common ornamental, has acute, entire, shiny leaflets; yellow to pink flowers in terminal panicles; and fruit pods 2–3 in. long and distinctively narrowed between the seeds.

Ebony Blackbead

Pithecellobium flexicaule (Benth.) Coult.

This is a common and beautiful shrub or small tree of the Texas Gulf Coast and banks of the lower Rio Grande into Mexico. It is characterized by bipinnate, few foliolate leaves, stipular spines, fragrant yellow flowers in cylindrical spikes, and thick legumes containing bright red-brown seeds. Huajillo, *P. pallens* (Benth.) Standl., also appears in Texas; *P. guadalupense* (Pers.) Chapm. and *P. ungis-cati* (L.) Benth. reach southern Florida.

Siberian Pea Tree

Caragana arborescens Lam.

This introduced tree has been extensively planted for shelterbelts and as an ornamental. It is characterized by even pinnate leaves with 8–12 leaflets and papilionaceous, yellow flowers, ½–¾ in. long, in fascicles of 1–4.

Black Locust

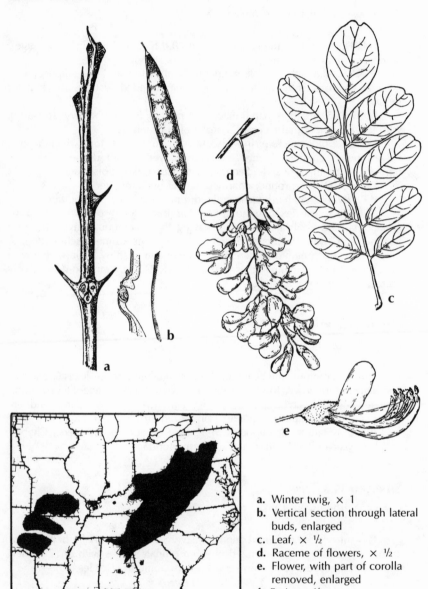

a. Winter twig, × 1
b. Vertical section through lateral buds, enlarged
c. Leaf, × ½
d. Raceme of flowers, × ½
e. Flower, with part of corolla removed, enlarged
f. Fruit, × ½

The *Robinia* Locusts

There are about 10 species of *Robinia,* all native to North America, with 4 reported to reach tree size.

KEY TO THE SPECIES OF *ROBINIA* LOCUSTS

1. Legume, twigs and peduncle glabrous or nearly so . . . .
. . . . *R. pseudoacacia* L., **black locust**
1. Legume and peduncle hispid, glandular, or viscid.
   2. Twigs glabrous; usually a shrub; eastern Tennessee and western North Carolina
   . . . . *R. kelseyi* Hutchins, **Kelsey locust**
   2. Twigs glandular pubescent or viscid.
      3. Glands not viscid; southern Colorado to Nevada, south to Arizona and west Texas . . . . *R. neomexicana* A. Gray, **New Mexican locust**
      3. Glands exuding a clammy, sticky substance; mountains, Pennsylvania to Kentucky, south to Alabama . . . . *R. viscosa* Vent, **clammy locust**

Black Locust

Robinia pseudoacacia L.

HABIT. A medium-sized tree 40–60 ft high and 1–2 ft in diameter (max. 100 by 5 ft); open, irregular crown.

LEAVES. Alternate; pinnately compound; 8–14 in. long; 7–21 ovate-oblong, entire, glabrous leaflets, 1½–2 in. long, dark blue-green above and paler below; deciduous.

FLOWERS. Papilionaceous; perfect; showy; fragrant; in racemes; calyx bell-shaped; corolla 5-petaled, white; stamens 10; ovary 1-celled; appearing after the leaves.

FRUIT. A smooth, dark brown, flat, linear-oblong legume, 2–4 in. long; 4–8 flat brown seeds about ³⁄₁₆ in. long.

TWIGS. Rather stout; red-brown; usually armed with stipular spines about ½ in. long. Winter buds: terminal absent; lateral minute, red-hairy, submerged, 3–4 superposed.

BARK. Red-brown to nearly black; deeply fissured into rounded, scaly ridges.

WOOD. Moderately important; very heavy and hard; very durable; dark brown or golden; used for posts, ties, insulator pins.

SILVICAL CHARACTERS. Intolerant; fast-growing; seriously threatened by locust borer (*Cyllene robiniae*); prefers moist, rich soils, but hardy on poor, dry sites; A clone of this species, which propagates only by vegetative means, is shipmast locust (*R. rectissima* Raber), which is widely planted and naturalized.

Hoptree

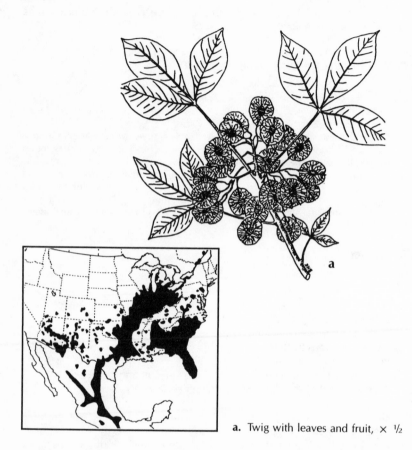

a. Twig with leaves and fruit, × ½

Hercules-club

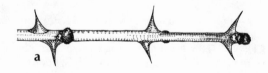

a. Twig with buds and thorns

RUTACEAE

Hoptree • Wafer-ash

Ptelea trifoliata L.

HABIT. A variable shrub or small tree 20–25 ft high with many intergrading geographical varieties.

LEAVES. Alternate, rarely opposite; compound, 3 (rarely 5) ovate leaflets; entire or crenulate-serrate; with translucent dots below; long-petioled.

FLOWERS. Regular; polygamous; in cymes or umbels.

FRUIT. Dehiscent samara; in drooping clusters; thin; nearly 1 in. wide; persistent into winter. Seeds: ⅓ in. long, oblong, dark red-brown.

TWIGS. Slender; round; dark brown; lustrous; marked by wartlike excrescences and conspicuous leaf scars. Winter buds: terminal absent; lateral small, depressed, pale, tomentose.

BARK. Smooth or warty; thin; bitter; ill-scented; dark brown.

WOOD. Rather heavy; hard; ring porous; unimportant.

GENERAL. California hoptree, *P. crenulata* Greene, is a shrub or small tree in central and southern California.

Hercules-club • Prickly-ash

Zanthoxylum clava-herculis L.

A distinctive small tree of the Coastal Plain ranging from Virginia to Florida, west to Texas, and north to Arkansas. It has spiny twigs; peculiar conical, corky growths on smooth gray bark; alternate, spiny-stemmed, late-deciduous, pinnately compound leaves, with 7–19 leathery, ovate, toothed leaflets; dioecious, clustered flowers; and an ovoid, brown, wrinkled capsule ½ in. long with a single black seed hanging from it at maturity.

Other usually shrubby eastern species reaching tree size are *Z. americanum* Mill., *Z. coriaceum* Rich., *Z. fagara* (L.) Sarg., *Z. flavum* Vahl, and *Z. hirsutum* Buckl.

Orange and Lime

Citrus L.

Three widely cultivated species of citrus have become naturalized in the Southeast: lime, *Citrus aurantifolia* (Christ.) Swingle in south Florida; sour orange, *C. aurantium* L., in Florida and Georgia; and orange, *C. sinensis* Osbeck in Florida.

Staghorn Sumac

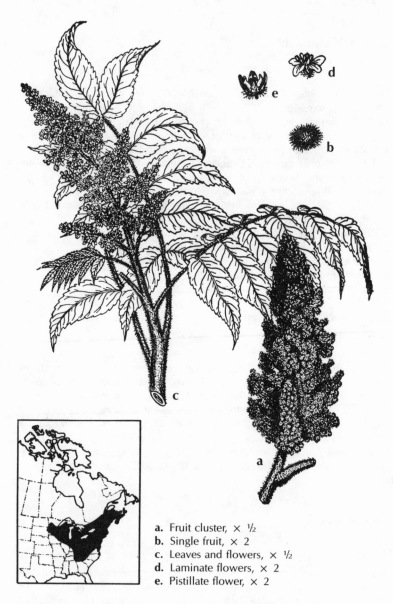

a. Fruit cluster, × ½
b. Single fruit, × 2
c. Leaves and flowers, × ½
d. Laminate flowers, × 2
e. Pistillate flower, × 2

ANACARDIACEAE
The Sumacs, *Rhus*

About 17 species are native to North America, with 10 rarely reaching tree size and keyed out below. Two species, poisonous to the touch, are placed either in the genus *Rhus* or *Toxicodendron;* these are poison-sumac, *T. vernix* (L.) Ktze., and poison ivy or oak, *T. radicans* (L.) Ktze.

KEY TO THE SPECIES OF SUMACS

1. Leaves simple or rarely 3-foliolate, leathery, evergreen.
  2. Leaves broadly ovate, entire; flowers in dense spikes; fruit red; California and Arizona . . . . *R. ovata* S. Wats., **sugar sumac**
  2. Leaves oval to ovate, rounded at apex.
    3. Fruit white in branched panicles; southern California coast . . . .
    . . . . *R. laurina* Nutt., **laurel sumac**
    3. Fruit red.
      4. Leaves toothed or entire; southern coastal California . . . .
      . . . . *R. integrifolia* (Nutt.) B. & H., **mahogany sumac**
      4. Leaves entire; Yuma County, Arizona and Baja California . . . .
      . . . . *R. kearneyi* Bark., **Kearney sumac**
1. Leaves pinnately compound, deciduous.
  5. Flowers in dense, terminal panicles; fruit red, hairy.
    6. Twigs and petioles velvety-hairy; leaflets serrate . . . .
    . . . . *R. typhina* Torn., **staghorn sumac**
    6. Twigs and petioles glabrous or hairy.
      7. Rachis terete; twigs glabrous and glaucous; leaflets serrate; most of North America . . . . *R. glabra* L., **smooth sumac**
      7. Rachis winged; twigs pubescent; leaflets nearly entire.
        8. Leaflets ovate-lanceolate; Maine to Wisconsin and Kansas, south to Florida and Texas . . . . *R. copallina* L., **shining sumac**
        8. Leaflets narrow-lanceolate, often falcate; south Oklahoma to Texas and New Mexico . . . . *R. lanceolata* Britt., **prairie shining sumac**
  5. Flowers not numerous in terminal or axillary panicles.
    9. Fruit red; rachis winged; leaflets less than 1 in. long; west Texas to Oklahoma and Arizona . . . . *R. microphylla* Engelm., **littleleaf sumac**
    9. Fruit white; rachis terete; leaflets ½–2½ in. long, entire; twigs yellow-brown. Quebec to Minnesota, south to Gulf . . . .
    . . . . *R. (or T.) vernix* (L.) Ktze., **poison sumac**

Staghorn Sumac

Rhus typhina Torn.

HABIT. A shrub or small tree to 40 ft high and 1 ft in diameter; commonly in broad thickets.

LEAVES. Alternate; deciduous; pinnately compound with 11–31 oblong, glabrous, serrate, dark green leaflets, 2–5 in. long.

FLOWERS. Regular; dioecious or polygamous; small; green-white; in dense, hairy panicles 6–12 in. long; after the leaves.

FRUIT. Compact, conelike clusters of red, hairy drupes, each ¼ in. long.

TWIGS. Thick; velvety-hairy; milky juice; thick pith. Winter buds: terminal absent; lateral ¼ in. long, conical, brown, hairy-silky, hidden.

BARK. Thin; dark brown; smooth, becoming scaly with age.

WOOD. Unimportant; soft and weak; ring-porous; orange-colored.

SILVICAL CHARACTERS. Intolerant; fast-growing; short-lived.

American Smoketree

a. Twig, leaves, and fruit, × ⅓

Ailanthus

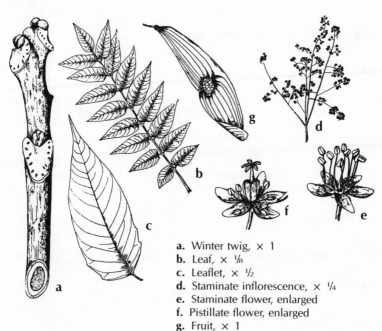

a. Winter twig, × 1
b. Leaf, × ⅛
c. Leaflet, × ½
d. Staminate inflorescence, × ¼
e. Staminate flower, enlarged
f. Pistillate flower, enlarged
g. Fruit, × 1

American Smoketree

Cotinus obovatus Raf.

This handsome shrub or small tree is rare and local in the highlands of Tennessee, Alabama, Arkansas, Missouri, Oklahoma, and Texas. It is characterized by simple, alternate, deciduous leaves 4–6 in. long, oval to obovate, entire, and dark green; dioecious, clustered flowers, many being abortive and hairy giving the tree its name; and a dry, compressed, oblong, brown, drupe about ⅛ in. long borne in loose panicles on stems 1–3 in. long.

Texas Pistache

Pistacia texana Swingle

This shrub or small tree extends to south Texas from Mexico. Characterized by alternate, persistent, pinnately compound leaves with 9–19 spatulate leaflets; small dioecious flowers without petals or calyx; oval, red-brown drupe ¼ in. long.

SIMAROUBACEAE

Ailanthus • Tree-of-heaven

Ailanthus altissima (Mill.) Swingle (*Ailanthus glandulosa* Desf.)

HABIT. A handsome naturalized tree 40–60 ft high and 2–4 ft in diameter; loose, open crown with very large leaves.

LEAVES. Alternate; deciduous; 1½–4 ft long; pinnately compound with 13–41 leaflets; leaflets ovate-lanceolate, 3–6 in. long, entire except for 1–2 glandular teeth at the base.

FLOWERS. Regular; polygamo-dioecious; small; yellow-green; in panicles; calyx 5-lobed; petals 5; after leaves.

FRUIT. Oblong, twisted samara 1–1½ in. long with seed in center; yellow-green; in crowded persistent clusters.

TWIGS. Very thick; velvety-downy; red-brown. Winter buds: terminal absent; lateral small, subglobose, brown.

BARK. Thin; gray; smooth; shallowly furrowed with age.

WOOD. Unimportant; soft; weak; pale yellow; ring-porous.

SILVICAL CHARACTERS. Intolerant; very fast-growing; short-lived; hardy on sterile sites and in smoky cities; root-suckers aggressively; a common city ornamental.

Holocantha • Crucifixion-thorn

Holocantha emoryi Gray

A distinctive shrub or bushy small tree of southern California, Arizona, and adjacent Mexico. Leaves present only on seedlings; branches spiny throughout; flowers dioecious and 7- or 8-petaled; fruit is small, nutlike drupe.

Chinaberry

a. Leaf, × ⅙
b. Fruit, × ⅓

Pawpaw

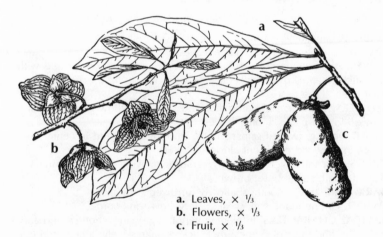

a. Leaves, × ⅓
b. Flowers, × ⅓
c. Fruit, × ⅓

MELIACEAE
Chinaberry • Umbrella-tree

Melia azedarach L.

HABIT. A small, attractive Asiatic tree commonly planted and naturalized from Virginia to California; with a spreading crown, or, in one common variety, with a dense, flattened crown like an umbrella.

LEAVES. Alternate; deciduous; bipinnately compound; 1–2 ft long; with many oval, acuminate, toothed or lobed, bright glabrous leaflets 1–3 in. long.

FLOWERS. Perfect, fragrant, purplish, ⅝ in. across clusters 4–8 in. long.

FRUIT. Yellow drupe; ⅝ in. in diameter; translucent; fleshy. Seeds: smooth, black, with a ridged stone.

TWIGS. Stout, circular, olive-green, brittle, with large, round pith. Winter buds: terminal absent; lateral ⅛ in. across, appearing naked.

BARK. Furrowed, gray-brown, with conspicuous pale lenticels.

WOOD. Unimportant; soft, weak.

SILVICAL CHARACTERS. Intolerant; short-lived; fast-growing.

West Indies Mahogany

Swietenia mahogani Jacq.

This is an important tropical timber tree, native to southern Florida.

ANNONACEAE
Pawpaw

Asimina triloba (L.) Dunal

HABIT. A large shrub or small tree 25–35 ft tall and 10–15 in. in diameter, scattered throughout the eastern United States.

LEAVES. Alternate; simple; deciduous; entire; obovate-oblong; 10–12 in. long and 4–6 in. wide; acute; base wedge-shaped; rank odor if crushed.

FLOWERS. Perfect; large; about 2 in. across; with 3 sepals and 6 purple petals; flower buds conspicuous.

FRUIT. An oblong, yellow, bananalike berry, 3–5 in. long; the pulp when yellow is sweet and edible. Seeds: several, dark brown, flattened.

TWIGS. Slender; brown; hairy; with diaphragmed pith. Winter buds: terminal present, flat, elongated, naked, rusty hairy, about ½ in. long.

BARK. Thin; brown to gray; with gray blotches; smooth or warty.

WOOD. Unimportant; light, soft and weak; yellowish green.

SILVICAL CHARACTERS. Intolerant; short-lived; with mixed hardwoods on moist bottomlands.

GENERAL. Seven other shrubby species are found in the Southeast. These are characterized by having smaller leaves and fruits.

Pond-apple

Annona glabra

This is a tropical tree reaching southern Florida. It is characterized by large, leathery, tardily deciduous, entire leaves 3–5 in. long and a distinctive compound fruit that is an aggregate of berries 3–5 in. long, ovoid, yellow.

American Holly

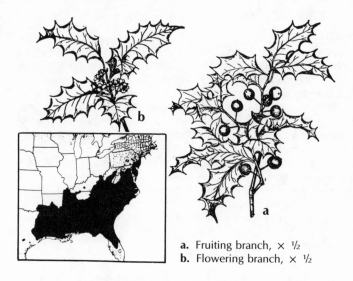

a. Fruiting branch, × ½
b. Flowering branch, × ½

Mountain Winterberry

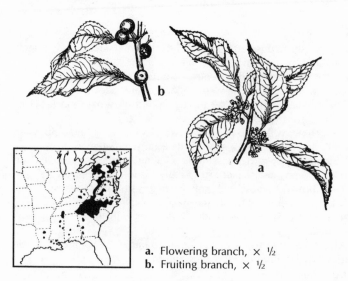

a. Flowering branch, × ½
b. Fruiting branch, × ½

AQUIFOLIACEAE

The Hollies, *Ilex* L.

About 13 species of *Ilex* are native to the eastern or southeastern parts of the United States, 6 of these commonly forming trees, and keyed out below. Most of the others, while typically shrubs up to 6 ft high, have been reported as rarely reaching tree size. The English holly, *I. aquifolium* L., is grown in plantations for decorations.

KEY TO THE SPECIES OF HOLLIES

1. Leaves persistent, thick and leathery; pedicels with bractlets.
   2. Leaves with spiny teeth or a spiny tip.
      3. Flowers and fruits usually clustered on last year's twigs; cultivated in warm areas .... *I. aquifolium* L., **English holly**
      3. Flowers and fruits usually single on current growth.
         4. Leaves less than twice as long as broad ... *I. opaca* Ait., **American holly**
         4. Leaves more than twice as long as broad; coastal plain, North Carolina to Louisiana .... *I. cassine* L., **dahoon**
   2. Leaves without spiny teeth or tip, entire to serrate.
      5. Fruit red; coastal plain, Virginia to Texas.
         6. Leaves oblanceolate to oblong-obovate, entire .... *I. cassine* L., **dahoon**
         6. Leaves oval with few crenate teeth .... *I. vomitoria* Ait., **yaupon**
      5. Fruit brown-purple; southern Florida ... *I. krugiana* Loes., **tawnyberry holly**
1. Leaves deciduous, not leathery; pedicels without bractlets.
   7. Leaves sharply toothed; apex pointed; Massachusetts and New York, south to Florida and Louisiana .... *I. montana* T. & G., **mountain winterberry**
   7. Leaves with few rounded teeth; apex obtuse; Maryland to Kansas and south ... . *I. decidua* Walt., **possumhaw**

American Holly

Ilex opaca Ait.

HABIT. The largest native holly forming a tree 40–60 ft high and 1–2 ft in diameter (max. 100 by 3½ ft); narrow, dense crown.

LEAVES. Alternate; simple; persistent 3 years; elliptical; 2–4 in. long; spiny-toothed or sometimes entire; with a spiny tip; leathery; yellow-green above; paler or yellow below.

FLOWERS. Regular; dioecious; small; solitary or in short cymes; green-white; appearing with the leaves.

FRUIT. A berrylike drupe persisting into the winter; bright red; ¼ in. long; bony nutlet in each of 3–8 cells of ovary.

TWIGS. Slender; glabrous; green with single bundle trace. Winter buds: terminal present, scaly, ⅛–¼ in. long, ciliate.

BARK. Thin; smooth; gray-white; with warty growths.

WOOD. Unimportant; hard and heavy; white; fine-textured; diffuse-porous; used for turning, novelties, finish.

SILVICAL CHARACTERS. Tolerant; slow-growing; reproduction sparse; commonly cultivated; rare near cities because of Christmas demand.

Canotia

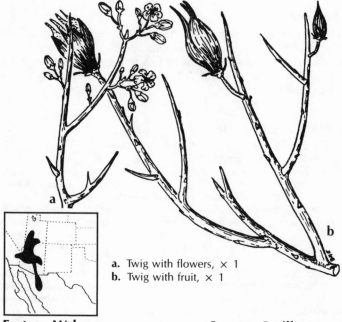

a. Twig with flowers, × 1
b. Twig with fruit, × 1

Eastern Wahoo

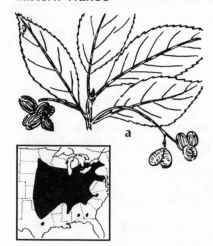

a. Fruiting twig, × ½

Swamp Cyrilla

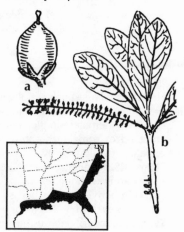

a. Fruit, × 6
b. Twig, × ½

CELASTRACEAE
Canotia • Mohavethorn

Canotia holacantha Torr.

HABIT. An odd, leafless shrub or small shrublike tree 20–30 ft high; trunk short and stocky; branches rushlike.

FLOWERS. Regular; perfect; small; in 3- to 7-flowered fascicles; calyx 5-lobed, persistent, minute; corolla 5-petale, white.

FRUIT. Dry, woody, ovoid, acuminate capsule 1 in. long; crowned with sublate, persistent style; 5-valved, splitting open at top. Seeds: solitary or paired; about ¾ in. long.

TWIGS. Slender; rushlike; round; alternate; glabrous; rigid; spine-tipped; pale green and carrying on photosynthetic functions; characteristic black, triangular, cushionlike processes located at base of each twig and flower.

BARK. Light brown; deeply furrowed.

WOOD. Heavy; hard; close-grained; light brown.

SILVICAL CHARACTERS. Intolerant; monotypic genus; on dry mountain slopes and mesas at 2,000–4,000 ft.

Eastern Wahoo • Burning Bush

Euonymus atropurpureus Jacq.

This widespread shrubby species reaches tree size in Arkansas and eastern Texas. It can be distinguished by its winged twigs; simple, opposite, petioled leaves; 4-part flowers; and fleshy, capsular seed enclosed in a thin scarlet aril. The shrubby western wahoo, *E. occidentalis* Nutt., is found in the Pacific Coast states.

CYRILLACEAE
Swamp Cyrilla

Cyrilla racemiflora L.

This common shrub, rarely a small tree, of wet sites in the coastal plain from Virginia to Texas is characterized by simple, alternate, oblong, entire, thick leaves 2–3 in. long; small, regular, perfect, white flowers in slender axillary racemes; 2-celled, ovoid, unwinged capsule ⅛ in. long

Buckwheat-tree

Cliftonia monophylla (Lam.) Britt.

This similar species ranges from Georgia to Louisiana. It differs in having glandular-punctate leaves; flowers in terminal racemes; and a 3- to 4-celled capsule ¼ in. long with 2–4 wings.

ACERACEAE

The Maples

Characteristics of the Genus *Acer* L.

HABIT. Deciduous trees or shrubs, with handsome foliage, usually assuming brilliant colors in autumn.

LEAVES. Opposite; simple or compound; deciduous; long-petioled; without stipules; simple leaves palmately 3- to 7-lobed; compound leaves pinnate, 3–7 leaflets.

FLOWERS. Regular; polygamous, dioecious, or rarely perfect; small; borne either in lateral fascicles from separate flower buds and appearing before the leaves, or in lateral and terminal racemes, panicles, or corymbs and appearing with or after the leaves; calyx colored, generally 5-part; corolla usually 5-petaled or absent; stamens 4–12, usually 7–8; ovary 2-celled, 2-lobed, compressed, 2 styles; ovules 2 in each cell, ascending.

FRUIT. Double samara united at base (key); each nutlike carpel laterally compressed and produced into large, obovate wing. Seeds: usually solitary by abortion; ovoid; compressed.

TWIGS. Slender to moderately stout; round; pith homogeneous, round; marked at base by bud scales with ringlike scars; leaf scars more or less U-shaped, with 3 (rarely 5–7) bundle scars. Winter buds: valvate or imbricated scales; inner scales accrescent; terminal buds larger than lateral.

BARK. Astringent and variable.

WOOD. Variable from soft to heavy and hard; diffuse-porous; pores all small and not crowded; rays distinct on cross section without lens; widely used for interior finish, etc.; sap of some species manufactured into sugar.

SILVICAL CHARACTERS. Mostly tolerant; fibrous root systems; widely used for ornamental and shade trees.

GENERAL. This genus contains over 100 species widely scattered through the Northern Hemisphere with one extending into Sumatra and Java. In the United States there are 13 native species. Several introduced species are planted extensively. Norway and sycamore maples are very common and better known than many native species (both included in the key). The distinctive Japanese maple, *A. palmatum* Thunb., has small, deeply 5- to 9-lobed leaves.

KEY TO THE SPECIES OF MAPLES

1. Leaves pinnately compound with 3–7 leaflets; twigs stout, smooth, green, with encircling leaf scars . . . . *A. negundo,* **boxelder,** p. 315
1. Leaves simple, palmately lobed (rarely compound in Rocky Mountain maple).
   2. Leaves with closely, often doubly, toothed margins and sharp-angled sinuses between lobes . . . . **soft maples**
      3. Winter buds bright green; leaves 4–7 in. across, 5-lobed, bluntly toothed; fruit wings 1½–2 in. long, diverging at right angle or less; Eurasian ornamental . . . . *A. pseudoplatanus* L., **sycamore maple**
      3. Winter buds red to brownish; native.
         4. Flowers appearing before the leaves; fruits maturing in late spring; buds with 4–8 visible scales; upper trunk bark smooth, light gray; eastern.
            5. Leaves very deeply 5-lobed, sides of middle lobe diverging, silvery-white beneath; young fruit woolly, wings 1½–2 in. long, widely diverging, petals absent . . . . *A. saccharinum,* **silver maple,** p. 307
            5. Leaves 3- to 5-lobed, sides of middle lobe usually converging toward apex, pale green beneath; fruit smooth, wings ½–1 in. long, slightly diverging; petals present . . . . *A. rubrum,* **red maple,** p. 307
         4. Flowers with petals, appearing with or after the leaves from leaf buds; fruit maturing in late summer; 2 (rarely 4) visible bud scales.
            6. Leaves essentially glabrous; flowers in corymbs; western.
               7. Leaves 7- to 9-lobed; fruit wings widely divergent; Pacific coast . . . . *A. circinatum,* **vine maple,** p. 309
               7. Leaves 3-lobed (rarely 3-part); fruit wings not divergent; through West . . . . *A. glabrum,* **Rocky Mountain maple,** p. 309
            6. Leaves hairy beneath; flowers in racemes; eastern.
               8. Leaves coarsely toothed, 3- to 5-lobed; fruit wings ½ in. long, diverging at about right angles; bark red-brown . . . . *A. spicatum,* **mountain maple,** p. 311
               8. Leaves finely doubly toothed, 3-lobed at apex; fruit wings ¾ in. long, widely diverging; bark green, white stripes . . . . *A. pensylvanicum,* **striped maple,** p. 311
   2. Leaf lobes entire or with few remote teeth, or slightly lobed; sinuses rounded between lobes; buds several scaled; flowers, with leaves . . . . **hard maples**
      9. Petioles red with milky juice; fruit wings 1½–2 in. long, widely diverging; leaves 5- to 7-lobed, 5–7 in. across; naturalized Eurasian species . . . . *A. platanoides,* L., **Norway maple**
      9. Petioles with watery juice; fruit wings usually diverging at right angles or less; leaves 3- to 5-lobed; native.
         10. Buds red, scales hairy on margins; western.
            11. Leaves 8–12 in. across . . . *A macrophyllum,* **bigleaf maple,** p. 313
            11. Leaves 2–5 in. across . . *A. grandidentatum,* **canyon maple,** p. 313
         10. Buds brown; eastern.
            12. Leaves 1½–3 in. across, hairy beneath; bark smooth, pale; Virginia to Missouri, Oklahoma, and south.
               13. Leaves pale beneath; fruit wings diverging at right angles . . . . *A. barbatum* Michx., **Florida maple,** pp. 303, 305
               13. Leaves green; fruit wings diverging at more than right angles . . . . *A. leucoderme* Small, **chalk maple,** pp. 303, 305
            12. Leaves 3–6 in. across; bark rough and dark; eastern.
               14. Twigs red-brown, large warty lenticels; buds light brown; leaves 5-lobed, glabrous beneath . . . . *A. saccharum,* **sugar maple,** p. 305
               14. Twigs orange, small lenticels; buds dark; leaves mostly 3-lobed, usually hairy beneath . . . . . . *A. nigrum,* **black maple,** p. 305

Sugar Maple

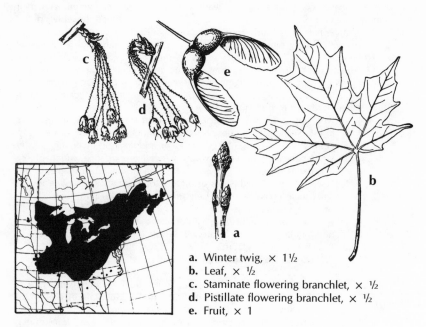

a. Winter twig, × 1½
b. Leaf, × ½
c. Staminate flowering branchlet, × ½
d. Pistillate flowering branchlet, × ½
e. Fruit, × 1

Black Maple

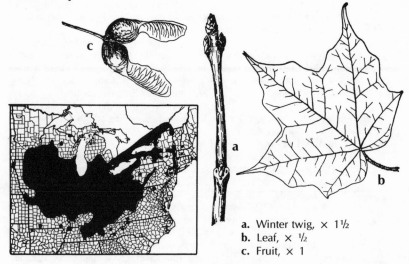

a. Winter twig, × 1½
b. Leaf, × ½
c. Fruit, × 1

Sugar Maple

Acer saccharum Marsh. (*Acer saccharophorum* K. Koch)

HABIT. A handsome tree 60–80 ft high and 2–3 ft in diameter (max. 135 by 5½ ft); dense, broad, rounded crown.

LEAVES. Simple; orbicular; palmately 5-lobed (rarely 3-lobed); 3–5 in. long; lobe margins entire or sparingly wavy-toothed with rounded sinuses; thin and firm; glabrous; bright green above; paler below; turning bright red or yellow in autumn.

FLOWERS. Polygamous; in crowded corymbs; apetalous; yellow-green; appearing with the leaves.

FRUIT. Key U-shaped, with nearly parallel wings about 1 in. long; red-brown; glabrous; maturing in autumn.

TWIGS. Slender; smooth; red-brown; shiny. Winter buds: terminal ¼–⅜ in. long, acute, red-brown, nearly glabrous, 4–8 pairs of visible scales.

BARK. Smooth and gray on young stems; becoming dark gray, thick, and deeply furrowed; often with long, scaly plates.

WOOD. Very important; hard; heavy; strong; flooring, furniture, etc.

SILVICAL CHARACTERS. Tolerant; rather slow-growing; long-lived; wide-spreading, lateral roots; important as an ornamental and as a source of maple syrup and sugar. The forms designated *A. barbatum* and *A. leucoderme* in the key are closely related and possibly should be considered varieties of *A. saccharum*.

Black Maple

Acer nigrum Michx.

This species very closely resembles the sugar maple, and many authors consider it to be a variety. It is distinguished from the sugar maple by the following characters: leaves mostly 3-lobed and lower leaf surface and petioles downy, leaf blades thicker and drooping at sides; twigs orange-brown; buds hoary-pubescent; bark often nearly black and more deeply and sharply furrowed.

Silver Maple

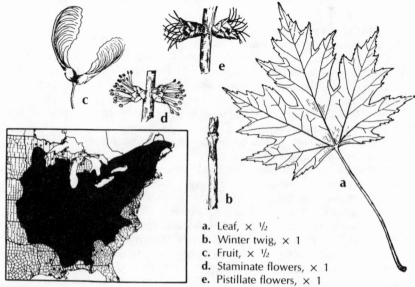

a. Leaf, × ½
b. Winter twig, × 1
c. Fruit, × ½
d. Staminate flowers, × 1
e. Pistillate flowers, × 1

Red Maple

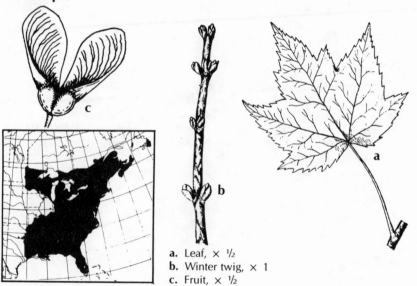

a. Leaf, × ½
b. Winter twig, × 1
c. Fruit, × ½

Silver Maple

Acer saccharinum L.

HABIT. A handsome tree 60–80 ft high and 2–3 ft in diameter (max. 120 by 7½ ft); trunk often separating near ground into several upright branches; crown broad, rounded.

LEAVES. Simple; orbicular; deeply 5-lobed, side of terminal lobe diverging toward apex; sinuses sharp-angled; 4–7 in. long; lobe margins sharply toothed; light green above, glabrous; silvery white below; turning pale yellow in autumn.

FLOWERS. Polygamous; in crowded fascicles; apetalous; red to yellow-green; appearing before the leaves.

FRUIT. Key with widely divergent wings 1½–2 in. long; greenish; glabrous; 1 samara often aborted; maturing in late spring and germinating immediately.

TWIGS. Slender; dark red; lustrous; with fetid odor when bruised. Winter buds: terminal ⅛–¼ in. long, blunt, dark red, 2–4 pairs of visible scales with ciliate margins.

BARK. Smooth and light gray on young stems; on old trunks becoming separated into scaly plates by narrow fissures.

WOOD. Moderately important; less heavy and hard than sugar maple and used as a substitute.

SILVICAL CHARACTERS. Tolerant; fast-growing; rather short-lived; moist sites; widespreading lateral roots; a common ornamental.

Red Maple

Acer rubrum L.

This species closely resembles silver maple and differs in the following characters:

LEAVES. Palmately 3-lobed (rarely 5-lobed) with short, broad lobes; sides of terminal lobe converging toward apex; sinuses sharp-angled; 2–6 in. long; lobe margins toothed; glabrous; light green above, paler and glaucous below; turning scarlet in autumn.

FLOWERS. Polygamous; petals present; reddish.

FRUIT. Key with slightly divergent wings ½–1 in. long.

TWIGS. Without fetid odor when bruised.

SILVICAL CHARACTERS. This species ranges from Canada to southern Florida.

Rocky Mountain Maple

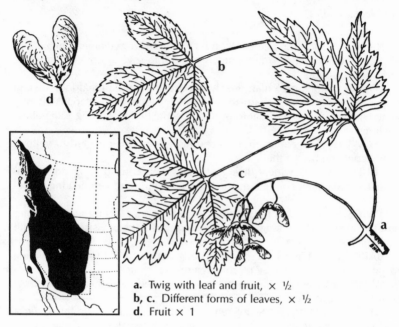

a. Twig with leaf and fruit, × ½
b, c. Different forms of leaves, × ½
d. Fruit × 1

Vine Maple

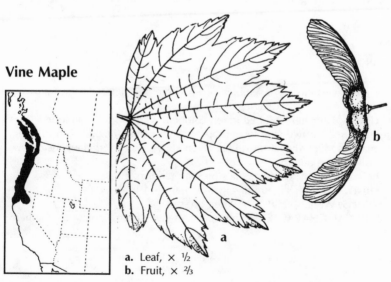

a. Leaf, × ½
b. Fruit, × ⅔

Rocky Mountain Maple • Dwarf Maple

Acer glabrum Torr.

HABIT. A shrub or small tree rarely 20–30 ft high and 6–12 in. in diameter; narrow crown with small branches.

LEAVES. Mostly 3- to 5-lobed and simple, but sometimes divided into 3 leaflets; 3–5 in. long; sharply and doubly serrate; glabrous; thin; dark green above; paler below.

FLOWERS. Mostly dioecious; in loose, racemose corymbs; petals yellow-green; appearing after the leaves.

FRUIT. Key with slightly spreading or nearly erect wings; ¾–⅞ in. long; glabrous; often rose-colored; maturing in summer.

TWIGS. Slender; glabrous; becoming bright red-brown. Winter buds: acute; ⅛–¼ in. long; bright red.

BARK. Thin; smooth; dark red-brown.

WOOD. Unimportant; heavy; hard; close-grained.

SILVICAL CHARACTERS. Rather tolerant; in moist locations; the northwestern form (var. *douglasii* Dibb.) has shallower leaf sinuses.

Vine Maple

Acer circinatum Pursh

HABIT. A shrub or small tree rarely 35 ft high; often vinelike or prostrate, forming dense thickets; irregular crown.

LEAVES. Simple; orbicular; 7- to 11-lobed; 2–6 in. long; lobes sharply doubly toothed; glabrous; light green above; paler below; turning red or orange in autumn.

FLOWERS. Polygamo-monoecious; in loose corymbs; petals greenish-white, shorter than red calyx; appearing with the leaves.

FRUIT. Key with widely divergent wings 1½ in. long; glabrous; red; maturing in late autumn.

TWIGS. Slender; glabrous; green to red-brown. Winter buds: terminal ⅛ in. long, obtuse, bright red.

BARK. Thin; smooth or with shallow fissures; bright red-brown.

WOOD. Unimportant; heavy and hard; used for handles and fuel.

SILVICAL CHARACTERS. Very tolerant; moist stream banks.

Striped Maple

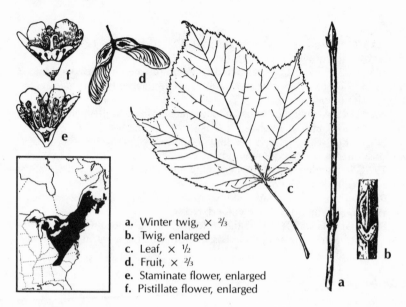

a. Winter twig, × ⅔
b. Twig, enlarged
c. Leaf, × ½
d. Fruit, × ⅔
e. Staminate flower, enlarged
f. Pistillate flower, enlarged

Mountain Maple

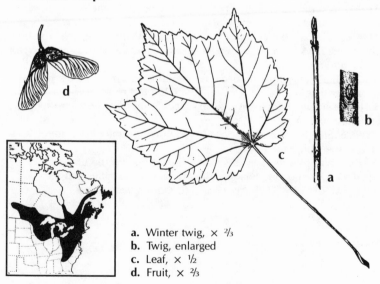

a. Winter twig, × ⅔
b. Twig, enlarged
c. Leaf, × ½
d. Fruit, × ⅔

Striped Maple • Moosewood

Acer pensylvanicum L.

HABIT. A shrub or small tree rarely 25 ft high and 8 in. in diameter; striped, upright branches with compact crown.

LEAVES. Simple; orbicular; shallowly 3-lobed above the middle; 5–6 in. long; sharply doubly toothed; glabrous; yellow-green above; paler below; turning pale yellow in autumn.

FLOWERS. Usually monoecious; in pendulous racemes; petals bright yellow; appearing after the leaves.

FRUIT. Key with widely divergent wings ¾ in. long; glabrous; red-brown; maturing in autumn.

TWIGS. Slender; smooth; red to green-brown; mottled. Winter buds: terminal ½ in. long, bright red, short-stalked.

BARK. Thin; red-brown to bright green; conspicuously marked by vertical, broad, white stripes.

WOOD. Unimportant; rather light and soft; pinkish brown.

SILVICAL CHARACTERS. Tolerant; cool, moist, shaded sites.

Mountain Maple

Acer spicatum Lam.

HABIT. A shrub or small tree rarely 35 ft high and 8 in. in diameter; upright branches, forming a compact, rounded crown.

LEAVES. Simple; orbicular; shallowly 3-lobed (rarely 5-lobed) above the middle; 3–5 in. long; coarsely toothed; dark green and glabrous above; white-downy below; turning red to orange in autumn.

FLOWERS. Polygamous; in erect, terminal racemes; petals yellow-green; appearing after the leaves.

FRUIT. Key with widely divergent wings ½–1 in. long; glabrous; bright red; maturing in autumn.

TWIGS. Slender; slightly hairy; red to brown. Winter buds: terminal ⅛–¼ in. long, bright red, more or less hairy.

BARK. Very thin; red-brown; smooth or slightly furrowed.

WOOD. Unimportant; rather light and soft; light brown.

SILVICAL CHARACTERS. Tolerant; cool, moist, shaded sites but less demanding of shade than striped maple; a common ornamental.

Bigleaf Maple

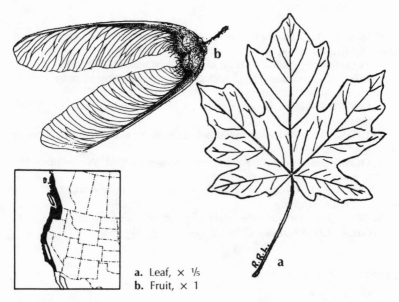

a. Leaf, × ⅕
b. Fruit, × 1

Canyon Maple

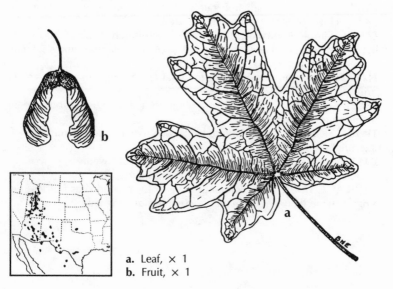

a. Leaf, × 1
b. Fruit, × 1

Bigleaf Maple

Acer macrophyllum Pursh

HABIT. A medium-sized tree often 80–100 ft high and 3–4 ft in diameter (max. 9 ft); narrow, compact crown.

LEAVES. Simple; orbicular; palmately 5-lobed; 8–12 in. long; lobe margins entire or sparingly wavy-toothed; glabrous; bright green above; paler below; turning bright orange in autumn.

FLOWERS. Polygamous; in pendulous racemes; petals present, bright yellow, ¼ in. long; appearing with the leaves.

FRUIT. Key with slightly diverging wings 1¼–2 in. long; wings densely hairy over seed cavity, nearly glabrous elsewhere; maturing in autumn.

TWIGS. Stout; smooth; red to green-brown. Winter buds: terminal ¼ in. long; blunt; 3–4 pairs of red-green, hairy-margined scales.

BARK. Smooth and gray-brown on young stems; becoming red-brown, deeply fissured, and broken into square scales on the surface.

WOOD. One of few important hardwoods on West Coast; medium hard and strong; veneer, furniture, flooring, etc.

SILVICAL CHARACTERS. Tolerant; moist sites; fast-growing; wide, shallow roots; vigorous reproduction; a common ornamental.

Canyon Maple • Bigtooth Maple

Acer grandidentatum Nutt.

HABIT. A small tree 30–40 ft high and 8–10 in. in diameter.

LEAVES. Simple; orbicular; 3- to 5-lobed; 2–5 in. in diameter; lobe margins entire or lobulate; dark green and lustrous above; paler and hairy below; turning red or yellow before falling.

FLOWERS. Polygamous; calyx yellow; petals absent.

FRUIT. Key with slightly spreading wings ½–1 in. long; glabrous or sparingly hairy; green at maturity in autumn.

TWIGS. Slender; glabrous; bright red. Terminal bud red, 1/16 in. long.

BARK. Thin; dark brown; with platelike scales.

SILVICAL CHARACTERS. Rather tolerant; moist sites; shallow roots.

Boxelder

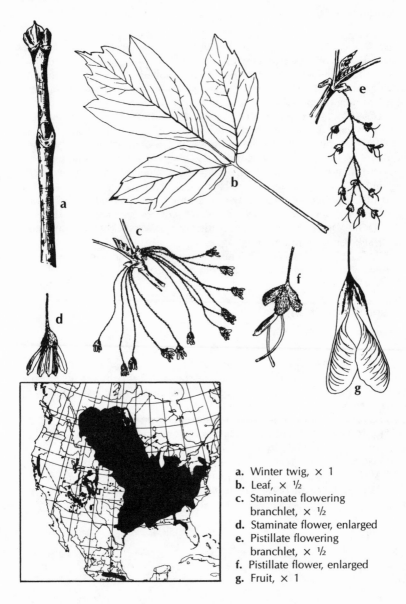

a. Winter twig, × 1
b. Leaf, × ½
c. Staminate flowering
   branchlet, × ½
d. Staminate flower, enlarged
e. Pistillate flowering
   branchlet, × ½
f. Pistillate flower, enlarged
g. Fruit, × 1

Boxelder

Acer negundo L.

HABIT. A small tree, rarely 75 ft high and 4 ft in diameter; trunk usually irregular and dividing near ground into several stout, widespreading branches.

LEAVES. Compound; 3–5 (rarely 7) leaflets; petiole long, slender, puberulous; leaflets ovate to lanceolate; 3–4 in. long, and 1½–4 in. wide; glabrous; acuminate; coarsely serrate and sometimes 3-lobed at base.

FLOWERS. Dioecious; minute; the male fascicled; the female in drooping racemes; appearing with leaves or a little before them; calyx 5-lobed, hairy, yellow-green; corolla absent; stamens 4–6 with slender, exserted, hairy filaments; ovary hairy, partly enclosed by calyx.

FRUIT. Pendent; 1–2 in. long; glabrous; ripening in autumn; in drooping racemes 6–8 in. long. Seeds: narrowed at the ends; smooth; bright red-brown; ½ in. long.

TWIGS. Moderately stout; greenish; pubescent, or rarely nearly glabrous; marked by conspicuous bud scale scars and crescent-shaped leaf scars that surround the twig. Winter buds: acute; ⅛–¼ in. long; reddish; tomentose.

BARK. Thin (¼–½ in.); pale gray or light brown; deeply divided by furrows into broad, rounded ridges.

WOOD. Light; soft; close-grained; weak; heartwood cream-white to yellow-brown, often streaked; sapwood thick; used occasionally for cheap furniture, woodenware, etc.

SILVICAL CHARACTERS. Upper Sonoran and transition zones; moderately tolerant; shallow-rooted, except on deep soils; hardy to extremes of climate; fast-growing but short-lived and usually of poor form; reproduction by sprout and seed plentiful.

GENERAL. Several intergrading geographical varieties have been recognized, including the following: *arizonicum* Sarg. in Arizona and New Mexico, with serrate leaves and glabrous leaves, twigs and petioles; *californicum* Sarg. in California, with coarsely serrate or nearly entire leaflets with matted hairs on the lower surface; *interius* Sarg. through the West, with hairy twigs and petioles; *texanum* Pax through the Southeast, with woolly twigs and lower leaf surface; and *violaceum* J. & B. through the northern half of the United States, with bluish glabrous twigs and entire or dentate leaves hairy on the lower surface. The distribution of all varieties is included on the map.

HIPPOCASTANACEAE

The Buckeyes and Horsechestnuts

Characteristics of the Genus *Aesculus* L.

HABIT. Handsome shrubs to medium-sized trees with dense, rounded crowns; commonly planted as ornamentals for their flowers or foliage.

LEAVES. Opposite; palmately compound; 5–9 serrate leaflets arising at end of long stem; deciduous; stipules absent.

FLOWERS. Regular; polygamo-monoecious; bell-shaped; many-flowered, showy, upright panicles; yellow, red, or white; flowers near base of panicles perfect and fertile; calyx 5-lobed (rarely 2-lobed); petals 4–5; stamens 5–8, inserted on the disk; ovules 3-valved, 2 in each cell; appearing after the leaves.

FRUIT. A large, leathery, smooth to spiny capsule, containing 1 or more large, lustrous, brown, leathery-coated seeds marked by a large light-colored hilum, which gives the name *buckeye* to this genus; poisonous.

TWIGS. Stout; round; marked by conspicuous triangular leaf scars with more than 3 bundle scars; pith large, circular, light-colored. Winter buds: terminal present, large, scaly, resin-covered in some species.

BARK. Intermediate in thickness; fissured and scaly; bitter.

WOOD. Moderately important; fine-textured; diffuse-porous; creamy-white; used for containers, novelties, furniture, etc.

SILVICAL CHARACTERS. Moderately tolerant; varied sites; fast-growing; short-lived; in mixed hardwood stands.

GENERAL. This genus contains about 13 species scattered over the Northern Hemisphere, with 6 species native to the United States; the European horsechestnut, *Aesculus hippocastanum* L., is widely planted and has escaped from cultivation in the northern states; the red buckeye, *A.* X *carnea* Hayne, is a hybrid of *A. hippocastanum* and *A. pavia* and often planted for its red flowers. Species hybridize frequently.

KEY TO THE SPECIES OF BUCKEYE

1. Winter buds thickly coated with resin; flowers white to pink (often red in A. X carnea).
    2. Leaflets usually 7 (rarely 5), sessile or nearly so; fruit 2–2½ in. long, with short spines; widely planted and naturalized ....
    .... Aesculus hippocastanum L., **horsechestnut**
    2. Leaflets usually 5, on stalks ½–1 in. long; fruit 2–3 in. long, smooth; California
    .... A. californica (Spach) Nutt., **California buckeye**
1. Winter buds not resinous, or slightly so; flowers yellow, white, or scarlet; leaflets stalked; eastern.
    3. Fruit spiny, 1–2 in. long; flowers yellow-green; bud scales prominently keeled.
        4. Leaflets 5 (rarely 7); small to medium-sized tree; Pennsylvania and Michigan to Nebraska and south .... A. glabra Willd., **Ohio buckeye,** p. 319
        4. Leaflets 7–9; shrub or rarely a small tree; Oklahoma and Nebraska to Missouri and Texas .... A. arguta Buckl., **Texas buckeye**
    3. Fruit nearly smooth, not shiny; bud scales not prominently keeled.
        5. Leaflets 5–7; flowers yellow or white.
            6. Flowers yellow with glandular-hairy calyx; fruit 2–3 in. long; large tree
            .... A. octandra Marsh. **Yellow buckeye,** p. 319
            6. Flowers white; fruit 1 in. long; local in Alabama and southwest Georgia
            .... A. parviflora Walt., **bottlebrush buckeye**
        5. Leaflets 5; flowers red to red-yellow with calyx not glandular-hairy; fruit 1–2 in. long; shrubs or small trees.
            7. Petals hairless but glandular on margin; North Carolina to Illinois, south to Missouri and Texas .... A. pavia L., **red buckeye**
            7. Petals hairy but not glandular on margin; Virginia to Tennessee, south to Georgia and Alabama .... A. sylvatica Bartr., **painted buckeye**

Yellow Buckeye

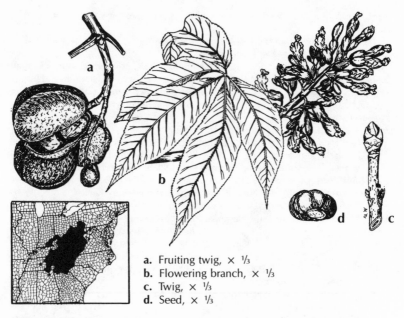

a. Fruiting twig, × ⅓
b. Flowering branch, × ⅓
c. Twig, × ⅓
d. Seed, × ⅓

Ohio Buckeye

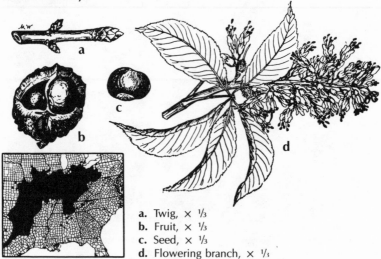

a. Twig, × ⅓
b. Fruit, × ⅓
c. Seed, × ⅓
d. Flowering branch, × ⅓

Yellow Buckeye

Aesculus octandra Marsh.

HABIT. A medium-sized tree 60–90 ft high and 2–3 ft in diameter (max. 110 by 5 ft); broad, rounded crown.

LEAVES. Five-foliate (rarely 7); 4–10 in. long; with elliptical, glabrous to tomentose-serrate leaflets; dark yellow-green above, paler below.

FLOWERS. Whitish-yellow; glandular-hairy calyx and pedicel; stamens inserted within corolla.

FRUIT. Capsule pale brown; 2–3 in. long; usually smooth; containing usually 2 red-brown seeds about 1–1½ in. long and poisonous.

TWIGS. Stout; hairy at first, becoming smooth and red-brown to gray. Winter buds: terminal ⅔–1 in. long, glabrous, pale brown, nonresinous, scales not prominently keeled.

BARK. Gray to dark brown; ¾ in. thick; thin scales.

SILVICAL CHARACTERS. Tolerant; moist sites; the largest American species.

Ohio Buckeye • Fetid Buckeye

Aesculus glabra Willd.

HABIT. A small to medium-sized tree 30–50 ft high and 1–2 ft in diameter (max. 90 by 3 ft); broad, rounded crown.

LEAVES. Five-foliate (rarely 7); 3–6 in. long; with ovate or oval, glabrous, finely serrate leaflets; yellow-green above; paler below; ill-scented when bruised.

FLOWERS. Yellow-green; hairy; small; stamens exserted.

FRUIT. Capsule red-brown; 1–2 in. long; usually spiny; containing a single brown seed about 1 in. long; poisonous.

TWIGS. Stout; hairy at first becoming smooth and red-brown to ash-gray; disagreeable odor when bruised. Winter buds: terminal ⅔ in. long, red-brown, nonresinous, prominently keeled scales.

BARK. Ash-gray; thick; deeply fissured and plated; ill-scented.

SILVICAL CHARACTERS. Tolerant; moist sites; becoming rare.

Western Soapberry

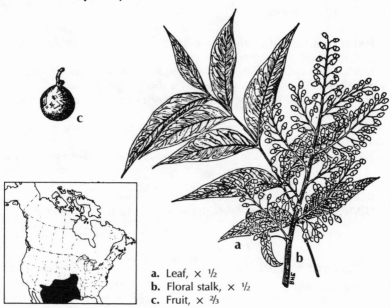

a. Leaf, × ½
b. Floral stalk, × ½
c. Fruit, × ⅔

Mexican-buckeye

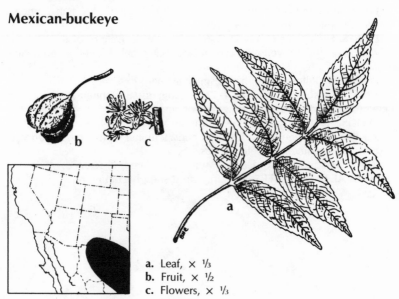

a. Leaf, × ⅓
b. Fruit, × ½
c. Flowers, × ⅓

SAPINDACEAE

Western Soapberry

Sapindus drummondii Hook. & Arn.

HABIT. A shrub or small tree rarely 40–50 ft high and 1½–2 ft in diameter; branches round, usually erect.

LEAVES. Alternate; pinnately compound with 4–9 pairs of lanceolate leaflets, each 2–3 in. long; margins entire; glabrous above; pubescent beneath; yellow-green; deciduous.

FLOWERS. Regular; polygamo-dioecious; minute; in many-flowered clusters 6–9 in. long; calyx 4–5 acute sepals; corolla 4–5 white petals; stamens 8–10; ovary 2- to 4-celled.

FRUIT. Drupaceous; ripening into a leathery, 1- to 3-celled, and seeded berry; ½ in. in diameter; glabrous; yellow, turning black in drying; persistent on branches until spring; formerly used as soap. Seeds: solitary in each carpel; obovoid; dark brown; smooth, bony coat.

TWIGS. Moderately stout; at first pubescent and pale yellow-green, becoming puberulous, gray. Winter buds: terminal absent; lateral small, globose, often superposed in pairs.

BARK. Thin (⅓–½ in.); red-brown; furrowed into long, superficially scaly plates; bitter and astringent.

WOOD. Unimportant; heavy; hard; strong; close-grained; ring-porous; heartwood light brown, tinged with yellow.

SILVICAL CHARACTERS. Intolerant. Florida soapberry, *S. marginatus* Willd., is a small tree from South Carolina to Florida. Wingless soapberry, *S. saporania* L., of South and Central America extends through Florida.

Mexican-buckeye

Ungnadia speciosa Endl.

This shrub or small tree of southern Texas and New Mexico has alternate, deciduous, pinnately compound leaves with 5–7 ovate-lanceolate leaflets, 3–5 in. long, thick, and dark green; small, irregular, polygamous flowers; leathery, 3-valved capsular, red-brown fruit 2 in. wide, containing black, shiny, leathery seeds about ½ in. long, reputed to be poisonous.

Goldenrain

Koelreuteria paniculata Laxm.

A small, graceful, Asiatic tree with pinnately compound leaves and crenate, serrate, or nearly lobed leaflets; yellow flowers; and a distinctive bladderlike fruit with papery walls and three black seeds.

Elephanttree

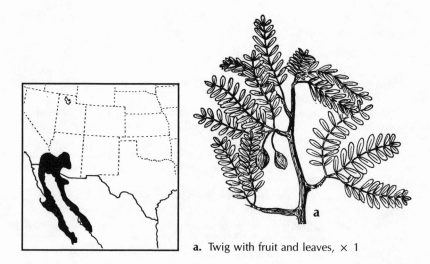

a. Twig with fruit and leaves, × 1

Tamarisk

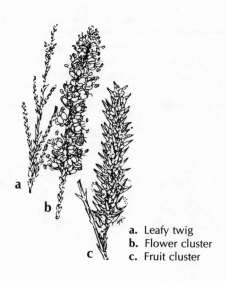

a. Leafy twig
b. Flower cluster
c. Fruit cluster

BURSERACEAE

Elephanttree
Bursera microphylla A. Gray

This rarely becomes a small tree in the desert in southern California and Arizona. It is characterized by alternate, deciduous, bipinnately compound leaves with 20–40 leaflets ¼ in. long; small, polygamous, white flowers; and a red, capsulelike drupe ¼ in. long. The fragrant bursera, *B. fagaroides* Engler., is a similar form in southern Arizona. Gumbo-limbo, *B. simaruba* Sarg., is native to southern Florida.

TAMARICACEAE

Tamarisk • Saltcedar
Tamarix chinensis Lour. (*Tamarix pentandra* Pall.)

This large shrub or small tree, which was introduced from Europe, is abundant and extensively naturalized along streams throughout the central and southern parts of the western United States. It is characterized by alternate, crowded, scalelike leaves, ¹⁄₁₆ in. long, and somewhat resembling those of junipers; showy pink, crowded small flowers in narrow clusters; small 3- to 5-valved capsular fruits containing many minute seeds; slender purplish twigs, which shed with the leaves; and red-brown bark.

Two smaller European species are planted and escaped across the United States. *T. gallica* L., French tamarisk, which is naturalized in southern Texas and Louisiana, and *T. parviflora* L., small-flower tamarisk, naturalized in California.

STAPHYLEACEAE

American Bladdernut
Staphylea trifolia L.

This shrub, or rarely a small tree, grows through most of the eastern United States. It is characterized by opposite, pinnately compound leaves with 3–5 ovate, serrate leaflets; greenish striped branches and a bladdery, inflated, 3-celled capsule.

Sierra bladdernut, *S. bolanderi* Gray, grows in northern to central California.

Cascara Buckthorn

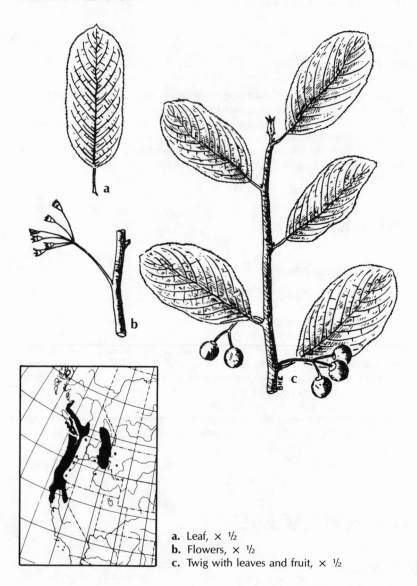

a. Leaf, × ½
b. Flowers, × ½
c. Twig with leaves and fruit, × ½

RHAMNACEAE

The Buckthorns, *Rhamnus* L.

A related shrubby form of buckthorn, *R. betulifolia* Greene, grows from southern Nevada and Utah through Arizona, New Mexico, and southwestern Texas. Four native and two naturalized species reach tree size.

KEY TO THE SPECIES OF BUCKTHORNS

1. Winter buds scaly; leaves oval to broad-ovate.
    2. Leaves deciduous, thin, opposite or nearly so, finely crenate-serrate; fruit black; naturalized . . . . *R. cathartica* L., **European buckthorn**
    2. Leaves persistent, thick, mostly alternate, spiny-toothed; fruit red; California and Arizona . . . . *R. crocea* Nutt., **hollyleaf buckthorn**, p. 327
1. Winter buds naked; leaves entire or finely toothed.
    3. Leaves deciduous, thin.
        4. Flowers in umbel-like cymes; leaves 2–7 in. long, 8–15 pairs of veins; native.
            5. Leaves 10–15 pairs of veins; peduncles longer than petioles; West Coast
            . . . . *R. purshiana* DC., **cascara buckthorn**, p. 325
            5. Leaves 8–10 pairs of veins; peduncles shorter than petioles; Southeast and central states . . . . *R. caroliniana* Walt., **Carolina buckthorn**
        4. Flowers fascicled or solitary; leaves 1½–2½ in. long, 8–9 pairs of veins; naturalized in the Northeast . . . . *R. frangula* L., **glossy buckthorn**
    3. Leaves persistent thick; southeastern California to Nevada and New Mexico . . .
    . . . . *R. californica* Eschsch., **California buckthorn**

Cascara Buckthorn

Rhamnus purshiana DC.

HABIT. A shrub or tree 20–40 ft high and 6–20 in. in diameter; wide, open crown with numerous stout branches.

LEAVES. Alternate, or rarely obliquely opposite; simple; broad-elliptic; 2–7 in. long; undulate margins finely serrate or nearly entire; thin; villous below and on veins above; deciduous; turning pale yellow before falling; petioles stout, hairy, ½–1 in. long; stipules minute, deciduous.

FLOWERS. Regular; perfect; small; in axillary peduncled cymes; long-pedicelled; calyx 5-lobed; corolla greenish, minute, 5-lobed; stamens 5; ovary 2- to 4-celled; ovules solitary, erect.

FRUIT. Drupaceous; subglobose; ⅓–½ in. in diameter; black; bearing remnants of style; flesh thin and juicy; 2–3 obovoid, 1-seeded nutlets with thin, gray or yellow-green shell.

TWIGS. Slender; round; pubescent, usually becoming glabrous; yellow-green or red-brown. Winter buds: terminal absent; lateral small, naked, hoary-tomentose.

BARK. Thin (¼ in.); gray to dark brown, often tinged with red; scaly; important because of laxative properties.

WOOD. Unimportant; rather light; soft; not strong; ring-porous; heartwood brown, tinged with red.

SILVICAL CHARACTERS. Moderately tolerant; prolific seeder, coppices freely; no taproot; few enemies.

Hollyleaf Buckthorn

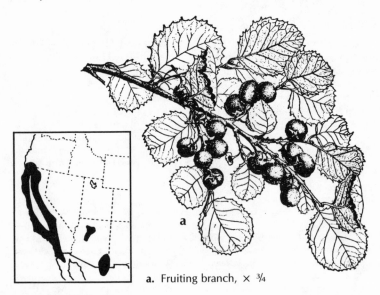

a. Fruiting branch, × ¾

Blueblossom Ceanothus

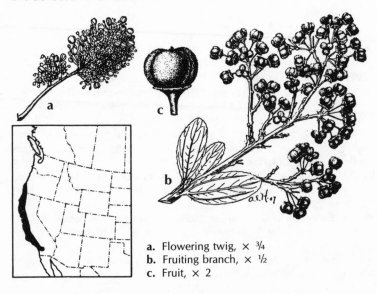

a. Flowering twig, × ¾
b. Fruiting branch, × ½
c. Fruit, × 2

Hollyleaf Buckthorn

Rhamnus crocea Nutt.

HABIT. A shrub or small evergreen tree rarely 25 ft high and 6–8 in. in diameter; crown round; branches stout.

LEAVES. Alternate or subopposite; simple; oval or orbicular; 1–1½ in. long; margin spinulose-dentate; leathery; glabrous; yellow-green above; often golden below; persistent.

FLOWERS. Regular; polygamo-dioecious; in small axillary clusters; calyx about ⅛ in. long, 4-lobed; petals absent.

FRUIT. Drupaceous; obovoid; ¼ in. in diameter; red; flesh thin and dry; 2–3 brown nutlets ⅛ in. long, hard.

TWIGS. Slender; round; rigid, often spinescent; red-brown; glabrous. Winter buds: terminal absent; lateral ¹⁄₁₆ in. long, scaly, obtuse, scales hairy-fringed.

BARK. Thin (¹⁄₁₆–⅛ in.); dark gray; slightly roughened by minute tubercles; acrid and bitter.

WOOD. Moderately heavy and hard; brittle; fine-grained; ring-porous; heartwood light yellow-brown; unimportant.

SILVICAL CHARACTERS. Intolerant; prolific seeder; on hot, dry hillsides; in pure groups or scattered.

Bluewood • Logwood

Condalia hookeri Johnst.

This velvety-pubescent shrub or small tree is one of the common chaparral species of central and southern Texas, commonly forming dense thickets. It is characterized by small (½- to ¾-in.-long), entire, tardily deciduous, alternate, or fascicled leaves; small axillary flowers; and a deep red, subglobose drupe ⅕ in. in diameter, to which the calyx is attached. *C. globosa* Johnst. is a shrubby species of the desert mountains of southwestern Arizona and southeastern California.

Blueblossom Ceanothus

Ceanothus thyrsiflorus Eschs.

This shrub or small tree is common in coastal forests from southern Oregon to central California. It is characterized by simple, alternate, minutely toothed, persistent leaves 1–1½ in. long; small, perfect, blue or white flowers; a subglobose, 3-lobed, dry drupe ¼ in. long, which separates into 3 nutlets; and scaly lateral buds. *C. arboreus* Greene and *C. spinosus* Nutt. are small trees in southern California.

American Basswood

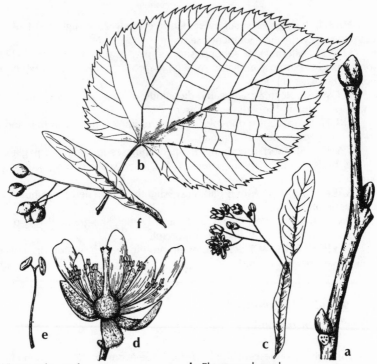

a. Winter twig, × 1
b. Leaf, × 1/3
c. Bract with flowers, × 1/2
d. Flower, enlarged
e. Stamen, enlarged
f. Bract bearing fruit, × 1/2

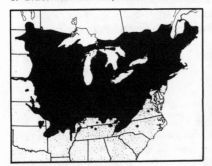

American Basswood

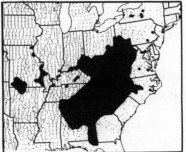

White Basswood

TILIACEAE

American Basswood • Linden

Tilia americana L. (*Tilia glabra* Vent.)

HABIT. A medium-sized tree 60–80 ft high and 2–3 ft in diameter (max. 125 by 4½ ft); dense, rounded crown.

LEAVES. Alternate; simple; deciduous; 5–6 in. long; broadly ovate; coarsely serrate; unequally heart-shaped base; glabrous; dull dark green above; paler beneath; petioles slender, 1–2 in. long; stipules falling early.

FLOWERS. Regular; perfect; in loose 6- to 15-flowered cymes, the long stalk attached to a leafy bract for half its length; yellow-white; fragrant; 5 sepals; 5 petals; many stamens; 5-celled ovary; appearing after the leaves.

FRUIT. A gray, globose, woolly, nutlike drupe ⅓–½ in. long; in cymes and attached to leafy persistent bracts.

TWIGS. Generally rather stout; green to red-gray, becoming dark gray; conspicuous stipule scars; pith circular. Winter buds: terminal absent; lateral subglobose, acute, red, lopsided, ¼ in. long, 2–3 scales usually visible.

BARK. Smooth and gray-green on young trunks; becoming thick, dark gray, furrowed, with narrow, scaly ridges.

WOOD. Important; light; soft; fine-textured; diffuse-porous; used for novelties, patterns, excelsior, containers, etc.

SILVICAL CHARACTERS. Tolerant; moist sites; abundant seed produced; sprouts vigorously; fast-growing; mixed hardwoods; deep lateral roots; prized as source of honey.

Other Species of *Tilia*

Some authors have recognized as many as 16 native species of *Tilia*, the differences being minor and variable. Three species are accepted in the 1979 checklist. *T. caroliniana* Mill. is an unimportant tree of the coastal plain and piedmont area from North Carolina to Florida, west to Texas, and north to Arkansas. White basswood, *T. heterophylla* Vent., is an important tree differing from American basswood by having leaves that are woolly on the lower surface and 10–25 flowers in a cluster.

Several European species are planted for ornamental purposes, the most common being the European linden, *T.* X *europea* L., with leaves 2½–4 in. long; and the small-leaved linden, *T. cordata* Mill., with leaves 1½–2½ in. long.

Fremontia

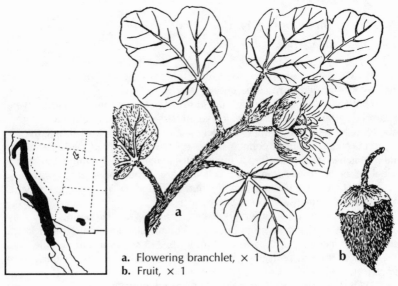

a. Flowering branchlet, × 1
b. Fruit, × 1

Allthorn

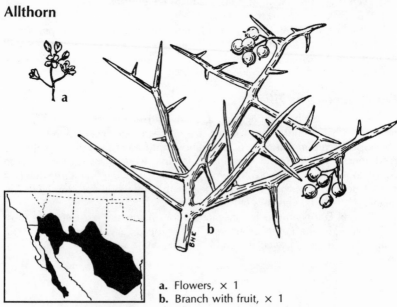

a. Flowers, × 1
b. Branch with fruit, × 1

STERCULIACEAE
Fremontia Flannelbush

Fremontodendron californicum (Torr.) Cov. (*Fremontia californica* Torr.)

HABIT. A shrub or small tree 20–30 ft high and 12–14 in. in diameter; crown open with stout branches.

LEAVES. Alternate, simple; broadly ovate; 1½ in. in diameter; usually 3-lobed; thick; stellate; rusty-pubescent below; persistent 2 years; petioles stout.

FLOWERS. Regular; perfect; solitary; calyx, deeply 5-lobed, yellow, 1 in. long; corolla absent; stamens 5; ovary 5-celled.

FRUIT. Ovoid, acuminate, 4-valved capsule; 1 in. long; densely woolly-dehiscent; inner surface villous-pubescent. Seeds: oval; small (about ³⁄₁₆ in. long); very dark brown.

TWIGS. Stout; round; stellate; rusty-pubescent at first, becoming glabrous and light red-brown. Winter buds: naked.

BARK. Thin; furrowed; dark red-brown.

WOOD. Unimportant; heavy; hard; ring-porous; red-brown.

SILVICAL CHARACTERS. Intolerant; on very poor, dry foothills; forming dense thickets; a monotypic genus. *F. mexicanum* Dav. is in extreme southern California and Baja California.

Chinese Parasoltree

Firmiana simplex (L.) Wight

This is an attractive ornamental with entire, palmately 3-lobed leaves 6–8 in. long and a fruit that is a leathery, leaflike follicle. It is widely planted, escaped, and locally naturalized in the southern United States.

KOEBERLINACEAE
Allthorn • Corono de Cristo

Koeberlinia spinosa Zucc.

HABIT. A shrub or small bushy tree rarely 20–25 ft high; often appearing to bear neither leaf, flower, nor fruit.

LEAVES. Alternate; simple; early deciduous, the tree usually leafless; scalelike and minute (not over ⅛ in. long).

FLOWERS. Regular; perfect; small; in short umbellike racemes; petals 4, green-white, much longer than sepals.

FRUIT. Small (³⁄₁₆–¼ in.), subglobose, 2-celled, black berry; flesh thin and succulent; cells 1–2 seeded. Seeds: coiled and shell-shaped; seed coat brittle and wrinkled.

TWIGS. Stout; glabrous; terminating in sharp, rigid spine; pale green in color. Winter buds: minute and inconspicuous.

SILVICAL CHARACTERS. Intolerant; on dry, gravelly plains and foothills; a monotypic botanical curiosity.

Gordonia

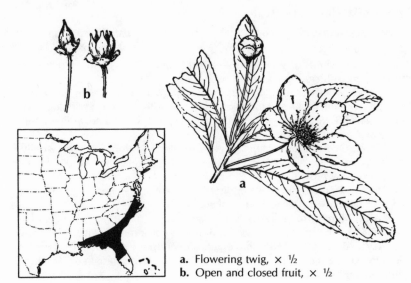

a. Flowering twig, × ½
b. Open and closed fruit, × ½

Devils-walkingstick

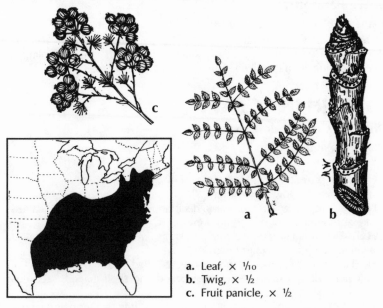

a. Leaf, × ¹/₁₀
b. Twig, × ½
c. Fruit panicle, × ½

THEACEAE
Gordonia • Loblolly-bay
Gordonia lasianthus (L.) Ellis

HABIT. A beautiful, medium-sized tree 60–75 ft high and 1–2 ft in diameter; narrow, compact crown.

LEAVES. Alternate; simple; persistent; 3–6 in. long; lanceolate to elliptic; leathery; shallowly toothed; dark green; turning scarlet before falling.

FLOWERS. Regular; perfect; showy; white; fragrant; 2½ in. across petals; sepals silky; ovary 3- to 5-celled.

FRUIT. A woody, oblong, 5-celled capsule ⅔ in. long; silky surface. Seeds: 1/16 in. long; flat; nearly square; winged.

TWIGS. Slender; dark brown; rough. Winter buds: terminal present, ¼ in. long, acute, silky-hairy.

BARK. Thick; red-brown; deeply fissured and ridged.

GENERAL. A rare shrub, franklinia, *Franklinia alatamaha* Bartr. (*Gordonia alatamaha* [Bartr.] Sarg.) with deciduous, lustrous, oblong leaves 6–9 in. long and creamy, cup-shaped flowers, is planted as an ornamental. Native to McIntosh County, Georgia, but not found growing wild since 1790.

Stewartia and Virginia Stewartia

The shrubby mountain Stewartia, *Stewartia ovata* (Cav.) Weath., with showy white flowers 4 in. in diameter and simple, deciduous leaves that are hairy-margined and minutely toothed, occurs in the mountains from Virginia and Kentucky to Alabama and to Georgia. The similar Virginia Stewartia, *S. malacodendron* L., occurs on the coastal plain from Virginia to eastern Texas.

ARALIACEAE
Devils-walkingstick
Aralia spinosa L.

HABIT. A prickly grotesque shrub or small tree rarely 35 ft high with few branches and a flat crown.

LEAVES. Alternate; doubly pinnately compound; deciduous; 2–4 ft long; pinnae usually bearing 5–6 pairs of ovate, serrate, thin, dark green leaflets 2–3 in. long and prickly.

FLOWERS. Regular; perfect or staminate; small; in many-flowered panicles 3–4 ft long; green-white.

FRUIT. Small, juicy, black berry ¼ in. long; tipped with persistent style. Seeds: 2–5, oblong; compressed; red-brown.

TWIGS. Stout (½–1 in. thick); orange; lustrous; armed with stout prickles. Winter buds: terminal present, conical.

CACTACEAE

The Cactuses

Characteristics of the Cactus Family

HABIT. Shrubs or seldom trees, rarely 50–60 ft high and 2 ft in diameter; stems commonly columnar, fluted, succulent, and branched; numerous spines springing from cushions of small bristles (areolae).

LEAVES. Alternate; simple; mostly reduced to spines or scales or absent; photosynthetic processes taking place in the green parts of the fleshy stems.

FLOWERS. Regular; perfect; usually single; large and showy; calyx of numerous sepals forming a tube, those of inner series petallike; corolla showy, of numerous petals; stamens many, inserted on calyx tube; ovary inferior, 1-celled, with several parietal placentae and numerous horizontal ovules, styles united into one, stigmas as many as placentae.

FRUIT. 1-celled, fleshy (rarely dry) berry, often edible. Seed: numerous, small.

WOOD. An internal, woody frame or skeleton, made up of a cylinder or a meshed network of strands.

BUDS. Modified into pulvini or cushions, which are usually depressions often consisting of a complex series of spines, wool, glands, and growing points.

SILVICAL CHARACTERS. Very intolerant; although seed generally produced abundantly, natural reproduction by seed is rather scanty because of unfavorable environment; vegetative reproduction common; typical of very dry desert areas where they are often the only woody plants.

GENERAL. This family contains about 120 genera and 1,200 species; there are 2 genera and 5 species reaching tree size in the United States in southern California, Arizona, and New Mexico. Saguaro, *Cereus giganteus* Engelm., is a large tree forming a conspicuous part of desert vegetation. Two species, *C. schotti* Engelm. and *C. thurberi* Engelm., of southern Arizona and Mexico, have columnar branches 20–25 ft high but cannot be considered trees as they do not have a definite trunk. *C. robinii* (Lem.) Ben. is very rare on the Florida keys. Cholla, *Opuntia* Engelm., has 4 species that may be considered treelike and are included in the key.

KEY TO THE ARBORESCENT SPECIES OF CACTACEAE

1. Branches and stems columnar, ribbed, not tuberculate, continuous; aeroles (growing centers) without glochids (minute bristles); leaves spinelike; tube of flower elongated; seeds dark-colored; spines not barbed; a tree often 50–60 ft high; the state flower of Arizona ....
   .... *Cereus giganteus* Engelm. (*Carnegiea gigantea* [Engelm.] B. & R.), **saguaro**
1. Branches and stems slender, columnar, tuberculate, conspicuously jointed; aeroles with both glochids and spines; leaves small, fleshy on young parts; flower tube short; seed light-colored; spines retrosely barbed; small plants not over 15 ft high ......
   .... *Opuntia*
   2. Tubercles of branches broad, full, and rounded below areolae; flowers pink or purple; fruit sparingly spiny or without spines.
      3. Flowers pink; fruit green, proliferous (one growing from another), usually spineless; joints pale olive-green, readily detached, freely falling, tubercles broad and ovoid; spines yellow .... *Opuntia fulgida* Engelm., **cholla**
      3. Flowers purple; fruit yellow, rarely proliferous, spiny; joints green or purple, not readily detached, persistent, tubercles elongated; spines white to red-brown .... *Opuntia spinosior* (Engelm.) Toumey, **tasajo**
   2. Tubercles of branches narrow, high, flattened laterally. Flowers purple, or green-tinted with red or yellow.
      4. Fruit smooth or but slightly tuberculate, spiny, green; branch tubercles ⅔ in. long; spines 5–11, ⅛ in. long or less, dark red-brown; flowers green, tinted with red or yellow .... *Opuntia versicolor* Engelm., **staghorn cholla**
      4. Fruit manifestly tuberculate, naked, yellow; branch tubercles ¾ in. long; spines 8–30, ¾–1¼ in. long, brown; flowers purple ....
         . *Opuntia imbricata* (Haw.) DC. (*Opuntia arborescens* Engelm.), **cane cactus**

EUPHORBIACEAE

Tung-oil-tree

Aleurites fordii Hemsl.

This tree of China is widely cultivated in subtropical regions for the commercial oil in the seeds. Grown in plantations in the coastal plain from Georgia to Texas, it has been reported as naturalized. It is characterized by large, simple, alternate, ovate, entire leaves that are palmately veined and have 2 red, lustrous glands at the petiole apex; a nutlike, capsular fruit 1½–3 in. long containing large, smooth, thick-shelled, poisonous seeds; thick twigs; and smooth, light gray bark.

Chinese Tallowtree

Sapium sebiferum (L.) Roxb.

A naturalized ornamental in the coastal plain from North Carolina to Texas, this Chinese tree is characterized by simple, alternate, entire leaves shaped like an inverted beet root; and a capsular fruit, 3-celled, ½ in. in diameter, and containing 3 white seeds with waxy seed coats.

Brazil sapium, *S. glandulosum* (L.) Morong, has been reported as naturalized in northwest Florida.

The Mexican jumping-bean sapium, *S. biloculare* (Wats.) Pax, with a 2-seeded capsule reaches southwest Arizona.

Black Tupelo

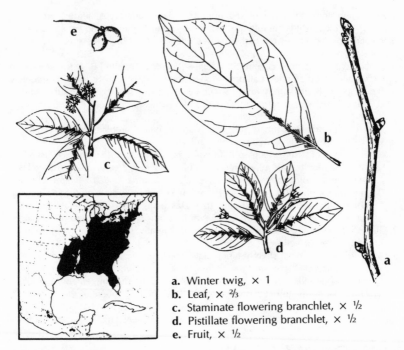

a. Winter twig, × 1
b. Leaf, × ⅔
c. Staminate flowering branchlet, × ½
d. Pistillate flowering branchlet, × ½
e. Fruit, × ½

Water Tupelo

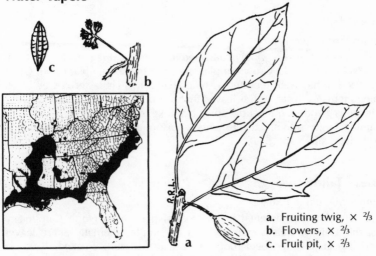

a. Fruiting twig, × ⅔
b. Flowers, × ⅔
c. Fruit pit, × ⅔

NYSSACEAE

Black Tupelo • Blackgum
Nyssa sylvatica Marsh.

HABIT. A medium-sized tree 40–80 ft high and 1–3 ft in diameter (max. 125 by 6 ft); rounded crown, horizontal branches.

LEAVES. Alternate; simple; deciduous; 2–5 in. long; obovate; entire or wavy; thick, lustrous; estipulate; dark green above, paler, often hairy below; scarlet in autumn.

FLOWERS. Regular; polygamo-dioecious; small; staminate in heads; green-white; appearing with the leaves.

FRUIT. Fleshy, ovoid, blue-black drupe ⅓–⅔ in. long, indistinctly ribbed pit (distinctly ribbed in swamp tupelo).

TWIGS. Slender; green to red-brown; smooth; pith diaphragmed; leaf scars with 3 bundle scars. Winter buds: terminal present, scaly, ¼ in. long, ovoid, yellow-brown.

BARK. Thick; red-brown; deeply fissured, broken into conspicuous square blocks.

WOOD. Important; rather heavy and hard; fine-textured; diffuse-porous; light-colored; used for furniture, containers, etc.

SILVICAL CHARACTERS. Intolerant; moist sites; fast-growing; shallow, lateral roots; scattered, never abundant. Swamp tupelo, *N. sylvatica* var. *biflora* (Walt.) Sarg., with somewhat narrower leaves and more distinctly ribbed pit, is common in southern swamps. The genus *Nyssa* is placed in the family Cornaceae by some authors.

Water Tupelo
Nyssa aquatica L.

This species, important for timber, occurs in pure stands or mixed with cypress in the southern swamps, often under water. It differs from black tupelo, having leaves 5–7 in. long, oblong-obovate, entire or sometimes irregularly toothed; fruit red-purple, 1 in. long, conspicuously ribbed pit; bark thin, gray-brown, scaly ridges; buds globose, not over ⅛ in. long; butt of the tree is often conspicuously swollen.

Ogeechee Tupelo
Nyssa ogeche Bartr.

This small, rare tree of the coastal plain from South Carolina to Florida resembles water tupelo and is distinguished from it by its red fruit containing a pit with broad, thin, papery wings.

Blue Gum

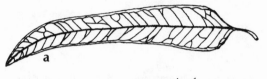

a. Leaf
b. Fruit

Silver Buffaloberry

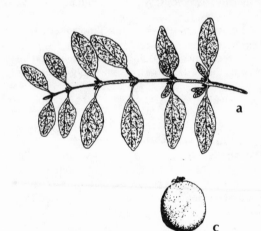

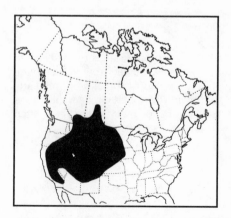

a. Twig with
leaves and
flower, × ½
b. Section through
flower, × 2
c. Fruit, × 2
d. Stone, × 2

MYRTACEAE

Blue Gum

Eucalyptus globulus Labill.

HABIT. A tall, fast-growing tree commonly planted as an ornamental or windbreak.

LEAVES. Alternate; simple; persistent; lanceolate; 6–13 in. long; margin entire; distinctively aromatic; short-petioled; sessile and opposite on young growth.

FLOWERS. Perfect; large; white; mostly solitary.

FRUIT. Woody capsule; ¾–1 in. long; warty; rough.

BARK. Outer deciduous and shedding; inner smooth, gray.

WOOD. Heavy; hard; cross-grained; used for timber and fuel.

GENERAL. About 500 species of eucalyptus are native to Australia and the Malayan region. Blue gum is the commonest of some 75 species planted in warmer parts of the United States.

ELAEAGNACEAE

Silver Buffaloberry • Buffaloberry

Shepherdia argentea (Pursh) Nutt. (*Lepargyrea argentea* [Pursh] Greene)

HABIT. A silvery, often spiny shrub or small tree rarely 15–20 ft high; stoloniferous, thicket-forming.

LEAVES. Opposite; simple; oblanceolate to oblong; cuneate at base; 1–2½ in. long; margin entire; densely silvery-scurfy on both sides with stellate hairs; deciduous; short, stout petioles.

FLOWERS. Dioecious; regular; small; yellowish; calyx urn-shaped; corolla lacking; ovary enveloped in receptacle.

FRUIT. Drupe; ovoid; scarlet; ½ in. long; juicy.

Russian-olive

Elaeagnus angustifolia L.

This introduced shrub or small tree is planted from New England to California and established in some areas. Drought and alkaline resistant, it is a common dryland ornamental and windbreak. It is characterized by alternate, lanceolate, silvery-scurfy leaves; silvery, often spiny branches; silvery-scurfy drupe ½ in. long.

Flowering Dogwood

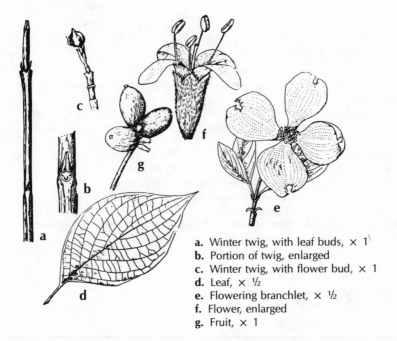

a. Winter twig, with leaf buds, × 1
b. Portion of twig, enlarged
c. Winter twig, with flower bud, × 1
d. Leaf, × ½
e. Flowering branchlet, × ½
f. Flower, enlarged
g. Fruit, × 1

Flowering Dogwood

Pacific Dogwood

CORNACEAE

Flowering Dogwood
Cornus florida L.

HABIT. A shrub or small tree rarely 40 ft high and 1 ft in diameter; bushy, flat crown; valuable ornamental.

LEAVES. Opposite; simple; deciduous; 3–6 in. long; oval; entire; thick; arcuately veined; hairy; bright green above; paler beneath; turning scarlet in autumn.

FLOWERS. Perfect; small; in heads; surrounded by 4 showy, 2- to 4-in., petallike, notched, white or pink bracts (red in variety *rubra* West.); appearing with leaves.

FRUIT. An ovoid, scarlet drupe ½ in. long; in clusters of 3–4; flesh bitter; containing a 2-celled pit.

TWIGS. Slender; glaucous; green or purplish. Winter buds: terminal present, ⅛ in. long, narrow-conical, acute, covered with 2 valvate scales; terminal flower buds subglobose, gray.

BARK. Thin; dark red-brown; broken into small, square blocks.

WOOD. Moderately important; very heavy and hard; fine-textured; diffuse-porous; in demand for shuttles.

SILVICAL CHARACTERS. Very tolerant; moist sites as "understory" species; slow-growing; lateral roots.

Pacific Dogwood
Cornus nuttallii Aud.

This small, handsome tree of the Pacific Coast is very similar to flowering dogwood in its appearance and differs in the following ways: petallike flower bracts not notched; often producing a second crop of flowers in late summer; bark remaining smooth on trunk.

Other Dogwoods

Nine other shrubby species rarely reach tree size. Red-osier dogwood, *C. stolonifera* Michx., covers most of North America. Eastern species are *C. alternifolia* L., *C. drummondii* Meyer, *C. racemosa* Lam., *C. rugosa* Lam., and *C. stricta* Lam. Western species are *C. glabrata* Benth., *C. occidentalis* (T. & G.) Cov., and *C. sessilis* Torr.

Wavyleaf silktassel, *Garrya elliptica* Dougl., is a shrub or small tree with wavy, evergreen, opposite, leathery leaves 2–4 in. long and a berrylike fruit that is persistent in long drooping clusters. It grows on coastal mountains from Oregon to southern California.

Pacific Madrone

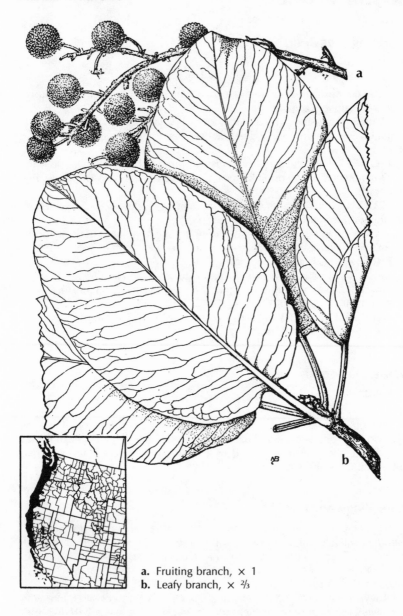

a. Fruiting branch, × 1
b. Leafy branch, × ⅔

ERICACEAE
Pacific Madrone • Madrona

Arbutus menziesii Pursh

HABIT. A medium-sized tree 20–100 ft high and 1–4 ft in diameter (max. 125 by 9 ft); rounded crown.

LEAVES. Alternate; simple; persistent; 3–6 in. long; oval to oblong; entire or toothed on vigorous growth; leathery; glabrous; dark green and lustrous above; glaucous beneath.

FLOWERS. Regular; perfect; in terminal panicles; white.

FRUIT. A globose, orange, semifleshy, glandular-coated, drupaceous berry ⅓–½ in. long. Birds eating fermented berries frequently becoming inebriated.

TWIGS. Slender; green to red-brown; glabrous. Winter buds: terminal ⅓ in. long, ovoid, scaly, bright brown.

BARK. Thin; distinctive; red-brown; separating into papery scales exposing the light red inner bark.

WOOD. Unimportant; heavy; hard; diffuse-porous; red-brown.

SILVICAL CHARACTERS. Moderately tolerant; varied sites.

GENERAL. Two other species are native to the Southwest. Texas madrone, *A. texana* Buckl., similar to Pacific madrone except for smaller leaves (1–3 in. long) and pubescent ovary, is a small tree on dry sites in southern Texas and New Mexico. Arizona madrone, *A. arizonica* (Gray) Sarg., with gray bark and a glabrous ovary, is native to southern Arizona and New Mexico.

Elliottia

Elliottia racemosa Muhl.

This is a rare tree now known only in eastern Georgia. It is characterized by simple, alternate, oblong, entire, deciduous leaves, 3–4 in. long; perfect flowers with 4 straplike petals; and small, globular capsular fruit.

Tree Lyonia

Lyonia ferruginea Nutt.

This is a small tree of coastal areas from South Carolina to Florida. It is characterized by simple, alternate, persistent, entire, obovate leaves 1–3 in. long and scaly below; by fascicled flowers ⅛ in. in diameter with a white, globular corolla; and by an ovoid, many-seeded, capsular fruit ¼ in. long.

Cinnamon Clethra

Clethra acuminata Michx.

This is a small mountain tree from West Virginia to Kentucky, Tennessee, and North Carolina to the northern tip of Georgia. It is characterized by simple, alternate, oval, deciduous, finely serrate leaves 3–6 in. long; white flowers in racemes; and a 3-valved capsule enclosed in the calyx.

Rosebay Rhododendron

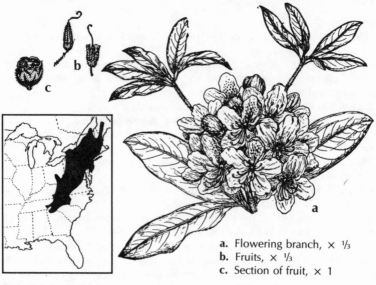

a. Flowering branch, × ⅓
b. Fruits, × ⅓
c. Section of fruit, × 1

Mountain-laurel

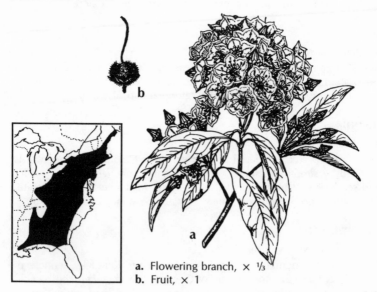

a. Flowering branch, × ⅓
b. Fruit, × 1

Rosebay Rhododendron • Great Rhododendron

Rhododendron maximum L.

HABIT. A beautiful shrub or small tree rarely 35 ft high and 1 ft in diameter; short, crooked trunk; bushy, rounded crown; an important ornamental.

LEAVES. Alternate; simple; persistent 2–3 years; 4–12 in. long and 1½–2½ in. wide; oblong; leathery; revolute, entire margins; dark green and lustrous above; paler beneath.

FLOWERS. Regular; perfect; showy; in 16–24 terminal flower clusters; white, pink, or purple; campanulate; 1 in. across; appearing after the leaves.

FRUIT. A woody, oblong-ovoid, red-brown, sticky, glandular-hispid, 5-celled capsule ½ in. long. Seeds: small, many.

TWIGS. Stout; glabrous; dark green to red-brown. Winter buds: terminal present, conical, green, scaly; flower buds 1–1½ in. long.

BARK. Thin; red-brown; broken into thin scales.

WOOD. Unimportant; heavy; hard; diffuse-porous; fine-textured; used for pipe bowls.

SILVICAL CHARACTERS. Tolerant; moist, cool, shady sites; often in thickets; does not like limy soils.

GENERAL. Two other species reach tree size. Catawba rhododendron, *R. catawbiense* Michx., with broader leaves 3–5 in. long, ranges from Virginia to Alabama. Pacific rhododendron, *R. macrophyllum* D. Don, ranges from British Columbia to California. The azaleas are shrubby species of this genus with deciduous leaves.

Mountain-laurel

Kalmia latifolia L.

This beautiful shrub or small tree resembles rhododendron and is a common ornamental. It can be distinguished by its flat, alternate, simple, persistent, elliptic-lanceolate leaves 3–4 in. long; its showy, white to rose-colored flowers with a saucer-shaped corolla with a short tube and 10 pouches below the 5-part limb; and the globose, woody, glandular-hispid, 5-celled capsule 3/16 in. in diameter, which splits at maturity into 5 persistent carpels releasing the many, minute, oblong, winged seeds.

Sourwood

a. Flowering branch, × ½
b. Fruiting branch, × ½
c. Fruit sectioned, × 1

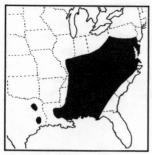

Sourwood

Tree Sparkleberry

Sourwood

Oxydendrum arboreum (L.) DC.

HABIT. A small to medium-sized tree 20–50 ft high and ⅔–1 ft in diameter (max. 80 by 2 ft); narrow, rounded crown.

LEAVES. Alternate; simple; deciduous; 5–7 in. long; oblong to lanceolate; thin; finely toothed; nearly glabrous; dark green and lustrous above; paler beneath; petioled; sour-tasting; turning scarlet in autumn.

FLOWERS. Regular; perfect; small; in delicate panicles of racemes 6–8 in. long; corolla white, bell-shaped, 5-lobed, ⅓ in. long; appearing after the leaves.

FRUIT. A 5-valved, 5-lobed, dry, persistent capsule ⅓–½ in. long; terminated by a persistent style; capsules often persisting on tree for over a year. Seeds: ⅛ in. long; pointed; pale brown.

TWIGS. Slender; glabrous; yellow-green to red-brown; leaf scar with single bundle scar. Winter buds: terminal absent; lateral small, scaly, red-brown, partially embedded in bark.

BARK. Thick; gray; tinged with red; furrowed; broad, scaly ridges.

WOOD. Unimportant; heavy; hard; diffuse-porous; red-brown.

SILVICAL CHARACTERS. Rather tolerant; dry, well-drained sites; does not like limy soils; an attractive ornamental; an important source of honey; a monotypic genus.

Tree Sparkleberry • Farkleberry

Vaccinium arboreum Marsh.

This shrub or small tree of the blueberry-cranberry genus is found on moist well-drained sites. It is characterized by alternate, simple, persistent (deciduous during winter in north) leaves obovate to oblong, entire or minutely toothed, leathery, dark green and lustrous above and paler beneath, and 1–2½ in. long; small, white, bell-shaped flowers either solitary or in racemes; and a black, globose, dry, scarcely edible berry about ¼ in. long, which persists on the branch into winter.

Gum Bumelia

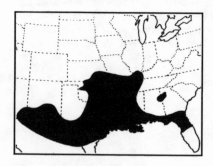

a. Flowering branchlet, × 1
b. Fruit, × 1

SAPOTACEAE

The Bumelias

Four native species sometimes become trees.

KEY TO THE ARBORESCENT SPECIES OF *BUMELIA*

1. Leaves persistent, thick and leathery, dull blue-green; Florida and Texas . . . .
. . . . *B. celastrina* H. B. K., **saffron-plum**
1. Leaves deciduous.
   2. Leaves glabrous or nearly so, Virginia to Illinois and south . . . .
   . . . . *B. lycioides* (L.) Pers., **buckthorn bumelia**
   2. Leaves hairy on lower surface.
      3. Leaves with silky, golden hairs; South Carolina to Florida . . . .
      . . . . *B. tenax* (L.) Willd., **tough bumelia**
      3. Leaves with reddish, dull, woolly hairs . . *B. lanuginosa* Pers., **gum bumelia**

Gum Bumelia • Gum Elastic

Bumelia lanuginosa (Michx.) Pers.

HABIT. A shrub or small tree 40–50 ft high and 1–2 ft in diameter; narrow crown with short, spinescent, spiny branches.

LEAVES. Alternate; simple; 1–3 in. long; oblanceolate to obovate; margins entire; thin; dark green above; soft, rusty-brown hairs below; tardily deciduous in winter; stipules absent.

FLOWERS. Regular; perfect; minute; in axillary clusters; corolla white, campanulate, 5-lobed.

FRUIT. Drupe; oblong; ½ in. long; black; solitary or in 2- to 3-fruited clusters; thick flesh. Seeds: ¼ in. long, shiny.

TWIGS. Slender; rounded; spinescent or with stout spines; red-brown to ash-gray. Winter buds: scaly; small; obtuse.

BARK. Thin; dark gray-brown; divided into scaly ridges.

WOOD. Unimportant; heavy; not strong; close-grained; ring-porous; light brown; producing clear, viscid gum.

SYMPLOCACEAE

Sweetleaf

Symplocos tinctoria (L.) L'Her.

This shrub grows in the coastal plain from Delaware to Florida, west to Texas and north in the Mississippi valley to Arkansas. It has oblong, nearly entire, thick, alternate, nearly evergreen leaves 5–6 in. long; small, yellow, fragrant flowers in dense axillary spikes; and a dry, brown drupe about ¼ in. long. It rarely reaches tree size.

Common Persimmon

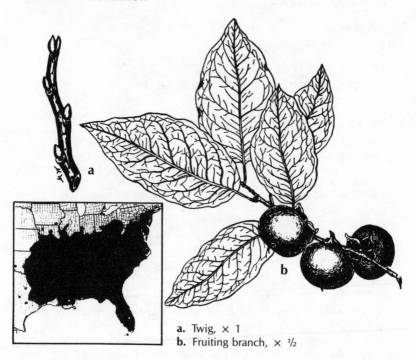

a. Twig, × 1
b. Fruiting branch, × ½

Carolina Silverbell

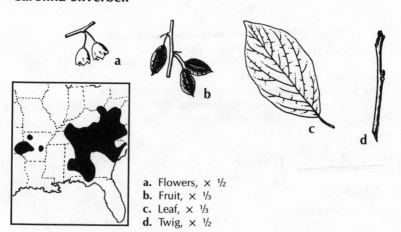

a. Flowers, × ½
b. Fruit, × ⅓
c. Leaf, × ⅓
d. Twig, × ½

EBENACEAE

Common Persimmon

Diospyros virginiana L.

HABIT. A small to medium-sized tree 25–50 ft high and 1 ft in diameter (max. 130 by 3 ft); broad, rounded crown.

LEAVES. Alternate; simple; deciduous; 3–6 in. long; oblong-ovate to oval; glabrous; entire; dark green and lustrous above; paler, sometimes hairy below.

FLOWERS. Regular; dioecious; ½–¾ in. long; corolla urn-shaped or tubular; yellow-green; appearing with leaves.

FRUIT. A globose, orange to purple berry 1–1½ in. long; subtended by 4 woody, persistent calyx lobes; astringent till frost, then edible.

TWIGS. Slender; gray-brown; leaf scar with single, elongated bundle scar. Winter buds: terminal absent; lateral, ⅛ in. long, red, 2 greatly overlapping scales.

BARK. Thick; hard; in distinctive square, scaly blocks.

WOOD. Moderately important; heavy; hard; strong; ring-porous; used for shuttles, golf clubs, billiard cues, brushes, etc.

SILVICAL CHARACTERS. Rather intolerant; varied sites.

GENERAL. This tropical genus contains over 200 species including the ebony of commerce. *D. texana* Scheele is a small Texas tree with small, wedge-shaped leaves and black fruit.

STYRACACEAE

Carolina Silverbell

Halesia carolina L.

HABIT. A small handsome tree; rounded crown.

LEAVES. Alternate; simple; deciduous; 3–4 in. long; oblong-ovate; finely toothed; yellow-green and glabrous above; pale and hairy below.

FLOWERS. Regular; perfect; showy; corolla white, bell-shaped, ½ in.

FRUIT. A dry, oblong, 4-winged drupe 1½ in. long.

GENERAL. Twigs slender; terminal buds absent; bark thin, scaly; moist sites; stump sprouts vigorously. Two other species form small trees in the coastal plain. *H. parviflora* Michx., with small flowers and club-shaped fruits, extends from South Carolina to north Florida and west to Mississippi. *H. diptera* Ellis, with a 2-winged fruit, from South Carolina to Florida and Texas.

The Snowbells

Bigleaf snowbell, *Styrax grandifolius* Ait., rarely forms a small tree. It ranges from Virginia to Illinois and Arkansas, south to northern Florida and east Texas. It is characterized by alternate, simple leaves 2½–5 in. long and white-woolly below; showy, white, bell-shaped flowers; a dry drupelike fruit; and stellate-hairy twigs.

American snowbell, *S. americanus* Lam., with leaves nearly smooth below, has a similar distribution.

OLEACEAE

The Ashes

Characteristics of the Genus *Fraxinus* L.

HABIT. Deciduous trees, or rarely shrubs; ornamental with handsome foliage; several species are important timber trees.

LEAVES. Opposite; odd-pinnately compound (rarely reduced to a single leaflet); without stipules; petiolate; deciduous; leaflets serrate or entire, sessile or petiolulate.

FLOWERS. Regular; perfect; dioecious or polygamous; small, but quite conspicuous in slender-branched panicles; appearing before or with the leaves; calyx 4-lobed or wanting; corolla usually 4-lobed or wanting; stamens usually 2 (rarely 3 or 4); single 2-celled ovary (rarely 3-celled); ovules suspended in pairs from inner angle of the cell.

FRUIT. Samara; 1-seeded (rarely 2 or 3); with an elongated terminal wing. Seeds: oblong; compressed; filling cavity in the fruit; chestnut-brown; albuminous.

TWIGS. Slender to stout; glabrous or pubescent; pith thick, rounded, homogeneous; leaf scars suborbicular to semicircular, sometimes notched on the upper edge; bundle scars numerous. Winter buds: terminal larger than lateral; both with 1–3 pairs of scales, the inner accrescent.

BARK. Thick and furrowed or rarely thin and scaly.

WOOD. Ring-porous; late wood with rather few pores not in distinct radial lines and with tangential bands of parenchyma; tough; straight-grained; not structural timber, but important for specialty purposes; sapwood not durable.

SILVICAL CHARACTERS. Rather intolerant trees; fast-growing; fibrous root system; reproducing well naturally and artificially; comparatively free from destructive attacks by insects and fungi.

GENERAL. This genus contains about 70 species of trees scattered through the Northern Hemisphere and extending into the tropical forests of Java and Cuba. In North America there are 16 recognized native species.

KEY TO THE SPECIES OF ASHES

1. Flowers with corolla, perfect, showy; leaflets 3–7, lanceolate, stalked; southwestern
   . . . . *F. cuspidata,* **fragrant ash,** p. 355
1. Flowers without corolla, dioecious or polygamous, in axillary panicles.
   2. Leaflets 3–7, ½–¾ in. long, black-dotted below, with winged petioles; southwestern . . . . *F. greggii,* **Gregg ash,** p. 355
   2. Leaflets 1–11, 1–6 in. long, with unwinged petioles.
      3. Twigs 4-angled; fruit compressed, oblong wing extending to base.
         4. Leaves 8–12 in. long, 5–11 leaflets; eastern . . . .
            . . . . *F. quadrangulata,* **blue ash,** p. 363
         4. Leaves 1½–6 in. long, 1–5 leaflets; southwestern.
            5. Leaflets 1 (rarely 3–7) . . . . *F. anomala,* **singleleaf ash,** p. 355
            5. Leaflets 5 (rarely 3).
               6. Arizona . . . . *F. anomala* var. *lowellii,* **Lowell ash,** p. 365
               6. California to Nevada and Utah . *F. dipetala,* **two-petal ash,** p. 357
      3. Twigs terete.
         7. Body of fruit compressed, wing extending to seed base.
            8. Leaflets 7–11, sessile; wing oblong, flat; northern and central . . . .
               . . . . *F. nigra,* **black ash,** p. 361
            8. Leaflets 3–7, stalked; fruit elliptic, often 3-winged; southeastern . . . . .
               . . . . *F. caroliniana,* **Carolina ash,** p. 361
         7. Body of fruit nearly terete, wing not extending to base.
            9. Wing terminal or not decurrent to below middle of seed cavity.
               10. Leaflets sessile or nearly so; local from southwestern Texas to Arizona . . . . *F. papillosa,* **Chihuahua ash,** p. 361
               10. Leaflets stalked.
                  11. Leaflets crenulate-serrate to entire, glabrous; twigs nearly glabrous, leaf scars notched at top.
                     12. Leaves 8–12 in. long, 7 (rarely 5–9) leaflets; eastern . . .
                        . . . . *F. americana,* **white ash,** p. 357
                     12. Leaves 5–8 in. long, 5 (rarely 7) leaflets; Texas and Oklahoma . . . . *F. texensis,* **Texas ash,** p. 357
                  11. Leaflets sharply serrate, at least above middle, glabrous to slightly hairy below; twigs glabrous to hairy, leaf scar truncate or slightly notched . . . . . *F. pennsylvanica,* **green ash,** p. 359
            9. Wing decurrent to below middle of seed cavity.
               13. Fruit 2–3 in. long, frequently 3-winged; leaflets soft-hairy below; eastern swamps . . . . *F. profunda,* **pumpkin ash,** p. 359
               13. Fruit not over 2 in. long; western.
                  14. Leaflets 3–7 in. long, usually sessile; West Coast . . . .
                     . . . . *F. latifolia,* **Oregon ash,** p. 363
                  14. Leaflets not over 2 in. long; southwestern.
                     15. Fruit 1–1½ in. long; leaflets glabrous . . . .
                        . . . . *F. berlandierana,* **Berlandier ash,** p. 365
                     15. Fruit 3–4 in. long; leaflets densely hairy below . . . .
                        . . . . *F. velutina,* **velvet ash,** p. 365

Privet

Ligustrum ovalifolium Hassk.

This Japanese shrub reaches tree size but has many stems. Widely planted across the southern United States, it has become locally naturalized. It is characterized by simple, opposite, entire, thick, nearly evergreen leaves; perfect flowers in erect panicles; and black drupes. Two other species planted from Virginia to Texas have become naturalized: Japanese privet, *L. japonicum* Thunb., and Chinese privet, *L. sinense* Lour.

Singleleaf Ash

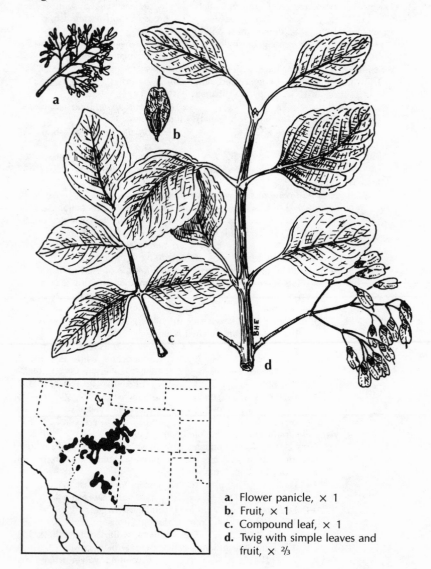

a. Flower panicle, × 1
b. Fruit, × 1
c. Compound leaf, × 1
d. Twig with simple leaves and
   fruit, × ⅔

Singleleaf Ash • Dwarf Ash

Fraxinus anomala Torr.

HABIT. A shrub or small tree 18–20 ft high; crown round-topped, contorted branches.

LEAVES. Usually single, but rarely 2–5 leaflets; broadly ovate or suborbicular; 1–2 in. long (smaller if compound); margins entire or sparingly crenate-serrate above middle; glabrous and dark green above, paler below.

FLOWERS. In short panicles; appearing with leaves; perfect or unisexual by abortion of stamens; calyx cup-shaped, minutely 4-toothed; corolla absent.

FRUIT. Obovate-oblong; ½ in. long; wing rounded or emarginate at apex, surrounding flattened seed cavity.

TWIGS. Quadrangular, slightly winged, and orange-colored at first; later round, ash-gray. Winter buds: terminal broad-ovoid, ⅛–¼ in. long, covered by orange tomentum.

BARK. Thin (½ in.); dark brown, slightly tinged with red; divided by shallow furrows into narrow, scaly ridges.

WOOD. Heavy; hard; close-grained; heartwood light brown; sapwood lighter colored and thick; no importance.

SILVICAL CHARACTERS. Intolerant; in the neighborhood of streams or on dry hillsides.

Fragrant Ash • Flowering Ash

Fraxinus cuspidata Torr.

A handsome shrub or low tree with showy, white flowers and small leaves; seldom a tree in the United States; upper Sonoran zone of Texas, New Mexico, Arizona, and Mexico.

Gregg Ash • Littleleaf Ash

Fraxinus greggii Gray

This shrub or small tree of the south Texas border and Mexico is rarely 25 ft high and characterized by 3–7 leaflets less than 1 in. long, usually entire, covered below with small, black dots, and obscurely veined; spatulate samaras, 1 in. long; twigs slender and round; and bark thin, separating into papery scales. Goodding ash, *F. gooddingii* Little, formerly included in *F. greggii*, is a small tree formed only on the southern border of Arizona and in Sonora, Mexico.

White Ash

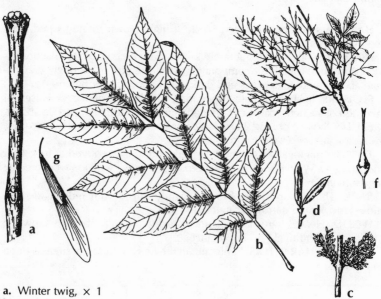

a. Winter twig, × 1
b. Leaf, × ¼
c. Staminate flowering branchlet, × ½
d. Staminate flower, enlarged
e. Pistillate flowering branchlet, × ½
f. Pistillate flower, enlarged
g. Fruit, × 1

White Ash

Texas Ash

White Ash

Fraxinus americana L. (*Fraxinus biltmoreana* Beadle)

HABIT. A medium-sized tree 50–80 ft high and 2–3 ft in diameter (max. 125 by 6 ft); open, pyramidal crown.

LEAVES. 8–12 in. long; 5–9 (mostly 7) leaflets, ovate to oblong-lanceolate, 3–5 in. long, entire or obscurely toothed, dark green above and paler and usually glabrous below, petiolules ¼–½ in. long.

FLOWERS. In loose panicles; dioecious; corolla absent; appearing with or before the leaves.

FRUIT. Lanceolate to oblanceolate; 1–2 in. long; wing terminal or slightly decurrent along seed cavity; persistent into winter on twigs.

TWIGS. Rounded; rather stout; gray-green; lustrous; leaf scars semiorbicular to U-shaped with deep to shallow notch. Winter buds: small; rounded; dark brown; nearly glabrous; inset in leaf scar; first lateral buds at base of terminal bud.

BARK. Thick; gray; closely fissured, narrow ridges around diamond-shaped areas.

WOOD. Important; hard; heavy; strong; ring-porous; used for handles, implements, containers, etc.

SILVICAL CHARACTERS. Intermediate in tolerance; moist sites; fast-growing; the most abundant and commonly planted species.

Texas Ash

Fraxinus texensis (Gray) Sarg.

This small tree of Oklahoma and Texas is very similar to white ash, differing from it in having smaller leaves (5–8 in. long) with 5 (rarely 7) leaflets 1–3 in. long.

Two-petal Ash

Fraxinus dipetala Hook. & Arn.

This shrubby species of northwest Arizona, southwest Utah, and southern Nevada extends to lower California. It is characterized by 4-angled twigs, a 2-petaled corolla, 5 leaflets, and flowers that appear before the leaves from leafless, axillary buds.

Green Ash

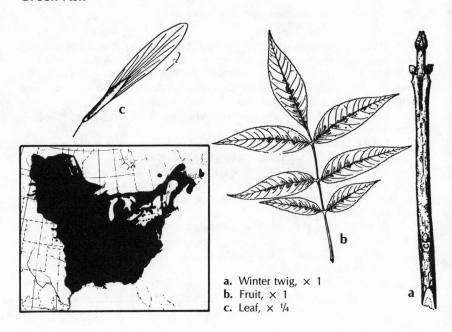

a. Winter twig, × 1
b. Fruit, × 1
c. Leaf, × ¼

Pumpkin Ash

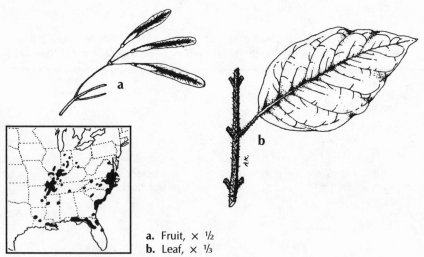

a. Fruit, × ½
b. Leaf, × ⅓

Green Ash

Fraxinus pennsylvanica Marsh.

HABIT. A small to medium-sized tree 30–60 ft high and 1–2 ft in diameter (max. 85 by 3 ft); broad, irregular crown.

LEAVES. 10–12 in. long; 7–9 leaflets, oblong-lanceolate to elliptic, 4–6 in. long, finely toothed or entire below middle, yellow-green above, paler and glabrous to silky-hairy below, petiolule ⅛–¼ in. long.

FLOWERS. In compact panicles; dioecious; corolla absent; appearing with leaves.

FRUIT. Narrowly lanceolate; 1–2½ in. long; wing terminal or extending to middle of terete, slender seed cavity; persistent through winter.

TWIGS. Rounded; rather stout; red-gray; glabrous to pale-hairy; leaf scar semiorbicular, truncate, or shallowly notched. Winter buds: small; rounded; red-brown; woolly; set above leaf scar; first laterals at base of terminal bud.

BARK. Thin; brown; shallow fissures and scaly ridges.

WOOD. Important; heavy; hard; ring-porous; like white ash.

SILVICAL CHARACTERS. Intolerant; moist sites, but hardy on dry sites; fast-growing; shallow roots.

GENERAL. This species closely resembles white ash and the glabrous form can best be distinguished by straight or slightly notched leaf scars and usually narrower leaflets and fruits. Formerly the hairy form was designated *F. pennsylvanica*, red ash, and the glabrous form *F. pennsylvanica* var. *lanceolata* (Borkh.) Sarg., green ash.

Pumpkin Ash

Fraxinus profunda (Bush) Bush

HABIT. A large, unimportant tree of coastal plain and Mississippi valley swamps and river bottoms. Characterized by prominently swollen base and a slender trunk.

LEAVES. 10–18 in. long; 7 (rarely 9) elliptic leaflets, 4–10 in. long, entire or slightly toothed, glabrous to hairy below, petiolules ¼–½ in.

FRUIT. Oblong; 2–3 in. long; wing extending from middle to base of terete seed cavity; frequently 3-winged.

TWIGS. Terete; stout; gray-brown; smooth to tomentose; leaf scars U-shaped. Winter buds: red-brown; outer bud scales with truncated tips.

BARK. Thin; light gray with shallow fissures.

Black Ash

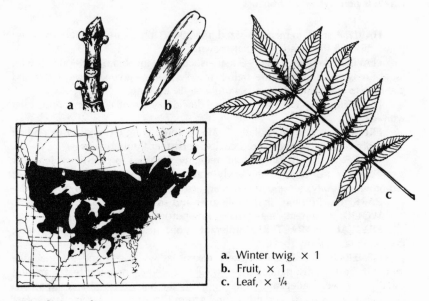

a. Winter twig, × 1
b. Fruit, × 1
c. Leaf, × ¼

Carolina Ash

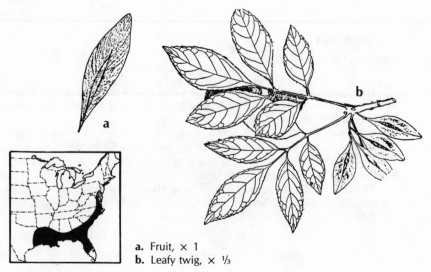

a. Fruit, × 1
b. Leafy twig, × ⅓

Black Ash

Fraxinus nigra Marsh.

HABIT. A medium-sized tree 40–60 ft high and 1–2 ft in diameter (max. 90 by 5½ ft); narrow, small, open crown.

LEAVES. 12–16 in. long; 7–13 leaflets, oblong to oblong-lanceolate, 3–5 in. long, finely toothed, glabrous, dark green above and paler below, sessile.

FLOWERS. In loose panicles; polygamo-dioecious; corolla and calyx absent; appearing before the leaves.

FRUIT. Oblong; 1–1¾ in. long; wing surrounding the flat, indistinct seed cavity; falling early or late.

TWIGS. Rounded; stout; gray; glabrous. Winter buds: ¼ in. long; ovoid-conical; nearly black; nearly glabrous; first laterals some distance below terminal bud.

BARK. Thin; gray; smooth, becoming scaly.

WOOD. Moderately important; softer and weaker than white ash.

SILVICAL CHARACTERS. Intolerant; wet sites.

Carolina Ash • Water Ash

Fraxinus caroliniana Mill. (*Fraxinus pauciflora* Nutt.)

HABIT. A small, unimportant tree of coastal or river swamps.

LEAVES. 5–12 in. long; 3–7 (usually 7) thin, mostly glabrous, long-stalked, coarsely toothed leaflets.

FLOWERS. Dioecious; appearing before the leaves.

FRUIT. Oblong-obovate to elliptic; 2–3 in. long; thin wing extending to the base of the compressed seed cavity that is more than half the length of the wing; frequently 3-winged.

SILVICAL CHARACTERS. Intolerant; wet sites.

Chihuahua Ash

Fraxinus papillosa Lingel.

This tree, local in the mountains from trans-Pecos Texas to southeastern Arizona, is characterized by nearly sessile leaflets with minute projections (papillae) on their lower surfaces.

Blue Ash

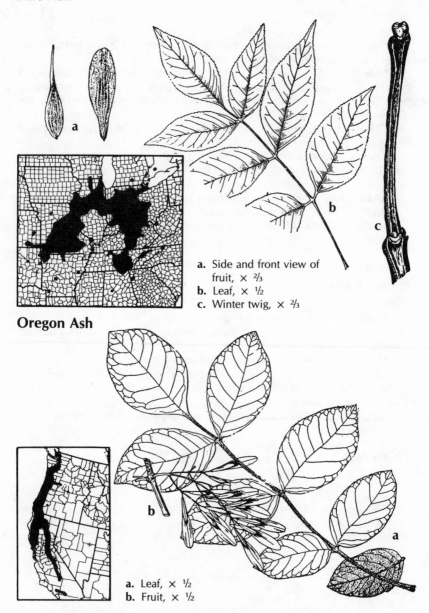

a. Side and front view of fruit, × ⅔
b. Leaf, × ½
c. Winter twig, × ⅔

Oregon Ash

a. Leaf, × ½
b. Fruit, × ½

Blue Ash

Fraxinus quadrangulata Michx.

HABIT. A medium-sized tree 40–50 ft high and 1–2 ft in diameter (max. 120 by 3 ft); narrow, open crown.

LEAVES. 8–12 in. long; 5–11 (usually 7) leaflets, lanceolate to ovate-oblong, 3–5 in. long, coarsely toothed, thick, yellow-green above and paler below, glabrous, short petiolules.

FLOWERS. In loose panicles; perfect; corolla absent; calyx reduced to ring; appearing before the leaves.

FRUIT. Oblong-ovate; 1–2 in. long; wing surrounding the compressed seed cavity; falling soon after maturing.

TWIGS. 4-angled and corky-winged; stout; orange-brown; red-hairy. Winter buds: small; rounded; dark red-brown; somewhat hairy.

BARK. Rather thin; gray; divided into platelike scales; often shaggy; inner bark contains material that turns blue on exposure.

WOOD. Moderately important; similar to black ash.

SILVICAL CHARACTERS. Similar to green ash; a scattered tree.

Oregon Ash

Fraxinus latifolia Benth. (*Fraxinus oregona* Nutt.)

HABIT. A medium-sized tree 60–80 ft high and 2–3 ft in diameter (max. 120 by 6 ft); narrow, compact crown.

LEAVES. 5–14 in. long; 5–7 leaflets, ovate to elliptic, 3–7 in. long, entire or finely toothed, light green above and usually hairy below, sessile or with petiolules up to ½ in.

FLOWERS. In compact panicles; dioecious; corolla absent; appearing with the leaves.

FRUIT. Oblong to elliptic; 1–2 in. long; wing extending to below middle of slightly compressed seed cavity.

TWIGS. Round; stout; woolly; red-brown. Winter buds: ⅛–¼ in. long; conical; brown; hairy.

BARK. Thick; dark gray; deeply fissured with broad ridges.

WOOD. Of slight importance; similar to white ash.

SILVICAL CHARACTERS. Rather intolerant; moist sites; mixed stands; the variety *glabra* Rehd. has glabrous leaves and twigs.

Lowell Ash

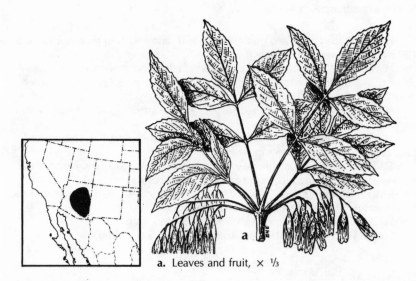

a. Leaves and fruit, × ⅓

Velvet Ash

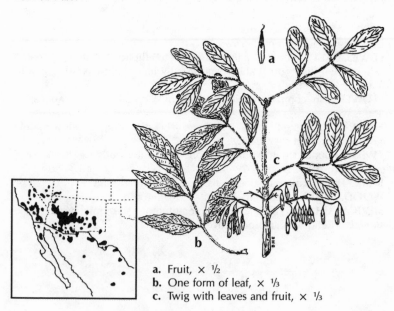

a. Fruit, × ½
b. One form of leaf, × ⅓
c. Twig with leaves and fruit, × ⅓

Lowell Ash

Fraxinus anomala var. *lowellii* [Sarg.] Little (*Fraxinus lowellii* Sarg.)

HABIT. A small tree 20–25 ft high.

LEAVES. 3½–6 in. long, stout petiole; 5 (rarely 3–7) leaflets, ovate to elliptic-ovate, 2½–3 in. long, remotely and lightly serrate, yellow-green, glabrous or slightly pubescent along midrib; sometimes single.

FLOWERS. In axillary panicle; corolla absent.

FRUIT. Oblong-obovate to oblong-elliptic; 1–1½ in. long; wing extending to base of compressed seed cavity.

TWIGS. Quadrangular; often winged; stout; orange-brown.

BARK. Rather thick; dark; deeply furrowed.

SILVICAL CHARACTERS. Intolerant; on dry, rocky slopes and in canyons. This tree is now considered a variety of *F. anomala*.

Velvet Ash

Fraxinus velutina Torr.

HABIT. A small, slender tree 20–50 ft high.

LEAVES. 3–6 in. long, broad, grooved, densely villous petiole; 3–9 (usually 5) leaflets, elliptic to lanceolate, 1–1½ in. long, finely crenate-serrulate above middle, thick, pale green, glabrous above, tomentose below; tardily deciduous.

FLOWERS. Dioecious, in pubescent panicles; corolla absent.

FRUIT. Oblong-obovate to elliptic; ¾ in. long; wing shorter than and extending to below middle of terete seed cavity.

TWIGS. Rounded; slender; velvety pubescent first year.

BARK. Thin; furrowed; gray, slightly tinged with red.

SILVICAL CHARACTERS. Intolerant; in dry mountain canyons and on banks of streams; hardy.

GENERAL. *F. velutina* passes into the following varieties: 1. *coriacea* Rehd., with leathery leaves. 2. *glabra* Rehd., with glabrous leaves and branches. 3. *toumeyi* Rehd., with lanceolate, acuminate leaflets, having petioles ⅛–½ in. long.

Berlandier Ash

Fraxinus berlandieriana A. DC.

This small tree of southern Texas and Mexico resembles *F. velutina* but has a longer fruit (1–1½ in.); glabrous leaves and twigs; and thin, dark green leaflets 3–4 in. long.

Fringetree

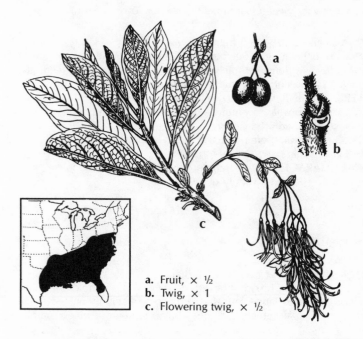

a. Fruit, × ½
b. Twig, × 1
c. Flowering twig, × ½

Swamp-privet

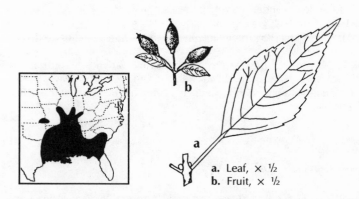

a. Leaf, × ½
b. Fruit, × ½

Fringetree
Chionanthus virginicus L.

HABIT. A beautiful shrub or small tree rarely 40 ft high and 1 ft in diameter; narrow, deep crown.
LEAVES. Opposite; simple; deciduous; 4–8 in. long; oval to ovate; entire; dark green above; paler and nearly glabrous below.
FLOWERS. Dioecious; showy; in drooping panicles 4–6 in. long; white, deeply divided corolla; appearing with leaves.
FRUIT. An oval, nearly black thin-fleshed drupe ½–¾ in. long; stone thick, ⅓ in. long.
TWIGS. Rather stout; green-brown; more or less hairy; slightly 4-angled; conspicuous lenticels. Winter buds: terminal present, ovoid, acute, ⅛ in. long, keeled scales.
BARK. Thin; scaly; red-brown.
WOOD. Unimportant; heavy; hard; fine-textured.
SILVICAL CHARACTERS. Tolerant; moist to wet sites; widely planted as an ornamental.

Swamp-privet • Forestiera
Forestiera acuminata (Michx.) Poir.

A rather rare shrub or small tree distributed along streams and in swamps. It is characterized by opposite, simple, deciduous, elliptic, long-pointed, glabrous, finely toothed leaves 2½–4½ in. long and yellow-green; by minute, dioecious or polygamous flowers without a corolla and appearing before the leaves in fascicles or panicles; and an oblong, purple, thin-fleshed drupe about 1 in. long. Desert-olive foresteria. *F. phillyreoides* Torr., is a shrubby form in southern Arizona. *F. angustifolia* Torr. is a shrubby form in Texas and Mexico, and *F. segregata* (Jacq.) Krug & Urban grows along the coasts of southeast Georgia and Florida.

Devilwood
Osmanthus americanus (L.) B. & H.

This is a shrub to medium-sized tree of the coastal plain from Virginia to Florida and Louisiana. It is characterized by opposite, simple, persistent, oblong, thick, entire, revolute leaves 3½–5 in. long, lustrous bright green; small, perfect or polygamous flowers in racemes or fascicles; and oblong, purple, thin-fleshed drupe ½–1 in. long. The tree gets its name from the wood, which is hard and difficult to work or split. Bigfruit osmanthus, *O. megacarpus* Small, is limited to central Florida.

Northern Catalpa

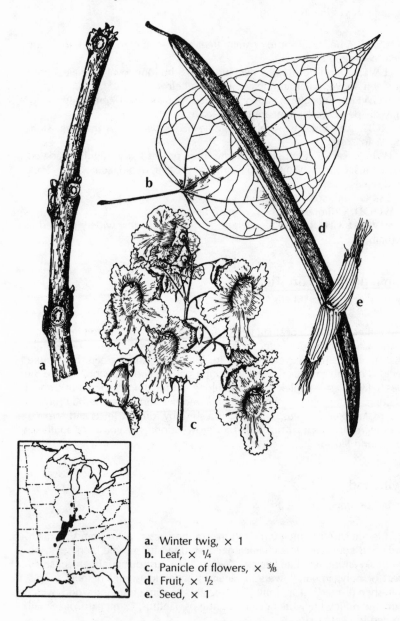

a. Winter twig, × 1
b. Leaf, × ¼
c. Panicle of flowers, × ⅜
d. Fruit, × ½
e. Seed, × 1

BIGNONIACEAE

Northern Catalpa • Hardy Catalpa
Catalpa speciosa Warder

HABIT. A medium-sized tree 30–60 ft high and 1–3 ft in diameter (max. 120 by 6 ft); broad, rounded crown.

LEAVES. Opposite or whorled; simple; deciduous; 8–12 in. long; heart-shaped; entire; thick; dark green above; paler and hairy below; petioles long, stout, round.

FLOWERS. 2-lipped; perfect; showy; in open few-flowered panicles; calyx hairy; corolla white, with inconspicuous yellow spots, 2½ in. across; appearing after the leaves.

FRUIT. A long, round, cigar-shaped, 2-celled, thick-walled capsule 8–20 in. long and ½ in. thick; persistent through winter. Seeds: numerous; flattened; rounded, fringed wings 1 in. long.

TWIGS. Very stout; brown; glabrous; orbicular leaf scar. Winter buds: terminal absent; lateral small, immersed in bark.

BARK. Rather thin; brown; broken into thick scales.

WOOD. Light; soft; weak; brown; durable; ring-porous; used for posts.

SILVICAL CHARACTERS. Intolerant; varied sites; fast-growing; taproot; widely planted as an ornamental and naturalized through all but coldest portions of United States.

Southern Catalpa
Catalpa bignonioides Walt.

This smaller and more southern tree, while native from Florida to Louisiana, has been naturalized as far north as New York. It is less hardy in cold sites than northern catalpa and is distinguished from it by having flowers 1½ in. across in many-flowered, crowded panicles with glabrous calyx and corolla with many conspicuous yellow spots and a thinner-walled fruit about ¼–⅓ in. in diameter.

Paulownia
Paulownia tomentosa (Thunb.) Sieb & Zucc.

This beautiful Chinese species has been widely cultivated in the eastern states and has become naturalized from New York to Texas and Georgia. In cold sites it winter-kills badly. It is characterized by opposite, heart-shaped, simple, deciduous leaves with entire margins, 5–8 in. long and densely hairy on the lower surface; by perfect, 2-lipped, showy, purple flowers 1½–2 in. long, which appear before the leaves; and by a leathery, ovoid, beaked, persistent, brown capsule 1–2 in. long.

Desertwillow

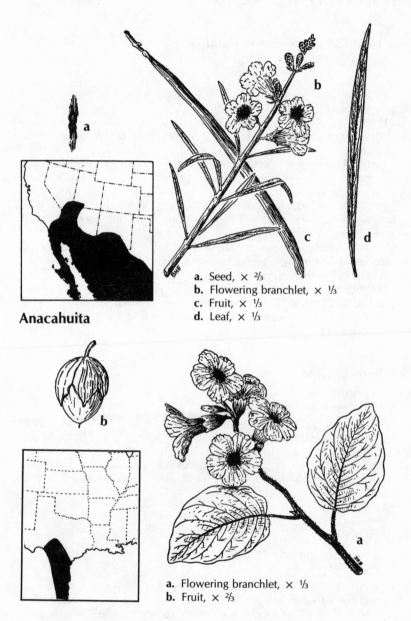

a. Seed, × ⅔
b. Flowering branchlet, × ⅓
c. Fruit, × ⅓
d. Leaf, × ⅓

Anacahuita

a. Flowering branchlet, × ⅓
b. Fruit, × ⅔

Desertwillow

Chilopsis linearis (Cav.) Sweet (*Chilopsis saligna* D. Don)

HABIT. A shrub or small tree rarely 20–30 ft high; trunk usually reclining; crown narrow with slender branches.

LEAVES. Opposite or scattered; simple; linear or linear-lanceolate; 5–12 in. long and ¼–⅓ in. wide; acuminate.

FLOWERS. Irregular; perfect; showy; in racemes; corolla white, yellow-spotted in throat, ¾–1½ in. long.

FRUIT. Slender, elongated, thin-walled capsule, 7–12 in. long and ¼ in. thick; splitting into 2 concave valves; persistent into the winter. Seeds: numerous; ⅓ in. long.

TWIGS. Slender; glabrous or densely tomentose; light brown. Winter buds: terminal absent; lateral minute, scaly.

SILVICAL CHARACTERS. Intolerant; short-lived; banks of watercourses in desert and low mountain areas.

Trumpetflower

Tecoma stans (L.) H. B. K.

A shrub or small tree extending through Mexico into the southern parts of Texas, New Mexico, and Arizona. Characterized by showy, bright yellow flowers; opposite, pinnately compound leaves with 5–13 leaflets; and a linear capsule, 4–8 in. long.

BORAGINACEAE

Anacahuita

Cordia boissieri A. DC.

HABIT. An aromatic shrub or small tree 20–25 ft high.

LEAVES. Alternate; simple; oval to oblong-ovate; 4–5 in. long; entire or obscurely crenulate-serrate; thick and firm; dark green above; woolly below; tardily deciduous.

FLOWERS. Regular; perfect; showy; in cymes; calyx tubular; corolla funnel-form, 2 in. across, white with yellow spot in throat.

FRUIT. Drupaceous; ovoid; 1 in. long and ¾ in. broad; acute; lustrous; bright red-brown; enclosed by orange-brown, tomentose calyx.

TWIGS. Stout; dark gray or brown; puberulous; marked by occasional large lenticels and elevated obcordate leaf scars.

SILVICAL CHARACTERS. Intolerant; dry limestone ridges and depressions; planted as ornamental.

Anacua

Ehretia anacua (T. & B.) Johnst.

This is a handsome, commonly planted tree of central and south Texas and Mexico, with small white flowers opening from autumn to early spring.

Common Buttonbush

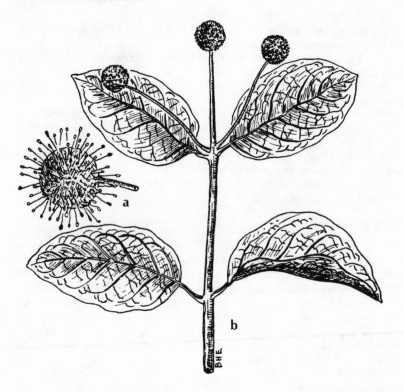

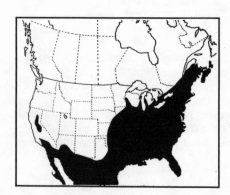

a. Flower, × 1
b. Leaves and fruit, × 2/3

RUBIACEAE

Common Buttonbush

Cephalanthus occidentalis L.

HABIT. A shrub or rarely a small tree up to 50 ft high and 1–2 in. in diameter; open, spreading crown.

LEAVES. Opposite or whorled in 3's; simple; ovate, lanceolate or elliptic; 2–7 in. long; acute or acuminate at apex; margins entire; thin; dark green and glabrous above; paler below, yellow midrib; tardily deciduous during winter; petioles stout, grooved, glabrous, ½–¾ in. long.

FLOWERS. Regular; perfect; minute; in dense, globose heads 1–1½ in. in diameter; fragrant; calyx tube 4- to 5-lobed; corolla cream-white, salverform, 4- to 5-lobed; stamens as many as and alternate with corolla lobes; ovary inferior, 2-celled, with protuding; threadlike style and capitate stigma.

FRUIT. Nutlike capsule; inversely pyramidal; splitting from base upward into 2–4 closed, 1-seeded portions; in heads ⅝–¾ in. in diameter; green tinged with red, becoming dark red-brown. Seeds: small; oblong; pendulous.

TWIGS. Stout; glabrous; thick pith; marked by large lenticels; opposite or in whorls of 3; light green at first, becoming red-brown. Winter buds: terminal absent; lateral minute, nearly immersed in the bark.

BARK. Thin; dark brown to nearly black; broad, flat, superficially scaly ridges; contains tannin.

WOOD. Moderately heavy and hard; fine-grained; diffuse-porous; light red-brown; unimportant.

SILVICAL CHARACTERS. Rather tolerant; reproduction abundant; on moist sites or in dry stream beds; often forming dense thickets.

Pinckneya • Feverbark

Pinckneya pubens Michx.

A very rare, small tree in the coastal plain from South Carolina to north Florida. It has awl-shaped stipules, trumpet-shaped flowers, a petal-like sepal, and a 2-valved, papery capsule about 1 in. long.

Blue Elder

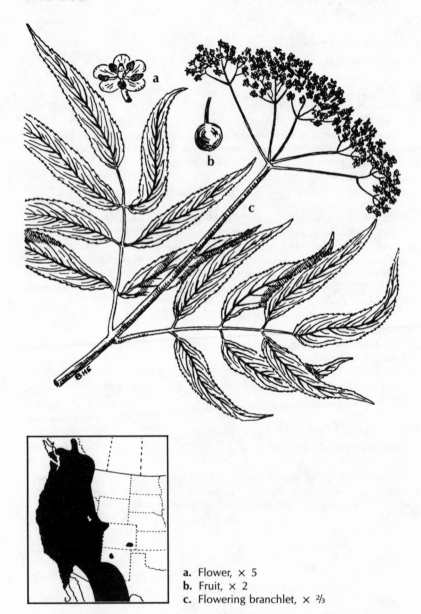

a. Flower, × 5
b. Fruit, × 2
c. Flowering branchlet, × ⅔

CAPRIFOLIACEAE

The Elders, *Sambucus* L.

Five native species rarely reach tree size.

KEY TO THE SPECIES OF ELDERS

1. Most of eastern and central North America . . . . . *S. canadensis* L., **American elder**
1. Western North America.
   2. Cymes flat-topped; fruit blue-black, commonly glaucous.
      3. Twigs and lower surface of leaf pubescent; leaves deciduous; western Utah and Arizona to California . . . . *S. velutina* D. & H., **velvet elder**
      3. Twigs and leaves usually glabrous or nearly so.
         4. Leaves persistent; leaflets 3–5, oblong-lanceolate to ovate; southern New Mexico to central California . . . . *S. mexicana* Presl., **Mexican elder**
         4. Leaves deciduous; leaflets 5–9, oblong-lanceolate . . . .
         . . . . *S. cerulea* Raf., **blue elder**
   2. Cymes pyramidal to ovoid; fruit red; leaflets 5–9, oval, slightly pubescent below; Pacific Coast from Alaska to northern California . . . .
   . . . . *S. callicarpa* Greene, **Pacific red elder**

Blue Elder

Sambucus cerulea Raf. (*Sambucus glauca* Nutt.)

HABIT. A shrub or small tree 30–50 ft high and 12–18 in. in diameter; compact, round-topped crown.

LEAVES. Opposite; unequally pinnately compound; petiolate; deciduous; 5–7 in. long; leaflets 5–9, ovate or narrow oblong, coarsely serrate margin, 1–6 in. long, green above, pale and glabrous to pubescent below.

FLOWERS. Regular; perfect; small (⅛ in. in diameter); in broad, terminal, long-branched corymbose cymes; corolla yellow-white, stamens 5; ovary inferior, 3- to 5-celled.

FRUIT. Dense clusters of small, blue, drupelike berries; ¼ in. in diameter, with sweet, juicy flesh. Seeds: 3–5 1-seeded nutlets in each drupe.

TWIGS. Stout; somewhat angled; pubescent first year; red-brown; nearly encircled by large, triangular leaf scars; thick, soft pith. Winter buds: terminal absent; lateral scaly, greenish.

BARK. Thin; dark brown, tinged with red.

WOOD. Light; soft; weak; coarse-grained; diffuse-porous; heartwood yellow, tinged with brown, durable; unimportant.

SILVICAL CHARACTERS. Intolerant; short-lived; reproduction abundant but scattered; coppices freely; moist porous soils; along streams, ravines, or moist hillsides.

Nannyberry

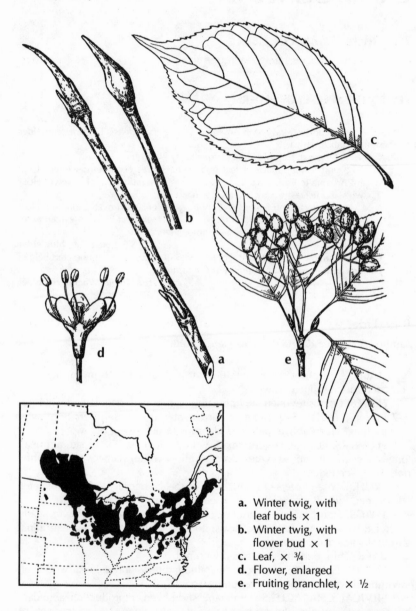

a. Winter twig, with
   leaf buds × 1
b. Winter twig, with
   flower bud × 1
c. Leaf, × ¾
d. Flower, enlarged
e. Fruiting branchlet, × ½

KEY TO THE SPECIES OF VIBURNUM

1. Leaves 3-lobed and palmately veined; flowers large and showy; drupes bright red; northern . . . . *V. trilobatum* Marsh., **American cranberrybush**
1. Leaves not lobed, pinnately veined; flowers small.
   2. Buds naked; drupes coral red; planted and escaped in northeast . . . . *V. lantana* L., **wayfaringtree**
   2. Buds 2-scaled; drupes blue or black.
      3. Leaves entire or crenulate.
         4. Cymes long-stalked; Connecticut to Tennessee, Arkansas and south . . . . *V. nudum* L., **possumhaw**
         4. Cymes short-stalked; coastal plain, South Carolina to Florida and southeast Alabama . . . . *V. obovatum* Walt., **Walter viburnum**
      3. Leaves sharply toothed, upper leaves on winged petioles.
         5. Twigs and buds red-woolly; buds oblong; Virginia to Indiana, Missouri, Kansas, and south . . . . *V. rufidulum* Raf., **rusty blackhaw**
         5. Twigs and buds not red-woolly; buds slender or flask-shaped.
            6. Leaves ovate, acuminate; northern . . . . *V. lentago* L., **nannyberry**
            6. Leaves oval, obtuse or slightly pointed; central and southern . . . . *V. prunifolium* L., **blackhaw**

Nannyberry

Viburnum lentago L.

HABIT. A shrub or small tree 15–30 ft high and 6–10 in. in diameter.

LEAVES. Opposite; simple; ovate; 2–4 in. long and 1–2 in. wide; sharply serrate; thick and firm; lustrous and bright green above; yellow-green and marked with minute, black dots below; deciduous; turning orange and red.

FLOWERS. Regular; perfect; small (¼ in. in diameter); fragrant; in stout-branched, scurfy, terminal cymes 3–5 in. across, corolla tubular, white.

FRUIT. Few-fruited, red-stemmed clusters of small, juicy, blue-black, ber-rylike drupes; each drupe oval or ovoid, flattened, covered with glaucous bloom. Seeds: solitary within oval; rough, flattened nutlet.

TWIGS. Slender; light green and hairy, becoming dark red-brown. Winter buds: enclosed by one pair of valvate scales; flower buds ¾ in. long, grayish, swollen; terminal leaf bud 1 in. long, light red, narrow, long-pointed.

BARK. Red-brown; irregularly broken into small, thick scaly plates.

WOOD. Heavy; hard; ill-scented; orange-brown; unimportant.

SILVICAL CHARACTERS. Intolerant; very hardy; attractive ornamental.

LYTHRACEAE

Crapemyrtle

Lagerstroemia indica L.

A handsome shrub or small tree from China widely planted and possibly naturalized from Maryland to Texas. It is characterized by profuse late summer bloom of showy pink, purple, or white flowers and dehiscent capsular fruit. Leaves are deciduous and mostly opposite, entire, elliptic to obovate or ob-long, and 1–2½ in. long. Twigs are 4-angled, glabrous; pointed buds with 2 outer scales. Distinctive grayish, exfoliating bark on fluted trunks.

Soaptree Yucca

a. Section of leaf, × 1
b. Fruit, × 1
c. Flower, × 2/3

LILIACEAE
The Yuccas, *Yucca* L.

These species, often called Spanish-bayonet, appear as shrubs to small trees with showy white flowers and conspicuous, rigid, sharp-pointed leaves. Nine species reach tree size.

KEY TO THE SPECIES OF YUCCAS
1. Southwestern.
    2. Fruit erect, dehiscent; flower clusters long-stalked; leaves filamentous, thin, pale yellow-green .... *Y. elata*, **soaptree yucca**
    2. Fruit pendent, indehiscent; flower clusters sessile or short-stalked; leaves concave.
        3. Fruit with thin, dry flesh; leaves blue-green, serrate; southwest Utah to Nevada, Arizona, and California .... *Y. brevifolia* Engelm., **joshua-tree**
        3. Fruit with succulent flesh; leaves with no, or minute, teeth.
            4. Panicle tomentose; leaves flexible, 2½–3 ft long; margins not filamentous; southern Arizona and New Mexico ... *Y. schottii* Engelm., **Schotts yucca**
            4. Panicle glabrous or puberulous; margins filamentous.
                5. Leaves 2½–4 ft long, dark green; Texas.
                    6. Leaves concave .... *Y. treculeana* Carr., **Trecul yucca**
                    6. Leaves flat .... *Y. faxoniana* Sarg., **Faxon yucca**
                5. Leaves 1½–2 ft long, light yellow-green.
                    7. Style elongated; Texas to New Mexico *Y. torreyi* Shaf., **Torrey yucca**
                    7. Style short; northwestern Arizona to southern Nevada and California .... *Y. schidigera* Roelz (*Y. mohavensis* Sarg.), **Mohave yucca**
1. Southeastern coastal plain, North Carolina, and south to Florida.
    8. Leaves serrate on horny margin; fruit succulent ..... *Y. aloifolia* L., **Aloe yucca**
    8. Leaves nearly entire; fruit thin dry flesh .... *Y. gloriosa* L., **moundlily yucca**

Soaptree Yucca • Spanish-bayonet
Yucca elata Engelm.

HABIT. A tree often 15–20 ft high and 7–8 in. in diameter with a deep, branched, underground stem; simple or branched at top; covered with pendent, persistent dead leaves.

LEAVES. Alternate; simple; 20–30 in. long and ¼–½ in. wide; thin and flat above; rounded below; glabrous; yellow-green; entire pale margins soon splitting into slender filaments.

FLOWERS. Regular; in compound, terminal panicles, 4–6 ft high; perianth cup-shaped, white, 3½–4 in. across.

FRUIT. Erect, oblong capsule, 1½–2 in. long; 3-valved; light brown, thin, and woody outside; light yellow inside; edible.

SILVICAL CHARACTERS. Lower Sonoran zone; intolerant; on desert plateaus; large roots used as substitute for soap.

Bigelow Nolina
Nolina bigelovii (Torr.) Wats.

This shrub or small tree of the Arizona and southern California desert resembles yucca, but it has a massive, unbranched stem 2–3 ft in diameter that bears stiff, grasslike leaves.

Washingtonia

a. Leaf petiole, × ⅓
b. Leaf, × ⅑
c. Part of fruit cluster, × ⅔

PALMAE

Washingtonia • California Palm

Washingtonia filifera Wendl.

HABIT. An evergreen tree 30–50 ft high and 1–2 ft in diameter; crown broad, consisting of large leaves; columnar trunk clothed with thatchlike mass of pendent dead leaves.

LEAVES. Clustered at top of stem; 3–6 ft long; fan-shaped; nearly circular; 40–70 ribbonlike folds deeply slashed ½–⅔ of distance to base; margins of the divisions separating into threadlike filaments; petioles 3–5 ft long, 1–3 in. wide, armed along margins with stout, hooked spines.

FLOWERS. Regular; perfect; minute; in compound clusters 8–10 ft long; appearing from axils of upper leaves; calyx tubular; corolla white, tubular; stamens 6; ovary 3-lobed, 3-celled with a single ovule in each cell.

FRUIT. Drupelike berry; ⅜ in. long; black when ripe in September; ellipsoidal; thin, dry, sweet pulp; produced in large quantities. Seeds: ¼ in. long; ⅛ in. wide; pale chestnut-brown.

BARK. Stem with thick barklike rind; narrowly furrowed; pale cinnamon to dull red-brown.

WOOD. Light; soft; spongy and fibrous; numerous, dark orange-colored, fibrovascular bundles; unimportant.

SILVICAL CHARACTERS. Moderately tolerant when young, becoming intolerant; reproduction plentiful; long, deep roots; alkaline soils; dry, warm, mountain canyons.

GENERAL. This palm often occurs in large numbers in canyons of desert mountains in southern California and southwestern Arizona.

Cabbage Palmetto

Sabal palmetto (Walt.) Lodd.

This species of the coastal plain from North Carolina to Florida forms a tree 40–50 ft tall and 1–2 ft in diameter. It resembles washingtonia in its fan-shaped leaves but can be easily distinguished by its unarmed leaf stalks. Two other species rarely reaching tree size are *S. minor* (Jacq.) Pers., dwarf palmetto, from North Carolina to Texas and *S. mexicana* Mart. in extreme south Texas.

Saw Palmetto

Serenoa repens (Bartr.) Small

Our most abundant native palm is usually a prostrate shrub but rarely forms a small tree. It is characterized by leaf stalks armed with sharp, rigid, curved spines. It ranges from South Carolina south to Florida and west to Louisiana in the coastal plain.

GLOSSARY

Abortive. Imperfectly or not developed; barren.

Accrescent. Increasing in size with age.

Achene. A dry indehiscent, 1-celled, and 1-seeded fruit or carpel.

Acicular. Slenderly needle-shaped.

Acuminate. Gradually tapering to the apex; long-pointed.

Acute. Sharply pointed, but not drawn out.

Adnate. Descriptive of unlike organs or parts fused together.

Aggregate. A compound fruit developing from separate pistils of the same flower.

Alternate. Scattered singly along axis; not opposite.

Ament. A scaly, bracted spike of usually unisexual flowers, frequently deciduous in one piece.

Angiosperms. Plants with seeds borne in an ovary.

Anther. The pollen-bearing part of the stamen.

Antherozoid. Male sexual cells.

Anthesis. The time when fertilization takes place or a flower expands.

Apetalous. Without petals.

Apex. Tip.

Apiculate. Ending in a minute, short, pointed tip.

Apophysis. That part of a cone scale exposed when the cone is closed.

Appressed. Lying close and flat against.

Arborescent. Attaining the size or character of a tree.

Arcuate. Leaf veins moderately curved.

Aril. An appendage or an outer covering of a seed, growing out from the hilum or funiculus.

Attenuate. Slenderly tapering; acuminate.

Auriculate. Furnished with earlike appendage.

Awl-shaped. Tapering from the base to a slender and stiff point.

Axil. The upper angle formed by a leaf or branch with the stem.

Axillary. Situated in an axil.

Baccate. Berrylike; pulpy throughout.

Berry. A fleshy or pulpy fruit with immersed seeds.

Blade. The expanded portion of a leaf.

Bloom. A powdery or waxy substance easily rubbed off.

Bole. The stem of a tree.

Boss. A raised projection, usually pointed.

Bract. A modified leaf subtending a flower or belonging to an inflorescence.

Bractlet. The bract of a pedicel or ultimate flower stalk; a secondary bract.

Bud. The undeveloped state of a branch or flower cluster, with or without scales.

Bud scales. Modified leaves covering a bud.

Bundle (leaf). Strand of fibrovascular tissue found in cross section of leaf.

Caducous. Falling off very early.

Calyx. The flower cup or exterior part of a perianth.

Campanulate. Bell-shaped.

Canescent. Gray-pubescent and hoary.

Capitate. Shaped like a head; in dense headlike clusters.

Capsule. A dry fruit of more than one carpel that splits at maturity to release its seeds.

Carpel. A simple pistil or an element of a compound pistil.

Catkin. The same as an ament.

Caudate. Furnished with a tail or a slender tip.

Cell. The unit of structure of living things; a cavity of an ovary or anther.

Chambered. Said of pith that is interrupted by hollow spaces.

Ciliate. Fringed with hairs on the margin.

Compound. Leaves made up of several individual leaflets.

Cone. A fruit with overlapping scales, usually woody.

Coniferous. Pertains to cone-bearing or to the order Coniferales.

Connate. United.

Coppice. Growth arising from sprouts at the stump.

Cordate. Heart-shaped.

Coriaceous. Of the texture of leather.

Corolla. Inner part of the perianth, composed of petals.

Corymb. A flat-topped flower cluster, the flowers opening from the outside inward.

Crenate. Dentate with the teeth much rounded.

Crenulate. Diminutive of crenate; finely crenate.

Crown. The upper part of a tree, including the living branches with their foliage.

Cuneate. Wedge-shaped, or triangular with an acute angle downward.

Cuspidate. Tipped with a sharp, rigid point.

Cylindric. Shaped like a cylinder.

Cyme. A flat-topped flower cluster, the flowers opening from the center outward.

Deciduous. Not persistent; falling away as the leaves of a tree in autumn.

Decurrent. Running down, as of the blades of leaves extending down their petioles.

Decussate. In pairs alternately crossing at right angles.

Dehiscent. The opening of an anther or capsule by slits or valves.

Deliquescent. Trunk dividing into several large branches.

Deltoid. Delta-shaped; triangular.

Dentate. Toothed, with the teeth directed outward.

Denticulate. Minutely toothed.

Diadelphous. Stamens formed into two groups through the union of their filaments.

Diaphragmed. Said of pith that is solid but with more or less regularly spaced disks of horizontally elongated cells with thickened walls.

Diffuse-porous. Wood in which the pores show little difference in size throughout the seasonal growth.

Dimorphous. Occurring in two forms.

Dioecious. Unisexual, the staminate and pistillate flowers on different individuals.

Disk. A development of the receptacle at or around the base of the pistil.

Dissemination. The spreading abroad of ripe seeds from the parent plant.

Divergent. Spreading apart; pointing away.

Dorsal. Relating to the back or outer surface of an organ; the lower surface of a leaf.

Downy. Clothed with a coat of soft, fine hairs.

Drupaceous. Resembling or relating to a drupe.

Drupe. A stone fruit, such as a plum.

E. A latin prefix denoting that parts are missing.

Eglandular. Without glands.

Ellipsoidal. Of the shape of an elliptical solid.

Elliptic. Of the form of an ellipse.

Emarginate. Notched at the apex.

Entire. Leaf margin without divisions, lobes, or teeth.

Erose. Descriptive of an irregularly toothed or eroded margin.

Excrescences. Warty outgrowths or protuberances.

Excurrent. Trunk extending to top of the tree.

Exfoliate. To cleave or peel off in thin layers.

Exserted. Prolonged beyond the surrounding organs, as stamens from the corolla.

Exstipulate. Without stipules.

Falcate. Scythe- or sickle-shaped.

Fascicle. Dense cluster or bundle.

Fibrovascular. Consisting of woody fibers and ducts.

Filament. The stalk of an anther.

Fluted. Regularly marked by alternating ridges and groovelike depressions.

Foliaceous. Leaflike in texture or appearance.

Follicle. A dry 1-celled fruit from a simple pistil dehiscent by one suture.

Fruit. Seed-bearing part of a plant.

Fugacious. Falling or withering away very early.

Fulvous. Tawny; dull yellow with gray.

Funiculus. The stalk of an ovule.

Furrowed. With longitudinal channels or grooves.

Gibbous. Swollen on one side.

Glabrate. Nearly glabrous or becoming glabrous.

Glabrous. Smooth, not pubescent or hairy.

Gland. Secreting surface or structure; a protuberance having the appearance of such an organ.

Glandular. Furnished with glands.

Glaucous. Covered or whitened with a bloom.

Globose. Spherical in form or nearly so.

Gymnosperms. Plants with naked seeds, i.e., not enclosed in an ovary.

Habit. The general appearance of a plant, best seen from a distance.

Habitat. The place where a plant naturally grows.

Halberdlike. Like an arrowhead, but with the basal lobes pointing outward nearly at right angles.

Hilum. The scar or place of attachment of a seed.

Hirsute. Covered with rather coarse or stiff, long hairs.

Hispid. With rigid or bristly hairs.

Hoary. Covered with a close, whitish, or gray-white pubescence.

Hybrid. A cross, usually between two related species.

Imbricate. Overlapping, like shingles on a roof.

Imperfect (flower). Containing one sex but not the other.

Indehiscent. Not splitting open; remaining closed.

Inferior ovary. Appearing to grow below the adnate calyx.

Inflorescence. Flowers appearing in clusters.

Infrastipular. Situated below the stipules.

Inserted. Attached to or growing out of.

Intolerant. Not capable of doing well under dense forest cover.

Involucre. A circle of bracts surrounding a flower cluster.

Irregular flower. Bilaterally symmetrical; similar parts of different shapes or sizes.

Keeled. With a central ridge like the keel of a boat.

Laciniate. Cut into narrow, pointed lobes.

Lanceolate. Lance-shaped.

Lateral. Situated on the side; not an apex.

Leaflet. One of the small blades of a compound leaf.

Leaf scar. Scar left on twig by the falling of a leaf.

Legume. Fruit of the pea family; podlike and splitting open by both sutures.

Lenticel. Corky growth on young bark that admits air to the interior of a twig or a branch.

Linear. Long and narrow, with parallel edges.

Lobe. A somewhat rounded division of an organ.

Lobulate. Divided into small lobes.

Lustrous. Glossy, shining.

Membranaceous. Thin and somewhat translucent.

Midrib. The central vein of a leaf or leaflet.

Monoecious. The stamens and pistils in separate flowers but borne on the same individual.

Mucro. A small and abrupt tip to a leaf.

Mucronate. Furnished with a mucro (bristle-tipped).

Multiple. A compound fruit developing from ripened ovaries of separate flowers.

Naked buds. Buds without scales.

Nut. A hard and indehiscent, 1-seeded pericarp produced from a compound ovary.

Nutlet. A diminutive nut or stone.

Ob-. Latin prefix signifying inversion.

Obconic. Inverted cone-shaped.

Obcordate. Inverted heart shape.

Oblanceolate. Lanceolate, with the broadest part toward the apex.

Oblique. Slanting or with unequal sides.

Oblong. About 3 times longer than broad with nearly parallel sides.

Obovate. Ovate with a broader end toward the apex.

Obovoid. An ovate solid with the broadest part toward the apex.

Obtuse. Blunt or rounded at the apex.

Odd-pinnate leaf. Pinnate with a terminal leaflet.

Opposite. Two leaves emerging at opposite sides from the same place on the twig.

Orbicular. A flat body circular in outline.

Oval. Broad elliptic, rounded at ends, and about 1½ times as long as broad.

Ovary. The part of a pistil that contains the ovules.

Ovate. Shaped like the longitudinal section of an egg, with the broad end basal.

Ovoid. Solid ovate or solid oval.

Ovule. The part of the flower that becomes the seed after fertilization.

Palmate. Radiately lobed or divided, veins arising from one point.

Panicle. A loose, compound, or branched flower cluster.

Papilionaceous. Butterflylike; typical flower shape of legumes.

Pectinate. Comblike, with narrow closely inserted segments.

Pedicel. Stalk of a single flower in a compound inflorescence.

Pedicellate. Borne on a pedicel.

Peduncle. A general flower stalk supporting either a cluster of flowers or a solitary flower.

Peltate. Shield-shaped and attached by its lower surface to the central stalk.

Pendent. Hanging downward.

Pendulous. More or less hanging or declined.

Penniveined. Having the form of a feather; secondary veins arranged parallel to each other and arising from a main vein.

Perfect. Flower with both stamens and pistil.

Perianth. The calyx and corolla of a flower considered as a whole.

Persistent. Remaining attached, not falling off.

Petiolate. Having a petiole.

Petiole. Footstalk of a leaf.

Petiolule. Footstalk of a leaflet.

Pilose. Hairy, with soft and distinct hairs.

Pinnate. A compound leaf with leaflets arranged along each side of a common petiole.

Pistil. Female organ of a flower, consisting of ovary, style, and stigma.

Pistillate. Female flowers; descriptive of unisexual flowers.

Pith. The central, softer part of a stem.

Pollen. The fecundating grains borne in the anther.

Polygamo-dioecious. Flowers sometimes perfect, sometimes unisexual and dioecious.

Polygamo-monoecious. Flowers sometimes perfect and sometimes unisexual, the two forms borne on the same individual.

Polygamous. Flowers sometimes perfect and sometimes unisexual.

Pome. An inferior fruit of two or several carpels enclosed in thick flesh; an apple.

Prickle. A small spinelike growth from the bark or epidermis.

Prostrate. Lying flat on the ground.

Puberulous. Minutely pubescent.

Pubescent. Clothed with soft, short hairs.

Pungent. Terminating in a rigid, sharp point; acrid.

Pyramidal. Shaped like a pyramid.

Pyriform. Pear-shaped.

Raceme. A simple inflorescence of stalked flowers on a more or less elongated rachis.

Racemose. In racemes; resembling racemes.

Rachis. An axis bearing leaflets, as in a compound leaf.

Receptacle. The more or less expanded portion of an axis that bears the organs of a flower or the collected flowers of a head.

Recurved. Curving downward or backward.

Reflexed. Abruptly turned downward.

Regular flower. Radially symmetrical; similar parts of the same shape and size.

Remotely. Scattered, not close together.

Reniform. Kidney-shaped.

Repand. With a slightly sinuate margin.

Reticulate. Netted.

Retrosely. Directed backward or downward.

Revolute. Rolled backward, margin rolled toward the lower side.

Rhombic. Having the shape of a rhombus.

Ring-porous. Wood in which the pores formed in the early spring growth are much larger than those formed later.

Rufous. Red-brown.

Rugose. Wrinkled.

Salverform. Tubular corolla with a spreading limb.

Samara. An indehiscent, winged fruit.

Scabrous. Rough to the touch.

Scarious. Thin, dry, membranaceous, not green.

Scorpioid. A form of unilateral inflorescence circinately coiled in the bud.

Scurfy. Covered with small branlike scales.

Sepal. A division of the calyx, usually bractlike.

Serotinous. Late in bearing or opening.

Serrate. Toothed, the teeth pointing upward or forward.

Serrulate. Finely toothed.

Sessile. Without a stalk.

Sheath. A tubular envelope, or enrolled part or organ.

Shrub. A woody, bushy plant, branched at or near the base and usually less than 15 ft in height.

Simple. Leaves consisting of a single blade.

Sinuate. With a strong, wavy margin.

Sinus. The cleft or space between two lobes.

Spatulate. Spatula-shaped.

Spike. A simple inflorescence of sessile flowers arranged on a common, elongated axis.

Spine. A sharp, mostly woody outgrowth in the position of a leaf or stipule.

Spinescent. With short, rigid branches resembling spines.

Spinose. Furnished with spines.

Stamen. The pollen-bearing organ of the male flower.

Staminate. Male flowers; provided with stamens but without pistils.

Stellate. Star-shaped.

Sterigmata. Short, persistent leaf bases found on spruces and hemlocks.

Stigma. The part or surface of a pistil that receives pollen for the fecundation of the ovules.

Stipe. The stalklike support of a pistil or a carpel.

Stipule. An appendage at the base of the petiole, usually one on each side.

Stoloniferous. Having lower branches or runners that tend to root.

Stoma. An orifice in the epidermis of a leaf used to connect internal cavities with air.

Stomata. Plural of stoma.

Stomatiferous. Furnished with stomata.

Strobile. A cone.

Style. The attenuated portion of a pistil between the ovary and the stigma.

Sub-. A Latin prefix denoting somewhat or slightly.

Suborbicular. Near round.

Subtend. To lie under or opposite to.

Subulate. Awl-shaped.

Succulent. Juicy; fleshy.

Superior ovary. Free from and inserted above calyx; hypogynous.

Superposed. Placed above, as one bud above another at a node.

Suture. A junction or line of dehiscence.

Syncarp. A multiple fleshy fruit.

Taproot. The primary descending root, which may be either very large or absent at the maturity of the tree.

Terete. Circular in traverse section.

Terminal. Situated at the end of a branch.

Ternate. In groups of three.

Thorn. A sharp, woody outgrowth in the position of a lateral branch.

Tolerant. Capable of enduring shade.

Tomentose. Densely pubescent with matted wool or tomentum.

Tomentulose. Slightly pubescent with matted wool.

Torulose. Cylindric, with swollen partitions at intervals.

Tree. A plant with a woody stem, unbranched at or near base, and at least 15 ft in height and 2 in. in diameter.

Truncate. Ending abruptly, as if cut off at the end.

Tubercle. A small tuber or excrescence.

Turbinate. Top-shaped.

Twig. A young woody stem; more precisely the shoot of a woody plant representing the growth of the current season.

Umbel. A simple inforescence of flowers with pedicels all arising from the same point.

Umbo. A boss or protuberance.

Undulate. With wavy surface or margin.

Unisexual. Of one sex, either staminate or pistillate.

Valvate. Leaf buds meeting at the edges, not overlapping.

Valve. One of the pieces into which a capsule splits.

Veins. Threads of fibrovascular tissue in a leaf or other flat organ.

Ventral. Belonging to the anterior or inner face of an organ; the upper surface of a leaf.

Vernal. Appearing in the spring.

Vesicle. A little bladder or cavity.

Villous. Hairy with long and soft hairs.

Viscid. Gluey or sticky.

Whorled. Three or more organs arranged in a circle around an axis.

Wing. A membranous or thin and dry expansion or appendage of an organ.

Woolly. Covered with long and matted or tangled hairs.

INDEX